Webmastering For Dummies®

A Webmaster's Bookmarks

Cheat Sheet

COMPUTER BOOK SERIES FROM IDG

Professional Webmastering

The Webmasters' Guild:
http://www.webmaster.org
A professional organization for Webmasters of all types

WebMaster Online: http://www.webmaster.com
News and archives from the magazine by the same name

The Webmaster's Reference Library:
http://www.webreference.com
Provides information on all aspects of building Web sites — from organization to execution

Site Builder Network:
http://www.microsoft.com/sitebuilder/
Microsoft's chatty, informative site about creating and maintaining a Web site

HyperNews Forums Web Mastery Resource Lists:
http://union.ncsa.uiuc.edu/HyperNews/get/
www/html/guides.html
A discussion forum for asking questions and sharing ideas

Talking Tech

BrowserWatch: http://www.browserwatch.com
Keep track of news in the world of Web browsers

Server Watch and WebCompare: http://
serverwatch.iworld.com and http://
webcompare.iworld.com
Feature-by-feature comparisons of Web-server software

Windows NT Resource Center:
http://www.bhs.com
All about running and administering Windows NT

How to Do a Searchable Database: http://
www2.ncsu.edu/bae/people/faculty/walker/
hotlist/isindex.html
Examines options for using a database with a Web site

Netscape DevEdge Online:
http://developer.netscape.com
For programmers and administrators using Netscape servers and other software

Information Systems Meta-List: http://
www.cait.wustl.edu/cait/infosys.html
Annotated pointers to all aspects of information systems

Look and Feel

Weblint Home Page: http://www.cre.canon.co.
uk/~neilb/weblint/
An installable error-checking script, Web gateways to use it, and HTML resources

Quadzilla: http://www.quadzilla.com
A design reference that covers everything from software to style sheets

Webmonkey: http://www.webmonkey.com
HotWired's learning center for Web design and HTML writing

CINet's HTML For Beginners: http://www.cnet.
com/Content/Features/Howto/Basics/
Excellent beginners' tutorials and advanced tips and tricks

ColorServe Pro: http://www.biola.edu/
cgi-bin/colorpro/colorpro.cgi
Lets you pick your hex color scheme with a few mouse clicks

Backward Compatibility Viewer:
http://www.delorie.com/Web/wpbcv.html
Shows how your page will look in various browsers

GIFWizard: http://www.gifwizard.com/
Simple software that helps you reduce the file size of your GIF images

Employment and Contracting

The Monster Board: http://www.monster.com
Work on your resume, or search job listings and employer profiles

Career Mosaic: http://www.careermosaic.com
Hosts online job fairs, as well as huge databases of jobs and resumes

Career Web: http://www.cweb.com
Specializes in technical, professional, and managerial job and resume listings

Yahoo! Employment: Use Yahoo! to find a job or an outsourcing firm. Try searching Yahoo! classifieds
(http://classifieds.yahoo.com/
employment.html), look up an Internet company
(http://www.yahoo.com/
Business_and_Economy/Companies/
Internet_Services/), or look into computer industry jobs (http://www.yahoo.com/
Computers_and_Internet/Employment/)

IDG BOOKS WORLDWIDE

D1501421

...For Dummies: #1 Computer Book Series for Beginners

Quality Assurance

What Is Good Hypertext Writing?: http://kbs.cs.tu-berlin.de/~jutta/ht/writing.html
Maintain both your Web pages and your grammar

The Slot: http://www.theslot.com
A copy editor's take on good and bad English usage

Sun Microsystems' Guide to Web Style: http://www.sun.com/styleguide
From page length to using Java, a great set of house rules

Tim Berners-Lee's Style Guide for Online Hypertext: http://www.w3.org/pub/WWW/Provider/Style/All.html
How to use HTML, from the guy credited with inventing the Web

The Yale C/AIM Web Style Guide: http://info.med.yale.edu/caim/manual/index.html
It's a manual, it's a tutorial, it's a great place to learn about HTML style

Web Pages That Suck: http://www.webpagesthatsuck.com
Learn HTML by (bad) example

Selling Online

Selena Sol's Public Domain CGI Script Archive: http://www.extropia.com
Include a shopping cart script, authentication and database management apps, and more

RSA Data Security: http://www.rsa.com
"The Most Trusted Name in Cryptography" offers detailed information on Internet security

CyberCash: http://www.cybercash.com
The popular option for online transactions

DigiCash & Ecash: http://www.digicash.com
Merchant technology for the online world and beyond

Intershop: http://www.intershop.com
Electronic commerce software here means online storefronts and online malls

Business Sense

The Excel Help Page: http://www.lacher.com
John Lacher, CPA, offers a newsletter on Excel, as well as sample macros and applications

The Spreadsheet User Group: http://www.sheet.com
Publishes two print magazines about spreadsheets

The Spreadsheet Page: http://www.j-walk.com/ss/
Everything you ever wanted to know about spreadsheets (including jokes!)

Legalese

The Copyright Web Site: http://www.benedict.com
An all-around guide to copyright, paying special attention to Internet issues

The Internet Legal Resource Guide: http://www.ilrg.com
An annotated guide to law, with local databases and articles and links

FindLaw: http://www.findlaw.com
An index of law resources online

e-THICS: http://home.earthlink.net/~ivanlove/
Attorney Ivan Hoffman posts articles about Internet law and publishing

Domain Names and Trademarks: http://www.law.georgetown.edu/lc/internic/domain1.html
From George Washington University Law School, an exploration of domain-name disputes

The Nolo Press Self-Help Law Center: http://www.nolo.com
Covers all aspects of law, including Smart Publishing (http://www.nolo.com/mag/index.html), Patent, Copyright & Trademark (http://www.nolo.com/ChunkPCT/PCT.index.html), and Independent Contractors (http://www.nolo.com/ChunkEMP/emp.index.html)

To Market, to Market

Search Engine Watch: http://searchenginewatch.com
About using search engines and indexes, what makes them tick, and what makes them work for you

Georgia Tech's WWW User Surveys: http://www.cc.gatech.edu/gvu/user_surveys/
Researches and reports on who's online

Submit-It: http://www.submit-it.com
Submits your site to search engines for a fee

Cool Site of the Day: http://cool.infi.net
An award you'd be proud to get — look at their picks to find out what's cool online

Liszt: http://www.liszt.com
Join a mailing list for industry news and to get the word out about your site and services

Link Exchange: http://www.linkexchange.com
Trade banner ads for free

Adweek Online: http://www.adweek.com
Online news about electronic advertising from the seminal advertising magazine

TM

References for the Rest of Us! ®

BESTSELLING BOOK SERIES FROM IDG

Are you intimidated and confused by computers? Do you find that traditional manuals are overloaded with technical details you'll never use? Do your friends and family always call you to fix simple problems on their PCs? Then the *...For Dummies®* computer book series from IDG Books Worldwide is for you.

...For Dummies books are written for those frustrated computer users who know they aren't really dumb but find that PC hardware, software, and indeed the unique vocabulary of computing make them feel helpless. *...For Dummies* books use a lighthearted approach, a down-to-earth style, and even cartoons and humorous icons to diffuse computer novices' fears and build their confidence. Lighthearted but not lightweight, these books are a perfect survival guide for anyone forced to use a computer.

> *"I like my copy so much I told friends; now they bought copies."*
>
> **— Irene C., Orwell, Ohio**

> *"Quick, concise, nontechnical, and humorous."*
>
> **— Jay A., Elburn, Illinois**

> *"Thanks, I needed this book. Now I can sleep at night."*
>
> **— Robin F., British Columbia, Canada**

Already, millions of satisfied readers agree. They have made *...For Dummies* books the #1 introductory level computer book series and have written asking for more. So, if you're looking for the most fun and easy way to learn about computers, look to *...For Dummies* books to give you a helping hand.

TM

IDG BOOKS WORLDWIDE

WEBMASTERING FOR DUMMIES®

Daniel A. Tauber
and
Brenda Kienan

IDG Books Worldwide, Inc.
An International Data Group Company

Foster City, CA ♦ Chicago, IL ♦ Indianapolis, IN ♦ New York, NY

Webmastering For Dummies®

Published by
IDG Books Worldwide, Inc.
An International Data Group Company
919 E. Hillsdale Blvd.
Suite 400
Foster City, CA 94404
www.idgbooks.com (IDG Books Worldwide Web site)
www.dummies.com (Dummies Press Web site)

Library of Congress Catalog Card No.: 97-73294

ISBN: 0-7645-0171-2

Printed in the United States of America

10 9 8 7 6 5 4 3

1O/SV/RR/ZY/IN

Distributed in the United States by IDG Books Worldwide, Inc.

Distributed by Macmillan Canada for Canada; by Transworld Publishers Limited in the United Kingdom; by IDG Norge Books for Norway; by IDG Sweden Books for Sweden; by Woodslane Pty. Ltd. for Australia; by Woodslane (NZ) Ltd. for New Zealand; by Addison Wesley Longman Singapore Pte Ltd. for Singapore, Malaysia, Thailand, and Indonesia; by Norma Comunicaciones S.A. for Colombia; by Intersoft for South Africa; by International Thomson Publishing for Germany, Austria and Switzerland; by Distribuidora Cuspide for Argentina; by Livraria Cultura for Brazil; by Ediciencia S.A. for Ecuador; by Ediciones ZETA S.C.R. Ltda. for Peru; by WS Computer Publishing Corporation, Inc., for the Philippines; by Contemporanea de Ediciones for Venezuela; by Express Computer Distributors for the Caribbean and West Indies; by Micronesia Media Distributor, Inc. for Micronesia; by Grupo Editorial Norma S.A. for Guatemala; by Chips Computadoras S.A. de C.V. for Mexico; by Editorial Norma de Panama S.A. for Panama; by Wouters Import for Belgium; by American Bookshops for Finland. Authorized Sales Agent: Anthony Rudkin Associates for the Middle East and North Africa.

For general information on IDG Books Worldwide's books in the U.S., please call our Consumer Customer Service department at 800-762-2974. For reseller information, including discounts and premium sales, please call our Reseller Customer Service department at 800-434-3422.

For information on where to purchase IDG Books Worldwide's books outside the U.S., please contact our International Sales department at 317-596-5530 or fax 317-596-5692.

For information on foreign language translations, please contact our Foreign & Subsidiary Rights department at 650-655-3021 or fax 650-655-3281.

For sales inquiries and special prices for bulk quantities, please contact our Sales department at 650-655-3200 or write to the address above.

For information on using IDG Books Worldwide's books in the classroom or for ordering examination copies, please contact our Educational Sales department at 800-434-2086 or fax 317-596-5499.

For press review copies, author interviews, or other publicity information, please contact our Public Relations department at 650-655-3000 or fax 650-655-3299.

For authorization to photocopy items for corporate, personal, or educational use, please contact Copyright Clearance Center, 222 Rosewood Drive, Danvers, MA 01923, or fax 978-750-4470.

is a trademark under exclusive license to IDG Books Worldwide, Inc., from International Data Group, Inc.

About the Authors

Daniel A. Tauber and **Brenda Kienan** met as employees of a computer book publishing company and immediately recognized each other as obsessive and highly geeky. Within a very short time, they set out to write books together, and in the course of that, Dan introduced Brenda to the Internet (well, newsgroups, really, because the Web and Web browsers were just glints in the eyes of their inventors at the time). They did much of the research for their early books on the Internet, and thus Dan made Brenda into the Internet junkie she became. Not too long after that, the Web debuted, Webmastering beckoned, and they both changed jobs.

Things got very interesting very quickly. You see, while these two had always enjoyed a good adventure, they didn't fully realize that being pioneers meant walking across the continent behind a wagon, dodging oxen poop. What's more, no one told them that no maps were yet available. They, along with a small army of other Webmaster pioneers, learned a lot of lessons the hard way, which maybe isn't so bad — after all, this book is the result of that experience.

Dan, by the way, holds a degree in computer science and in the course of his career as an Internet professional has led technical development of Web sites for Fortune 500 companies and the publishing industry. Brenda has created, acquired, and produced Web content for the publishing and search engine industries, and has managed Web teams ranging from two to 46 people.

Together, Daniel A. Tauber and Brenda Kienan have written eight books, including four that cover Internet topics. This is their first for IDG Books Worldwide. They're married now (to each other), and live in the San Francisco area with five computers and two cats.

You can visit their Web site at http://www.dnai.com/~vox.

ABOUT IDG BOOKS WORLDWIDE

Welcome to the world of IDG Books Worldwide.

IDG Books Worldwide, Inc., is a subsidiary of International Data Group, the world's largest publisher of computer-related information and the leading global provider of information services on information technology. IDG was founded more than 30 years ago by Patrick J. McGovern and now employs more than 9,000 people worldwide. IDG publishes more than 290 computer publications in over 75 countries. More than 90 million people read one or more IDG publications each month.

Launched in 1990, IDG Books Worldwide is today the #1 publisher of best-selling computer books in the United States. We are proud to have received eight awards from the Computer Press Association in recognition of editorial excellence and three from Computer Currents' First Annual Readers' Choice Awards. Our best-selling ...For Dummies® series has more than 50 million copies in print with translations in 31 languages. IDG Books Worldwide, through a joint venture with IDG's Hi-Tech Beijing, became the first U.S. publisher to publish a computer book in the People's Republic of China. In record time, IDG Books Worldwide has become the first choice for millions of readers around the world who want to learn how to better manage their businesses.

Our mission is simple: Every one of our books is designed to bring extra value and skill-building instructions to the reader. Our books are written by experts who understand and care about our readers. The knowledge base of our editorial staff comes from years of experience in publishing, education, and journalism — experience we use to produce books to carry us into the new millennium. In short, we care about books, so we attract the best people. We devote special attention to details such as audience, interior design, use of icons, and illustrations. And because we use an efficient process of authoring, editing, and desktop publishing our books electronically, we can spend more time ensuring superior content and less time on the technicalities of making books.

You can count on our commitment to deliver high-quality books at competitive prices on topics you want to read about. At IDG Books Worldwide, we continue in the IDG tradition of delivering quality for more than 30 years. You'll find no better book on a subject than one from IDG Books Worldwide.

John Kilcullen
Chairman and CEO
IDG Books Worldwide, Inc.

Steven Berkowitz
President and Publisher
IDG Books Worldwide, Inc.

*Eighth Annual
Computer Press
Awards 1992*

*Ninth Annual
Computer Press
Awards 1993*

WINNER

*Tenth Annual
Computer Press
Awards 1994*

*Eleventh Annual
Computer Press
Awards 1995*

Dedication

To Lori, Jessie, and Kevin, with bright hopes for their futures.

Authors' Acknowledgments

This one was a dash to the finish. For their efforts and support we'd like to thank the many people who made it possible.

At IDG, our thanks go to Gareth Hancock for signing us up, to Bill Helling for shepherding us through development and keeping the faith, to John Edwards for buffing the manuscript to a sparkle, to CJ Yem for offering ace technical feedback, to Sherry Gomoll and all the production crew for forging edited manuscript into printed matter, and to everyone in the Dummies groups for their gung-ho enthusiasm. Thanks also to the folks who brought to life and keep alive www.idgbooks.com and www.dummies.com.

J. Tarin Towers, Wendy Van Wazer, Ann Navarro, Vivian Perry, and Valerie Singer researched or drafted chapters in this book; we couldn't have done this without their able contributions and on-time delivery.

Grace Allison, Barbara Bruxvoort, Diane Rowett Castro, Debra Goldentyer, Tamra Heathershaw-Hart, Carolyn Lamont, Claudia L'Amoreaux, Marcy Lyon, Ralph the Wonder Llama, Ann Marie Michaels, Faith Renee Sloan, and Akemi Tazaki contributed thoughts, ideas, URLs, and more; our thanks to each of them. From the Webmasters' Guild, Cybernauts, Bay Area Editors' Forum, and the San Francisco chapter of Webgrrls, we received invaluable insights and tidbits; our thanks to everyone in each of those groups.

Dave and Sherry Rogelberg at Studio B are just the best. Our thanks go to them, as always, for all they do. Thanks also to Asha Dornfest, who was kind enough to bail us out on that other book and prop us up with bread products just when we needed it most.

Many thanks to Barbara Cohen, Karen Emery, and Kent Gerard, who kept hearts, health, and hearth pasted together; and to Vivian Hoffman and Jan Jobert, who more than understand the oddball hours of a deadline-driven life.

Our family and friends have our constant gratitude if not our constant attention—thanks as always to Joani and Jessica Buehrle; Sharon Crawford and Charlie Russel; Kevin, Caitlin, and little Kevin Cunningham; Jerry Doty; Rion Dugan; Femmes Who Feast; Fred Frumberg and Robert Turnbull; Jessica, Martin, and Lori Grant; Caroline Heller; Mai Le Bazner, Katri Foster, and Peter Bazner; the McArdle and Undercoffer families; Carolyn Miller; Lonnie Moseley and Cordell Sloan; Wynn Moseley and her family; Freeman Ng; Margaret Tauber; Ron and Frances Tauber; Judy Tauber and Lauren Yohan; Savitha Varadan; and Robert E. Williams III.

Publisher's Acknowledgments

We're proud of this book; please register your comments through our IDG Books Worldwide Online Registration Form located at http://my2cents.dummies.com.

Some of the people who helped bring this book to market include the following:

Acquisitions, Development, and Editorial

Project Editor: Bill Helling

Acquisitions Editor: Gareth Hancock

Media Development Manager: Joyce Pepple

Associate Permissions Editor:
Heather Heath Dismore

Copy Editor: John Edwards

Technical Editor: Chandrama "CJ" Yem

Editorial Manager: Mary C. Corder

Editorial Assistant: Donna Love

Production

Project Coordinator: Sherry Gomoll

Layout and Graphics: Dominique DeFelice, Pamela Emanoil, Angela F. Hunckler, Jane E. Martin, Mark C. Owens, Anna R. Rohrer, Brent Savage

Proofreaders: Kelli Botta, Nancy Price, Rob Springer, Karen York, Carrie Voorhis, Ethel Winslow

Indexer: Ty Koontz

Special Help

Terri Morgan

General and Administrative

IDG Books Worldwide, Inc.: John Kilcullen, CEO; Steven Berkowitz, President and Publisher

IDG Books Technology Publishing: Brenda McLaughlin, Senior Vice President and Group Publisher

Dummies Technology Press and Dummies Editorial: Diane Graves Steele, Vice President and Associate Publisher; Mary Bednarek, Director of Acquisitions and Product Development; Kristin A. Cocks, Editorial Director

Dummies Trade Press: Kathleen A. Welton, Vice President and Publisher; Kevin Thornton, Acquisitions Manager

IDG Books Production for Dummies Press: Michael R. Britton, Vice President of Production and Creative Services; Cindy L. Phipps, Manager of Project Coordination, Production Proofreading, and Indexing; Kathie S. Schutte, Supervisor of Page Layout; Shelley Lea, Supervisor of Graphics and Design; Debbie J. Gates, Production Systems Specialist; Robert Springer, Supervisor of Proofreading; Debbie Stailey, Special Projects Coordinator; Tony Augsburger, Supervisor of Reprints and Bluelines

Dummies Packaging and Book Design: Robin Seaman, Creative Director; Kavish + Kavish, Cover Design

◆

The publisher would like to give special thanks to Patrick J. McGovern, without whom this book would not have been possible.

◆

Contents at a Glance

Cartoons at a Glance

By Rich Tennant

page 335

page 5

page 117

page 273

page 211

Fax: 978-546-7747 • E-mail: the5wave@tiac.net

Table of Contents

Introduction

· ·

A few years ago, when we left our more traditional jobs and ventured into the Web world, we said we wanted to be pioneers. This was our chance to zip off toward the frontier, and we couldn't have been more optimistic. We sent out some résumés, got our new jobs, and headed bravely into the unknown. Sheesh. Someone might have told us that being a pioneer means walking across the continent behind a wagon, dodging oxen poop all the while, and feeling never quite sure you're headed in the right direction.

This is the book we wish we'd had when we started out. It's packed with the sum of our experience on the wildest adventure we might have imagined. It's also packed with tips and tidbits we picked up from a lot of other smart people who headed out into Web work with bright shining eyes but no idea what they were all getting into.

Who You Are and What You Already Know

You may come from any of several backgrounds. Not all Webmasters are programmers or system administrators; some are content people, designers, production folk, even managers. Truth be told, when we set out to write this book, we thought one of us was a Webmaster but one of us was not. One of us, a techie, had gotten it in mind way back when the Web was being born that he wanted to put together a Web server, and he spent evenings and weekends doing just that, right under his company's nose, without them knowing. That's how lots of Webmasters came into being, and it was clear to both of us that he (Dan) was a Webmaster. His path started with that first server, and led to technical development of very big Web sites.

Meanwhile, the other of us (Brenda) went about the business of creating and developing content, without knowing for a long time exactly what to call herself professionally. Content manager? Style constable? Online publisher? Producer? Not a programmer and no system developer, she was never inclined to call herself a Webmaster, but she felt confident in her skills as a content developer and Web team manager, and had no trouble finding work in an industry that for a good while had no agreed upon title for her.

Finding the Webmasters' Guild definition of a Webmaster (quoted at the beginning of Chapter 1) was a great revelation to us — at last a clear, comprehensive description of what a Webmaster is and does. Voilà — we were *both* Webmasters. (There's nothing like a little external validation in life.)

You may have opted for Webmasterhood because you thought it would be a lot of fun (it is), or you may have had Webmasterhood thrust upon you as part of your job. In either case, this book is for you. It's also for those who manage and hire Webmasters, and even those who are investigating Web strategies to see what's best for their company. You may be an executive, a hiring manager, a system administrator, or an HTML jockey. Whatever your position in the scheme of things, we think this book will provide you with strategies you can use in creating and implementing your Web endeavor from budget through concept, staffing, implementation, and maintenance. We even cover promoting your site and measuring your success.

We do assume that you have knowledge of the Internet and its tools, and that you're comfortable talking the talk of browsers, ftp, servers, and clients. You needn't be a programmer, nor need you aspire to becoming a programmer. You don't even have to know HTML, though you do know what HTML is.

What This Book Covers

From soup to nuts, this book covers Webmastering — all sorts of Webmastering, including content development, design, production, tech stuff, and management. Above all, this book is about how to create a strategy, how to follow through successfully, and how to know you have succeeded. Sure, we talk about how to create a smashing site, but we also talk about hiring a team, jobbing out to Web shops, creating a budget, legal pitfalls, selling on the Web, promoting your site, and more.

Part I: Who You Are and Where You Start

Logically enough, we start with what Webmasters do, where they get their credentials, how to hire them if you're a hiring manager, and where Webmasters can meet each other to trade tips and technologies. We also cover setting goals for your site, because that's the foundation on which a winning site is based. We delve into selling on the Web, so you can determine whether that's a worthy goal for your site, and we finish off with the one-two combination of budgeting and some legal bugaboos you should watch out for. This is all basic stuff you need to know about to get going.

Part II: Planning a Smashing Web Site

Planning and creating a site is a big job. We cover these topics from beginning to end, telling you all about the all-important selecting and registering of a domain name, organizing content, creating directory structures, working out a design document, and so on. We also walk you through HTML and the super-duper stuff that jazzes up plain Web pages. Then we cruise you through the ins and outs of working with Web job shops big and small, offering scads of tips gleaned from working in the industry. You'll want to make sure your site's quality and standards are strong and that they remain strong after launch, so we cover quality assurance and document control, too.

Part III: Under the Hood: Server, Database, and Search Engine Strategies

This is no server administrator's book (there are plenty of those around), but every Webmaster should know enough about the tech end to be able to make sound judgments, so in Part III we open the hood to have a look at servers and other tech head delights. Here we cover Web servers, firewalls, types of connections, and databases. We also cover dealing with ISPs, IPPs, and database developers (who sometimes seem to speak a different language than the rest of us). We wind up with a look at using search-engine technology on your site to enable users to find in a heartbeat what they seek.

Part IV: Winning: Promoting and Assessing Your Site's Success

Once you've created a winning Web site, you'll want to let others know about it. In Part IV, we cover listing your site with online indexes and search engines (Yahoo!, AltaVista, and the like). We tell you how to find out how many backlinks lead from other sites to yours. We also cover promoting your site in a variety of creative ways ranging from using traditional print media to . . . well, you'll see. And finally, we cover the various ways you can measure success in an industry that just a year ago offered few standards and fewer means of measuring. All in all, we tell you how to win and how to know you have won.

Part V: The Part of Tens

As an added bonus, we offer three chapters at the end that are filled with quick tips, tricks, and ideas you can put into play right away. We describe ten Web sites you won't be able to live without, ten tools you can use to jazz

up your HTML, and ten types of live content you can implement today —
many of which require no programming knowledge at all!

How to Use This Book

You needn't read this book cover to cover. Simply flip to the sections that
interest you as you face one challenge or another. Or, if you want to get a
complete overview of the craft of Webmastering, go ahead and read the
whole thing — we're not stopping you!

Icons Used in This Book

This book is dotted with nifty icons marking text that's of special interest.
Here's what all those nifty icons mean:

This one points out important bits of information you won't want to forget.

Shortcuts, tricks, winning tactics — they're all marked with this icon. To
save yourself time and cut straight to winning strategies, look here.

The world won't end if you fail to heed advice marked by this icon, but you
probably ought to listen up anyway. You'll save yourself a lot of grief if you do.

As a Web enthusiast, you probably already know that the Web is teeming
with information — this icon flags URLs that will help you in your
Webmastering endeavors. You'll want to bookmark many of these.

To find out what others who've gone before you have to say, look for this icon.
It marks quotes from experienced Web folk, anecdotes based on our own
experience in the field, and stories from the real world of Webmastering.

Off You Go

This book is meant to act as your guide to the wonderful world of
Webmastering. Just because we ventured into the frontier unprepared
doesn't mean you have to. It's still a brave new world out there, and you're
headed for a big adventure. Keep this book beside you, and as you go, flip to
the section you need. Have fun!

Part I
Who You Are and Where You Start

The 5th Wave   By Rich Tennant

"WHAT CONCERNS ME ABOUT THE INFORMATION SUPERHIGHWAY IS THAT IT APPEARS TO BE ENTERING THROUGH BRENT'S BEDROOM."

In this part . . .

Some people are born Webmasters (well, not many), some become Webmasters, and some have Web-mastering thrust upon them. Whichever description fits you, and whatever your focus (content, tech, design and production, or management), you need a firm foundation in what you do and where to start. That's what this part is all about.

In Part I, we tell you all about the different types of Webmasters, where they trade strategies and get credentials, how to hire them, and what groups and associations they frequent. We also walk you through setting goals for your Web endeavor, creating a budget, and legal bugaboos you ought to know before you get rolling.

Chapter 1

What Webmasters Do and Where to Find Them

*I*t's the hippest, coolest job anyone could have, isn't it? `<wonder>` Now, what is it you do, exactly? `</wonder>` Ask any ten people in the industry what a Webmaster is or does, and they'll offer a bunch of different answers. Guess what? They're probably *all* correct. This chapter covers the topic of Webmastering for the aspiring or newly minted Webmaster and hiring for those looking for Webmaster talent.

Basically, a Webmaster is the person who owns a Web site. That's simple enough, and most folks in the industry can agree up to that point. But beyond that — at the point where you start talking about what skills, credentials, and qualities a Webmaster should have — opinions take off in every direction. Depending on who is doing the talking, a Webmaster may be a fresh-faced, entry-level programmer or a marketing manager with years of experience. According to the Webmasters' Guild (`http://www.webmaster.org`), "The goal of a Webmaster is to design, implement, and maintain an effective World Wide Web site. To achieve this, a Webmaster must possess knowledge of fields as diverse as network configuration, interface and graphic design, software development, business strategy, writing, and project management. Because the function of a Webmaster encompasses so many areas, the position is often not held by a single person but by a team of individuals."

In many cases, the first person who stood up in the company and advocated having a Web site became the Webmaster by default. That's not so bad — evangelizing is actually an important part of running a Web site. First, there is the evangelizing that led to getting a green light from top management to create a site and then the evangelizing of the site to the world at large. But skills of persuasion alone don't make a Webmaster — he or she must also show a keen understanding of the company's core business, knowledge of the Internet and its technologies, solid marketing savvy (especially if the site's purpose is marketing), ability to put himself or herself in the user's shoes, and so on. Perhaps the most important qualities a Webmaster can show are vision — you *are* inventing the future, after all — combined with hard-nosed practicality and a dash of deep curiosity.

There are Webmasters and there are *Webmasters.* Some are the technical sort, who administer servers, and some are more responsible for the site's content, its look, or perhaps its overall management. In this book, when we refer to a *Webmaster,* we're talking about the person who "owns" a Web site — the guy or gal who has overall responsibility for running the thing. In cases where the job is done by a cast of two or even thousands, we're still going to call that collective group the Webmaster (except when we call them the *Web team*). Now, what is it that the Webmaster does again?

Webmaster Roles and Reasons for Being

When the Web was very, very young (say, in 1994), there were maybe a handful of people who called themselves *Webmasters,* and they were mainly tech folks who, for one reason or another, figured they should put together a Web server. In those days, the Webmaster may have set up the server and maintained it, he or she may have done all the programming or HTML coding, and then he may have whipped up a nifty design (well, at least it was nifty to that person's eye). The self-appointed Webmaster probably also wrote every speck of copy for the thing. Sites were simple back then. Henry Ford once said you could have a Model T in any color as long as it was *black;* similarly, in the "old" days of Webmastering, the constraints of HTML were such that you could create a Web site in any color, as long as it was gray, with simple black text and blue links.

Ah, but those days are long gone. One day someone in the company caught on to the technical whiz's secret hobby — it may have been about the time the Internet became a familiar phrase on television. Suddenly the Web site became *important.* Today, creating a company Web site is more often a high-profile activity that involves a whole team. That team may include someone to plan and manage the thing, someone to write or edit the content, a marketeer, a designer, a tech wizard, and maybe more. Even in a small one-person operation, where a single soul is charged with creating a Web site, the roles and responsibilities of that person are increasingly diverse.

Tim Berners-Lee may easily be considered the original Webmaster. His home page (`http://www.w3.org/pub/WWW/People/berners-lee`) even says something to the effect that he invented the World Wide Web — which he did.

The Webmaster as visionary

Unfortunately, many folks cling to the familiar. Adventurous as the human spirit may be, human beings also fear what they don't know, so the relationship of our species to change is ambivalent at best. We do explore — we head for new continents, new planets, new ideas, new technologies. Then, when we get there, we try to make whatever we discover into what we already know. We settle new lands by re-creating our home culture, and we interpret new ideas by comparing them to the familiar — sometimes by even failing to comprehend the new idea just because it is unfamiliar and other times by turning what's new into the familiar! It takes people a while to willingly embrace and weave into their lives the new and the different.

A Webmaster must not only be able to see into the future but to invent it. A Webmaster — even a Webmaster working in solitude on a small site — must be able to envision the site and how it is to look, work, and fulfill its promise. A great Webmaster can embrace new technologies and apply them as appropriate to fulfill the Web initiative's goals. What's more, a Webmaster should be able to describe that vision of the future in such clear terms that he or she can win others over to it.

The Webmaster as evangelist

Powers of persuasion come in very handy for the Webmaster. In the course of events, he or she may find it necessary to first sell the Web itself to the company and then sell the idea that a Web initiative is a worthy cause. After the first rush of excitement the Web inspired, many companies began to realize that a Web site was not a free ride, and for much of 1996, *retrenchment* was the watchword. Did the site make money? Where were the riches everyone expected to roll in so easily from the company's Web presence? (Luckily, people got a better grip in 1997.) A Webmaster's role may include assessing the company's strategy and persuading the powers that be that the described Web initiative is the way to go, but that role may also involve reeling in expectations and focusing on what the Web can realistically do for the company.

Evangelizing the site to the outside world — marketing the site itself — is the subject of Chapters 13 and 14.

The Webmaster, who has presumably embraced an evolving, dynamic world filled with change, must also help foster in others some level of comfort with change. On the Web, things change very quickly. It may not be clear to a company's decision-makers that new tools are needed every few months to keep up with the dynamic rate of movement on the Web. It may take some selling to convince certain executives that the Webmaster's request for a Sun Sparc workstation or a T1 line is not frivolous but is indeed well thought through. To get and keep confidence that the site is worthwhile and that investing in new tools is not throwing good money after bad, the Webmaster must continue to evangelize the Web, the site, and the ability of the Web to fulfill the company's business goals. (See Chapter 2 to look into setting goals for the site that align with company goals.)

The Webmaster as business strategist

A company's Web site shouldn't be just a company hobby. Like everything else the company does, the Web site — to be successful and to be seen as successful — should further the company's overall ambitions. A company Web site should operate based on a business plan that's geared toward making and keeping the Web initiative effective and manageable. In this case, the Webmaster acts as a business strategist, defining and prioritizing goals for the Web site and generally managing the fulfillment of the site's mission. The site's goals, of course, should be based on those of the company. (See Chapter 2.)

At first, a Webmaster may find that keeping a tight rein aimed at a focused goal is the way to go. As with any business initiative, early successes can lead to the kind of recognition that brings bigger budgets and the resources needed for more ambitious projects. When dealing with a Web endeavor, striking out toward a bold result can also lead to bigger budgets. Whether that or the narrow-focus strategy is best in a given company is one of the many business judgments a Webmaster may make.

The intrepid Webmaster, fulfilling the role of business strategist, often finds that various departments in the company have differing — or even conflicting — wishes for the way the Web-site strategy should go. Here, again, is an opportunity for the Webmaster to act as a business strategist, in this case judging which is the best direction from an overall business perspective. Forget going in all possible directions — trying everything and seeing what works is never a good idea.

Keep in mind that most business endeavors succeed if they have less than three key objectives. Prioritizing those objectives up front is also usually a wise move. Chapter 2 is geared toward helping you focus on your goals.

It's up to the Webmaster to help the company see the opportunities available in having a Web presence, and to exploit them fully. By their very nature, and because the medium is in its infancy, Web initiatives are a risky business. A Webmaster may be called on in the most conservative of blue-suited companies to propose a risky venture and to predict its success with little hard data to back up the plan. A clear sense of business judgment and confidence in assessing the suitability of the venture can really come in handy. Skill at adapting to frequent, large-scale change is an asset, as is an ability to help the company and its people to adapt similarly on the fly.

The goal of the site is *always* to advance the goals of the company. This means that, while the Webmaster may yearn deeply to be first on the block to implement push technology, for example, he or she has to consider the business implications of every aspect of the site, including the relative wisdom of implementing new technology.

The success of a Web site from a business viewpoint can be hard to measure. The Web is too young and has grown too quickly to allow universally accepted mileposts to have developed. As a result, it falls to the Webmaster to guide the company in developing its expectations of the Web initiative and then to manage the company's expectations as things change. Chapter 15 covers measuring success as it is currently seen.

The Webmaster as manager of expectations

Someone has to see to it that everyone whose opinion counts in a company understands what can and can't be done on, through, and to the company Web site. The first barrier to implementing a Web site is often the fact that people don't understand the Web and what can be done. They have no expectations of the site because they don't know what to expect.

Oddly enough, in the next phase — the enthusiasm phase — people get all excited and want to post everything within reach on the company Web site. They may imagine that millions are going to flock to the site just because it's been launched or that millions are going to buy their wonderwidget just because it's shown on the company site. These are cases where expectations have risen to an unreasonable level, making the likelihood that the site is going to be *seen* as successful very slim, even if it actually *is* successful.

The Webmaster's task is to guide the company in clearly setting and understanding realistic goals for the site and in assessing what resources are needed to meet those goals. Both actual costs and opportunity costs have to be considered: If we post *x* on the site, we are spending our resources and can't do *y* — is that the right business choice? It's up to the Webmaster to lay out a thoughtful plan, to manage expectations as they arise, and to manage the perception of results. (You may think of the Webmaster as sometimes slipping into the role of spin doctor!) Measuring success is the topic of Chapter 15.

The Webmaster as creative implementer

With all of the roles a Webmaster has — acting as visionary, evangelist, business strategist, and manager of expectations — at the end of the day, the Webmaster must have implemented a winning site that runs reliably 24 hours a day, 7 days a week. To make that so, he or she must engage in a long list of ordinary activities, which range from server and database maintenance through checking links and logs and ending, perhaps, in creatively implementing content.

For many Webmasters, the tasks involved in maintaining the site are a joy. Many Webmasters love doing server maintenance — somehow it seems like polishing or tinkering with a fine car. There is surprising room for creativity in everyday tasks, and for the Webmaster, devising a better system for checking the error logs may be one of the special, warm-hearted moments of Webmastering.

What's more, because the site's basic purpose is to further the goals of the company, the Webmaster sometimes has to simply implementing content or methodology that someone else sees as urgent. In those moments, it's the Webmaster's task to bring forward the best in that content, making it as easy to navigate and as dynamic and useful as any of his or her own pet content. The Webmaster's responsibilities are to the user, to the site, and to fulfilling the site's mission.

The Four Types of Webmasters

Today's Webmaster may have overall responsibility for the site or one specific assignment. He or she may be the person who administers the technical end of things or may be someone like a film producer, who is responsible for making the project come alive. He or she may be like an executive who is responsible for the overall project but who has never laid eyes on the server itself. In the sections that follow, you can take a quick look at the various jobs a Webmaster may have.

There are four basic types of Webmasters. However, in many cases, all the jobs described in the following sections are taken on by a single Webmaster in a one-person-band approach. This is certainly the case in a one-person Web job shop, in a small company, or in a company where the Web site is not mission critical or where the Web initiative's budget is small. If that's the case where you are, it's still important to know and understand the various roles a Webmaster may have and how these roles interact.

The tech Webmaster

In a first-things-first world, the one, true Webmaster is the person who keeps the technical underpinnings of the site shiny and running smoothly. This person may be responsible for setting up the server (or maybe even *servers* if the site is a very big one), for keeping the connection going, for seeing to it that any database back ends are nicely integrated into the site systems, and for reading the log files and responding to any problems that may occur.

The tech-type Webmaster may also be called on to do programming, coding, scripting, database development, and search-engine configuration, or to spec and buy hardware and software or get bids from vendors. (Whew!)

It's not strictly necessary for the tech Webmaster to have a degree in computer science — a solid background in system administration does quite nicely. Someone who has been responsible for keeping a LAN or a big database running has the basic skills needed for this job. Knowledge of TCP/IP is a big plus — almost a requirement. If that person also has programming skills in C++ or Perl, so much the better.

Tech Webmasters absolutely must have a fundamental curiosity about the tools of their job. This is because they have to stay on top of technological trends. That means if you are hiring a tech Webmaster, you need to find someone with a high degree of enthusiasm and a sense of intellectual adventure. On the other hand, this person has to be diligent enough to read log files regularly and disciplined enough to stay on top of what those log files reveal.

The tech Webmaster position is obviously very important — without the server, there is no Web site. What's more, the tech Webmaster's job is being done best when the effects of the work are invisible to others. Think about this: If the server is running well and the connection never goes down, it's easy for the clueless to start wondering what the tech Webmaster is doing with his or her time. We've seen cases where the techie looks like a hero for repairing systems that crash all the time. Keep in mind that the truly heroic tech Webmaster is the one who maintains a stable, smooth-running, trouble-free system.

It's also *very* important for other members of the Web-site team to consult the tech Webmaster before forging ahead with plans to alter the site; all too often, some piece of the technical underpinnings may be at stake. For example, production folks may think it's a fine idea to use *server includes* to repeat a piece of content or a navigational element on every page in the site. If they were to consult with the tech Webmaster, they could find that server includes would trip up the server's successful handling of online transactions that some other part of the team was in the process of implementing.

The bottom line is that, while the techie's job, when done successfully, is often seemingly invisible, the techie's presence in matters of creating and implementing what goes online should be very high profile. It is a bad idea to simply expect this person to find a way to implement whatever the rest of the team thinks should be done. When anyone on the Web-site team has a scheme for implementing just about anything that doesn't already exist on the site, the first step should always be to consult with the tech Webmaster.

The content Webmaster

Face facts: It's pretty unlikely for one person to have the hard-core technical skills of a tech Webmaster *and* be well versed in creating content. If you're putting together a Web-site team and you can hire only two people, those people should be a techie and a content Webmaster. The content Webmaster is typically responsible for, well, creating and managing content. That can mean as little as writing, editing, and posting static Web pages or as much as driving strategy for a large-scale Web site using state-of-the-art technologies for live content, audio, sound, and *push* (or actively broadcast) content.

The content Webmaster in a larger Web team may also be charged with establishing standards for look and feel, for how the interface works, for the style of writing and how it's presented, or even for the whole shebang of what the site is actually like. Often this person is called a *producer,* which is a bit of a holdover from the multimedia field that preceded Web development by a few years.

What's a Webmaster to you?

Akemi Tazaki, who frequents the Webgrrls mailing list, answered from the tech viewpoint, "A Webmaster is a system administrator with Internet technology knowledge and skills — a computer (professional) with multimedia/ Internet computing and good hardware knowledge. He or she knows several programming languages, like C++ and Java, *and* knows how to document and manage a software program.

(An applet or a CGI script is actually a small software program.)" She also suggests that a Webmaster needs a BS degree with on-site training or significant experience in and tremendous curiosity about high-tech matters. "Basically," she says, "you need to get turned on deeply by the technology and have really *good* reading skills so you can make yourself an expert."

What I really want to do is *produce*

In the movies, the person who calls the shots (no pun intended) is called a *director.* In television, that person is called a *producer.* (In movies, the producer is more of a business type who gets the financing and puts deals together but does not — usually — direct the content.) In the multimedia milieu, the shot-caller is again called a *producer,* as in television. That language has carried over to professional Web teams, where the person who calls the shots and carries forth the site's mission is often called a producer rather than a Webmaster. Producers, however, typically have pretty good technical knowledge. If they don't do the scriptwriting and HTML production work, they can at least carry on an intelligent conversation in those areas. At best, they can press themselves into service doing the scripting and HTML work to keep a project on track.

If you're really strapped and can hire only one person for your Web team, go for the content Webmaster. Why? Because a lot of site maintenance can be jobbed out to your Internet service provider, and design can be jobbed out to a design firm. But someone is going to have to figure out what the content is going to be and tell the ISP and design firm which end is up in that content. That person must be familiar with your company's products, strategy, and positioning among competitors. The person should also be familiar enough with Web technology to be able to talk intelligently with the techie or the ISP, and he should have enough grasp of the technology to envision and imagine ways to create and expand lively content.

It is often said that on the Web, content is king. Yet, oddly enough, many companies think first about hiring a tech Webmaster when they search for someone to be on staff. They seem to expect this person to be a programmer, writer, editor, designer, and marketing strategist all rolled into one. Don't fall for that. If you do, you end up with a site with possibly strong underpinnings but probably weak content. Think about it — how many people visit a Web site to admire its server and elegant scripting?

In a Web *job shop* — a company that specializes in creating Web sites — the content Webmaster or producer is often the person who has the most contact with the client. In that case, this person may be called on to help the client focus on goals and concepts, to define the site and maintain the schedule and budget, and to report to both the client and the job shop on progress. (Chapter 8 covers working with Web shops.)

In a best-case scenario, the content Webmaster or producer has writing and editorial skills along with HTML ability, at least a basic understanding of layout and navigation in an online world, perhaps some ability to do scripting in CGI or perl, and if you're very lucky, some actual design training or basic programming background. Given that precious few people have both college credits in these topics (in an online setting) and enough world experience to have developed judgment and supervision skills, it may be best to consider those with transferable skills to fill the spot of content Webmaster. We've found that people with experience as multimedia producers make good content Webmasters — as do people with backgrounds as high-level editors in print media.

That last one may surprise you. But consider that an editor's job has to do with putting himself in the shoes of the reader (the user, in this case) and figuring how to help shape that reader/user's experience as that person navigates the material. In print media, like magazines and books, the editor often has to consider where to break material to appear on a deeper page and which stories are most appropriate for the front page, while in nonfiction books, the editor also considers what topics warrant cross-referencing (hmmm . . . kind of like *linking*) to other places in the text or to other documents. And heaven knows editors of print media have to be well versed in copyright law, which is increasingly important in Web publishing.

It may be tempting to save a few bucks by assigning responsibility for your company Web site to someone in a seemingly related department — for example, marketing — as something to do in his or her spare time. Remember that this makes fulfilling such a responsibility a very low priority to that person. If your site is important enough to create, it's probably important enough to assign to someone who knows what he or she is doing.

Again, if your Web team is really a one-person band, go for a content whiz with as many technical and design skills as possible. That person should also be able to strategize, organize, edit, and control documents as well as manage projects and hire and oversee outside contractors. You'll have to contract out the tech and design sides, but that's not difficult.

What one Web wizard does

Web diva Tamra Heathershaw-Hart says, "Yes, you do have to be a designer and an engineer and a marketer if you're a one-person-band Web shop . . . I have to know how to make beautiful art work at 216 colors, how to do animated GIFs, how to lay out sites using table codes (and still make them readable to older browsers), how to make server-side includes work on an NT server, how to create database-driven sites, how to hook up to Cybercash and set up secure ordering, how to set up mailing list software, how to write proposals, and how to market my clients' sites so they get visitors. And don't forget knowing how to install chat software!"

The production Webmaster

In the Web world, production often means design, and design often means page layout. The fact is that few companies or Web shops can manage to hire a designer, an illustrator, a couple of HTML production people, and a creative director to keep 'em all on track. Instead, someone is often hired who falls somewhere in that continuum and who is then expected to fill all of those roles. So what else is new in the business world?

A couple of years ago, there was such a shortage of people with design skills who knew anything about the Web that anyone with the slightest design experience could easily get work on the Web. We still see postings every day on e-mail mailing lists for Web designers, but those doing the hiring now have higher expectations — not just any designer who can use a Web browser can get the big bucks today. Instead, a designer is expected to be familiar with HTML, electronic typography, Adobe Photoshop, deBabelizer, compression software, the 216-color palette, and more. Luckily, design schools are seeing this need, and many now have programs for training people to do Web design work. NYU and UCLA have notable programs, for example.

A production Webmaster may be a Jack or Jill of all trades. He or she may handle everything from overall site design through spot illustrations that go on the pages, creation of page templates that make production simpler, HTML production itself, scanning art, and maintaining tags that specify certain types of links. In smaller organizations, this person also tracks the work flow and hires out art jobs as needed. For tips on outsourcing Web design or other production work, turn to Chapter 8. The main things to remember about the design personnel that you hire are:

- ✔ They should have a style compatible with your site.
- ✔ They should have the special technical skills the Web requires.
- ✔ They should be able to understand and visually interpret the goals of your site. For example, if your site is primarily a source of functional information, the designer should make navigation easy, whereas if your site sells fine furniture, you probably need a more designerly look that is compatible with the style of the furniture itself.

The executive Webmaster

Simply speaking, this is the boss. The boss on a Web team may come from the tech world, the content world, or the production world. Or, he or she may just come from the management world with a background in marketing, editorial, or even operations; this person may in fact have no Web experience, though this is not the wisest way to go. While many non-Web-world skills, such as managing a LAN or editing print media, are highly transferable to the Web, it's a big handicap to try to manage a Web team with no background in the Web at all.

If you're in a position to hire the boss of a Web team, it's important to find someone who has experience managing projects and preferably has experience managing the technical, content, or production side of a Web site. Even having a little experience in any of those areas combined with some solid project management and business background can work out well. If you are a manager who finds yourself thrust into the role of running a Web team and you have no Web experience, consider jobbing a great deal of stuff out until you are up to speed with the technology.

The person who is charged with directing a Web team is often called a senior producer, an executive producer, a content director, or an executive content director. These titles, which are similar to those used in multimedia and somewhat similar to titles used in film and TV, all roughly correspond in print media to the title of editor-in-chief.

The executive Webmaster's role often includes making and tracking the overall budget, and creating strategic partnerships or making business alliances. This is a business role, and traditional business and management skills are transferable here.

In the early days of Web development, running the Web site often fell to the person who first got the idea and the impetus to set up a fledgling site. As the industry matures, this job is more often assigned to a manager. If the Web initiative's mission is to market stuff, the Web-team boss may be a marketing manager. If the site is to publish strong content, go for a content type. If it's supposed to be offering the company or the public whiz-bang technology, a tech type — maybe from information services — may be the chosen one.

Finding Webmasters and Finding a Job as a Webmaster

Little Webmasters can be found in cabbage patches under the leafy purple stuff — too bad this isn't true. As of this writing, there is no officially sanctioned Webmaster certification. Universities and technical seminars are training programmers and system administrators, and as time goes on, more colleges and extension programs will be training people with the specialized skills that are involved in creating and running a Web site. But the field is still quite new, and while the Internet may exist in fast-forward mode, the education system certainly does not.

It's tough for a hiring manager to know how to assess a Webmaster's skills and abilities, and taking the short route of simply hiring someone with years of Java experience is a big mistake. As we've discussed throughout this chapter, *Webmaster* is a title that can describe a wide variety of charters and tasks. While it may be reassuring to the corporate hiring manager to think a certificate assures someone's legitimate skill level, the Webmaster community argues that it's really tough to test technical skills that change at the speed of light, let alone more abstract skills like the ability to imagine this design and that functionality working together smoothly.

The perfect Webmaster may be someone with an MBA in marketing, two bachelor's degrees (one in computer science and one in multimedia design), and a minor in English or journalism. Of course, this person should also probably have five years of project management experience as well! This is hardly reasonable to expect in one person. The bottom line is this: Don't bother looking for degrees or certification when you try to hire a Webmaster; instead, look for shining accomplishments and demonstrated skills.

Web technologies move so fast that, even if there were a certification program, this year's degree may be next year's bird-cage liner. It's vision, accomplishment, drive, and demonstrated skills that count, along with a clear understanding of the site's objectives and an ability to carry them out.

In-house staff with transferable skills

Don't overlook the folks you already have. Think about it — they know your business, they know the company values, and they know their current fields. A small Web team may consist of someone from marketing, someone from the technical side, and someone from editorial in a publishing house (or perhaps from your in-house design department if your company creates its own marketing collateral). It's tough to have these people work on the Web initiative in their spare time, though. The company's core business, which is presumably generating revenue, is usually thought of as a first priority, with the Web work slipping to a much lower spot on the priority scale. To create a Web team that puts its best effort into the Web initiative, if you pull people from in-house, truly *pull* them — place them in a separate team that can gel and work toward a focused goal.

Avoid the inclination to believe no one in-house is qualified to be Webmaster. The job is too broad for any one person to be fully qualified, and there are no universally reliable certification standards. Furthermore, an in-house Webmaster's primary responsibility is to fulfill the mission of the company's Web initiative, and who knows your company's mission better than in-house people?

Other fields

If you go outside to seek a Webmaster, first try to determine the purpose of your site and where your in-house staff is strongest. If you have a solid IS department but no one in marketing who knows the Web, you may find that a content Webmaster is a better choice than a techie. If your site is going to deliver a great deal of text as its content, you may look for someone with an editorial background. You may have to get creative about where you look for a Webmaster. Don't overlook editors, database administrators, marketing folks, and so on. But try to get someone who has a fundamental understanding of your business along with the mix of skills that make up a good Webmaster.

Universities, colleges, and training programs

Some colleges and universities have taken a plunge into the future by offering Webmaster courses or even short-term certification programs; these programs are often cobbled together out of existing courses in various departments. As of this writing, Los Angeles City College, DePaul University, Marquette University, UC Santa Barbara (through the extension), and the New Jersey Institute of Technology are on board; others are sure to follow quickly.

If you're thinking about becoming a Webmaster and you're looking for where to start, you may put together your own quick-study program that pulls together coursework in network and system administration, graphic production, interactive marketing, and programming. Many colleges and universities grant independent study degrees if you have a well-thought-out course plan that you can present. Alternatively, just having the right mix of coursework on your resume can, in combination with the smallest measure of demonstrated skill, get you a job in this field.

Take some classes and build a good portfolio

According to freelance Web developer Ann Marie Michaels, "If you have a good portfolio, that says much more about your ability than a degree. In fact, some of the best graphic designers and programmers I have worked with had no college education. They taught themselves. Then there are others, just as talented, who went to a two-year trade school. Still others went to a university. The point is, what you do to get the skills doesn't matter. It's what you do with your skills that is important. I think it's smart to take some classes (even part-time) to ramp up your skills — this is much faster than trying to learn on your own. Don't worry about completing a degree."

Where to place and find Webmaster job listings

As manager of a Web team or a hiring manager, you may have to think creatively about hiring Webmasters. Look for Webmasters through the usual hiring channels, but post notices in online venues, too. Online is where these people (especially the experienced, qualified ones) hang out. Here are some national venues that post job listings, including Webmaster listings:

- The Monster Board (http://www.monster.com) is a huge site with listings for all sorts of jobs.
- Career Mosaic (http://www.careermosaic.com) is another biggie.
- CareerPath.com (http://www.careerpath.com) includes ads from newspaper classified sections around the United States.
- Career Web (http://www.cweb.com) specializes in listiing jobs in the tech industry.

You'll also find that many print newspapers and trade magazines have online versions; often their classified ads appear in both the print and online worlds.

Don't forget, too, to look into professional organizations and guilds such as those listed in the next section, and to post ads to discussion groups or mailing lists that accept ads (such as the Webgrrls list noted in the next section). Not all discussion groups and mailing lists accept ads, but hey, if you can find one that's populated by Webmaster types and accepts ads, too, where better to look for qualified people? If you aren't sure whether a given group or list does accept ads, ask who's moderating the thing and inquire with that person — even if you can't place the ad there, you may get word of mouth going.

Webmaster Guilds and Groups

So you want to be a Webmaster — or maybe you already are one — and you're looking around for other Webmasters to network with. Where are your colleagues trading tips and strategies? They aren't gathering around the water cooler at your job — that is, unless your job is at a Web job shop or a search-engine company. Here are some handy sources of Webmaster information.

The Webmasters' Guild (`http://www.webmaster.org`) has as one of its noble goals the standardizing of a certification for professional Webmasters. At this point, there are local chapters only in San Francisco and Boston, but you can stay in touch online. At the site, the guild offers a job board and a QA section; there are also a couple of mailing lists, particularly about intranets and e-commerce.

WebMaster magazine (`http://www.web-master.com`) is a great online service for Webmasters, including content from the magazine itself and a highly useful archive of articles, discussion forums, and listings of people looking to hire a Webmaster. Contributors to the magazine include organizers and members of the Webmasters' Guild, among others.

The Webmaster's Reference Library (`http://www.webreference.com`) provides information on all aspects of building Web sites — from picking a server to tools you can use to produce cutting-edge pages.

You can also look for local groups. Here in San Francisco, we've found the Webgrrls mailing list a constant source of good information; there is a national Webgrrls site at `http://webgrrls.com`. Additionally, The Bay Area Internet Users Group (`http://www.baiug.org`) sponsors a monthly meeting with speakers about Internet issues.

Speaking of mailing lists, look into Iconocast for a gathering of fellow Webmasters. To subscribe, send a message to `majordomo@iconocast.com`; in the body of your message, type **subscribe iconocast**. Subscriptions to Iconocast are free. In return, you agree to receive no more than 12 sponsored e-casts per year.

Throughout this book, we highlight additional online resources of special interest to the well-rounded Webmaster. And in Chapter 16, we tell you about ten sites that can save your life.

Chapter 2

Your Site's Goals Define Everything Else

In This Chapter

▶ Defining your site's goals

▶ The six basic goals a Web site can fulfill

▶ Looking into your audience

▶ Creating community and what that counts for

▶ Revenue models and other resource issues

▶ A quick look at measuring success

▶ Writing a mission statement

*B*efore you build your Web site, you must plan your Web site. And before you plan your Web site, you must have a pretty clear idea of where you want to go. This is only logical, right? No one would build a house without a plan. To build a house, most folks would hire an architect or at least a skilled contractor, who would come up with a plan based on the answers to a series of questions about the purpose of the building, the budget, the sort of look the client is hoping for, and so on. To build anything, one starts with defining the goal for that thing. In the case of a Web site, you may hire a Web job shop and have those folks do the detailed planning, or you may appoint yourself architect of your own site. In either case, it is up to you to determine just what your site is supposed to accomplish.

It's always a good idea to keep in mind your future goals as well as your current goals. That's because you don't want to have to undo today's work when you decide to implement something new six months from now. So as you define your goals, think about them in terms of what you want to accomplish in the short term and the longer term. On the other hand, keep in mind that on the Web, the short term is pretty immediate, while the long term is 6 to 12 months from now.

Keep Your Eyes on the Prize

Things move so fast on the Web that it's often a temptation to zip on past the planning stages of building a Web site and move directly into implementing. This is a big mistake. Trust us — you only wind up spending that same time unknotting all the problems that arise daily from doing things so much on the fly. If we make one point repeatedly in this book, it's going to be this: Like a finely trained athlete, you, the wonder Webmaster, need to stay light on your feet but keep your eyes fixed firmly on the prize.

It's true that, unlike other forms of media — print, for example, where you must dot every *i* and cross every *t* before you go to print — the Web lends itself to incremental development. You can put up the home page today, expand a certain area tomorrow, and introduce entirely new subject matter and technologies any time you like. While this makes things so that almost anyone with a word processor and an Internet-access account can start building a Web site in the next half hour, it also makes it more possible for things to get out of hand.

What happens when you lose focus

One of the worst things that can happen to a Web site is what we call *Winchester Mystery House syndrome.* You see, smack dab in the middle of Silicon Valley, in San Jose, California, there is this house — the Winchester Mystery House. It was built by a dotty old rich woman, and she believed that if she ever stopped building that house, she would die. So there are rooms upon rooms, and they go willy-nilly in every direction. It's very funny, and tourists go there, but do you want your Web site to resemble a dotty Victorian fun house or does it have a true purpose?

Now imagine Winchester Mystery House syndrome applied to your budget, your staffing, or your site's concept. The mind just boggles, eh?

What you gain by setting goals and planning

Okay, it's true that coming up with a clear plan is going to cost you time and maybe even money in the short run. You may think this means it's going to take longer to launch that oh-so-important Web site, but here we offer you a money-back guarantee: In the long term, we guarantee you that focusing on your goals before you plan your site can save you both time and money.

Remember, your purpose is not to go to launch with a complete site that includes every bell, whistle, and piece of brilliant content you envision for your site. You don't have to have every single content area or useful gizmo in place at the start. In fact, if you wait for your site to be "finished," you may never launch. Your goal is to launch with a site that is focused and that can support your vision. To do that, you want to create a plan that makes the site you launch a building block — not a road block — to the site you've envisioned.

One more thing: Over time, your plans for your site are going to change. This is bound to happen — it's just the nature of the Web. As new technologies become available, your organization is going to have new and different ideas for its Web initiative, and so are you. Don't worry — be happy. Stay light on your feet, with your eyes on the prize.

What Exactly Are We Doing Here?

Before you start planning your Web site, ask yourself — and whomever is footing the bill — a few questions. Here's where you put on your marketeer and business-strategist hats. The basic questions are:

- ✔ What is our purpose?
- ✔ Who are we trying to reach?
- ✔ Who are our competitors?
- ✔ What resources do we have?
- ✔ What expectations of success do we have?
- ✔ How will we measure our success?

After you've considered these questions, you're in a good spot to start planning your site. (Chapter 6 covers actually creating the architecture of your site.)

Throughout this chapter, we talk about setting goals and show you a lot of example sites. Think of this as a shortcut tour through the possibilities. You can and should take your own online tour of sites that may be similar to what you have in mind. We're just getting you started.

What is our purpose?

In most cases, you find that the company for which you're creating that nifty Web site already has clearly set, company-wide goals. They probably sell or provide a product or a service — most organizations do. In that case, the overriding goals of the site should parallel those of the company.

Specify no more than three important goals for your Web site, and be sure to prioritize them. For example, your site may have as its goals (a) promoting the company's image and products, (b) providing purchase support to potential customers or clients, and (c) selling your product or service directly via the Web site.

However, the goals of the Web site can *parallel* the goals of the company and may not match them exactly, at least at the surface. To get a clear picture of this, read on.

The basic goals of Web sites

At their most basic, Web sites usually serve some combination of six basic purposes. Some sites serve several of these purposes, while others are more purely focused. But in general, most sites attempt to do at least one of these:

- Entertain
- Inform
- Sell
- Promote
- Distribute
- Research and report

Your mission, then, is to determine which of these purposes (or which combination of purposes) is suitable for your site. In the sections that follow, we look a bit more closely at some examples to help get you started.

You also need to consider whether your site exists for profit or not for profit — the difference is not quite the same as the difference between a profit-driven company and a nonprofit organization. One can get an official nonprofit designation if that's to allow a different tax status. In this case, all we mean is that your site should be geared directly toward making money or not.

Sites that entertain

Many sites have entertainment as their sole purpose, although few really big entertainment sites live on without underwriting by a large corporation. The Spot is (or was) a famous serial (or online soap), a creation of American Cybercast Network (http://www.amcy.com), and as of this writing has been sponsored by Toyota. Another serial, Ferndale (http://www.ferndale.com), is run by Songline Studios (which, in turn, is funded by America Online).

Some companies don't have online tech support to offer, and they really have nothing to promote other than their brand name. For them, entertainment content is often the way to go, as shown by sites like Mama's Cucina, the Ragu site (http://www.ragu.com). It offers lessons in cooking and the Italian language, and it's barrels of fun to click through. Similar entertainment sites that also serve to sell or promote a product include Crayola (http://www.crayola.com), Ben & Jerry's (http://www.benjerry.com), and Tanqueray (http://www.tanqueray.com).

The IRS is certainly not known as an entertainment enterprise, but visitors to its Web site (http://www.irs.ustreas.gov) may be surprised and delighted by the user-friendly, fun, and warm presentation the content is given (see Figure 2-1). This is particularly laudable considering the other content the IRS has to offer — tax forms, filing guidelines, tax laws, and so on.

Cool Site of the Day: An entertaining case study

Since 1994, Cool Site of the Day (http://cool.infi.net/) has achieved enormous success based on an extremely simple concept: Find a cool link, and point everyone there. Although the link-a-day operation has been copied countless times, CSOTD is undoubtedly the most successful (and most frequently visited) Web site that does nothing but serve up noteworthy links. While Glenn Davis, the original arbiter of Cool, has moved on to create his own (quite similar) page (at http://www.projectcool.com), and CSOTD has expanded to include other "cool" editorial features, the main premise hasn't changed: Tell people what to look at, and they will. What keeps the site going? It's run by Infi.net, an ISP from Norfolk, Virginia. One may imagine that Infi.net scores quite a few customers just because "it's the ISP that runs Cool Site of the Day. They must know what they're doing." What's more, Infi.net was started by Landmark Communications, whose partners include Gannett and Knight-Ridder, the newspaper people. They started the ISP to put those newspapers online.

Figure 2-1:
The IRS
softens its
image
through this
entertaining
but
practical
and
informative
site.

Perhaps the least surprising entertainment sites are those offered by entertainment giants like 20th Century Fox (http://www.foxinc.com), Paramount (http://www.paramount.com), and Disney (http://www.disney.com). (And by the way, just *what* is 20th Century Fox going to do in a couple of short years when the 20th century sounds like yesterday's oatmeal?)

Sites that inform

An excellent example of a largely informative site that serves to promote a company almost invisibly is the Ultimate Band List (http://www.ubl.com). (We're not sure obscuring the company is the best way to go, but there you are.) American Recordings, a record company, maintains this huge index of music-related Web pages with nary a mention that the site is a product of American Recordings. Music artists from every label get equal time on the site, which is attractive to music fans who rarely limit their tastes (or their buying habits) to records from only one label.

The Web site of any magazine, radio station, newspaper, television network, or news service is always a dual effort in providing information — which is the commodity these companies sell to begin with — in other media. What's interesting about extremely successful news sites like CNN (http://www.cnn.com), ESPNet Sportzone (http://www.espnet.sportszone.com), and HotWired (a Web endeavor of Wired Ventures, at http://www.hotwired.com) is that they also feature original content that is not available outside of the Web. HotWired is pretty close to a virtual-only model, as is CNET (http://www.cnet.com), but all of those sites also serve to promote another service, in paper or on television.

Completely information-based Web sites often come in the form of news and features (the magazine model, as seen in Salon at http://www.salon1999. com), but these are often the most useful when they're also resources *about* the Internet. Women's Wire (http://www.women.com) is successful not only because it offers a wealth of information for and about women, but because it features a huge catalog of other resources for women on the Internet. This sort of model — the Web resource plus news and entertainment resource — is what most of the major Internet directories use these days. Infoseek (http://www.infoseek.com) and Yahoo! (http://www.yahoo.com) are particularly good examples of sites that offer both virtual and real-world information — there is no physical product involved at all.

Online chats can be said to be informing — in this case, instead of the Web publisher informing an audience, the "audience" may be informing each other. One site that both informs and creates community is Parent Soup (http://www.parentsoup.com). Centered around live chats as well as informative articles, Parent Soup attracts parents who either want to take a break from parenting or learn more about it. A similar site, ParentsPlace (http://www.parentsplace.com), also offers chats for parents. Parent Soup and ParentsPlace are both owned by iVillage (http://www.ivillage. com), which has sponsors ranging from Acutane to Polaroid to UPS.

Sites that sell

Although Amazon.com (http://www.amazon.com) has the obvious purpose of selling books over the Internet through secure transactions, which are described in Chapter 3 (and at large discounts — another big selling point), it also makes efforts to inform its audience. Its site includes not only a searchable database of book titles and authors but additional information for book lovers, such as listings of Pulitzer Prize winners, *New York Times* bestsellers, and top titles in fields such as mysteries and science fiction. Book lovers enjoy this type of information, and the addition of editors' and critics' picks on special topics like Web development and Women's History Month serves to entertain the audience and spark sales. Similar efforts can be seen at CDNOW (http://www.cdnow.com), which sells CDs and video-tapes.

Walnut Creek CDROM (http://www.cdrom.com) is a huge manufacturer and distributor of CD-ROMs that has preserved customer loyalty through its huge archive of freeware and shareware. Anyone can access the archive through Walnut Creek's FTP (file transfer protocol) site. Give the customers free stuff, and they think of you when they need to buy similar products. That's the apparent thinking behind TUCOWS (http://www.tucows.com). TUCOWS is in the business of giving away software for free, and it also sells a CD-ROM that archives the best of TUCOWS. In this case, TUCOWS is banking on people wanting to avoid downloading all the free software in their archives by ordering the CD.

Travelocity (http://www.travelocity.com) is an online travel-agent service that lets visitors plan vacations and purchase tickets and hotel reservations via a Web browser. In addition to convenience, the site offers contests, discounts, and other promotions through partnerships with large travel companies. Travelocity wouldn't be so successful, however, if it didn't provide some content in the form of travelogues, travel guides, photo essays, and chat rooms. People come to Travelocity to get tips and ideas for planning their vacation, and buying the tickets is often an added convenience rather than the main reason for visiting the site.

Sites that promote

While it isn't feasible just yet to actually buy a new car online, the large car manufacturers all have a Web presence that serves as a promotional vehicle. (Yuck, yuck.) There isn't much appeal in visiting a billboard in the form of a Web site, so most of these manufacturers embellish their sites with some form of entertainment content, in addition to specs on new models and features. Toyota's site (http://www.toyota.com) features a section called Car Culture, which is about driving, road trips, travel, and other car stuff. Interestingly, Toyota used to have a section called The Hub, which featured several different online *zines* (electronic magazines). That was kind of clever in that it re-created the sort of upscale magazines in which car companies usually advertise. (Don't go to the audience, bring the audience to you!) Now Toyota has distilled its online content venture from an amalgam of sports, living, and entertainment to the basics: cars. You can see similar approaches at Volkswagen's site (http://www.vw.com), which focuses on younger drivers, and at BMW's (http://www.bmwusa.com), which uses the appeal of both online technology and sports car engineering to sell its sedans.

Marketing genius is nowhere more evident than in the Levi Strauss site (http://www.levi.com). Having posited its product, blue denim jeans, as more of a cultural icon than an article of clothing, levi.com follows up on this premise by offering a good deal of history on blue jeans. But a historical site wouldn't appeal on its own to Levi's target audience (which ranges from 15 through baby boomer). The rest of the site (see Figure 2-2) is entertainment based; it includes not only fashion, but nightlife around the world and occasional spotlights on recording artists or other completely non-jeans-related material. It helps that the site looks *amazing*.

A tried-and-true promotion strategy is the *charity affiliation*. When corporations sponsor or donate to a popular cause, they can't help but look good. Of course, what they're promoting is not only their own service but the

Figure 2-2:
The Levi
Strauss site
is a piece of
marketing
wizardry.

altruistic goals of the organization. An excellent example of this model is
Organic Online's Amnesty International site (http://www.organic.com/
Non.profits/Amnesty/index.html). Organic (http://www.organic.com)
is a Web and multimedia design firm, and although its look alone is enough to
attract clients, its pro bono work can only add to the appeal, especially for
young or progressive clients. Interestingly, Amnesty International maintains
another Web site (http://www.amnesty.org), which is updated more
frequently but doesn't look half as good.

Sites that distribute

Online software distribution makes sense. It eliminates the middle man (and
all of the packaging) and delivers the software directly to the computer that
is to run it. Netscape Communications Corp. (http://home.netscape.com)
is the most obvious model of online distribution for money. Other sites,
such as Progressive Networks (http://www.real.com) and Macromedia
(http://www.macromedia.com), distribute a free software product online
in hopes that the promotional aspect of the free stuff carries over into the
market for their larger, commercial products. What all of these sites do
extremely well is to offer extensive technical support for their products
online, while at the same time showcasing the best of the Web sites that use
their technologies. In Netscape's case, any really good Web site is fine, while
Progressive Networks' RealAudio and Macromedia's Shockwave are specific
Web technologies that caught on largely because of the canny distribution
techniques of the parent companies.

A corporate image site

Merck's Web site (http://www.merck.com) does not sell the company's products (at least not directly). Instead, the site offers information that promotes the company. Press releases detail Merck's impressive recent discoveries and new projects that the company has taken on. A wealth of information about health and drugs in general makes the site informative. This is a whizzy site that's designed to tout the image of Merck as a premier drug company.

From Merck's home page you can access areas about Merck's various divisions and information that Merck publishes — like the *Merck Manual of Diagnostics and Therapy,* an online version of a handy book. This gives both professionals and laypeople a good, solid reason to visit the site repeatedly — for reference. When they get there, some folks may click around and get the rest of the Merck news.

The primary purpose of a corporate-image site like this one is to promote the company. Corporate image sites can consist of a few pages or thousands of pages. The Merck site is well done, with some big, impressive information available. However, it does not, as of this writing, include one element that many sites of this type provide — a stockholder-relations section. Such an area may contain a copy of the company's annual report, along with copies of any other filings with the SEC and other financial news. It may also be linked back to those oh-so-informative press releases.

Whether your company is large or teensy, you may find a corporate-image site works well. Your site's size has little to do with the size of the company (but everything to do with the size of the budget and the amount of attention you want to devote to content maintenance). Just keep in mind in this case that your goal is to *promote,* and make the site represent the company well.

A more niche-oriented example of online distribution is id Software (http://www.idsoftware.com). Creator of such popular (and violent) games as Quake and Doom, id became the success it is today based on an ingenious distribution model that today is commonplace in both gaming and other software products. id was one of the first companies to offer a free, scaled down, demo version of its games over the Internet and through online services — starting in 1992! — that game players could download and play to the end. Not satisfied, of course, the gamers would need to go to the store and buy the full version. (This became known affectionately as the "drug dealer" model.) Today, id offers online purchase for many of its games as well as an excellent Web site that's geared toward both hard-core fans and prospective gamers.

Perhaps the main model for online distribution is seen in software, but a few other companies have successfully managed to sell information (meaning the content of their Web site), and perhaps that is something of a model for the future. Newspapers, for example, may charge a fee to subscribers, who receive the paper copy and get access to the Web site. The most successful of the newspaper sites in the fee-for-access game is the *San Jose Mercury News* (`http://www.sjmercury.com`). Its Mercury Center Web site offers headline access to everyone free of charge, but access to many in-depth stories, as well as the searchable archives, are only available to paid subscribers. Papers such as *The New York Times* and the *Wall Street Journal* haven't had as much success making their online paper available only to paying subscribers, however. Maybe that's because they offer nationwide distribution of their print versions, while the *Mercury News,* a Silicon Valley rag of interest to tech watchers everywhere, is not distributed nationally in print form. Another example of an information-distribution service is Quote.com (`http://www.quote.com`). Quote.com offers stock information for free to any visitor while reserving real-time stock quotes and in-depth information for paying subscribers.

TIP

A software publishing site

Some sites offer giant collections of software that you can download either for free or for a small fee that's paid to the publisher of the software; Shareware.com (`http://www.shareware.com`) is of that variety. Consider another type of site — one that's run by a single software company and focuses only on software that is published and distributed by that one company. This type of endeavor can be put forth by small one-person shops or multimillion dollar software development companies competing with each other, and the big guys don't always do it better.

A particularly tasty example is the WinZip site (`http://www.winzip.com`). If you use Microsoft Windows, as so many people do, odds are that you also use WinZip, a handy utility for compressing and uncompressing files. If you use WinZip, you may have downloaded it from the WinZip site, a real beauty that's resisted loss of focus. When you visit the site, its purpose is clear: to get WinZip onto your computer. The home page greets you with direct links to downloading the latest version of the software in an evaluation version, along with access to online documentation. You can also purchase an "unlock" key online to convert the evaluation version of WinZip into a registered copy. This is all very handy.

An example of a less closely focused software publisher site can be seen at Symantec (`http://www.symantec.com`). From the Symantec site you can download evaluation versions of some of their software, access online documentation and support files, and partake in online discussion groups that are monitored by support engineers. Our point here is that the site is not focused on the single purpose of selling software. It apparently has (at least) a dual purpose in that it also functions as a corporate image site.

Sites that research and report

Getting information *from* users or the general population is a fantastic use of the Web, and using the Web for this purpose is a real boon to marketers, researchers, and informants alike. Most of the sites we mention in the sections on stats and demographics in this chapter got their data by putting up a questionnaire or form on a Web site, letting people respond, and then compiling the raw data to create information which could then be fed back to visitors to the site. This is something you can do on your own site through customer service or marketing questionnaires; it can also be the whole purpose of a research or survey site like those demographics gatherers.

In another example, BrowserWatch (`http://www.browserwatch.com`) is a brilliant piece of work that has saved our butts more than once. This site tracks the popularity of Web browsers, plug-ins, and ActiveX controls by gathering statistics on the software used to visit the site itself. (It also tracks the emergence of upcoming betas!) Anyone interested in Internet technologies, including not only developers, administrators, and Webmasters but journalists and regular surfers, can visit BrowserWatch on a curiosity basis. Want to find out what stage the next Netscape beta is in? Here's the place. To get software that's listed on the site (if it's been released, that is), visitors can click on the Download Software button, which leads them through to a section of iWORLD, BrowserWatch's parent site. iWORLD is the Web home of Mecklermedia, which produces Internet-related magazines and trade shows.

Firefly (`http://www.firefly.com`) is said to make its business selling customer profiles to other customers. Visitors to the Web site log in with a free username and password, and from there they can choose to chat or go to the music or movies sections. These latter two sections are based on *agent* technology — users rate their favorite bands or movies using Firefly's ratings scale. After a user has rated enough products to create a basic profile, the agent computer scans the profiles of users with similar interests and suggests music and movies that people with similar tastes have reported to enjoy. These types of "recommendation services" are interesting in the novelty sense. But the real trick is in selling average profiles (or the technology itself) to their advertisers, who can then target different ads to, say, an Alanis Morissette fan or a Nine Inch Nails fan. It's almost a coup — a marketing survey that people submit a great deal of information to, for fun.

You can have more than one goal

Note that many of the sites that we just described have more than one purpose. Sure, we picked sites that do mainly one thing to make our point, but many of them also have a secondary or even third-level purpose. If your company sells music on CDs, the site can provide content to inspire the purchase of the music on these CDs from a handy retailer, it can sell music on CDs directly to the public, or both. (Of course, along the way, it should also promote the company's image.) If the company makes or sells cars, it is unlikely that you are going to sell something that big via the Net, but you can provide purchase support information that can inspire users to zip on out to a handy dealer and buy this car over its competition. You can then point them in the direction of nearby dealers. You can also provide prefinancing via the Web, through the use of a secure server that protects people's credit information in an online setting.

If the company manufactures a product that is then sold by others, its Web site may be geared toward bringing in the correct audience for that product, providing them with information about the product's sterling virtues, and then offering them links to where to buy or a Zip-code database that lets users find a retailer near them. Think for a moment about a film company's Web site — it can offer clips of films, audio or video interviews with stars, behind-the-scenes glimpses at the making of the film (notice that these are all purchase-support items!), and screening schedules (which is a lot like pointing to a retailer near you).

Keep in mind as you consider goals that your Web site should not be just a billboard or brochure. It's a primary principle on the Web that you must give into it as well as reap from it. Perhaps just as importantly, the Web's true power is in content. Users come to your site only if there is something of value there. (Something informative or entertaining also works.) This isn't all that surprising — would you watch television if there were nothing there to illuminate or entertain you? Even commercials generally have some content — some cute story line or seemingly informative pitch.

Take a quick look at the Pacbell site (`http://www.pacbell.com`). Of course, its ultimate goal is to sell Pacific Bell telephone service to California residents. But pointing directly to that goal — simply putting up a site that says "buy your phone service from Pacbell" — would probably not be best. First of all, people would only drop by when they had a specific question or concern — like getting service started or stopped. Traffic wouldn't be all that it could be. Second, a number of opportunities would be lost, for example, the opportunity to promote in the minds of potential customers the image that Pacbell believes can reel those customers in. So what does it do? When we stopped by, the company had extended the theme of its current television and print ad campaign to the Web, focusing on how you can use its service by offering stories from presumably real people saying how they used Pacbell phone service. Then Pacbell offered the opportunity to send in your own story — this is very clever. It provides the company with a mailing list, and it appears to create *community,* which is another watchword of Web content development. Oh, and by the way, Pacbell also offered information about its services and about solutions to your communications needs. These folks clearly know their audience.

Who are we trying to reach?

When you know your product, the next item of business is to identify who wants it — your *audience.* In truth, whomever developed the product probably had scads of input from marketing types, who identified the audience (the customer) and thought a lot about *positioning* — the creating of a personality for the product to make it attractive to the audience — before anyone even thought about a Web site.

If you are in a position to define your audience, you may ask yourself questions about its gender, age group, income and education levels, desire for accessibility vs. sophistication, and how these people access the Internet. (Turn to "Demographics and other justifications for existence," later in this chapter, to find out more about demographics and Web audiences.) The basic question you want to answer is: Who wants what we plan to offer?

After that, in traditional media, the follow-up questions may be where are those people and how do we get to them. This is where the Web is widely believed to be the great leveler. Theoretically, it costs very little to have a Web presence, meaning that on the Web, you can reach your audience cheaply, while in other media — television, radio, and print — ad space ain't cheap. Hardly anyone would think of launching a whole magazine or TV show to promote his or her own product. (That wouldn't be very cost-effective, now would it?) The reality is increasingly that you have to be very clever or have a good-sized budget to launch a viable and exciting Web presence. However, there is truth to the truism. The fact is that, while in other media you have to go after the audience by targeting the right media and the right venues, on the Web, the audience can come to you — as long as you remember that other maxim, that *content is king,* and as long as you make that content intriguing or useful to your audience.

Demographics and other justifications for existence

There are two basic reasons why you want to know about demographics. One is that demographic information can help you know your audience and focus on your goals, and the other is that demographic information can buck up your proposals.

Again, because your company probably has a good idea who its customer base is, it also probably has a pretty good idea about the demographics of that customer base — both for the company and for individual products or services. This should be true, because even start-up companies generally need to know who their customers are before hanging out their shingles. Find out from your company who it sees as who you're talking to — who's going to be the target audience for your site?

In the course of your career as a Webmaster, you may write a great deal of proposals long and short. You may propose buying a new server, redesigning the site, and maybe even creating the site to begin with. Take note: Demographic information makes a proposal a lot stronger. What's more, demographic information can tell you about your site.

After you get your site launched, you can use a variety of methods — tracking log files, using site-statistics software (see Chapter 15), gathering data via registration forms, and so on — to find out more about who is using your site. In the meantime, you need to know about who's using the Web. How many people are using the Web? Who are these people, and how many of them are members of your target audience? How many of them are using which sort of Web access? Knowing who can and will and who can't or won't visit your site makes a *very* big difference in planning. If you know just who you're catering to, you can actually cater to them!

The Graphics, Visualization, and Usability Center at Georgia Institute of Technology's College of Computing does an annual study that may help you. What have they found? In general, they found that the Web is composed of a diverse group of people. While people who use the Web tend to have higher incomes and more education than the typical American — a college degree is typical for a Web user — they also found that users range across all ages and income and education levels. To find out percentages of each group and check out the latest version of the study, visit `http://www.cc.gatech.edu/gvu/user_surveys/`.

Internationalism and regionalism

Among the bits of wisdom that you may glean from that Georgia Tech study is that, while American Web users outnumber those in any other country, responses to the survey came from all over the world. It turns out that the typical European Web user is similar to the American user. He or she tends to be a few years younger and have more education, and that person is more likely to be accessing the Web from work or school (rather than home) than American users. Outside of that, American and European users are pretty darn similar. This begs the question about whether you need to accommodate international users.

If your product or service is international in scope, you should provide multilingual versions of your site or offer standalone sites for your international compadres. If not, there is no reason to worry about this point — just focus on your target audience.

Stats, get your red-hot stats right here

Looking for more stats and demographics? The Web is now crawling with them. This is lovely, because just a year before the writing of this book, there were practically none. As the industry matures, look for more that are even more sophisticated. The following are a few sources to get you started:

✔ **Cyberatlas** (http://www.cyberatlas.com) is basically a digest/news report that summarizes everyone else's studies. You can use it as sort of a benchmark and then visit the other studies from there.

✔ **Emerging Technologies Research** from FIND/VSP (http://etrg.findsvp.com/index.html) offers big reports that aren't free, but try the Demographics (http://etrg.findsvp.com/internet/demograph.html) and Survey Highlights (http://etrg.findsvp.com/internet/highlights.html) links.

✔ **O'Reilly Research** (http://www.ora.com/research) offers two studies: The State of Web Commerce is a trendcasting report on online transactions (encryption, digital signatures, secure transactions, and so on), while Defining the Internet Opportunity is a user-profile study that determines the demographics of the average Internet user. It includes separate demographic profiles for online service subscribers and general Internet

users. Dated for 1995, it includes forecasting for growth that still may help you.

✔ **Hot 100** (http://www.hot100.com) rates the popularity of Web sites based on (probably subjective) analyses of Web traffic, which is in turn based on selected access and referrer logs. Hot 100 includes Top 100 sites in various categories; what's interesting here is that some topics are popular enough to rate their own Top 100 list (sex, kids, and cars), saying a lot about the demographics of the Internet.

✔ **Cyberstats** (http://www.cyberstats.com, also http://www.internetstats.com) compiles kazillions of Internet statistics, some original and some digested, and offers to e-mail a file of the raw data to you.

✔ **The Hermes Project** (http://www-personal.umich.edu/~sgupta/hermes) study focuses on commercial uses of the Web, although the data that they use to compile info is largely from the Georgia Tech survey that we've mentioned elsewhere in this chapter.

✔ **Nielsen Media Research** (http://www.nielsenmedia.com) is notable mainly for its recognizable name. Its demographic study indicates that "of the 220 million people over 16 in the United States and Canada, 23% are using the Internet."

On the other hand, if your product or service is priced differently for different regions within your own country, or in your country and another country (say the United States and a European country), you may want to provide different information to people in those areas. Unfortunately (or fortunately), there is no way to prevent people in one region from accessing information that you put on the Web. If you're in a situation like this, you may want to consider not putting the questionable information online. Just skip it. Or, you may want to offer two paths from your home page. Using the United States versus Europe challenge as an example, you can link to each from your home page. Then, in each section, you don't restrict what you say, and you probably use the local language. If someone who is located in one region enters the area designed for the other region, that person knows about the varying information, but it is also clear that the information for the other region is not focused to him or her.

Some folks may think that if the Web is global, it isn't an appropriate venue for local companies. If you run a small restaurant, what's the point of putting up information about your restaurant so that people from around the world can access it? Okay, maybe you'd catch a few tourists swinging through town, but is it worth the trouble?

 Just because seemingly everyone is on the Web, you don't have to include everyone in your audience — just focus on your target audience and ignore everyone else. We've created sites for nonprofit agencies serving only the San Francisco Bay Area. Was it a problem that people all over the world could access the site? Not at all — they're welcome to visit, and if they find something of interest there, it's all well and good. But the audience was primarily local.

In announcing a regional site, though, you may want to focus more closely on regional guides like Yahoo! San Francisco (`http://sfbay.yahoo.com`). More of these local directories are bound to appear, focusing more tightly on single geographical areas and providing information for residents or visitors there. Yahoo! San Francisco is shown in Figure 2-3, and announcing and otherwise promoting your site is covered in Chapter 14.

The friendly business of creating community

Ah, community. It seems like everyone's been talking about that for some time — the Web as the vehicle for global community, for communities of interest, and so on. Create a sense of community for your target audience, and they are going to come back. You can use a variety of techniques to build community for your audience, including the following items:

- ✔ Mailing lists
- ✔ Discussion groups
- ✔ Chats

All of these venues can provide your target audience with a place to know each other, but perhaps just as importantly, they provide you with direct communication from your audience that you can then monitor — you have a great opportunity to get to know them as a group, and in some cases, individually. Chapter 7 talks more about implementing mailing lists, discussion groups, and chats. Here we'll describe them generally.

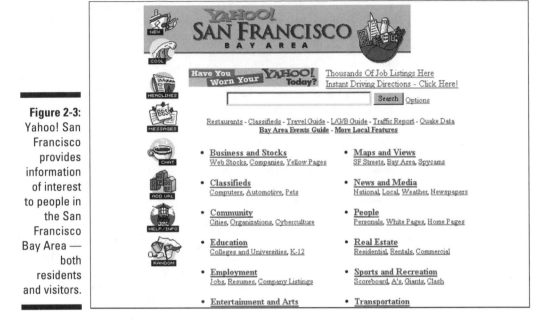

Figure 2-3:
Yahoo! San
Francisco
provides
information
of interest
to people in
the San
Francisco
Bay Area —
both
residents
and visitors.

Mailing lists

A mailing list that uses e-mail as a vehicle for discussion can provide a means of discussion among a group of people, or it can provide a means of communication directly from you to a group.

In the discussion setting, one person hosts — or maintains — the mailing list and often acts as its moderator. The list is usually focused on a topic — perhaps Web development, computer-book publishing, or marmosets as pets. People who share interest in that topic subscribe to the list; whenever any of these list members sends a message to the list, every other list member gets a copy. If someone on the list responds, the response may go to the group or to the individual who posted to the list, depending on how the list is set up. The upshot is that all of the list members are taking part in a group discussion that may grow to include dozens or hundreds or even thousands of people. In a typical scenario, only a small percentage of those on the list actually participate in the discussion at any given time — the rest are *lurking* (listening in, a perfectly acceptable habit on the Internet). This provides an opportunity to generate ongoing interest in your site. Just pick a broad topic that's central to your site, set up a list server, and off you go.

In the direct communication from the Webmaster setting, you can use a mailing list to inform users about what's new on your site, encouraging them to stop by for a visit. HotWired's HotFlash mailing list does just this. So does the mailing list for Car Talk (http://www.cartalk.msn.com). Of course, only people who have requested that they be added to such a mailing list should receive this sort of mail, and an unsubscribe option should clearly tell people how to remove themselves from the list. You don't want to mail-bomb unsuspecting users but rather to keep interested people updated and invite them back.

The sending of unsolicited e-mail, that is, *spamming,* is very unpopular on the Internet. You don't want to be known as a *spammer.* To avoid this, take care when sending bulk e-mail to the users of your site. When you collect e-mail addresses from your users, make it clear how they are to be used, and always include, in bulk e-mail, instructions for unsubscribing from your mailing list.

Discussion groups

Discussion groups function similarly to mailing lists at the surface, although they use Usenet news servers as their basis rather than e-mail mailing lists. More companies use discussion groups to foster communication both between their customers and between customers and the company. Both Netscape (`http://www.netscape.com`) and Microsoft (`http://www.microsoft.com`) use discussion groups extensively to support use of their products. Not only do these discussion groups allow users a chance to communicate with each other, trading tips and tricks, but they allow users to communicate to each company's support engineers any problems with the company's software. Presumably, these users feel fully able to get support and offer feedback; this fosters in them product loyalty and a sense of community with other users and the company.

Chats

Chats, real-time conversations that happen on the Web, usually require some special software. One that's very common is Internet Relay Chat (IRC), although many Java-based chat *applets* (Java applications) are appearing. These nifty items let you place a chat area right in a Web page, eliminating the need for users of the chat area to have additional software. (The software that's needed for the chat is downloaded right along with the Web page.)

Chats are occasionally set up so that users can chat with each other, but more commonly, they take the form of an informal meeting, where one person — an author, for example — is interviewed or hosted in a loosely organized conversation. Users may submit questions to a monitor who asks the questions, or they may ask questions outright. Sometimes the questions are submitted via the chat program, while at other times they are sent in via e-mail. Either way, this is a great way for users to interact on your Web site about some issue that relates to your site.

Getting demographic feedback

The last thing to consider is getting feedback from your users. You can set up forms and have users fill them out to find out all types of things about them. If you are providing a site with original content, you can even set things up so that users must fill in a questionnaire before they can access the site. Be careful with this. You don't want to put roadblocks in the way of people using your site. If you have a commercial site, the last thing that you want to do is to make your site harder to access than that of your competition. Figure 2-4 shows a simple form that gathers information about a user.

One good way to get people to fill out an online questionnaire is to offer rewards for completed forms. Offering a weekly drawing — you don't have to give away much to get people interested — can greatly increase the number of respondents. If you have a software company, for example, you can offer a licensed copy of your software to one winner a week.

Who are our competitors?

Another definition of positioning may be "how your product is focused against the marketplace and its competitors." To know how to position your site — how to put the right spin on the site's purpose(s) and know which goals may be best to pursue in the course of the Web initiative — you must know what your competitors are up to. That's a lot easier when you're creating a site for an existing company that actually has competitors. In that case, you can simply surf their sites (if they have sites) or imagine what they may do, given their corporate personality. Make it your habit to surf the sites of competitors every day or two, especially after you've launched your company's site.

If you're in the very interesting position of creating a site that is so original that it has no competitors, don't imagine that it never will. A newly launched idea on the Web — if it's successful — has about a 15-minute chance of being the only one of its type, and that's only if no one knew a thing about it two weeks earlier. We've seen cases where one site announced a batch of nifty new features two weeks before its launch, and a competitor beat them to the punch. This is a fast, fast business. To stay on top, you need to anticipate the competition.

If you're a freelance Web developer or if you work for a Web job shop and you're working on a site for a client, ask them right away who their main competitors are. Make it one of your first tasks to look closely at the content and organization of those companies' sites. If the company's competitors don't yet have a Web presence, question your client closely about their competitors' images, their products, and how they perceive what differentiates them from their competitors.

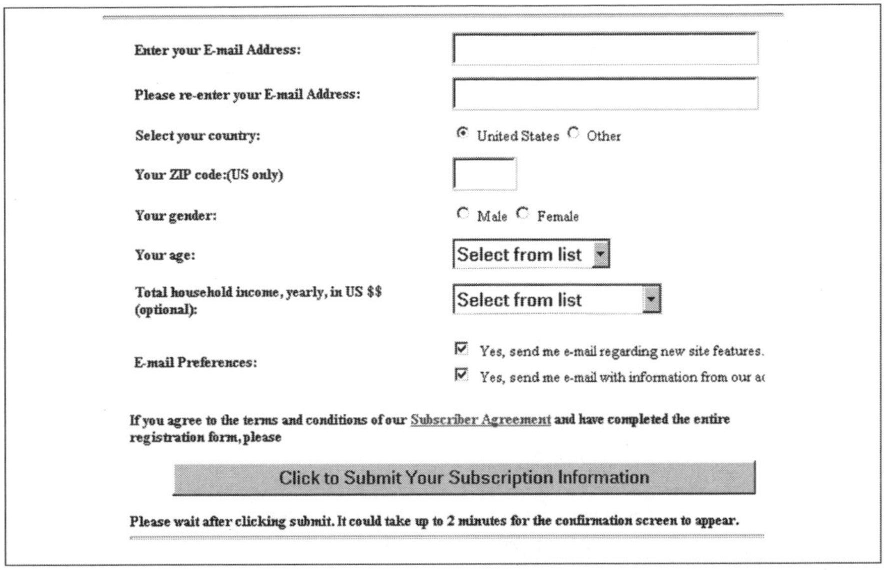

Figure 2-4:
This
questionnaire
allows the
Webmaster
to collect
information
about the
site's users.

What resources do we have?

First, you need to know where the funding is coming from. You must know who holds the purse strings and whether the funding is coming from an existing source, anticipated revenue, or anticipated investment. This is very important. It tells you a lot about where the Web initiative is positioned in importance, how stable the endeavor's financial foundation is going to be, and how far you can go in building a site and a team to run it. Then you need to know what people and equipment resources are budgeted.

Revenue models we know and love

Some sites make money, some save money, some are for fun; let's focus for a moment on how sites make money or save it.

Advertising and subscriptions: It should work, but does it?

You may think that your paid subscription to a magazine funds the magazine's publication and that all those ads are just gravy for the publisher. In fact, in many cases, subscriptions are a relatively small piece of the revenue pie, and ads are what count big time. There is a general principle in magazine publishing that individual publications are either *circulation driven,* meaning that most of the revenue comes from paid subscriptions, or *ad driven,* meaning that most of the revenue comes from ads.

The circ-driven publications have relatively few ads and a high percentage of editorial content — they also have relatively few subscribers and often charge a great deal for subscriptions. Some professionally oriented reference publications are like this. These publications are not trade magazines that you get for free if you're in the right demographic group but rather the sort of materials that you may keep in a binder for professional reference over a period of time. In fact, trade magazines illustrate the ad-driven type; they are often given away for free (you can get a free subscription to Web Week easily if you fill out that form inside with the right demographic info to get approval). That gives the magazine a high circulation rate so they can charge big bucks for ad space — it's the ad space that's paying the bills. Similarly, in local, alternative newspapers that are distributed for free, it's the ads — both display ads and the classifieds — that pay the bills. Those publications don't even charge for single-copy issues; they simply drop the paper on your doorstep and at strategic locations around town, and count their circulation as the number of copies they've dropped off.

Perhaps it's worth noting that, in the case of *Web Week,* you, the "subscriber" are motivated to read the publication because you want the professional news. Many magazines — especially those that are more oriented toward your extracurricular interests — charge for subscriptions *and* are full of ads. (Take a look at *Vogue,* which is both a trade magazine and of interest to the public — well, at least some of the public.) Or look into *Vanity Fair,* which is not so trade oriented. In the case of subscriptions, the subscription itself "proves" the subscriber's motivated commitment to the publication.

One may think that the subscription/advertising models would easily apply to the Web. For a while, everyone thought that this was the way to go — that it was a no-brainer. However, there are some built-in problems. One, quite simply, is that to have strong circulation for your publication — be it print or Web — you need whiz-bang editorial content. And while some of that exists on the Web, the Web is also seen as the place where anything goes and anyone can publish. As a result, some sites get the traffic (read: *circulation*) and some don't. If they don't, charging for advertising isn't viable.

Another is that, while magazines and newspapers get unbiased, external audits from recognized auditors to prove their circulation levels, Web sites have yet to establish that system. (Chapters 14 and 15 talk about this quite a bit more.) In fact, in the Web-site world, we're still figuring out what constitutes a unit of measurement for this — a hit, an impression, or what? And how on earth, given the state of technology, can we measure it ourselves let alone get an external auditor to verify it? And what, if there is no model for proving circulation, can advertisers accept as proof that their money was well spent? It's in this context that some advertisers began to turn the tables by declaring that they would only pay for *clickthroughs* (instances where the user actually clicked on the banner ad to go to the advertiser's site). At least *that* was verifiable and measurable. (Again, see Chapter 15 for more on units of measurement.)

Also, in the magazine world, it's believed that the fledgling publication is going to bleed money for three to five years before it starts to turn a profit, if it ever does. (Not all magazines survive.) Most people launching a Web endeavor naively expect to cut a profit in year one, if not the first six months. They start out underfunded and have unreasonable expectations, which are perhaps built on the early press that suggested that the Web was the locale of this century's gold rush. Well, in a way it was, but not everyone who rushed to California in the mid-nineteenth century turned up rich. And not every Web endeavor is going to have millions of visitors, a loyal following that visits every day, and high enough circulation to warrant other companies paying for ad space there.

There is also a basic problem in the way that ads appear on Web sites — as banner graphics somewhere on the page. Often, the banner ad appears in a given location. Advertisers prefer the top of the page, while site designers prefer a lower location — and they rotate. That means different ads appear each time a user loads the page. That also means (assuming that there are at least several ads) that users don't see the same ad repeatedly. Given that one of the watchwords of advertising is *repetition,* there is a question about whether the ad is offering adequate bang for your buck.

However, users don't like a Web site that's crowded with ads, which is how magazines and newspapers solve this problem. (There is so little screen real estate on an average-size monitor that even two ads start pushing out the content, and that drives away readers.) Figure 2-5 illustrates this dilemma. Note, too, that when more ads appear on your Web page, the user is experiencing more invitations to leave your site — your ad revenue can cost you traffic in more than one way.

Finally, there is the question of subscriptions. Many sites today ask you to subscribe by registering. In exchange for offering some demographic info like your profession, income and education levels, and so on, you often get access to some special area of the site. Early on, some sites experimented with charging fees for subscriptions — a notable case was *USA Today,* which is a respected publication with loyal readership and strong editorial content. No go. *USA Today*'s attempt to charge for subscriptions to its online version went down in flames. So far, the Web seems to have retained some of its original character in that those who frequent the Web don't like to pay — they expect free content. We hear Bill Gates plans to charge for content produced by Microsoft (he said so himself on television), and maybe this model will succeed in the future. But bear in mind if you go this route that the really high traffic area of your site is going to be the free area.

To wrap it up, advertising may indeed be the way to go for your site, but think about it — you're going to need a great deal of traffic and solid content that brings in a loyal following day after day. Paid subscriptions are a long shot unless you offer both very strong content that users can access for free *and* even stronger content in a special area that's accessible to only those who pay.

The ad

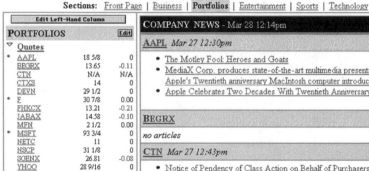

Figure 2-5:
These two
sites accept
paid
advertising—
appearing
as banner
graphics —
to help with
funding.

The ad

Licensing: selling your content to others

With a strong following and plenty of traffic — the sort of stuff that inspires one to take in paid advertising — you can also consider licensing content to others. Here's how this works: You create the content, and it's very popular. Your rep then contacts a company with deep pockets but no content to speak of, and you agree that they can use your content on their site, preferably in a cobranded situation that shows users that you created the content. This has worked somewhat for many big-content companies — for example, some of the big search-tool companies like Excite have licensed their content to AOL and others. Similarly, some highly popular entertainment sites, such as those with story lines and ongoing characters, have been launched by entrepreneurs who licensed the content to big companies. We even know of a case where a print editor created a series of online magazines and licensed them to an advertising agency, which in turn licensed them to a major client — a car company — to pull traffic into the client's site. This can work, but it takes a lot of attention to the licensing deals. Perhaps you'd need a rep on staff to make the deals, negotiate favorable contracts, and tend your relationships with cobranding partners.

Sponsorship: The PBS model

Sponsorship takes three forms, two of which are used by PBS, the noncommercial television network. The third is actually the simplest — that's when a company sponsors its own Web site and calls all the shots; we're not going to dwell on that much here. (If your company is sponsoring its own site and does not expect external revenue, you know where the funding is coming from.)

In the PBS model, sponsors come in two basic forms: (a) corporate or organizational sponsorship, where a company or group pays for production or distribution of a production to be broadcast and is visibly recognized as the sponsor and (b) individual sponsorship, where interested parties pledge and send in donations to keep the station going. (Note that this second method is somewhat like the model of software that's distributed as shareware — if you like it, you voluntarily pay for it.)

Figure 2-6 shows the Band of the Week section of IUMA, the Internet Underground Music Archives Web site (http://www.iuma.com/IUMA-2.0/bow/). You can see that the band of the week is being sponsored by that famous maker of jeans, Levi Strauss. There are no ads, and in this case, there are no links to the Levi Strauss Web site (although that is not unheard of in sponsored sites). But the sponsor is associated with a Web site that's highly trafficked by exactly the sort of people who buy a great deal of jeans. Levi products are touted near the Band of the Week banner, and on every page, IUMA gives Levi Strauss credit for sponsoring the contest.

Welcome to IUMA's **501® Band of the Week** game show! Each week we'll be choosing three IUMA bands to be voted on by **YOU**! And by voting, you'll have a chance to win a pair of 501® jeans and an IUMA CD each week! When a year is up, all of the continuing champs will duke it out to become the **Band of the Year Grand Champion** and press a CD. It's YOUR chance to break a band so join our studio audience and check out *This Week's Contestants!* To get the complete lowdown, read the rules.

Evidence of sponsorship

Figure 2-6:
The Band of the Week section of IUMA is sponsored by Levi Strauss.

In other areas of the IUMA site, other revenue models apply — some areas include banner ads, for example. And this is a site that sells a product — music — but also offers such high-quality content and gets so much traffic that it can justify charging for banner ads and sponsorship. You may want to browse here for a while.

Paid placement: an alternative to advertising and sponsorship

So you're sitting there watching some big Hollywood movie, and there in the scene, the characters are quietly (or not so quietly) using products like soft drinks or books — and you recognize the brand name. Is this a lucky accident for the companies whose products are shown? No! They went to a lot of trouble — and usually some expense — to get that stuff up there on the screen in front of you and millions like you. This is known as *paid placement.*

In the Web world, paid placement occurs when a company ponies up to have its logo placed strategically on a site — it looks a bit like sponsorship. The Car Talk site (http://www.cartalk.msn.com) — discussed earlier in this chapter as a good example of an entertainment-oriented site — takes paid placements. Look at the Car Talk banner graphic in Figure 2-7, and you see boxes labeled Yahoo!, while Microsoft references are also scattered around the room. The clock on the wall is a Valvoline clock, and the car in the garage is a Nissan. This is no accident (so to speak). Click on these items, and you find that they are linked, just as a banner ad would be. The difference, however, is that these links are integrated into the site — they aren't tacked on as a banner ad would be.

Figure 2-7:
These paid
placements
work
because
they fit in as
part of the
humor.

If you don't want to interrupt your site with obvious ads or if sponsorship doesn't work for you, paid placement may be the way to go. Again, though, note that in the Car Talk example, ads work well because the site is funny, and the paid placements are funny, too. Be sure that you use paid placements in a way that fits in with the overall theme of your site.

Customer and purchase support: It does work

This may seem subtle to those who expected to rush into the Web and scoop up the gold, but it is true that your Web initiative can *save* you money in some cases, and isn't that as good as making money? Well, maybe not always, but look at it this way: If you have to provide customer support or you want to support people in choosing your product over the competitor's, the Web can be a highly cost-effective tool. It can save you customer support costs *and* provide increases sales.

The customer support thing is pretty obvious. At its simplest, you post a FAQ or a searchable database of questions and answers, and make your URL very prominent on the product packaging and elsewhere, and (poof!) you can reach more people with less overhead. (Calculating the savings is up to you, as circumstances vary.) For some companies, this alone can financially justify having a Web site.

Purchase support can be very powerful in an online setting, although it may be somewhat tough to measure its effect in real numbers. (This is also true of advertising and public relations efforts. If your company does not believe in advertising, it is going to be hard to sell the company on purchase support as justification for a Web site.)

In most cases, figuring which sales came from print advertising, which from a Web presence, and which from some other promotional efforts is tough. Anecdotally, we can tell you that we once were offered free ad space on a big search engine as a perk for working on the site. We spent $500 to have two banner ads designed and linked the ads to a small Web site promoting the two books that we were advertising. (We are authors, so our products are books.) We were not selling the books from our site; we simply put up some sample material from our books (with permission from our publisher) along with a few bonus items. (This, folks, is a simple form of purchase support — the purpose of the material was to persuade people to buy our books.) The results we got were astonishing — book sales popped up so dramatically in the next two months that our publisher was amazed. So were we, to be honest.

For a long time, the Western Digital Web site (http://www.wdc.com) was singular among its competitors for providing online documentation for the hard drives it manufactured. The company didn't have banner ads up on anyone else's site, and it didn't charge for access to its site — anyone could access any of the information that the company offered. Did the site pay for itself? Yes — by offering cost-effective customer support *and* purchase support in a one-two combination that persuaded potential customers that this company supported its products.

The idea behind online purchase support is to give a potential customer every thing he or she needs to make a purchase decision 24 hours a day, 7 days a week, with relatively low overhead. (Running a 24/7 Web site is a lot cheaper than running 24/7 storefronts or even phone lines.)

Call centers are expensive to run. Providing a Web site with a full set of troubleshooting notes for your product can reduce the overall number of phone calls and e-mails to your support organization. Reduced phone calls to your 800 number spell real cost savings to your organization. This alone may cover the expense of building your Web site. Also, having support information available on your site empowers your customers to solve their own problems using your product. This makes for positive customer experiences, and how can that translate into anything but sales?

Reduction of distribution costs: the software model

Just as a Web presence can reduce customer service costs, it can also reduce the costs involved in distributing some products. This is an especially effective way to distribute software, which is downloadable. In this case, the costs that are usually associated with packaging, shipping, and distributing via retailers are outright nixed — only the pure product is delivered. And in a real coup, it gets to market a *lot* faster.

Symantec sells Symantec Visual Cafe via a Web site (http://www.symantec.com), and Netscape (http://www.netscape.com) sells its products online, too. In fact, Netscape pretty much led the way in this method and revolutionized software delivery in the process. Another application of this idea can be seen in IUMA's distribution of music via download. (IUMA was discussed earlier in this chapter, in "Sponsorship: The PBS model.")

The costs you save if you can deliver your product electronically are astronomical. It's certainly possible that this idea may also apply to information products or perhaps even services in the future — it will be interesting to see how this shakes out.

Budgeting people and equipment

Let's face it: In most endeavors, when you begin putting together a new division, company, or department, there are models to fall back on. You've usually worked in that kind of setting before, so you can re-create some processes and procedures that you know have worked before. And usually, you have a rough idea of what's needed to get the job done. You know that you are going to need certain equipment, and you can work out a pretty clear idea of how many people are needed to get the job done. If you're setting up an IS department, a restaurant, or an office-supply store, you can rely on past experience and perhaps even books on the topic to point you on your way. But specifying what you need to set up your Web initiative is often a crap shoot. Sure, you can say that you need this sort of server and that sort of connection. The big challenge is in anticipating the workloads of various team members and in specifying how many people you need to get the job done. It's especially tough to anticipate what it's going to take to keep the site fresh — what it takes to create a new site is a lot easier to plot. And as any manager can tell you, managing the workload and the cost of labor to accomplish that workload is a big part of keeping things in line.

Perhaps the best way to determine what resources are needed is to start with what the budget is going to be, and then figure what you can do within that budget. The alternative is to figure out what you want to do and ask for hardware, software, and head count. It's often difficult to get a budget if you don't have a specific plan in mind (especially if the holder of the purse strings isn't clear about what it takes to run a Web site).

Frankly, you're in trouble if your resources consist of borrowed time from various people in various departments. In that case, the Web initiative often falls to the bottom of those people's priority lists repeatedly, in favor of the most urgent tasks that are involved in the company's core, profit-making business (that is, unless the core, profit-making business *is* the Web initiative).

In a best-case scenario, you are presented with a budget, and you can use that as a starting point. Then you can either point out to those who approve the checks that, for *x* dollars they can accomplish *x* goals, staying within the budget. Or, you can put on your evangelist hat and persuade them that, to accomplish the higher goals that you've set for the Web endeavor, you need a more generous budget. To sort through what resources you may need, review the chapters in Parts II, III, and IV of this book; to look into writing a budget, turn to Chapter 4. When you propose a budget for consideration, the more concrete information you have, the more credible your request is going to be.

FIELD NOTES

Promises, promises

Promises are easy to make and even easier to break. Promising visitors to your Web site that there's more to come is one way to make them want to come back and see what you've added. The crucial mistake made by Webmasters large and small, however, is promising content that's never delivered — or is delivered too late. In the following example, provided by freelance Web site reviewer J. Tarin Towers, substitute the topic of *your* Web site for the words *pickled cabbage*.

"Suppose I visit your site, which you've proclaimed is 'soon to be the premier Internet resource for pickled cabbage!' Okay, I say to myself. There aren't too many sites about pickled cabbage right now, so we'll see what they do. The first time I visit, your site (`pickledcabbage.com`) is about a month old. Much of it is under construction, with 'Coming Soon' plastered across about half the proposed sections. Now, if I'm really a dedicated pickled cabbage fan, I *may* deign to revisit the site a month or two later and find out what's cooking. What I want to see is what you promised me when I first found your site: the premier Internet resource for pickled cabbage lovers. Unless you've filled in all the blanks, you won't get a third visit from me, much less a link on my Web page or a glowing recommendation to my friends who also adore pickled cabbage. If you have filled in all the blanks, congratulations. I'm your fan, and I'm going to keep my eye on your page. But bear in mind what I'm going to expect to see. Pickled Cabbage News, for instance, just better have *new* news from the world of pickled cabbage, while Pickled Cabbage Link of the Moment should certainly be a different link from the last time I visited. In surfing the Net for sites about some of my own interests, such as comic books, computer games, and Web page design, I can't tell you how often I've had my high hopes for a new site dashed on the rocks of neglect. Make me a promise you can actually fulfill, and then follow through, and I'll be your fan. Promise me the stars, then give me a couple of asterisks, and I'll grumble about you to all the other pickled cabbage lovers I know."

What expectations of success do we have?

When it comes to expectations of success, you can expect two extremes: Some people in your company are going to have no picture of success, because many folks don't know what to expect, and some are going to have unabashed visions of sudden wealth and wild, widespread fame. Notice that we said *and* not *or.* You usually find both of those extremes occurring. What's more, it is a rare CEO that springs for a budget and resources for a Web initiative or any other project without a vision of success.

Remember, part of your role as Webmaster is to manage expectations. You need a clear picture of what success means in your company in general — for example, is success measured by numbers or by the meeting of goals? Then, you need to know what the vision of success for the Web site was. With those items in mind, you are in a position to help guide or shape that vision of success. You can help guide expectations by researching what has happened for sites like yours over the past year or so, but again, because you are in a pioneering field, you may find yourself the first to wander down the path you are on.

You may be tempted — because, for example, it may seem appropriate to get the big budget — to suggest very high expectations for your site. You may want to believe that you are going to launch, and in minutes, you'll be selling millions of Acme Wonderwidgets, or that through the fine service your site is going to offer, you can end world hunger within a few months. Okay, so maybe that's a little extreme. Maybe you just think you are going to get a million hits per month. Here's your dilemma: While it's often true that high expectations inspire bigger budgets, it's also true that you can be setting up your Web endeavor for a big fall if you inflate expectations to unreasonable levels or fail to manage any overly high expectations in others. When considering what the site can do — what is going to show its success — it's generally best to err on the conservative side. Then you (and the site) look brilliant when you do succeed.

How do we measure our success?

You can measure success in your Web site using as your criteria any combination of traffic, sales, acceptance by the public of an online transaction system, savings in costs (for example, the cost of customer support may drop because the site has succeeded in doing that job), and media presence (attention the site is getting from the press). Your company's values and the goals you've set for the site will contribute to how success is viewed and how it's measured.

Make sure the measurement of success is in line with the site's goals and that it's attainable. Set success benchmarks that are within reasonable expectations (remember, as described in Chapter 1, part of your role as Webmaster is to manage expectations). Chapter 15 goes into detail about measuring success; before you take another step review that material so you have a full grounding in appropriate measurements and how the actual quantifying of traffic can occur.

Writing a Mission Statement

As a quick exercise for focusing on the purpose of your site, write up a quick mission statement. Don't slave over this — its reason for being is just to get you going. It's not meant to have historical significance. Start by jotting down a few pieces of information:

- ✔ Exactly what product or service does your company provide?

- ✔ Name three to five important goals your company hopes to achieve. Some of these goals may be as simple as selling x product. Some may address promoting a certain image or reaching a certain group of people. If you aren't sure of your company's goals, a quick conversation with the marketing honchos or a check of the corporate values may help.

- ✔ What three words describe your company's corporate image?

- ✔ Who is your customer or audience?

- ✔ How can the Web initiative help to achieve the company goals or reach the audience?

- ✔ What types of content or technology are available, especially within the limitations of your budget? (Don't dwell on this — just brainstorm very briefly.)

- ✔ What does the success of your Web initiative look like to your company, given the nature of your site's goals?

Now use this information to write a quick mission statement for your Web initiative. Keep it simple — don't try to recreate the Constitution. Just string all of the pieces of information together into sentences. If one goal seems to conflict with another, look for priorities, and consider dropping the less-important goals. If one piece of information appears to be out whack with others — for example, if the corporate image is fun, fresh, and sassy but the audience is blue-suited executives — seek clarification from the marketing department. Now tack your mission statement up where you can see it, and file a copy of it for handy reference. You can refer to it when you've forgotten what you're doing here, and you can place it in some edited form into important documents like proposals and reports.

Chapter 3

Selling on the Web

● ●

In This Chapter

▶ What sells online and what doesn't

▶ What makes selling work

▶ How online shopping works

▶ Understanding security and commerce

▶ Secure servers and transaction systems

▶ Mastering the challenge of fulfillment

● ●

*O*kay, so you've set the goals for your site and among them is to sell, sell, sell. Now what? First off, you need to think through whether your product or service can sell online. Then you need a strategy for selling it, and finally you need to know how to implement that strategy through technology.

Many folks think of the Web as the great business leveler, where a couple of Joes with a good idea can hang out a virtual shingle and make a million, or where a mom-and-pop shop has the same chance of success as a giant multinational corporation. It's true that the cost of launching a Web site is far less than the overhead involved in launching a big company. And it's dang sure true that some products — like software — can be distributed via the Web at tremendous savings in packaging, promotion, and distribution. (Do you know anyone who actually bought Web-browser software *in a box through a store?*)

However, not every Web-based business has experienced success, and selling on the Web can be dicey business. In this chapter, we discuss the special issues that surround selling on the Web. We start by looking at those items that move on the Web — what sells and what doesn't sell. We also talk about building trust with users — if they don't trust you, they aren't going to buy from you. That's followed by a look at security and how security impacts commerce on the Web. And we take a look at how you can sell on the Web — the software packages, payment schemes, and even prepackaged storefronts that may work for you. Finally, we look into *fulfillment* — getting your product to your customers in a timely, reliable way.

What Sells Online and What to Forget About

There is no selling-regulations bureau on the Web to stop you from trying to sell whatever you want. If you want to get out there and push smokeshifters, gumballs, or snailtraps, you can give it a whirl. No one is going to stop you. The big question is, are people going to buy what you offer? Underlying that question are more basic questions regarding why some things sell and some don't. We make no claims to be the final word on these topics. We can report what we've seen, but the Web is such a wonder that no one knows what's going to come up tomorrow or next week.

As of this writing, we can report the success to varying degrees of Web sites selling the following items:

- ✔ Hard deliverables, like flowers, wine, CDs, cigars, and books

- ✔ Software (and other stuff) that can be delivered via download

- ✔ Services, like those offering package shipping, travel packages, investment brokerage, or the best price on new or used cars

- ✔ Information, like news from a reliable journalistic source

We can also report some notable flops:

- ✔ *USA Today* launched an online version of its well-known newspaper and charged for access to it via subscriptions. This venture went down in flames. We think that happened because *USA Today* was so widely available in print and because the online version offered no substantial advantage over the print version.

- ✔ Web Review was a wonderful source of news about the Web. Produced by Songline Studios, it made quite a splash at first. In an interesting spin on the PBS pledge-drive model, a call went out for individual pledges of financial support. Not enough came in, and Web Review caved. Of course those PBS pledge drives look like they take a *lot* of time and energy.

In upcoming sections we take a look at some of the successes and what may make them tick.

Hard deliverables fly

We can name so many cases of *hard deliverables* (physical objects that are easily shipped) selling on the Web that it's tempting to say that this is the big winner. It makes sense; after all — these are many of the same items that sell well through catalogs, by fax, and by mail order. The attractions? For one thing, you as the user/customer generally know what you're going to get. You can see pictures of the merchandise, or maybe you already know the products or the company's reputation. The stuff is real, solid, and tangible, and you have a reasonable expectation of it arriving on your doorstep in one piece. The convenience of catalog shopping is strong motivation. Many folks think that buying through catalogs is fast, easy, and convenient and offers free parking to boot. All of those qualities transfer directly to an online environment, assuming that the online shopping system is orderly (so to speak), understandable, and secure.

It's still kind of tough to make money selling items that cost less than about $10 online. This is because *microtransactions* (sales involving as little as pennies), long promised and technically feasible on the Web, have not yet caught on — there are still a few snags in the systems. We talk about the limitations of selling online throughout this chapter and discuss payment schemes in particular in "The Deep Skinny on Transaction Systems," later in the chapter.

In the sections that follow, we describe some notable Web sites that sell hard deliverables. Some of these are examples of companies that started with a phone, mail, and fax order business that segued into online shopping; others started out online, and some even exist only online.

Lands' End

Lands' End, which sells clothing and household goods through a longstanding and respected print catalog, now also sells via a Web site (http://www.landsend.com). Lands' End (Figure 3-1) is certainly an established brand, and it has fast shipping options and a no-risk return policy going for it. This, along with quality merchandise and reasonable prices, has kept Lands' End at the forefront of selling via catalog for quite a while. People trust Lands' End. Trust translates into sales. (See "Selling Is About Trust — Building It and Keeping It," later in this chapter.) Lands' End has been able to leverage its brand name, consumer confidence level, and an online catalog that's bigger than its print catalog into a solid selling operation on the Web.

The around-the-clock service that an online storefront can offer is a great advantage to users. Someone looking for an item can find and purchase it with a few mouse clicks anytime day or night. For sellers that are already in the catalog business, selling on a Web site offers a new sales channel. For new companies, it offers a sales channel with low overhead. In both cases, the expense of running the site is considerably less than the expense of running a fully staffed call center.

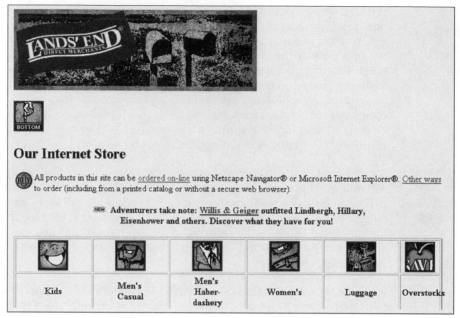

Figure 3-1:
Lands'
End's
respected
mail order
business
translates
well onto
the Web.

CD Now

Easy access to a great deal of information about musical artists (including their bios and release lists) makes for sterling content at CD Now (http://www.cdnow.com). Even without the huge inventory of CDs available for purchase, this site would be a winner. A handy search form appears right on the home page, minimizing the number of links that customers have to click before they can make a purchase. (Long ago, a wise marketeer told us, "To sell, remove all the barriers to buying.") The option to preorder yet-to-be-released CDs and have them shipped automatically when they're pressed makes music fans feel like they have special access to what's hot, and digitized sample music that's delivered using RealAudio provides plenty of purchase support. (RealAudio enables users to hear music without having to first download the sound files.) Meanwhile, the site offers a variety of payment options — a shopping cart system with DigiCash and ecash options, a credit card payment option using a secure form, and the choice to set up an account over the phone. (Later sections of this chapter cover shopping systems and so on.) Convenience is the order of the day; you can save the contents of your shopping cart and continue purchasing items a few days or even weeks or months later. When it comes to solid content, hot products, and ease of payment, this site has it all.

Make buying easy as pie

Every step you make a user take before buying is a barrier to purchasing. Keep your shopping system as simple as possible while still being clear — don't confuse the users, and don't make them click around excessively. A Buy button should be prominent and should go *directly* to purchasing — not to some explanation of purchasing. Also, the more options for payment and delivery that you can offer, the more opportunity the user has to buy. Use the sites that we describe in these sections as models for your payment systems.

Amazon.com

Watch out, booksellers. Amazon.com (`http://www.amazon.com`) hit the business by storm, going from start-up to "the world's biggest bookstore" in a flash. Where is this bookstore? Only — absolutely *only* — online. Amazon.com carries so many titles (2.5 million "in stock"), we have heard that its database is quietly replacing the venerable Books in Print in many people's minds. Instead of going to Books in Print to look up a title, people in the book business (and the public) are turning to this resource. Amazon.com discounts books (some as much as 40 to 50 percent) but then charges a fee for shipping; it offers shipping options from fast to fastest. Users who have ordered become part of a mailing list that is not abused; they don't get junk mail from Amazon but do get very rare notices of some importance. (Amazon sends out holiday gifts like mousepads via snail mail.) Users can also request automatic notification by e-mail when books by authors of interest to them are released.

Where on Earth is Amazon storing all these books? It must be a really huge warehouse somewhere, right? Nope — the company has no warehouse. Instead, it orders directly from the same distributors used by big bookstore chains. The big difference is that, when the big bookstores order, the books (which have already been shipped by their publishers to the distributor) have to be shipped from the distributor to the bookseller's warehouse(s), and then to individual bookstores. All of this distribution costs a pretty penny, which Amazon saves. (*Fulfillment* — sending out the stuff that's ordered — is an important issue for an online storefront. You can get fulfillment, or at least information about fulfillment, at the end of this chapter.)

Remember purchase support

Take a look at the sites of companies that deliver big-ticket items, such as Dell Computers (`http://www.dell.com`) and Ford Motor Co. (`http://www.ford.com`), and you can see that they are in fact conducting online commerce. (*Commerce* means business, right?) While no one is (yet) selling computers or cars via Web sites, they are providing *purchase support* — all of the info that you need to support your decision to buy their products. Does this work? You bet it does. Twenty-four hours a day, seven days a week via its Web site, Ford pumps out a great deal of information about models, safety features, options, nearby dealers, and so on; it also lets users see the car of interest in a range of color choices using a nifty Java applet. This all leads to increased sales that can be documented.

Purchase support via the Net is very viable and may well segue in the future into providing the choice to buy these big-ticket items, too. In the meantime, to make a purchase-support site succeed, you need to provide online answers to every question that a customer may ask about your products. A site that aims for purchase support pays for itself not through direct sales but through mind share, which, in a marketing truism, "precedes market share." You may find a purchase support site preferable regardless of the size of your product, because it involves less overhead than implementing and maintaining a transaction system.

Downloadable software moves

The Internet has revolutionized the software industry in a number of ways. One is that selling software online is so successful. Now that people can both download software and pay for it via the Web, there is no need for a software company to create packaging, cut millions of disks or CDs, print documentation, or maintain a warehouse or third-party distribution system. The expenses of manufacturing and distribution go way, way down. What's more, the software company, which had been paying large percentages of the purchase price to distributors and retailers as their cut, no longer has to share. It's possible for software to be less expensive to the user while the manufacturer's profit margins grow, too. (However, it's more likely that the profit margins will grow than that the savings will be passed on.)

Selling software online has been successful for companies both large and small. In Chapter 2, we described a couple of success stories that are worth taking another look at in the context of this chapter.

WinZip

The WinZip site (`http://www.winzip.com`) is tightly focused on the goal of getting WinZip to your computer and thus making a sale. Neatly organized and easy to use, the site provides easy download links right on the home page, along with a convenient system for registering your copy of the software; registration keys are available (for a price) online. There's no wait, no problem, and no barrier to getting the product. And there is no confusion — one product, one easy-to-use Web site.

Consider getting a domain name for each product and tightly focusing a distribution site in the model of this example. The advantage is that users don't have to search for your product among a host of other products. When someone wants WinZip, he or she can go straight to `www.winzip.com` and get it.

Symantec

Symantec is the software giant that brings you Symantec C++; two important Web-development tools, Café and Visual Café; and the venerable Norton Utilities. The Symantec Web site (`http://www.symantec.com`) is something of a purchase support site in that it offers discussion groups (which are monitored by support engineers) about Symantec products along with special areas providing updates for some developer products. What's more, at the Symantec site, users can get fully functioning sample software for free via download on a rotating basis. When we visited recently, WinFax for NT and CrashGuard for Windows 95 were being offered. All of this brings a great deal of traffic to the site, where users can easily purchase the Web-development tools mentioned, choosing whether they want the stuff right now via download or shipped on CD.

You can combine the three goals of selling, purchase support, and promoting the company in a single Web site by following the Symantec site's model.

Netscape

Okay, these are the folks who invented this concept. Come to think of it, these are the folks who invented the concept of graphical Web browsers as well as a couple of other nifty items. The phenomenal success of Netscape has been well documented. Consider how Netscape distributes software via the Web. First, the company provides multiple links to its site from the browser itself and from millions of other people's Web sites that are adorned with that cute Netscape Now button. Many of those buttons initiate a download of Netscape software directly from other sites. Those clever folks at Netscape aren't just using their own site to distribute software, they're using everyone else's sites, too! Meanwhile, back at the Netscape site, users have quick, convenient access to payment through a secure payment system that, again, Netscape invented. Also available are loads of purchase support information and technical support in the form of FAQs and online discussion groups that are geared toward both users and developers.

Create a nice logo icon for your product and offer it for free to other Webmasters, who can place your logo icon on their sites with a link back to yours for easy download of your product. You can, if you really, really want to, grab a copy of Photoshop and create your logo icon yourself; unless you are a bona fide designer, however, we strongly recommend you hire a designer instead. Remember, this icon is going to represent you to the world.

Services sell

Service is by its very nature virtual — there are no goods to be delivered in service companies. Services sell on the Web, but the trick here is that the service has to be as good as or one up on nonvirtual services of the same type that are offered in the real world. In some cases, an online setting allows a company to offer a special service that it could not provide its customers except through a Web site.

FedEx

FedEx (`http://www.fedex.com`) offers something online that could never have worked otherwise: instant package shipping and tracking. Using special software that's easy to download from the FedEx site, users can create an airbill and send it electronically to FedEx; they can even request pickup. Users can also find out in a few mouse clicks what would have taken much longer via telephone — *exactly* where that in-transit package is and when it's going to arrive. What's more, they can see the signature of whomever signed for the thing when it did arrive. The FedEx site leverages brand recognition and plenty of visibility in print and TV advertising — FedEx is no penny-ante operation — but the real kicker is the online service itself, a work of sheer brilliance that defines the term *value added*.

A model of distribution and selling

Taking a quick look at one model of distribution can help to focus your efforts. Here, as usual, we encourage you to use several tactics in implementing your overall strategy. For example, to sell shareware online, you may consider the approach of creating a tightly focused site like WinZip's and then getting your product listed at CNET's highly successful shareware.com site (`http://www.shareware.com`). While you're at it, hit all of the computer-book Web sites, where there are often whole areas of the site devoted to downloadable software. Use the create-a-nifty-logo-icon idea (see the section of this chapter on Netscape) to encourage Webmasters everywhere to make your product's presence known. The point here is to maximize your visibility. Then, at your site, make downloading a breeze, and offer two or three simple payment systems: perhaps a phone/fax/mail order system with a simple form provided, and if you're up to it, a form-based secure server system. (A shopping cart seems like overkill here.) As always, the point is maximum visibility followed by easy access to both the product and payment. That works for many products, not just shareware.

AutoByTel

Do you know anyone who actually enjoys buying a car? New or used, it's always an ordeal — why, even our cousin, who sells cars, hates walking into a dealership as a customer. AutoByTel (http://www.autobytel.com) takes the pain out of car buying by removing the haggling and yet guaranteeing customers a low price on the auto of choice. AutoByTel is closely integrated into a number of other sites, including Edmunds (http://www.edmund.com) and Microsoft CarPoint (http://www.carpoint.com), that offer information to help users choose which car from which manufacturer they want. After that decision is made, the customer can click over to AutoByTel, describe the car of interest via a simple e-mail form, click on Send, and sit back in comfort. Very quickly, a price quote arrives from a dealer within 60 miles of the user's home — and the quote is for a rock-bottom deal!

AutoByTel offers a service to both customers and dealers, for whom this is an added sales channel. The car buyer pays nothing for the service; this means that AutoByTel doesn't have to run a secure server or process payments from users. Instead, the service is paid for through subscription fees paid by the car dealers. AutoByTel has created one of the most profitable sites on the Web using this model.

Just in case you're interested, we bought a car through AutoByTel, and the whole deal ran so smoothly, we've been telling everyone we know for months; even our sales-rep cousin was astonished! So there you have it — AutoByTel has a good word-of-mouth campaign going, too.

Information is oddly challenging

The Web has been touted by many as one of the most important developments in information delivery since . . . television! The telephone! The *printing press!* (No one seems to go quite so far as to say that it's as important as the development of written language.) And yet, Web publishing — a thriving idea — has not yet paid off in big bucks the way that many thought it would. Perhaps that's because the tradition on the Net has been to offer information for free. Perhaps the trick is that, on the Web, publishers have to add value to the basic information they publish and charge for the value added rather than just for the delivery of information.

If this is so, it makes publishing substantial information on the Web hard to justify. For publishers, a question arises about whether the venture is cost effective. Publishing is not an inexpensive business, and where can publishers recoup their costs if they offer big-time information content and cannot charge for it? In Chapter 2, we discussed various revenue models, with a look at advertising and subscriptions included. There are special problems in using that model in an information-publishing context — traffic has to be mighty high to attract advertisers, and examples of successful sites with paid subscription income are rare. Again, there's that information-is-free tradition on the Web. In the next couple of sections we take a look at some successful information sites and see what makes them tick.

Mercury News

The *San Jose Mercury News*'s Mercury Center (`http://www.mercurycenter.com`) quickly gained a reputation as a sterling source of online information — it was one of the first newspapers published in a Web edition. This online edition was also able to trade on both the *Mercury News*'s existing journalistic reputation and the paper's proximity to the Silicon Valley scene, where so much online development was occurring. The print version of the paper already focused on technology and Silicon Valley news; its target audience — and that of the online version — has had one of the highest rates of adoption of computers, Internet connections, and Web technologies in the world. What's more, while *The New York Times* and *The Wall Street Journal* are distributed in print version to subscribers all over the United States, the *Merc* is not — the Web version opened a brave new world for the *Merc*.

Stop by the site, and you can see that its design matches its journalistic integrity. Unlike some news sources that "slap up" wire-service stories without any design or thought to editing the content to make it dynamic online, Mercury Center is well designed and attractive. The site provides content beyond the newspaper's, with extended versions of stories and bulletin board areas for reader comments. Access to selected articles is free, while a fee is charged for subscriptions that offer access to the meatier content. Special discounts are available to those who subscribe to the print edition of the paper, and inexpensive subscriptions are available to those who don't subscribe to the print edition. In a nice touch, custom news delivery allows readers to personalize the "paper" they receive according to their own interests.

Quote.com

Is it an information site or a service? That's hard to say, because the added value here is so closely integrated with the information that's offered. Quote.com (`http://www.quote.com`) publishes stock quotes (with a 15-minute delay) and other investment information that's attractive to its audience — so much so, we have to call it an information publisher. A great deal of that stuff is free, though. When you get more deeply into Quote.com's offerings — which include e-mail delivery of content to subscribers, daily e-mail delivery of closing prices, e-mail throughout the day of news headlines, and even e-mail warnings when your stocks get above/below specified price points — the added value component is clear.

For added value, users have to register; they can get some stuff for the simple cost of registering, while other material costs money. Fees are stepped up in a range that depends on the information and service offered — the *top* subscription price is $99.95 per month. This system of stepped-up service and fees allows users to pay only for the services that they want, and it affords Quote.com a way to upgrade users to more expensive options along the way. It also allows Quote.com to broaden its product base, content, and potential revenues as new information services become available — users of new stuff don't usually balk when told they have to pay for it.

Selling Is about Trust — Building It and Keeping It

So you walk into a sporting goods shop, a restaurant, or a big department store, and what do you want to know before you lay down your hard-earned moolah? You want to know that you are buying a good thing, that you are going to get what you pay for, that it is going to be delivered in good condition, and that, if something goes wrong, someone is going to make it right. Much of the evaluation you do before making a purchase involves answering these questions, and if you are over nine years old (you are, aren't you?), you probably know the importance of being a savvy consumer. You also want to know — though you may not think consciously of this — that whomever is selling to you is not going to abuse the trust that you place in your (however brief) business relationship with that company.

Every day, millions of consumers fork over their credit cards to waiters, gas station attendants, phone order clerks, and sales reps. We all write 'em on magazine subscription forms, too. Any one of those folks that you've given your credit card number to could take, use, and even distribute it to whomever they bump into on the street, for fun or for profit. But we go ahead, calmly handing over our credit cards and letting total strangers simply walk out of sight with them for minutes at a time. Why do we do that? We do it because we trust the system. On the whole, we believe that the gas station, store, or restaurant looks okay and does not sanction abuse of customers by its employees, and that the vendor we are dealing with and the credit card company itself are going to cooperate with each other and with us to resolve any problems. We feel a sense of . . . *security.*

When to bill a credit card

Keep in mind that ethically, and perhaps even legally, you really shouldn't bill a customer's credit card until you ship the order. This is how mail order works, and it goes a long way toward your customers having confidence in you. The downside is that it requires a two-part transaction, but in the long run, it's really the best way to go.

It is that sense of security that you want to instill in your online customers. To do so, you may first look at the real-world successes of catalog and mail order companies like Lands' End (whose Web site is shown in Figure 3-1), L.L. Bean, Harry & David, and so on. The model they present is perhaps as close as any can get to what works online. People buy from these companies because mail order is convenient but also because the companies are known to provide good merchandise in a trustworthy manner. They follow a few simple guidelines that you too can use:

✔ **Look credible.** Project a professional and trustworthy image, whatever that means in your industry. If you're selling CDs for garage bands, it means something different than if you're an investment firm. Your Web site is your storefront, and a customer's first visit to it forms an overall impression of your credibility. There's no need to make the site too designer oriented — unless you're selling design services or fashion accessories — but do at least make it attractive and easy to navigate. (Accessibility to products is crucial.)

✔ **Leverage the familiar.** If your company is well known and has spent bundles creating a corporate identity, you're in. But if yours is a fledgling outfit, you may consider partnering with established companies to make yourself seem credible, touting that famous client that you snagged, or even getting testimonial quotes from well-known backers or supporters. At the very least, use recognized, credible systems for payment and for your underlying technology. Even just saying that you use a Netscape secure server makes you seem more credible than if you use an obscure payment scheme and a homemade security system.

✔ **Give the customer all of the information needed to make a purchase decision.** Don't go overboard, though — one picture of that super-duper ergonomic chair and a list of available colors are enough. There's no need for slow-to-download 3D animated representations of all nine color choices.

✔ **Make placing an order easy.** Place a simple Buy button where it is most visible without pushing it in your customer's face. Also, remove all barriers to placing an order, including the barrier of not understanding. Confused customers often don't ask for help; they simply leave the store. Make sure that your forms are simple but complete, and that your ordering system walks people through the steps without making them hop through so many hoops they tucker out and take off.

✔ **Provide understandable, familiar ways for the customer to pay.** If you use a shopping-cart system that features a secure server or some payment scheme like CyberCash, offer information about why that system is safe. You may also want to offer a couple of alternative ways to pay so that if a secure shopping-cart system seems too avant-garde to some, they can print the order form and use the more familiar faxing technique.

- **Make the point when the transaction is actually going through very clear.** Don't leave people wondering whether their attempt to buy actually worked. Offer them a chance to review their purchases and the option to put things back or add to their purchase. As they approach the moment of actual payment, let them know it's occurring, and afterward, acknowledge their purchase, tell them when to expect delivery, and *thank them*. It's also a good idea to give them an order number they can use to track the purchase should they wonder what's up later.

- **Explain your system for delivering what you sell.** A simple link to a "How this Shopping System Works" page can go a long way toward building customer confidence.

- **Back up your products with assurances that you will make things right if something goes wrong.** Make sure you've posted your return policy; this is law in many states but good business everywhere. Again, it's a matter of inspiring customer confidence. Also, keep in mind the power of the unlimited money-back guarantee. Not many people send the merchandise back for silly reasons, but many people buy based on the idea that they have a guarantee.

- **Treat your customers with respect.** Don't reuse information you get from your customers. If they gave you their e-mail address as part of a transaction, don't use it to spam them with announcements. No one likes getting junk mail. And above all, don't *ever* sell or otherwise provide your customer list to another company or person without offering your customers an option out of that. You may not get off the Internet alive if you do.

How Online Shopping Works

There are many ways to place an order. Perhaps your online customers will order by sending you return e-mail, by filling out an online form that can be printed and faxed to you, or by browsing your virtual storefront, placing items in a virtual shopping cart and checking out through a secure payment system. Which of the many available shopping systems you use depends on your products, your audience, and the level of complexity that you, the Webmaster, feel is worthwhile.

You may want to offer more than one ordering system on your site. It's a general rule in sales that you want to make buying as easy as possible, and offering some combination of ordering systems is sure to increase the percentage of people who see your system as easy to use.

The sales tax shuffle

Once upon a time, sales tax was a relatively simple matter — as a merchant, you collected your state or local sales tax at the point of purchase (your store) and paid up to the state or local tax board. You didn't have to pay sales tax on merchandise purchased by those in other states and shipped there. Simple enough, eh?

But things have changed. If you plan to sell online, you must, must, must learn your state and local sales tax codes and comply with them. Pay attention to complications — for example, in California, sales tax varies from county to county. If yours is such a situation, to collect the proper tax, you may have to track a purchaser's zip code and cross reference it (electronically, of course) against the tax code for that locale. And some states have cross-taxing agreements such that if you are in State A and selling to someone in state B, you have to charge that state B resident sales tax.

Note, too, that in this context that nifty borderless quality of the Web — the quality that makes where the server is actually located of no apparent consequence — cuts both ways. Because your virtual storefront is considered by some tax boards to have no actual locale, you may be considered to be doing business in all 50 U.S. states and thus required to collect sales tax from everyone. This could be a real mess. In fact, it may turn into not just an American mess but an international one, if tax boards around the world get it in mind that you're doing business in their countries, too.

The fact is that this matter is really up in the air. Our best advice is to consult a professional tax advisor and your state and local tax boards to find out the law where you do business. Best of luck to you, and to us all.

Viewed from behind the scenes, a typical order-taking and fulfillment system may be as basic as a simple Microsoft Access database on a PC or as complex as a multimillion dollar computer system with servers and clients spread across the world. Usually, there is a front end of some sort — it may be an interface that's tacked onto a flatfile or relational database — and the database back end. If your company has such an existing system, small or large, your online order system can be connected to it. If not, you must take into consideration the lengths to which you want to go in setting up an order-taking and fulfillment system.

The deciding factor is volume of business — you need more back-end support for higher volumes of orders. Even if you're not using a flashy shopping-cart system, if your shopping system is as simple as accepting e-mail orders, for example, you need a more robust order-taking and fulfillment back end if the orders start flying in at the speed of light. In the sections that follow we take a look at various systems that your customers can use to place orders and what makes them handy.

Phone and mail order systems

What could be more understandable to users? You publish your "catalog" of products on the site, long or short, along with a phone number or simple instructions for sending in a mail order, and it's all no big deal. This option certainly has the advantage of being understandable to the customer, and dang, you can just use your existing order-taking and fulfillment systems (if you have them). This may be the way to go if you are in no position to set up a more ambitious system — after all, secure servers aren't cheap, and they do take some maintenance.

Even if you use other more-sophisticated systems to sell on your site, include a simple phone and mail order system. It shouldn't add much expense, and you want to provide as many options for buying as you can within your budget.

E-mail ordering

Many sites publish their catalogs online and then, as a buy option, they provide a simple link to an e-mail form. Okay, so it isn't slick, but it's easy — significantly easier for users than having to pick up the phone or mail an order request. They're sitting there, and they have their mouse pointer poised....

Payment via e-mail is an issue, however. Don't ask users to send their credit card numbers in an e-mail message — it's about as safe as dangling your credit card out the car window as you drive through Vegas. Instead, you may want to ask that your customers open an account by calling in or faxing an application. You can then give them a unique account number to use in placing orders. The account information would specify where to ship the stuff as part of the "permanent" record. In a worst-case scenario, someone may steal the account number, but the would-be thief would only be able to order merchandise that would then be shipped to the customer who set up the account. That's no fun for the thief, now, is it?

Forms for faxing or simple online ordering

There are forms, and there are forms. One of the simpler ways to take orders is to post a nice-looking, easy-to-fill-out form on your site and ask people to print it and fax it to you to place an order. No sweat. This is a variation, really, on the tried-and-true phone and mail order scheme we described in a previous section. It's neat and simple, and it costs very little to implement, assuming that you're using existing fulfillment strategies.

The form in this scenario probably includes a brief list of products, along with check boxes or text boxes into which a quantity can be entered, and some other text boxes that may be labeled Name, Address, City, State, Zip, and so on. A payment method should be specified somewhere on the form, and it's always a good idea to offer a couple of payment-method choices. (However, if you offer the "Bill Me" method, count on losing a fair amount of revenue.)

In a slightly more sophisticated version, the form has a button on it that says something like Submit Order. When the customer clicks on the button, the order is placed via a secure server or a payment system like CyberCash (described later in this chapter). The server programs involved in doing this can be very simple, as long as all that's happening on the back end is logging the sale into a file that then gets dealt with by your existing order-entry system. (In fact, if you're not doing many transactions, your order-entry system may be as simple as a person just grabbing the list of orders and packing and shipping the merchandise.)

If you expect big volume, you should integrate this type of a form into a robust back-end order-taking and fulfillment system. You can either connect to your existing system, or you have one built. In either case, get a database pro to give you a hand. Many existing order-taking and fulfillment systems are old databases that never expected to meet up with the Internet. A new database, on the other hand, can become the backbone of your ordering system — you want it to work and be flexible enough to grow with your business.

If you do decide to go the route of connecting your shiny new order form to an existing database, you may want to look into using Web Objects from Apple. This tool for developing Web applications runs on Windows NT and UNIX operating systems and includes a component that makes connecting to older databases easier.

Shopping carts

Picture yourself as Wanda Webuser. You are attracted by the winning content at the Acme Wonderwidget site, and you toodle around there, noticing as you go the fine widgets the company offers for sale. One by one, you view them, and when one strikes your fancy, you click on a Buy button to plop it into your virtual shopping cart. After a while, you think, "I wonder how many Wonderwidgets I have in my cart?" You click on the handy What's in My Cart? button, and change your mind about one or two items. Then, with the click of another button, you head for checkout, where you provide some simple information via a brief set of order forms, pony up your payment, and *click* — you're done. In most cases, Acme sends you an e-mail confirmation of your order, and the order itself arrives within a specified time, via a real-world shipper.

Shopping-cart systems like these consist of a front end that's composed of a series of Web page forms, a bunch of CGI scripts (special programs that run on the server) that enable the user to add and remove items from the cart (as well as just peek into it), and perhaps a database of products. Anyone with scripting skills can write a shopping-cart system, but you may want to skip some of the hard work. Intershop, Microsoft Merchant Server, and other prepackaged storefronts include the scripts you need, although you must customize them for your products and systems. We discuss these products later in this chapter. Selena Sol's Shopping Cart (Figure 3-2) is a public domain shopping-cart system you can use on your site. (It takes some modification, too.) Selena Sol's Shopping Cart and other public domain scripts can be found at `http://www.eff.org/~erict/Scripts/`.

Just as with the simple form-ordering system that we described in the section titled "Forms for faxing or simple online ordering," big sales volume in a shopping cart situation can mean you need a big back-end order-taking and fulfillment system. You can either connect to your existing system or have one built. Have a database pro help you with this, however; existing order-taking and fulfillment systems often exist as old databases that balk at working with the younger, flashier Internet. If you have a new database developed, it's bound to become the backbone of your ordering system, so make it flexible enough to grow with your business.

You also need a two-part transaction system working with your shopping cart to allow users to pay using their credit cards. One part logs the transactions into a database, letting individual transactions be tracked. The other part handles payment. This is either through a secure server or through a payment system that's provided by another company, like CyberCash. The balance of this chapter describes the issues involved in secure transaction systems.

Figure 3-2:
Selena
Sol's public
domain
shopping
cart.

Selena Sol's
Public Domain CGI Script Archive

HOME

Archive Home
Announcing
Scripts
In The Press
FAQ's
Help Found
Research Links
Offsite Goodies
Web Kudos

Welcome to Selena Sol's Public Domain Script Archive, a public service website developed out of the late-night scripting expeditions of Selena Sol and Gunther Birznieks. Feel free to browse through the resources we have compiled and sign the guestbook or the Mailing List if you like what you find. Also, to discuss installation and customization issues with others, please visit the The Selena Sol Script Archive Discussion Forum generously maintained and donated by John Cesta.

Why is This Page Here?
The goal of the site is mainly to document the CGI work that Selena Sol and Gunther Birznieks have done so that perhaps other programmers can learn from the way we do things and hopefully evolve our ideas so we can learn too.

Those Not-So-Identical Twins: Security and Commerce

Those twin issues of electronic business, *security* and *commerce,* capture a lot of headlines. Lots of folks think there are big bucks to be made online as soon as the twins mature a bit more. Security and commerce are closely interrelated, that's for sure (increased security on the Web encourages conducting Internet commerce, and interest in Internet commerce encourages development of Web security), but they aren't quite the identical twins they often seem to be.

Why this counts

To put together a nifty shopping system — to conduct *commerce* — you'd need to provide your users with security. You must give them the knowledge that when they engage in a transaction on your site, they can do so without fear of intrusion or theft. You can do that using a secure server or through third-party payment software. In either case, knowing the underlying technology can help you understand and build a secure transaction system.

Security and commerce basics

Many people think that someone — some evil person or group — is lurking in the electronic shadows about to pounce. This evil entity wants your credit card number, can get it in a snap, and then can distribute it at will to millions of other evil ones who can use it for unscrupulous means. Are these realistic fears? Probably not. Do you have to take these concerns seriously? You bet.

Oddly enough, the security systems now in place for Web commerce are much safer than those used when you fork over your credit card in a store, restaurant, or some other real-world business. When you stroll into a store and charge a purchase, you give your credit card number and signature to a total stranger, who can easily jot down the number or simply lift the carbon. Most bank processes involve the handling of the transaction by any number of individuals. Anywhere along the path of the transaction, your credit card number could be stolen fairly easily.

By comparison, the schemes used in electronic commerce are a lot tougher for an unscrupulous individual to get into. These schemes, the basic building blocks that allow confidential data to move over a public network like the Internet without third parties listening in, are based on two basic technologies: *encryption* and *digital signatures.* Encryption and digital signatures make secure servers and payment software, such as CyberCash and ecash, both possible and functional.

Encryption

Encryption is the process of taking data (for example, the contents of a Web form that includes a credit card number) and using a mathematical formula to scramble it such that you need a *key* (a digital code) to decrypt and read it. Encryption is nothing new — a form of encryption called the *Caesar Cipher* was used in the Roman Empire to protect Roman communications that could fall into enemy hands from being read. Encryption has been used extensively during the American Civil War, World War II, and most other conflicts.

Today's uses of encryption have spread beyond the military to all types of commerce, and the combination of advances in *cryptography* (the branch of mathematics that includes encryption) and the rapid growth of inexpensive, powerful computers make encryption important to all of us. One of those advanced forms of encryption that was until recently of interest only to military intelligence units — RSA public key encryption — is now often used to make Web pages that are stored on a secure server remain secure.

Public key encryption — a special kind of encryption that is used extensively to protect information on the Web — is based on the notion that some mathematical functions are much easier than their inverse. For example, think about multiplication and division. Most people can multiply two numbers fairly quickly. But those same people pause and have to think a bit harder when asked to reverse the process and divide those numbers. They may even need to pull out a calculator! That isn't because these folks aren't as smart about division — it's because division is by nature a tougher calculation.

Exploiting the idea that some functions are easier to accomplish than their inverse allows the possibility that anyone can encrypt data using what is called a *public key* (a method of encryption that's based on something similar to but far more mathematically complex than multiplication). In *public key encryption,* everyone gets two keys: one that is publicly known, as mentioned, and another, the *private key,* that is not publicly known. Each of these keys can decipher the data the other encrypted. Having a two-key system like this solves many problems of cryptography.

Public key encryption was invented by a group of people that formed the company RSA Data Security. RSA owns patents for public key encryption; Netscape, Microsoft, and most other major Web-related companies license this technology from RSA. The RSA home page at http://www.rsa.com is full of information about public key encryption.

Digital signatures

A related technology, *digital signatures,* is based on the idea that a unique electronic "signature" is like a real signature — like the one with which you sign your checks. Digital signatures are pieces of electronic data that are at the bottom of a document (but you don't actually see them); they guarantee the identity of the author of the document and that no on has modified the document in transit. Digital signatures don't hide the contents of the document; they merely prove the document's legitimacy. But again, it's private key encryption at work behind the scenes here.

Secure Servers and You

Secure servers are, simply, servers that operate in a secure way. The use of a secure server in conjunction with a secure Web browser allows confidential information to travel over the Internet without the likelihood that the information is going to be intruded upon by those whose business it is not. Secure servers use technologies such as encryption and digital signatures (described in preceding sections) in a scheme known as *secure socket layer* (SSL) to protect the confidential information as it travels. SSL makes it possible to securely send information as diverse as credit card numbers, medical records, stock portfolios, and even simple confidential messages over the Internet. SSL manages the security of Web pages that are sent from the secure server to a Web browser and back again in the sort of exchange that takes place when a user fills out a Web-page form and submits it. The form can be a simple order form, a request for medical records, or the result of a user looking into his or her own stock portfolio.

SSL provides security between the server and the Web client (the browser). Both have to support SSL for this to work, but that's not much of a problem these days, given that Netscape Navigator has always supported SSL, Microsoft Internet Explorer started supporting it in version 2, and even the AOL browser has now gotten on the bandwagon.

Secure server advantages

SSL offers a way to set up the secure environment you need to provide for financial transactions on your site, but it's not the only option. A number of companies — such as CyberCash and DigiCash, both of which we describe in the following sections — provide secure payment software that you can use. The advantage of using SSL, however, is that it can secure *any* type of data — not just a financial transaction — while third-party payment software can handle only *payments*. This becomes important when you're exchanging confidential information with users beyond just payment information — for example, medical records or bank statements. The advantage of using payment software, on the other hand, is that you get a complete package that's designed to handle payment — something that you don't get with SSL. If you need the complete works — a secure server for encrypting confidential data like bank records and a fully integrated payment package — you may want to consider integrating something like CyberCash with your secure server, or you can have a custom payment system built by a pro.

What you need

To use SSL security on your Web site, you need Web-server software that supports SSL. This is no big a deal — both Netscape Enterprise server and Microsoft Internet Information Server (IIS) support SSL. You also need to *enable* SSL security on your server — SSL is disabled by default on most servers. To enable SSL, you must get and install a digital certificate. A digital certificate (described earlier in "Security and commerce basics") is comprised of both of the two keys used in the public key encryption system that is part of SSL. You purchase your certificate from a *certificate authority* — a company that is authorized to sell certificates. VeriSign is one such company, which you can reach at `http://www.verisign.com`. VeriSign offers various grades of certificates; each is designed for different types of transactions. During the process of purchasing a certificate, you must provide proof of your identity — you may be required to have the application stamped by a notary public, or you may have to send in a copy of your business license or fictitious name statement. It all depends on the type of business you're doing.

Your users must use a Web browser that supports SSL security. Netscape Navigator and Microsoft Internet Explorer both do. According to some surveys, 92 percent of Web users are using one of these two browsers. What's more, the newer versions of the AOL browser also support SSL, so you're pretty much covered.

What security "looks like"

Typically, not everything on a site is confidential, so an entire site does not have to be protected using SSL. A home page certainly is not likely to be secure, and informational areas of a site probably need not be secure. However, when a user enters a sensitive area of the site — perhaps an area that includes the person's bank records — a secure server can kick in and start using SSL to encrypt the data as it travels from the server to the browser.

A number of clues may tell the user whether a Web page is secure:

- The URL for a page encrypted with SSL starts with `https:` instead of `http:`.

- A dialog box heralding the fact usually appears as the user enters or exits a secure area (although this depends on the browser used, and the message can often be disabled by the user).

- Various browsers offer their own specific visual clues; for example, Netscape Navigator 3 shows a broken key in the lower-left corner of the screen for nonsecure pages and an intact key for secure pages.

Security and online transactions

It's quite important that you as the Webmaster understand the role of SSL in the world of online transactions. SSL does not "do" transactions — it doesn't collect payment information or gather information about the things a user wants to buy. SSL addresses the important issue of securing information as it travels over the Internet. SSL stops third parties from eavesdropping on data going from the server to the browser and back again — and it stops third parties from impersonating you or your user. It can be used in conjunction with special scripts, such as shopping-cart scripts, to create an online shopping environment; but in and of itself, it is not the payment system. For a shopping system that includes a secure server, you need to have either your own proprietary payment scheme or one that's provided by a third-party company. Creating proprietary payment systems is beyond the scope of this book — we recommend that you get a pro to handle it if that's the way you want to go. What we can delve into, though, is payment systems that are offered by third-party companies. Tally ho!

The Deep Skinny on Transaction Systems

A *transaction system* lets users buy something — in this case, on the Web. A transaction system consists of a secure server and a specially created payment scheme that are custom built for you (see preceding sections), or it may be a payment system that's provided by a third-party company; in the latter case, you don't necessarily have to have a secure server. In that case, the necessary level of security is provided by the payment software that you get from the payment-software company.

Today there are scads of companies selling and promoting systems for doing secure transactions on the Web. The first question you must ask yourself is whether the company you're considering is reputable. As everyone knows, there's plenty of snake oil on the Web. In the sections that follow we take a look at some of the larger, better known companies — those with established credentials. This can give you a good overview of what's available. Then you can decide whether to do it yourself or to rely on a third party to handle your transactions.

Handy-dandy payment systems

In general, payment systems fall into two categories, and each uses a different processing system. One processing system requires your customers to run special software and makes most of the details of conducting commerce on the Web invisible to you, the Webmaster. You simply open an account, set up the software, and let it run. CyberCash and DigiCash are of this type. The processing system uses software that lets you collect a credit card number — usually sent to your Web server via a secure SSL channel — and then charge against it. This system usually requires that you do more custom programming to integrate the processing software into your site — that's the downside. The upside is that this system does not require your customers to run any special software on their computers. A customer only needs to enter his or her credit card number into a standard Web form when shopping. ICVERIFY, which we discuss later in this chapter, is an example of this type of system.

CyberCash

The CyberCash system is based on use of two pieces of software — the client-side CyberCash Wallet and the server-side CyberCash Register. To conduct a transaction, you and your customer must both have accounts with CyberCash. You set yours up before you set up your payment system. Your customers set theirs up when they initiate their first transactions using your payment system.

CyberCash's Web site, at `http://www.cybercash.com`, provides the information and software that you need to start using CyberCash on your site. You can find out all about becoming a CyberCash merchant, meanwhile, at `http://www.cybercash.com/cybercash/merchants/ getstarted.html`.

Your customer can set up an account with CyberCash in a quick and easy online process while installing the CyberCash Wallet software. This software is available for free download from CyberCash's Web site, to which you can link from your site quite simply. During the process of setting up an account, your customer can specify either a credit card or a bank account to which purchases can be billed. All the purchases that customer makes anywhere via CyberCash are consolidated monthly and billed by CyberCash. If the customer makes many small transactions, they all appear as one lump-sum charge on the credit card bill or the bank account transfer.

As you may know, credit card companies charge merchants for transactions. They often charge a percentage of the transaction, with a minimum fee specified. So if a merchant lets you charge a 10-cent item on your credit card, the merchant may pay the credit card company 50 cents for providing you with that privilege. (This is why many merchants don't accept credit cards for purchases under $10.) The CyberCash system of bundling purchases made by a single customer through CyberCash and then charging all of those small purchases as one lump debit makes doing small transactions much more practical for merchants (like you).

CyberCash Wallet software is available in both Windows and Macintosh versions. The CyberCash register software runs on most of the popular platforms for Web servers — Windows NT, Solaris, Sun OS, HP-UX, and IRIX.

Like the Wallet software, the Register software is free. You don't need a secure server on your end to use the CyberCash system. The CyberCash Wallet application (which runs on the customer's machine) and the CyberCash Register application (which runs on your Web server) create a secure channel between them using encryption. However, this only provides security in the occurring financial transaction; it has nothing to do with security of sensitive documents (see "Secure Servers and You," earlier in this chapter). The general process of a CyberCash transaction is shown in Figure 3-3.

It's pretty easy to set up a CyberCash system and get it going. You can integrate it into your existing Web pages, and you don't have to do any special programming. You don't even have to deal with security issues, because security is handled by the software provided by CyberCash. The only real downside is that your customers must have an account with CyberCash and the CyberCash Wallet software installed on their computers to use the system, but that's simple enough for even the most technophobic users to manage.

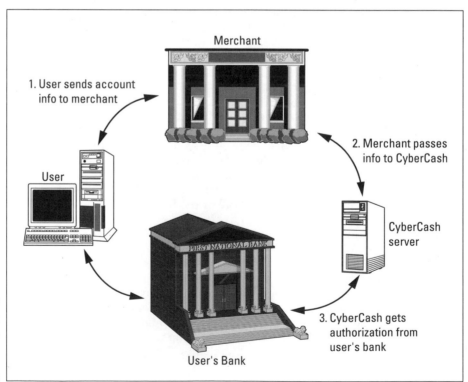

Figure 3-3:
A
CyberCash
transaction.

DigiCash and ecash

DigiCash offers a payment system that allows users to trade in the electronic equivalent of currency — *ecash* — on the Internet. DigiCash's system includes simple client software, which your customers must run to use the system, and server software, which you must install on your server to make things go. Figure 3-3 shows a typical ecash transaction. DigiCash's system relies on real banks — instead of credit card companies — for transactions.

DigiCash and CyberCash may seem similar, but there are some interesting differences between them. While the CyberCash system involves CyberCash acting as a financial go-between, DigiCash provides only the transaction software and doesn't get involved in the transaction. In a DigiCash transaction, when the user makes a purchase, he or she withdraws electronic currency from a real bank, and the currency is traded in the transaction. No credit card charges apply, and no interest is charged on the account, as is the case in a credit card transaction. (This is a *currency system*, not a credit system.)

DigiCash's client software is available in both Windows and Macintosh versions. The server software works with almost all Web servers — regardless of the server hardware that you are using.

To install DigiCash ecash on your server, you need to download the software from DigiCash's Web site at `http://www.digicash.com`. You must also open an account with a bank that accepts ecash. A list of those banks is found at DigiCash's Web site.

You don't need a secure server to set up and use an ecash system on your site. Just as with CyberCash, you can integrate an ecash system into your existing Web pages without special programming. You also needn't deal with security issues, because security is handled by the DigiCash software. Again, the downside is that your customers must have an account and must have the client software installed on their computers to use ecash, but anyone can manage that. DigiCash supports European currencies and is better accepted in Europe than it is in the United States, although U.S. users are growing in number.

ICVERIFY

ICVERIFY is a credit and debit card authorization system. It works in much the same way as the system you use in actual stores when you swipe your credit card or ATM card through that little machine — except, of course, that there's no little machine and instead the authorization takes place over the Internet. The general process of using ICVERIFY to conduct a transaction is shown in Figure 3-4.

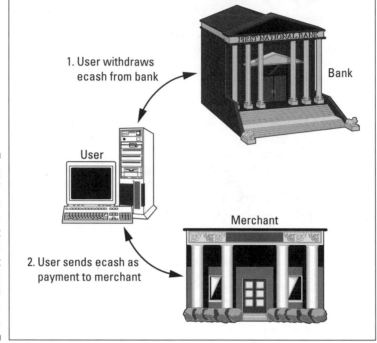

1. User withdraws
ecash from bank

Bank

User

2. User sends ecash as
payment to merchant

Merchant

Figure 3-4:
ICVERIFY
enables
users to
conduct
credit card
and debit
card
transactions
via a
Web site.

When a customer uses ICVERIFY, he or she submits a credit card number directly onto a secure Web form — the person doesn't have to set up accounts with anyone (except the credit card or debit card people) and he or she doesn't need to have any special software (other than a Web browser). At your end, the form must be processed using a custom script, and more than likely, someone will need to write the script for you. This script passes the information along to ICVERIFY. There, their software contacts a bank, gets an approval number for the transaction (assuming that the credit card is good), and returns that information to the script running on your Web server.

ICVERIFY software (found at `http://www.icverify.com`) runs under Windows 95 and Windows NT, but no Mac version is available. ICVERIFY is not a Web-specific application — and does not require your customers to run any special software — so you definitely need a secure server to make the system work. Your secure server can provide the secure channel necessary to conduct transactions with your customers. The upside here is convenience to your users, who don't have to create yet another account in their lives. The downside is that you have to invest some energy and perhaps capital in custom programming to launch this system.

All about prepackaged stores

We want to be clear about this: A prepackaged store is not quite what it seems. You don't pull a freeze-dried storefront from a box, pour on a little steamy water, and — poof! — move in for business. A prepackaged store is a suite of software that contains all of the components you need to put your storefront on the Web, but it still requires some custom programming. A number of companies are putting these conveniences together; they usually include in them components for publishing your catalog (actually the contents of a database), taking orders, and processing payments (usually with CyberCash as the payment system). Using a prebuilt system like this does save you the time and trouble of setting up all of the databases, creating all of the scripts, and most importantly, debugging the system. A prepackaged solution may allow you to concentrate on your products and market them, and it can be a real convenience if you aren't a programmer or don't want to hire one.

The drawback in using a prepackaged solution is that it can never be as flexible as something that's custom-built. (Ain't that the way it is in life?) You are stuck with certain assumptions the suite developer made about businesses in general, and that may not be right for your business. Maybe the thing doesn't display information in quite the way you'd prefer, maybe it makes customers jump through some unnecessary hoops, maybe it doesn't support the payment system that you would prefer. And, finally, it may just lock you into using a certain Web server.

Prepackaged solutions do not work "right out of the box." Depending on the one that you go with, you still have to do more or less of creating the HTML pages for your online store, populating the database with your products, and some connective programming or script writing. These beauties also don't come cheap. We've seen prices ranging from $3,500 to $18,000 for various packages. But again, what you're paying for is convenience. If you're prepared to compromise customization for easier setup, this may be the way to go, and depending on how elaborate your customization plans were, it may even save you a bit of moolah.

Microsoft Merchant Server

Microsoft Merchant Server is probably the heavyweight here. It includes modules that work along with IIS, the Microsoft Web server, and with other Microsoft BackOffice products, such as SQL Server. Using Merchant Server, you can set up a complete electronic store, including catalogs, shopping carts, and payment systems.

While Merchant Server includes some prebuilt sample stores that you can start using right away, it's really designed to be customized for your particular needs. You need to get developers to customize it for you — unless of course you are a developer, in which case you can do it. Merchant Server also includes a number of sample storefronts that you or a developer can customize for your needs. But it really shows its stuff if you start from scratch and build your store from the ground up using the Merchant Server components. (Warning, warning! — real programmer definitely needed here!) Merchant Server includes modules for handling database access to any ODBC database, including Microsoft SQL Server, and modules for handling credit card transactions. (ODBC is a standard by which programs and databases communicate.)

In terms of operating systems, unlike the other products that we discuss in this chapter, Merchant Server is designed to run only with Windows NT Server. And to really make use of Merchant Server, you need other parts of the Microsoft BackOffice suite of programs as well — most notably Microsoft SQL Server. (This is not going to be cheap.)

You can find out all about Microsoft Merchant Server at `http://www.microsoft.com/merchant/`.

You can find a list of sites using Merchant Server at the following URL: `http://www.microsoft.com/merchant/shop.htm`.

Tower Records (`http://www.tower.com`) used to sell a hefty catalog of 150,000 CDs. At the Tower Records site, you can see all of the aspects of Merchant Server form a user's perspective. Here, it was used to publish a giant catalog of inventory, take orders, and conduct financial transactions.

As mentioned, Merchant Server runs under Windows NT Server; it requires at least a Pentium-based machine with 64MB of RAM and 55MB of hard disk space. You can supposedly run all of the servers required to use Merchant Server — Merchant Server itself, Internet Information Server, and SQL Server — on a single Windows NT Server machine, but in reality, you probably need multiple machines. It's common to have IIS and Merchant Server running on one NT machine and SQL Server running on a second machine.

Merchant Server is sold as two pieces, and you need both pieces to use the system. The first piece is the core Merchant Server software, which retails for $14,995. If you end up running the Merchant Server software on multiple servers — say you have a real popular site — you need a core Merchant Server software license for each of the servers. In addition to the core software, you also need a store administrator license for each store that you run. The store administrator license costs $3,495. It's possible to run multiple stores on the same server; while this requires only a single core license, it also requires distinct store administrator licenses for each of the stores.

Microsoft runs a large and very well-known program for training and certifying developers in different Microsoft products, but as of this writing, it doesn't certify Merchant Server developers. This means that you aren't going to be able to find anyone carrying a handy sheepskin from Microsoft saying that he or she knows the system and can set you up. In hiring a developer to help you build a system based on Merchant Server, your best bet is to be sure that that bloke or lassie has built sites with it before — check those references! Microsoft does offer training and certification in some of the other servers that are used with Merchant Server, especially the Internet Information Server and SQL Server, so try to get someone who at least has those certifications.

Intershop Online

Intershop Online provides a complete shell of an online store, which you can then customize to your heart's content. Remarkably, Intershop Online lets you launch an online store without writing any scripts. It's pretty much ready to go as soon as you get it.

Intershop Online includes a server, which is the core of the online storefront; Sybase SQL Server, a database server; and the CyberCash payment system software we discussed earlier in this chapter. When you install Intershop Online, it installs all of these components — all set up to work with each other — there is no fussing with configuration files. Supposedly, you can just start selling today.

One of the more interesting features here is that you can administer the thing via a Web browser. This means that you can administer your online store from any place that you can access the Web — at home, a hotel room, you name it. You don't have to trot down to where the server is located. This can be a great help if your site is housed at an Internet service provider.

What's not to like? You sacrifice some robustness compared to Merchant Server, and you may prefer some other payment system than CyberCash. If so, you have to integrate some other payment system.

Intershop Online is available for both the Windows NT Server and UNIX operating systems. Both versions require 64MB of RAM (128MB is recommended) and 200MB of hard disk space. The Windows NT version requires Windows NT Server version 3.51 or 4.0 running on a Pentium-based machine and costs $5000. The UNIX version requires a machine running Sun Solaris 2.5, HP-UX 10 running on an HP 9000/800, AIX 4.1 running on an RS 6000 – based machine, or IRIX 5.3 running on any Silicon Graphics machine. It costs $8000.

You can download a 30-day trial of either version from Intershop's Web site at http://www.intershop.com/.

Having someone else do the selling for you

Maybe you want to sell online but you really don't want to get into all this techno-nightmare. If you have no substantial reason (say a big catalog of products and realistically high sales expectations), there's nothing to say that you must have a full-blown storefront of your own. In the sections that follow we look at some ways you can piggyback, sell through others, and generally avoid unwarranted headaches.

Third-party retailers

Sometimes the most obvious solution, the one right in front of you, is as invisible to you as your nose. If your company manufactures things for resale — books or toys or snailtraps — the quickest and easiest way for you to sell that stuff online may be to get someone else to do it for you. You simply need a deal with a single retailer that carries your products and has an online storefront that's set up, and you're in business. You can create your own site that reels in traffic and promotes your product and then link from your site directly to the part of the retailer's site where your stuff is sold. Your users may never realize that they've jumped servers as they purchase your product.

The advantage here is that you don't have to create and maintain a shopping system. But given that most companies sell their products at discount to the distributors and retailers, and that through direct sales you could be raking in the full product price instead of the maybe 50 percent you get when you sell through a retailer, the disadvantage is that you don't get that extra dough. Basically, you're just directing a customer to one of your retailers. It's not a bad idea, you just don't get the whole pie. On the other hand, more than one CFO we know thinks that selling to individual customers is a losing proposition. Fulfillment is expensive, after all, especially if you're fulfilling many orders of single units of your $15 product.

In choosing this kind of a system, keep in mind that you don't want to seem like you're favoring one of your retailers over others. The last thing you want is one of your major retailers shaking a fist at you because you partnered with its competition. The best way around this problem is to offer links to *all* of the retailers that sell your products. This sort of deal is offered by Farallon (`http://www.farallon.com`), a maker of networking products. On that company's site, it offers users a list of retailers that carry Farallon products, with links to retailers that take orders online.

A second possible drawback in using this scheme is that you may be directing your customers to a retailer that also sells products that compete with yours. If a customer comes to your site, he or she is probably interested in one of your products. If that person clicks a link that says Buy It, that shows some serious interest. If your Buy It link then takes the ready-to-buy customer to a site that offers other options, well — you can probably see the dilemma.

If you can link directly to a Buy It page on the retailer's site that is about your product only, there's no problem. If the retailer's site offers your product on a page with other products that compete with yours, this is a problem with no good solution. You can try to get the retailer to agree not to display those other products on the same page, or to make it cumbersome to get to them. But our experience is that it takes some hard persuasion to get folks to agree to this condition, and even if they do agree, it may be technically challenging to get it to work, unless they have a database like Amazon.com's, with a single product displayed on each catalog page. In this case, you don't have a problem.

If yours is a small site that perhaps promotes your products and if you can link to a retailer who sells those products but does not display others that compete with yours on the same page, this can be a really nifty way to go. (We use it ourselves to help sell our books — take a look at `http://www.dnai.com/~vox`.)

Online malls

If you happen to be a retailer instead of a manufacturer, then directing customers to someone else's site to place an order there is obviously a bad idea. Likewise, if you're a manufacturer and you want to retain control over the entire sale process, you want to avoid sending your customers off to a retailer. Perhaps you should consider setting up shop in an *online mall*.

The definition of an online mall is not as firm as the definition of a real-world mall — you pretty much know the difference in the real world between a big, fancy mall and a simple shopping center. One of the big differences is that the actual mall is anchored by a few big, relatively nice department stores, and it usually offers more to do than just dash into the pharmacy or grocery store and leave. The first online malls started up as overall shopping sites where more than one store shared one domain on the Net. The idea behind all the stores sharing the same URL was that the online mall would get popular and in and of itself would attract traffic. That's not so different from a real-world mall, eh? Similarly, some online malls try to get well-known anchor stores.

However, as time has gone on, more online stores have their own URLs. Some are still associated with malls, but with all the URLs involved, it's getting hard to tell which stores actually belong to the same online mall. Often the individual stores in an online mall don't provide links to the other stores in the mall — it's as if you couldn't walk from one store into another in a real mall. So at most, many online stores provide only a link on their home page to the home page of the mall, and the mall offers only individual links to the several stores. Figure 3-5 shows a fairly typical online mall.

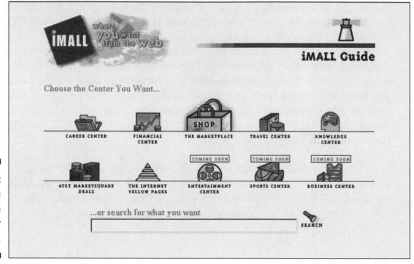

Figure 3-5:
An online mall may be the way for you to go.

Nonetheless, working with an online mall offers a big advantage for some — the company that runs the mall often helps put together your storefront, acting as a presence provider by designing the retail site and providing systems for accepting payments. Going with this kind of deal can get you the services of people who have done it before and can sell you their expertise. (For more on what Internet presence providers, or IPPs, do, see Chapter 10.)

You can easily tell what type of work the mall company does for its clients by looking at other stores located in the same mall. Look critically at the level of design expertise shown. Many of these places have the technical know-how to sell on the Web — they can set you up with the databases, Web servers, and other components you need to open your store. But many lack the high-impact and cutting-edge design skills that are needed to produce a compelling shopping experience. To produce a really hot shopping site, you may want to contract only for tech services with the mall people and then hire your own designers. We talk more about hiring Web design people in Chapter 8.

The Myriad Challenges of Fulfillment

People are funny when it comes to shopping — if they buy something, they actually want to receive it. They find that . . . *fulfilling*. Maybe this sounds obvious to you, but when it comes to selling on the Web, it's a topic that's often forgotten until the orders come in. Oddly enough, while the weird and wacky issues of publishing online catalogs and conducting secure financial transactions grab the headlines in articles about online commerce, one of the toughest challenges is actually shipping the merchandise to the customer.

This may seem less of an issue if your product is downloadable, and to some extent, it is — you don't have to wonder if downloaded software is going to break on the truck, as you would wonder about glass. Nonetheless, if you're distributing software, you have to track purchases and verify payment. On the other hand, if you're distributing software, you probably have software engineers on hand who can set up a nice custom tracking program for you with a nifty database back end.

The issues of fulfillment include:

✔ Attaching an order number to a given order so you can track it

✔ Checking and maintaining inventory

✔ Tracking the order so you know it's been paid for (and ultimately delivered)

✔ Providing the customer with e-mail verification of the order and a method for tracking it, too

✔ Shipping the order and closing the record

Be sure to review the section titled "Selling Is about Trust — Building It and Keeping It" earlier in this chapter for information about the reassurances people want when they buy from you. Much of what they want is a method for knowing where their order stands. You can set up a simple e-mail system that confirms the order, provides tracking info, notifies the customer of items that are out of stock or on back order, and so on. Use a sequential numbering system to identify orders and make it easy for you and your customers to track them.

If your company has an existing system for fulfilling orders, much of the handling and shipping aspect of fulfillment may be handled just by having that department do fulfillment for your Web initiative. Depending on your order system, this may be a simple matter — surely your fulfillment department is set up to handle phone, fax, and mail orders, for example.

Stepping things up, if you're using a shopping system, you can program your online store to interface with your existing inventory system. When a customer submits an order, the inventory can be checked, and if any of the ordered items are not available for immediate shipping, an automatic response can be sent to the customer. The customer can then choose whether he or she wants to place the item on back order or (heaven forbid!) cancel the order. Sounds nice, doesn't it? But connecting your online store to existing back-end systems is no easy task. Some of the prepackaged store software we discuss earlier in this chapter can help smooth the process, but they all require some custom database work. This may include writing special database queries or even writing special programs that run on your Web server and query your database to retrieve inventory information and add shipping records. This is not easy stuff, and it shouldn't be attempted by amateurs. To implement an online shopping system with a sophisticated fulfillment system that provides you with good reports and keeps the customers happy, hire professionals and do it right. Obviously, you don't want to do this unless you have a good reason for it — maybe a big inventory or high-volume sales expectations.

If you've chosen to align yourself with an online mall, and the operators say they can help you with fulfillment, beware. Look into this carefully — their system may not be able to "talk" to your database back end; in any case, someone is going to have to pack the stuff and ship it out. It's a rare online mall that does that for you.

In terms of getting the merchandise out the door, you (or your lackeys) can pack it yourself, or you can contract a distributor or fulfillment house to do this. Amazon.com has a nice deal with various book distributors — remember, book distributors receive really huge shipments from publishers (at least the publishers hope so) and then ship less-huge quantities to book stores everywhere. Amazon.com does not keep a large inventory — instead, it relies on the distributors to maintain inventory, and simply takes the orders and passes them electronically to the distributor, who actually ships the books. You can use this model in your industry if your sales figures are high enough to interest the distributors.

Of course, distributors and fulfillment houses don't provide their services for free — they usually charge a portion of the purchase price of the item for their cut. For example, if an item sells for $19.99, the distributor or fulfillment house may get $11.99! Be sure to investigate the costs of fulfillment before you launch your super Web site selling millions of Wonderwidgets.

Chapter 4

Building a Better Budget

Somewhere in the world there are probably people who think budgeting is a barrel of fun. To many, budgeting is a terrible chore. But to build and run a sterling Web site, you've got to face budgeting squarely and make it your friend. A good budget will help you make solid business decisions and keep costs in line. It's also a total necessity when you outsource some or all of a Web project. A budget is a good tool for projecting and assessing the *return on investment* (ROI) your Web initiative enjoys. Finally, you pretty much can't get funding without budgetary approval, so you've got to have a budget if only for providing something to your boss to sign. Basically, you need a budget and you must build one.

Yes, that's right, *you* must do it. Don't let a budget be suggested by a contract Web shop or imposed on you by someone who knows little of Web matters. A contractor cannot know your business dealings. It may be tough enough for you to put together a budget — after all, you are still in a start-up endeavor in a start-up industry even if you've been at it since the birth of Web browsers. But you must do it, and in the end, you'll be glad you did. (Hmm. We're starting to sound like our mothers.)

 Your company may already have a budget process in place. If it does, you should have an easier time because you can get guidance in putting together your budget. If you know nothing of budgeting, we recommend *Managing For Dummies*, by Bob Nelson and Peter Economy (IDG Books Worldwide, Inc.), which includes an excellent chapter on the basics of budgeting.

In this chapter (in this book), we clue you in to some general budgeting tips and then the specific budget categories you need to consider in creating an overall budget for a Web endeavor.

How Often to Budget

It's interesting to note that while most companies have an annual budgeting process, things change a lot faster than that on the Web. You may well find that the budget you create in May to submit for approval for a fiscal year that ends in September has less to do with reality come the middle of that fiscal year than you'd like. Because of the rate of change on the Web, you may have to create interim budgets and adjust your budgetary thinking throughout the year. Nonetheless, an annual budget is the way to go for planning purposes and to fit in with your company's overall systems.

Remember that a budget is an important management tool whether you are on a tight budget or have unlimited funds. Either way, producing a budget helps you to understand what to spend money on and in which areas you should concentrate your fiscal management efforts.

Tips for Approaching the Budgeting Process

As a Webmaster, you probably won't have history to fall back on. That's how most budgeting processes work — the new budget is based on the old budget, with a little shifting from this category to that and some rounding up for some items and rounding down for others based on last year's experience and your overall judgment regarding how next year will go. You, luckily or unluckily, work in a new field, and as such, you probably get to build your budget from scratch. Here's a quick game plan you can use to approach the budgeting process:

- ✔ **Look into your company's budgeting processes.** Start by finding out what documents, if any, your company provides to managers to guide them in the budgeting process. Read these guidelines thoroughly, and follow them. Your budget may not be approved if it is not understandable to the accountants and execs, and following their guidelines is always a good idea.

- ✔ **Do research and meet with the people involved.** Get models wherever you can. Look into what other departments have done, and call around for estimates and price quotes. Meet with your Web team if you already have one, and get their input. Meet with other departments to find out how they imagine your online endeavor could fulfill their needs.

- ✔ **Develop an overall strategy for your Web endeavor.** Based on your findings and meetings, project what the Web endeavor might involve in the coming year. Think about revamping your site goals, whether you need a redesign (you probably do), where your database and server stand, what's needed to maintain the existing site, to expand it, and to fulfill the needs of other departments in your company.

✔ **Exercise judgment.** While budgets are supposed to be about facts and numbers, the building of them includes a healthy dash of judgment. As Webmaster, you need to look through all the information you've gathered and consider options. You may need to sort through expectations and revamp your strategies several times over.

✔ **Play with the numbers.** In the course of your thinking and planning, create a spreadsheet. (We cover this in upcoming sections.) Attach specific numbers you've gathered through your research into specific items, tally things up, and see what you see.

✔ **Think it all through yet again.** Don't think that your first pass at making a budget will be your last. Go back, examine your assumptions, play with adjusting your strategy, consider dropping unnecessary expenses, and then see what happens. Now do it again. You'll find as you do that different considerations occur to you each time. This is good. This allows you to strategize more thoroughly. This is budgeting.

Take it from us, there are tried-and-true tricks for making your budget fly and keeping it in line. Here are some quick tips learned in the trenches:

✔ **Pad a few things.** Selectively padding an item here and an item there gives you a bit of room to maneuver. Remember, nobody looks smart by going over budget, but coming in under budget makes you a genius.

✔ **Consider the company values as you create your budget.** If your company values quality, tie a special budget request to improving quality in your Web site. If your company is in a consolidating mode, tie requests to savings. You get the picture, right?

✔ **Create an item or two that are specifically meant to be expendable.** You're a team player, right? And you sure don't expect to have the whole of your first budget proposal approved. You may want to add a couple of items to it that can easily be axed without harming your Web endeavor. Pop in something you know won't pass, and think of it as the sacrifice that saves an important but little understood item. Do this cautiously, though — if your budget seems like fiction, the whole thing might get the ax.

✔ **Tie big items to a big payoff.** When you make big requests, make sure you note what the payoff is and when to expect it. The payoff does not have to occur within the fiscal year, but it should not be so far off that it becomes unimaginable. Try something like, *if we purchase this Sun Sparc workstation, we'll be able to handle the projected increase in traffic for the next two years. That will bring in at least a 300% increase in ad space revenues.*

What Budgets Look Like

In a nutshell, every cost associated with your site should be represented as a line item somewhere on your budget. Some budgets are long and complex (hey, when the federal government budget is printed it goes to *volumes*), some go into projecting future requirements and expenses, and some are much, much simpler. You don't have to write the federal budget to account for what you're going to do with your Web site. All you have to do is whip up a few good spreadsheets. Figure 4-1 shows a spreadsheet containing a typical budget for a Web site. (It does not include the ongoing expenses associated with keeping an in-house Web team on staff.) One line exists for each item of expense, and the amount of the projected expense is indicated. No big deal.

To take things a step further, items are grouped into general categories, and each category is summed up. At the bottom of the budget, the whole shebang is summed up, so anyone can see what the Web endeavor is going to cost.

One special category, however, does not fit into the final sum shown, and that is *ongoing expenses*. In budgeting tradition, these are regular expenses you'll encounter year-to-year; for example, staff salaries, travel expenses, continuing education, staff bonuses, rent and other overhead, and so on. If you want to expand out your budget to create line items for these expenses, simply follow the pattern shown of setting up categories, columns, and rows.

Figure 4-1: This is a typical budget for a medium-sized Web site.

Item	Hours	$/Hour	Fixed Cost	Total Cost	Notes
Content Dev't/Edit					
Concept	25	95		2375	Needed early for initial go-ahead
Editorial	25	75		1875	Needed early
Define target audience	6	65		390	Work w/ Marketing
Create/edit original mat'l	42	65		2730	Before coding begins
Architecture/Navigation					
Flowchart	5	65		325	
Navigational scheme	4	65		260	Before coding begins
Design					
Roughs			5000	5000	Provide to ad agency
Storyboards			650	650	Ad agency will create
Repeated design elements	10	65		650	Estimate will depend on design
Pictures and artwork	20	45	5000	5900	Original and stock
Production					
Media conversion	15	60		900	
HTML	40	60		2400	
Custom scripts	15	75		1125	For catalog and guestbook
Site Testing					
Review roughs	8	65		520	
Review mock-ups	8	65		520	
Reviewing HTML	8	65		520	
Test navigation	16	65	200	1240	Recruit review team from company
Upload Content					
Upload, final test, launch	8	95		760	
Marketing					
Online promotions			2000	2000	
Admin and Maintenance					
Server admin	8	95		760	Preparing server
			Total:	$30,900	

The Spreadsheet User Group, at `http://www.sheet.com`, publishes two print magazines about spreadsheets. Another beauty, The Spreadsheet Page (`http://www.j-walk.com/ss`) includes everything you ever wanted to know about spreadsheets — even jokes!

Elements of the Spreadsheet: Columns and Rows

As you probably know or have noticed, a spreadsheet, and therefore a budget (or is it the other way around?), consists of columns and rows. Look again at Figure 4-1, and you'll see that we have included these columns in the spreadsheet:

✔ **Item** is basically the heading for a column of short words to describe each item in the budget. As you read this chapter we'll suggest some line items that are commonly placed in a Web site budget.

✔ **Notes** is the heading for a column that allows one to describe the items in further detail. The notes column may be a good place to indicate to whom you are contracting something out or what exactly is included in the scope of the item listed.

✔ **Hours** is the heading for a column that describes the number of hours worked by in-house people. Here you can indicate the estimated number of hours in-house people will spend working on a given item. You can also use this column to show the estimated hours a contract person will take to do a given job, if you're paying them hourly. If you're contracting out to a Web job shop (see Chapter 8) some part of the work on your site, leave this item under this heading blank and enter the estimated costs in the fixed cost column instead.

✔ **$/Hour** is the heading for a column that shows the estimated hourly cost of your in-house people on this item. This is not the same as the Hours column, which shows the number of hours — this column shows the money involved. You may want to go with a general estimate and keep it the same for all items that in-house people will work upon, or you may want to enter more realistic numbers that are based on the type of work involved. For example, someone doing CGI scripting will usually be paid more per hour than someone writing editorial copy.

✔ **Fixed Cost** is the heading for a column showing the nonvariable cost of an item. This may be the cost of physical stuff, like computers, or it may be an item like work you plan to contract out to an outsider. Basically, if you think you'll pay a fixed amount for someone's work instead of an hourly rate, show that amount here. Sometimes you'll have both an hourly and fixed cost associated with an item. That's no problem — just indicate both and sum them up in the next column, *total cost.*

> ✔ **Total Cost** is the heading for a column showing the (you guessed it) total cost for the item. It is the sum of the hourly cost and the fixed cost. This is the number you look at to see what the item actually is going to cost (or at least what you hope the item will cost).

The spreadsheet's rows show the categories of expense involved in putting together a Web site. In our example spreadsheet, the categories shown are:

- ✔ Content Development/Editorial
- ✔ Architecture and Navigation
- ✔ Design
- ✔ Production
- ✔ Site Testing
- ✔ Uploading Content
- ✔ Marketing
- ✔ Administration and Maintenance

We talk in more detail about these categories throughout the rest of this chapter, so read on to explore them.

Excel resources at your service

Microsoft Excel is the product of choice for many spreadsheet number crunchers. To delve into Excel and what you can do with it, you may want to consider these handy online resources:

The official Microsoft Excel home page at `http://www.microsoft.com/msexcel` offers an overview, as well as tutorials, links, and tips.

Microsoft Excel Support is at `http://www.microsoft.com/MSExcelSupport`.

The Insider's Guide to Office '97: Excel Tips (`http://www.cnet.com/Content/Features/Howto/0fc97tips/ss04.html`) is CNET's page on Excel, packed with Internet and Web tips for using Excel.

The Excel Help Page (`http://www.lacher.com`) by John Lacher, CPA, offers a newsletter on Excel, as well as sample macros and applications.

The Unofficial Microsoft Excel Page (`http://www.vex.net/~negandhi/excel`) provides tech hints and great pointers to online help and discussions about accounting with Excel.

General Types of Expenses

In putting together a budget for your Web endeavor, you obviously have to consider the types of expenses you'll encounter. This, of course, is true of every budget for every endeavor, but it's a trickier matter in this case, because the Web business is so new. In the sections that follow, we offer pointers for categories to consider. You may find that your needs are quite different or that your needs will evolve with time, but this should provide you with a starting point. In the broadest sense, you can split your costs into three general categories: infrastructure, production, and ongoing support, each of which represents a distinct part of building and running your site.

Infrastructure

In this book, when we talk about infrastructure, we are not talking about what Al Gore is when he talks about infrastructure and the Internet. We're just talking about what you need in place to do business and run a Web site. Depending on the size of your site and how much of your site you plan to outsource, your "infrastructure" may be limited to one person, a computer, and a dial-up account with an Internet service provider, or at may be a 70-person group with workstations and a dedicated T1 Internet connection. Infrastructure is all the stuff you need to do your job. This might include office space, the Internet connection, general telephone service, network servers, the depreciation or rental of computers, and more.

In many cases, infrastructure costs are the hardest to pin down. Often you can ignore this aspect of your budget because it is included in your company's overall budget. Or you may find that you have to consider some parts of it but not all of it. For example, if your company has an IS department that runs the company's Internet connection, it's likely that the cost of that connection appears in the IS department's budget. It need not also appear in yours. You can simply ax that item from your budget. Likewise, if every employee in your company is provided with a computer automatically, you won't have to budget that basic piece of equipment for your team, because it is accounted for elsewhere in the company's budget.

How infrastructure costs fit into your budget varies tremendously from one company to another. Some companies split these costs across all projects over the course of a year. Other companies ignore these when putting together a specific project's budget. Just follow the norms for your company.

Production

Production is all about producing the site. Production in this sense may include everything from conceptualizing and planning through design, technical implementation, HTML production, and all that's involved in actually launching. Production does not include ongoing support.

Ongoing support

The cost of running your site day-to-day after launch is quite easy to overlook. Don't forget that you must keep content fresh, maintain the server and databases, and generally keep things humming. Depending on the size of your site and your plans for updating content, ongoing support may consist of a few full-time people working away on developing zippy new content and marking it up in HTML, or a single person spending a few hours a week reviewing your log files. Whatever the size of your site and your ambitions for it, you'll need to provide appropriate ongoing support. Remember to account for that in your budget.

Specific Activities that Inspire Budget Categories

The trickiest part of setting up a budget is getting all of the budget categories correct. It's treacherously easy to overlook entire categories when figuring how much a project will cost. In the Web world, this gets compounded by the newness of the medium and the speed at which it evolves. What's more, things change from one Web site to another. We offer you some categories for consideration; think of these as a starting point as you develop your own, more specific set.

Content development and editorial

On the Web, content is king, and you'll need to devote some funding to developing that content. How much funding you'll need depends on what sort of content you plan and how much of it involves hands-on creation rather than repurposing. Content development may mean simply reviewing existing material or it may involve writing new copy and creating new graphics for your site. Consider which of the following areas are relevant to your Web endeavor:

- ✔ Concept development (see Chapters 2 and 8)
- ✔ Editorial development, copy editing, and review (see Chapter 9)
- ✔ Defining the target audience (see Chapter 2)
- ✔ Creating and editing original material

Architecture and navigational maps

One of the trickier aspects of putting together a good Web site is setting up easy navigation — how people move around the site. You may need to budget for:

- ✔ Flowcharting the site (see Chapter 6)
- ✔ Determining the navigational scheme (again, see Chapter 6)

Design

The cost of design can vary widely depending on the designers you choose (see Chapter 8). If your company has an established corporate image you will want to take into account whether in-house designers can create a design consistent with other media the company puts out. If not, outsourcing may be the way to go. In the design section of your budget, consider:

- ✔ Creating "roughs" of each *type* of page (see Chapter 6)
- ✔ Creating actual storyboards of key pages (see Chapter 6)
- ✔ Creating repeated design elements (like buttons and logos) to be used throughout the site (see Chapter 6)
- ✔ Creating or procuring any pictures or other artwork used in the site (see Chapter 5 to learn about buying and licensing art)

Production

Production is highly visible work, but having in place the proper funding for activities that occur before production — like planning and design — can reduce the time and cost involved in production by a large margin. What is actually involved in producing a Web site varies depending on the type of content included. Some typical categories to account for here are:

- ✔ Turning graphics and other media into appropriate formats for the Web (see Chapter 6)

- Creating all HTML pages based on the roughs, final designs, and storyboards (see Chapter 6)
- Writing any custom scripts, including CGI scripts, JavaScript, and any custom applets (see Chapters 6 and 8)

Reviewing and site testing

This category is too often overlooked. When you create your budget, include a line item for review processes and site testing. Budget time you can devote to an in-house testing procedure that may be as simple as a few folks taking a day to pound on the site to see if it works or as complex as a review team looking at every page and another testing all functionality. Let us just say here that more testing is always better. Chapter 9 of this book covers review processes and some testing issues. In budgeting, consider these site testing categories:

- Reviewing roughs
- Reviewing mock-ups of key pages
- Reviewing HTML as it's produced
- Testing navigational elements of the site
- Verifying links
- Verifying that the site works after alpha and beta stages, and before launch

Uploading content

Generally speaking, your site will be created on a "staging" server. (See Chapters 6, 8, and 9.) It will have to be moved from the staging server to its true home on your Web server before launch. You'll need to budget time to have someone move files from the staging server to your live server. Then you can launch. Here are some tasks to be done and budgeted for:

- Making any changes to configuration files on the server as required by the new site content
- Uploading the site files to the final, live server
- Verifying that content is working and correct on the final server before launch

Changing your mind is never cheap

Unlike print, where you have to settle all the details of text and design before you actually go to print, the Web is a medium of incremental change, which is one of its advantages but also a bit of a booby trap. Because you can change almost anything on your Web site any time, it is often a temptation to never make up your mind. You may think, for example, that once you have hired a design firm you can revamp your concept and design several times over, both before and after launch, without a "deadline." Watch yourself — Web endeavors are highly prone to *feature creep* (defined in Chapter 8), a condition in which people get all kinds of brilliant thoughts about what can be done without thinking about whether those ideas are cost-effective.

Further, if you never settle on visual and editorial standards (see Chapter 9), or if you don't create and stick to a workable directory structure (see Chapter 6), your staff may wind up reinventing the wheel daily, because they simply don't know that one decision or another has been made. Exercising creativity is a fine thing, but to keep your budget in line, you (meaning either you the manager or the collective you if a group is making decisions) simply must make up your mind and then help others to know and apply what you've decided. Otherwise, you are wasting time, and as we all know, time spells money.

Marketing the site

To make your site a success, you'll need to promote the thing. In Chapter 15, we cover a variety of methods for marketing and promoting your site. You need not spend a fortune on this, but you ought to consider any expenses involved as you create your budget proposal. This is a great place to tie in specific references both to the site's goals (Chapter 2) and future payoffs. Marketing your site can include registering your site with search engines and directories like Yahoo!, trading links with related sites, purchasing banner ads on other popular sites, and using more traditional print and television promotional efforts. Of course, marketing is a very creative process and you'll probably think up whole new ways to market your site.

If your company conducts an advertising campaign, you may be able to use some of the money budgeted for it to advertise or promote your Web site. We've worked with one client that simply added its URL to all of its TV and print media advertising to build traffic for its Web site.

Here are some marketing activities you may need to consider in building your budget:

 ✔ Registering the site with search engines and indexes (see Chapter 13)

✔ Adding your URL to print and television/radio advertisements (see Chapter 14)

✔ Adding your URL to business cards and letterhead (see Chapter 14)

✔ Trading links with other similar sites (see Chapter 14)

✔ Buying banner ads on especially popular or highly targeted sites (see Chapter 14)

Administration and maintenance

After your site is launched and marketed, it will have to be maintained. You'll need to create, acquire, and add new content, freshen up what's there, fidget with navigation to improve it, write and edit new pages, implement new technologies as appropriate, and more. You'll also have to maintain the server(s) and database(s) (see Chapters 10, 11, and 12), monitor log files, and track your success (see Chapter 15). Remember to budget for all of these activities.

ROI Meets Management Buy-In

The big talk these days when it comes to the Web and even intranet sites is ROI (*return on investment*). According to a recent International Data Corporation group report, an intranet site can easily show an astounding 1000 percent ROI. This means that for every $1 you spend on a internal Web site, you can expect to get a $100 return on the investment. To investigate this report and consider what ROI your Web endeavor may show, see `http://home.netscape.com/comprod/announce/roi96_idc.html`.

It's very important to remember that ROI is what managers and executives want to see. It's a poor business that shows no profit, and while one can consider that a Web site is succeeding based on any of a number of criteria, the bottom line is the bottom line after all. You must, must, must keep your finger on the pulse of how your site's success is showing return on the investment made in it. This is crucial to getting management buy-in for expanded endeavors in the future, and it's often even more crucial to keeping your job!

Watching the bottom line

Lonnie E. Moseley, president of a technical solutions company, points out that "Keeping costs in line matters as much as how much business walks through the door. Yours can be the busiest shop on the block, but if you don't keep your eye on profit and ROI, all you have is a hobby."

Chapter 5

Legal Bugaboos for the Lay Webmaster

· ·

In This Chapter

▶ Who owns what on the Web

▶ Respecting copyrights that are held by others and protecting your own

▶ Understanding the public domain and fair use

▶ Looking into licensing

▶ All about ™ and ®

▶ Owning look and feel (trade dress)

▶ Art you can and can't use

▶ The law on linking

▶ Freeware and shareware

· ·

A few short years ago, the Internet seemed as lawless as the Old West, and many people liked it that way. But as overall popularity and commercial development grew, the law started to move in — at first, everyone was confused. Now, as things settle down, it appears as though the Internet, while certainly a new medium, is *just* a medium in many ways. The laws that apply to and protect other media (print, television, film, music, and so on) are easily adapted to this one.

Fewer and fewer Webmasters have delusions that everything on the Web is in the public domain, but just in case, we offer some quick pointers here. The first is that, to be a Web publisher, you should know the law. It not only prevents you from copying and using material that was created by others as if it were your own, but it prevents others from doing the same to you. In most cases, the laws that protect us all on these topics are pretty sensible, and after you get a few basic concepts in mind, following them (and notifying others that they should, too, when they visit your site) is as easy as negotiating traffic laws — for the most part, it's all a matter of judging situations.

We are not attorneys. Nothing written here is meant to be legal advice. Even if we were attorneys, we would have to say that last part. To get the lowdown on your specific legal situation, if you have one (and don't we all?), the person to see is an actual attorney.

One more thing: This chapter may worry you. Keep in mind that as a publisher (which is what you are — you publish a Web site), you must take into account business risks of all sorts, including legal risks. It is up to you to determine how to assess any potential risks and how to handle them.

Intellectual Property and Web Real Estate

So you launch your browser and open a Web page. It includes text, perhaps graphics or video snippets, a sound file or two, a Java applet, and certainly a bunch of code lurking behind the page. To you the Web page looks like a whole thing, and if it has a copyright notice on it (and if you happen to read that copyright notice), you may think that the entire page belongs to Wilma Webwanderer, who created it. But this is not necessarily so. True, the page is Wilma's, but that video may be licensed and rights to use that sound byte may be assigned, and if Wilma used a Web shop to create the page, the code itself or perhaps the Java applet may belong to the Web shop and not Wilma.

Who "owns" intellectual property is a question that gets at the heart of the Information Age. At one level, the answer may seem simple: *Intellectual property* (stuff that's created by someone who thinks it up) is owned by its creator. What's created is called *the Work* in copyright laws and contracts. However, how ownership of the Work is claimed and protected and transferred to others is not quite so simple — nor is the matter of defining what intellectual property actually is.

Intellectual property law and indeed ownership laws in general haven't evolved as quickly as technology. The Web has grown a lot faster than people's understanding of who owns what on the Web or even who owns the Web itself! Because of this and because there simply have not yet been many cases appearing in the courts to test and set precedents for the application and handling of intellectual property law as it applies to the Internet, you may not get much in the way of specifics when you delve into these issues.

As previously mentioned, a Web page often consists of diverse elements: coding, graphics, text, design, and more. Who created which part has a great deal to do with who owns what — remember, the creator of the Work owns the Work, at least at first. There may be four or more creators involved as well as copyright, trademark, trade dress, and licensing concerns. The fact is, even in the traditional world of publishing, intellectual property laws are not black-and-white.

Our advice is to provide yourself with a good understanding of how intellectual property law, copyright law, trademark law, and licensing have been understood in more traditional media, and start with the basic assumption that someone owns everything. You cannot assume that anything on the Internet is in the public domain. It's best for now — unless you don't care who owns what or who may sue you — to err on the side of caution. It's also more ethical in general to assume that, if you want to use something that you find on the Internet on your own Web site, you must at least get permission and perhaps even sign a licensing contract or similar document.

Intellectual property laws are, essentially, a bundle of rights. Various rights associated with intellectual property include those known as copyrights, patents, trademarks, trade dress, industrial/trade secrets, circuit layouts, registered designs, and confidentiality. The five major intellectual property laws in the United States that are important for Webmasters to know and consider include:

- ✔ Copyright law, which protects original works of authorship (known individually in contracts as *the Work*)
- ✔ Patent law, which protects new, useful, and nonobvious inventions and processes
- ✔ Trademark law, which protects words, names, and symbols used by manufacturers and businesses to identify their goods and services
- ✔ Trade secret law, which protects valuable information that is not widely known and has been consciously kept secret by its owner
- ✔ Trade dress law, which protects packaging, general look, or in the case of the Internet, the look and feel of a proprietary site

Of these, copyright law may be the most relevant and commonly applied one; it's also one that's among the toughest to pin down in some ways.

Copyright protects the expression of an idea, not the idea itself. When it comes to the expression of ideas, a Web site is no different from a magazine, book, or even a CD-ROM. They all contain some combination of text, graphics, video, and audio, which someone created.

Use of materials on a Web site does involve some unique issues. For example, because of the borderless nature of the Internet, any licenses that you may obtain for using material that was created by others on your site should specify worldwide rights. We discuss this further in upcoming sections. First, we're going to dig into copyright.

Online legal resources for you and me

To look into the basic legal issues described in this chapter, start with these online resources:

✔ The Internet Legal Resource Guide, at http://www.ilrg.com, is an annotated guide to law, including both local databases and articles and links to outside help.

✔ FindLaw is an online Yahoo!-style index of Internet law resources, while the Cyberspace Law Center (http://www.cybersquirrel.com/clc), focuses on hot legal topics that relate to the Internet world.

✔ The U.S. House of Representatives Internet Law Library is at http://law.house.gov. Of special interest to discussions in this chapter are Intellectual

Property (http://law.house.gov/105.htm) and Computers and the Law (http://law.house.gov.95.htm).

✔ At e-THICS (http://home.earthlink.net/~ivanlove), attorney Ivan Hoffman posts useful articles about Internet law and publishing based on his professional legal experience.

✔ For a peek into entertainment and multimedia law, explore Multimedia Law Repositories & Related Links at http://www.batnet.com/oikoumene/mmlinks.html. You'll find articles, guides, databases, and many other valuable links.

We describe more online legal resources throughout this chapter.

The Large and Small of Copyright Law

Copyright (and patent) law sprang up in most western countries to encourage the evolution of tools. It all started when a king granted to owners of early printing presses the *right* to make *copies.* Practically speaking, artisans of the day needed to believe that they would gain something from their efforts and that their work would be protected — otherwise, what was the point? Because it was believed by others that to protect the work of artisans would benefit the public, copyright law was born.

The Copyright Web Site, at http://www.benedict.com, is an all-around guide to copyright law that anyone can use, and it includes special attention to Internet issues.

What is a copyright?

A *copyright* is a right of intellectual property that gives (for a limited time) certain exclusive rights to authors for works that they create. (Note that the author in this case is anyone who has created an original work.) In the United States, copyright law is a federal law. It's a civil law (not a criminal law), so violators may be sued but generally not jailed.

Copyright law protects any material that's fixed in a tangible form beginning the moment it's fixed (for instance, e-mail is considered copyrighted the moment you type it). It does not cover ideas, factual information, blank forms, systems, or specific words, just *the expression of an idea* in an original work. It also doesn't extend into any existing material that an author may incorporate into *the Work.*

The key word here is *originality.* However, the standard by which originality is judged is pretty generous. How To Play Golf in Ten Seconds needn't be utterly different from the thousands of how-to golf books that preceded it; it need only have minimal inventiveness and be solely the work of the stated author. And the author need not officially register the Work to be protected under copyright law (although registering the Work is very valuable if you ever have to drag someone into court), nor does the author have to include a copyright notice.

Seven rights of copyright law are recognized:

- The right to reproduce the work by any means and in all media
- The right to prepare derivative works based on the copyrighted work
- The right to distribute copies of the work
- The right to perform the work in public
- The right to display the work in public
- The right to claim authorship and to prevent use of the author's name on a work that he or she did not create
- The right to prevent distortion of the protected work

You can "sit in on" a Harvard class called Business and the Internet: Strategy, Law, and Policy at `http://www.law.harvard.edu/courses/tech97`. This site includes class and lecture notes, links, and student Web presentations that may be of interest.

> ## You can view the source, but don't take it
>
> As you surely know, when you set out to design and publish a Web page, you come up against a boggling array of issues to consider, even as you scribble ideas on a napkin. Design and content may seem to be the biggest considerations. Like most people setting out to author an original, creative piece, you probably find yourself trekking out to see what others have done.
>
> Many Web browsers let you view "the source" — the code behind a given Web page. This is really handy in that you can peek into what makes up a successful Web page. What's more, this ability to openly see what's what is part of the culture of the Internet. Lucky you — this is like being a newly minted architect and getting to see blueprints of the Coliseum or
>
> I.M. Pei's glass pyramid. It's very cool and even a big convenience. But a serious issue lurks in this convenience.
>
> Because accessing the process behind the design is so easy, it seems harmless to many to cut and paste that code, perhaps modifying it or perhaps just telling yourself that you're "borrowing" the tools to make your site. After all, you may say, it's right there for the taking, and who is going to know? However, this is both unethical and illegal. Even if the owner of the site has not marked it saying that you may not take anything, everything there is intellectual property — even the code — and you may not legally snag that code for your own purposes.

How copyright law works

In traditional media, copyrights straightforwardly cover books, maps, musical lyrics, poetry, screenplays, and so on. They are all fixed (printed) forms of original works. New media like the Web can present different considerations. For example, a Web page is unlike other media in that, when it is viewed using different Web browsers, it looks different. One may wonder if this means that the expression is different in each browser. But the foundation of a Web page consists of a fixed arrangement of elements — text, graphics, audio, video, VRML, and so on. As long as that stuff is in an original layout, the page design is copyright protected. As soon as you've created an original work, it is copyrighted. Whether it's printed, created on a machine or device, or stored on a floppy disk or hard drive matters not. If it exists in fixed form, it's protected.

Proof of copyright

At one time, if a work wasn't marked with a copyright notice, it wasn't protected, but today most nations follow the rules of the Berne Copyright Convention; these rules indicate that no written notice is actually needed. In the United States, by default, almost everything created after April 1, 1989, falls under protection, regardless of whether a notice appears. A notice does aid in copyright protection by warning people, however. And if litigation involving a work that's marked by a copyright notice is won, a larger monetary amount may be awarded by the court as damages because the infringer cannot claim "innocent infringement." Placing a copyright notice on your Web pages is always wise.

The correct form to use for your notice is *Copyright [date] by [author/ owner]*. You may substitute the familiar © symbol for the word "Copyright" if you like — either is correct. Note, however, that a standard HTML code for that © symbol does not exist — at least not for all browsers. You can use the code #169; to produce the symbol in most browsers, but because you want your copyright notice to be legible to all, we recommend the word rather than the symbol.

The phrase *All rights reserved* isn't required in the United States as of this writing; however, certain countries require it for copyright protection there. Additional language may be suggested by your attorney, depending on your circumstances and the degree of protection that you need.

Registration with the Copyright Office is optional but carries with it certain rights, which you may want to look into through the Web sites mentioned earlier in this chapter. You do have to register a copyright before filing an infringement suit, and registering may allow you, in certain cases, to receive attorney's fees as well as damages should you win the case.

While it was not always the case, copyright is never "lost" unless it is explicitly given away. Beginning in 1978, the term for an author's copyright became the author's life plus 50 years. (It is transferable to heirs, and may be assigned or sold in some cases, too, as described in upcoming sections.) The term *copyright* varies somewhat for certain special circumstances (for example, when a work is created by an independent contractor who is paid to create it); again, we suggest that you look into how this may affect you.

Infringement myths and realities

In the Web world, there are many urban myths floating around along with an unfortunate naiveté surrounding copyrights. The following are some common questions and misunderstandings:

> ✔ **Shouldn't the author of a work simply be flattered if I showcase the work on my site?** Many are not. At the very least, they almost certainly want you to get permission. They may prefer that you pay a licensing fee, and if you don't, they may sue you.

✔ **I credited the author when I posted his or her work on my site; isn't that enough?** Unless you get explicit permission, you are infringing copyright law. You've only saved yourself from being a plagiarist (someone who illegally passes off the work of others as his or her own).

✔ **I changed the work a bit before I posted it on my site, so now it's okay, right?** No. Don't expect to evade liability by altering a work that you've illegally copied. If you do so, you're not only violating copyright laws, but you've infringed on the author's right not to have the work modified.

Penalties can be costly and time consuming. It's far better to be safe than sorry, and furthermore, would you want someone to nab your work and use it, change it, or pass it off as his or her own?

Public Domain and the Fair-Use Follies

Some works exist in what's called the *public domain*. A work that is in the public domain can be used by anyone for any purpose. Works can enter the public domain in several ways: Perhaps the copyright expired, the copyright owner didn't renew a copyright that was granted under the Copyright Act of 1909, or maybe the owner failed to use a proper copyright notice before the rules changed again in 1989. (Copyrights can be both renewed and inherited.) The specific rules of public domain are beyond the scope of this book; they're very complex and vary from country to country. Suffice it to say that the plays of William Shakespeare and other very old stuff are in the public domain; Marilyn Monroe's diary is not.

It can be very tempting, when you're in the thick of trying to track down copyright owners and get their permission, to happily deceive yourself into thinking that something is in the public domain just because it's on the Net. This is not true. We've seen cases where otherwise ethical people have picked up images and writings from Web sites (some of which claimed to be, for example, clip-art sites offering work that anyone could use for free), assuming the stuff to be in the public domain. A quick glance at the material with a practiced eye revealed that this photo was from *Sports Illustrated,* while that piece of writing was lifted from a well-known book — this is bad news for everyone involved.

The *fair use* rule was created to allow people to quote or reproduce portions of a work in reporting events, reviewing the work, creating educational materials, and creating parodies. Under this doctrine, an author or Webmaster may make limited use of a work that was created by another without permission, but only for limited purposes and only in limited amounts. Fair use is a privilege, not a right. And the qualifying word *limited* is of paramount importance in applying the idea of fair use. It's pretty tough to know when the use of a piece is actually fair use, so it's best to be very conservative — the only way to "prove" fair use is in court, and many authors are quite willing to let a judge or jury decide. Get to know the rules, ask experts, and use good judgment and common sense.

One aspect of fair use is that the use should not deprive a copyright holder of income. For example, if a teacher makes five copies of a newspaper article for educational purposes, that may be fair use (assuming that the class is not a profit-making venture). Other uses that *may* be deemed fair use include the following:

- ✔ A short passage or quote appearing in an article or news report
- ✔ A short passage or quote appearing in a criticism or commentary on the work to illustrate a point or give a flavor of the work
- ✔ A short passage or quote appearing in a scholarly, scientific, or academic work for illustration, clarification, or footnote purposes

Modern technology unfortunately makes copyright infringement easy. One can retrieve whole works in digital form with no trouble and attach them to an e-mail message that can then be spread within seconds to hundreds or thousands of people. Because of this, fair use on the Internet actually lacks clear parameters. In most cases, copying of a work or a portion of a work online is not considered fair use and is considered a violation of copyright law.

Again, courts usually consider a clear case of infringement to have occurred when the user's motive is for monetary or commercial gain. As an illustration of this point, consider a case involving *The Nation* magazine, which obtained President Ford's memoirs before their publication. In an article of 200,000 words, the magazine quoted a few hundred words verbatim from the memoirs. Was it fair use? It was a small amount of the memoir, after all, in an article. The case went to the U.S. Supreme Court, which ruled that this was not fair use. The reasoning was that in this case the *amount* of the material did not matter. The quoted material dealing with the pardon of President Nixon was found by the court to be at the very core of the book. It was seen as "the most interesting and moving aspect of the entire manuscript," which, having now been published in a national magazine, reduced the book's commercial value and impaired the ability of both the book's author and its publisher to gain income from the book. The use of the material in the magazine was also seen as having been used to further the magazine's commercial appeal.

As is true of so much of copyright law, the question of fair use is one of context, intent, and other subtle matters. As always, our advice is to consult professionals regarding specific cases and to learn the law so that you can exercise good judgment.

As a general rule, most of what appears on Web sites is copyrighted material. If you want to use something you find on someone's site, simply assume that the stuff is not in the public domain and that your use is not fair use; *get permission*. Having considered all this, you say that you've decided to be a moral and upright Netizen and now want to know your options?

A Licensing Lowdown

You have two choices when it comes to securing the rights to publish material that others own: You can request permission, which is usually a relatively simple matter of asking for it and being granted it. Or, you can license the use, which may carry with it special restrictions or may require paying a fee. Permissions don't have to take special form, although your legal department may prefer that you follow a certain format.

Gaining a license to use copyrighted work is something like renting a house or a part of it. The owner of a copyright can lease as many licenses as he or she wants, even at the risk that one renter's use may overlap another's. For the most part, a license grants use within such limits as a specified time or specified venues but does not transfer ownership. Here are some typical license structures:

- ✔ **Nonexclusive licenses** are permissions to use a work in specified ways. For example, a photograph may be licensed for six months of use in a particular blue jeans ad in a specified national magazine. (Note that the law does not require a nonexclusive license to be in writing, although a verbal nonexclusive agreement is terminable at will by the owner.)

- ✔ **Exclusive licenses,** on the other hand, grant to only one licensee at a time the right to use that same photograph in a specified way.

- ✔ **Assignment of copyright** is like selling the copyright itself for a lump sum or a portion of income produced by the work. For example, a graphic artist may transfer a portion of his logo-design ownership to a Webmaster in return for money and/or a promise that the Webmaster markets the graphic and directs more work toward the designer. Any purchaser of an assigned right may sell that right unless specifically prohibited in writing.

Written assignments of copyright or exclusive license agreements may be recorded in the Copyright Office to document the particular rights involved. This is not necessary, but it is an option. The most important benefit of recording such documents is that a public record is established (which helps prevent "innocent infringement"). The Copyright Office offers registration applications, publications, and related materials via the Internet at no charge; the Copyright Office home page is at `http://lcWeb.loc.gov/copyright`.

Work-for-Hire and What It Means

Copyright can be transferred via assignment of copyright or by licensing (both discussed in preceding sections) or through *work-for-hire* agreements. In a work-for-hire agreement, party A hires party B to create a work on party A's behalf; party A pays party B, and party A owns the copyright. Works made for hire belong to those who hired the creator, including graphic artists in an advertising agency, for example. The law states that works created by freelancers after January 1978 cannot be considered works-for-hire unless a specific written document is signed by both parties agreeing to it.

Ignoring this matter can bring about hefty consequences. Consider an example in which two people create an online interactive game. One is an artist who is hired by a product manager, and the other is the product manager. If the game sells well, who owns the copyright? The artist may own half, or her work may be considered a work-for-hire and be owned by the person who hired her. Millions could be at stake. As usual, check copyright statutes or consult a professional for more information.

Work-for-hire agreements are very common in the world of Web shops and outsourcing projects. We cover working with Web shops in Chapter 8.

For online resources related to contracts (including work-for-hire agreements), look into `http://www.courttv.com` (no kidding), where the small business section includes a library of legal forms, contracts, and agreements. Also try `http://www.sbaonline.sba.gov`, the Small Business Administration online.

Trademark Tricks and Tips

A trademark is a first cousin to copyright, but there are important differences between the two. A *trademark* is a right of ownership that is placed on a word, phrase, or symbol that is used to identify a product or a service in the market-place. This is quite different from a copyright, which is ownership of a given work. The title of a book cannot be copyrighted, but the name given to a series of books (for example, ...*For Dummies*) can be trademarked (and it is).

Rights to a trademark begin only when the trademark gains some relevance and commercial worth. For example, before Ronald McDonald was widely recognized as the mascot for the hamburger chain, he was just another clown. Now he's a trademarked clown. In fact, just about any use of the prefix *Mc* is trademarked by McDonald's. Unauthorized use of a trademark is considered a serious infringement.

The International Trademark Association (INTA), at `http://plaza.interport.net/inta/index.html`, promotes the use of trademarks and includes convenient guides to using them correctly.

What a trademark protects

Trademark protection is available for words, names, phrases, symbols, and logos that distinguish the owner's products and services from others. A trademark that describes only a class of goods (for example, athletic shoes) as opposed to a specific product (GymJets) is not protectible. The statute is also clear that if a trademark (or trade dress, described in an upcoming section) is designed to closely resemble a trademark already in use in the United States, so as to cause consumer confusion, it is not protectible and thus cannot be registered.

In general, trademark laws protect your commercial identity, including goodwill, reputation, and marketing investments, by ensuring you the exclusive right to use the trademark for the goods and services you're marketing. Any person who uses a trademark in connection with goods and services in a way that's likely to cause consumer confusion can be busted as an infringer. As the trademark owner, you can sue the infringer to make him or her not only stop infringing but also pay lost income and damages.

In January 1996, the U.S. Congress passed the Federal Trademark Dilution Act to protect famous trademarks. *Dilution* is defined as the "lessening of the capacity of a famous mark to identify and distinguish goods and services . . ."

For example, you may not be able to use the trademarked tag line *Brings Good Things to Life* for your new sheep-cloning company. That line is already associated with and trademarked by General Electric, and even if your company would not be in direct competition, you cannot use the tag line.

This new dilution statute should provide trademark holders with a more effective remedy against those who own very similar domain names, for example. Trademark rights are usually recognized within a narrow class of goods, typically allowing companies to hold similar marks in different industries (for example, Delta Airlines and the Delta faucet company). But if Delta Airlines registered `delta.com`, the faucetmaker would be blocked from using its trade name as its domain name. This would be a bummer for the faucet folks but not a trademark infringement. However, if Computer Company X registers `ibm.com` for its domain name, it can expect a phone call from Big Blue.

The Nolo Press Self-Help Law Center, at `http://www.nolo.com`, includes sections on Smart Publishing (`http://www.nolo.com/mag/index.html`) and Patent, Copyright, and Trademark (`http://www.nolo.com/ChunkPCT/PCT.index.html`).

The difference between ™ *and* ®

Did you ever wonder about the difference between the TM mark (™) and the R in a circle (®)? The ® means that the trademark is registered with the U.S. Patent and Trademark Office (PTO). The ™ symbol is used when a trademark has not been registered. A ™ is usually used for trademarks when an application for registration is on file at the PTO; however, you can use the ™ whether you have an application on file or not. Registration is not required for protection, although (as we mentioned in preceding sections) it can strengthen protection considerably.

Getting a trademark

For the most effective protection you can get, file a federal trademark registration application via the Patent and Trademark Office in Washington, D.C. File your application as early as you can to gain the most protection. You can even file an application before you start using the trademark — consult a legal professional for more information on this. Federal law protects unregistered trademarks, but protection is limited to a geographical area (the country and state), and not registering a trademark is trademark suicide in a borderless medium like the Internet. To get state protection, file an application with your state trademark office.

Trade Dress Is Look and Feel

Especially relevant to Webmasters is the idea of *trade dress,* which is simply the look and feel of a product (for example, your Web site). Examples of protected trade dress include the interior look of theme restaurants such as Hard Rock Café and the look of the cover of this book. As a protected right, trade dress is enjoying more significance and is growing as a legitimate concern. Trade dress is essentially packaging and any recognizable design that is associated with a company, including colors and total appearance. Although more widespread rights may be recognized in trade dress than in trademarks, the same legal standards apply here as with unregistered trademarks (see the preceding section). Courts in trade-dress suits evaluate design and layout, graphics, and similar elements.

It's been mentioned that interfaces of creatively designed Web pages are likely to enjoy trade dress protection.

Clip Art, Photography, Sampling, and You

Everything on the Net is owned — if you doubt that, read all that's preceded this section of this chapter. Every scrap of art that you see is owned by someone. Some kind souls, however, make their art available inexpensively or for the free use of others as *clip art*. Be forewarned that, unless you find a statement that clip art, or any kind of premade art, is public domain, you must assume that it's copyrighted and should not be used without permission and perhaps a small payment. Of course, some clip art *is* free for you to use, and that stuff is often easy to find on any number of clip-art sites and bulletin boards.

Using stock photography or graphics, which are often presented on CD-ROM, is also a quick and painless way to get art for your site. You can look into getting such art through design shops (see Chapter 8) or at software stores. Each stock art CD carries its own licensing agreement, and you must pay attention to what you're agreeing to by buying the CD. For example, it's a virtual certainty that you may not distribute the art for use by others.

Today, almost anyone with a scanner or digital camera, the right software, and some talent can nab and manipulate video tapes, images, and audio. There seems to be no end to what can be created using premade images as a toolbox. The possibilities for copyright infringement are just as broad, but is there any case where altering and using the work of another is acceptable? With *very* few exceptions, the answer is no. The law seems pretty clear in this area (for once). Most instances of electronic manipulation can be litigated and can result in damages.

Of course, tampering can be done with any digital information, including audio. Digitalization, or *sampling,* is pretty common, especially in rap music that sometimes uses bits and pieces of existing works. In sampling, short fragments of composition can be easily reproduced and blended to compose new melodies or enhance them.

The main concern for the originating artist in this case is maintaining the integrity and quality of the original work. The law does not provide exact guidelines for "fair use," so you need to use your best judgment and the advice of your legal advisor to keep yourself out of hot water. The general rule: If you use another artist's work to create a new work, you may find yourself at the wrong end of a lawsuit. Our advice, as always, is to get permission to use even excerpts of recordings on your Web site.

What You Buy when You Buy Original Art

There is a big difference between buying art and licensing it; licensing is usually a contractual matter between you and, say, a designer or a stock photography house. (See preceding sections for more on licensing and who owns what in general.) As a single end user of stock photography, what you usually purchase is a nonexclusive, nonsublicensable license to use an image in prescribed ways. You may not sell or otherwise provide the art to anyone else, and you may not use it in any way other than that for which you've licensed it. The license agreement clearly spells this out.

As special note to Web designers, the licenses usually denote that the images you've licensed for your site cannot be detached from the page and made available for downloading or permanent storage. Also, if you license an image from a stock house, you cannot use it in the design of your trademark.

On the other hand, if you commission a photographer, graphic artist, or designer to create an original work of art, you own it (see the previous section on work-for-hire agreements). But there may still be copyright laws against modifying/altering the image in ways that the artist didn't intend. This applies especially in a public forum like the Net. Talk to a legal professional for more information about this complex concept.

What's in this picture?

When you purchase an original piece of art, such as a photographic portrait of your family or a sculpture from your local art gallery, you own the physical piece of art but you *do not* own copyright to it. All of the copyrights in that piece of art (as discussed earlier in this chapter) are retained by the artist. We know of an interesting case in which a photographer was commissioned to shoot a photo of the company's corporate headquarters for the cover of the company's annual report. The company obtained permission from the architect (yes, architecture is protected by copyright) but not from the artist who created the sculpture the company had purchased to decorate the front of the building. The inclusion of the sculpture in the photo without the sculptor's permission was copyright infringement.

Linking and the Law

The Internet seems to invite unlimited public access. The very nature of the Web, in fact, is one of an interconnected network with hyperlinks that lead everywhere. By putting a presence on the Web, it is often believed that you've implied permission to the public to link to your page and that you have unlimited implied permission to link to their pages in return.

Be prepared, however, for the natural tendency to associate you with the company that you keep. If the Corrupt Skinheads of America decide to link their home page to yours (even if your Web site sells handmade I Love Everyone bumper stickers), do you have some right to demand that they desist? No one is yet quite sure. The questions raised are legally and psychologically interesting; they're also complex. But they remain unanswered. We must wait and see how things play out in the courts on this one. The tendency, however, is to think that URLs (and therefore links) are probably not copyrightable themselves because they are facts, not expressions. (See the previous sections on copyrights.)

Linking seems to be a question of proper Netiquette, the informal but governing law on the Internet, rather than legality. If your site is being linked to from questionable sites, monitoring is the best control. Seek out references to your page and information on incoming hits. (You can find out how to check backlinks of your site in Chapter 14.) Then send e-mail to the Webmasters of those sites that you don't want to link to you, and request that the link to your site be removed. All that you can do, at least as of this writing and in the face of no legal precedents, is to ask.

Have a question about your liability in maintaining a kid-safe site? If you advertise yourself as such, create and post a policy for your users saying how deeply (one link deep?) you investigate those sites that you link to; post a disclaimer, too. Get your attorney's help with this — it's a very sensitive issue.

Winging It through Freeware and Shareware

Downloadable files and software are very popular online. When this stuff is literally free, it's called *freeware*. When it's distributed to others who are expected to try it and then pay a fee to its creator if they like it and want to keep it, the material is called *shareware*. Freeware often carries with it rules for use, if no fee. You are usually not allowed to sell, alter, or modify freeware (although there are some notable exceptions to this). Shareware carries both rules — which vary enormously — and a fee for continued use. In both cases, if you want to distribute the stuff via your site, you need to look into the rules governing the particular material that's of interest. The specific rules are usually attached to the freeware or shareware in some type of readme file.

Part II
Planning a Smashing Web Site

In this part . . .

There's planning a site, then building the site — that's the glam part — and then finally there's maintaining the site. As Webmaster, you are master of the whole process from soup to nuts. Part II offers the step-by-step map we wish we'd had when we started out.

In this part, you discover how to build a site from the ground up. You start with organizing content and building a directory structure for your site, and looking into HTML and lots of even jazzier stuff. Then you find out about successfully outsourcing some or all of a project to a Web job shop. You also learn the ins and outs of establishing style guidelines and review processes, appointing a style constable, and generally maintaining quality assurance.

Chapter 6

Creating Your Site's Framework

In This Chapter

▶ Getting your content together

▶ Building your site's hierarchy

▶ Establishing your site's directories

▶ Deciding if your site needs a database

▶ Documenting your plans

*B*uilding a site is no mysterious process. It's a step-by-step operation. First, you must pull together potential content. Then you organize your glowing and wonderful content into a hierarchy. As you build the hierarchy, you identify the different types of pages that you want to have on your site. With the hierarchy thought through, you build a site map that charts out the pages on your site and the potential links between them. There are a number of ways to do this — we describe several for you to consider. After that, the site map evolves into a plan for setting up directories on your Web server. In this chapter, we talk about all of that and strategies for organizing your content on the server and about some special directories that you should have on the server to make your life easier.

This may seem like a lot of legwork up front, but trust us. Paying attention to these details now can help you keep a well organized site. Just as a good directory structure on your PC makes life easier, and just as a good file system in the office makes life more productive, a solid and understandable directory structure is going to make your site maintenance much smoother. A good directory structure can help you identify outdated content in a moment and remove those files as soon as they are no longer needed. It also makes finding and linking to images and other items easier as you create new pages.

If you've contracted out development of your Web site, then those folks can probably come up with a way to organize your site and its files. Even so, you still need to know about these topics. For one thing, it helps you with the process of evaluating and approving their work; for another, if you can go to them with a preliminary plan, you may shave a few bucks off their fees.

Remember, even if your freelance Web developers know more about the Web than you do, you know more about what you want the site to do today — and in the future — than they do. It's important that the directory structure that's used to build your site is flexible enough to support any new content that you may want to add in the future.

Pulling Together Content

Where content comes from is a pretty big question. A certain amount of what you work with will come from existing documents. For example, you can probably pull together a large portion of the material you might post for your human resources department from material they have on hand describing the company, the benefits of working for the company, and perhaps even the city or community where the company offices are located. Your company's public relations and marketing departments almost certainly has on hand information about the company itself, awards, press releases, and so on. And it's really hard to imagine that the company doesn't have scads of material describing its products or services. Finally, the customer service department probably has a list of commonly asked questions and stock answers that can easily be made into a FAQ (frequently asked questions) list.

Another portion of the material that becomes your content will probably be fresh —newly created for the Web initiative. That might come from any of many sources. Perhaps you'll hire an IPP or ad agency or a content developer to conceptualize or create it (see Chapter 8). Perhaps your Web team, your marketing group, or some other department within your company will conceptualize and create it.

Whichever approach you decide to take, be sure to look through at least Chapters 2, 7, 8, and 9 of this book before you finalize your plan. That will help you get a grip on what good content is and how to manage it. Chapter 2, which covers setting your site's goals, and Chapter 7, which talks about HTML and Web technologies, are especially urgent in your current research. Look around the Web, too; not just for sites similar to your own, but for sites whose concepts and approaches seem appealing in the context of your site's goals. As you plan your content, you must constantly review whether a given piece of stuff will further the goals of your site, whether it will add to the user's experience, and whether it will be cost-effective to implement and maintain. You must also consider whether what you want to do will work within the Web's technical, navigational, and legal boundaries. We'd all like to think the Internet is boundless, but it isn't — again, review the chapters in this book that cover technical and legal matters for tips.

You may want to take all the papers and documents and notes that comprise your planned content and shuffle them around organizationally, considering these matters and tossing and sorting stuff before you move on to actually constructing your site. At least sketch out an initial plan on paper; it also helps to draw it out on a big whiteboard and just stare at it for some time, thinking things through and moving bits and pieces and even cutting and adding things as you go. Above all, keep your eyes squarely on the goals you've set for the site.

With your organized content in hand, you're ready to turn your attention to the actual structure of your site. This is where the foundation building begins — up to this point, you were gathering information. But now we're headed into the real-deal conceptualizing.

Grouping Content and Activities

The first step in mapping your site is to group your content. Figure 6-1 shows the map of a Web site that has been built based on a fairly typical grouping process.

The purpose of grouping content is to figure out what goes with what, that is, which pieces of content are logically related to which others. In doing this, you determine where you should place links, what common items can be linked to rather than repeated, and what links should appear on your site's navigation bar. You also take a big step toward figuring out how to organize files on your Web server.

Identifying types of content

One good way to identify the types of groupings your site may fall into is to look at the content — study it like a puzzle, considering which items are logically similar to others. Two commonly used big-picture ways to think about this are grouping by content and grouping by task.

We describe those more specifically in the next few sections. Note for the moment that they are not mutually exclusive. You may find that grouping some items by task and others by content is the way to go — and if you think up your own grouping system, more power to you. You may find that you want to group based on which department of your company (say marketing or customer support) is responsible for the content or by the intended audience of the material (current product owners, potential customers, the press, and so on). But as you group your content, do keep your audience in mind. Distinctions between departments in your company may make no sense at all to your customers or others who visit your site; the organization you create should be geared toward the audience's experience, not toward recreating the company's structure.

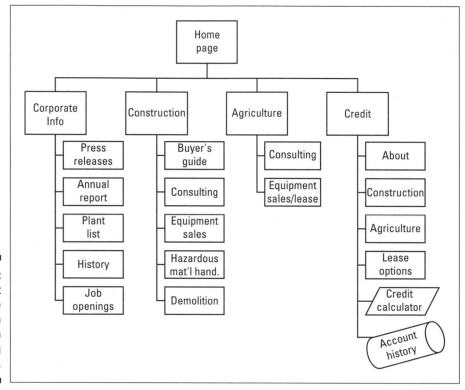

Figure 6-1:
We built
this site
map for an
information
publishing
site.

As we describe groupings, we're going to ask you to do some quick exercises to see if they work for you. Don't slave over this — it's just a way to start thinking about things. In the upcoming section titled "Doing the grouping two-step," we walk you through the actual grouping process, and then you can use what you learned in the briefer exercises described in these next few sections.

Grouping by subject

Perhaps the easiest and most obvious way to group the content of your site is by the subject of that content. For example, if your site is about cooking, you can group the content related to breakfast, lunch, and dinner, and within that, break down dinner into types of entrees: meat, fish, poultry, pasta, and vegetarian. You may have another category for tools (pans, knives, and so on) and yet another for seasonal menus. How you group your content by subject depends on your industry. Look to the real world for models. Apply whatever logic drives your industry to the logic of your site. Figure 6-2 shows a sample list of subjects and corresponding pages for a construction company site.

```
Corporate Info
        Press Releases
        Annual Report
        Plant List
        Corporate History
        Job Openings

Construction
        Buyer's Guide
        Consulting Services
        Equipment Sales
        Hazardous Material Handling
        Demolition

Agriculture
        Farming Consulting Services
        Farm Equipment Leasing/Sales

Credit
        About Credit
        Construction Project Financing
        Agricultural Project Financing
        Equipment Leasing Options
        Credit Screen
        Account History
```

Figure 6-2:
This
content is
grouped by
subject.

Try shuffling your site content by subject, and see what you come up with. Jot down headings, and under each heading, list the bits of content you have on hand until they all fit in somewhere. If you find that some don't fit, you may need to add a category or rethink your subject categories from scratch. If the whole thing is working, in the end you will have categorized all of your content. If not, don't worry — just read on.

Grouping by task

Alternatively, you may find it better to group your content based on the tasks a user may do when coming to your site. Perhaps a user hops over to your nifty software company site. The user may seek information, download the software, register it, and pay for it. He or she may also want to look into customer service, get tech support, or purchase T-shirts and accessories or books on the subject of the software. He or she may also want to download patches to the software. Hmmm — doesn't that go in *download?* Doesn't the purchase of books go in *purchase?*

As you identify tasks that users may do on your site, jot them down as categories. Then go through your content, and consider which pieces of content relate to which tasks. Place those pieces of content under the appropriate task-oriented headings. You may find yourself adding or deleting headings as you move along. In the end, if all of your content seems to fit into this system, you're set. Figure 6-3 shows a list of pages grouped according to tasks. If all of your content doesn't quite fit into this system, keep reading.

Figure 6-3:
This
content is
grouped
by the
tasks that
users may
accomplish
at the site.

```
Managing Your Finances
        Banking
        Bill Payment
        Expense Reports
        Personal Income Tax Advisor

Managing Your Business
        Banking
        Bill Payment
        Expense Reports
        Business Tax Advisor

Investing
        Investor's Guide
        Retirement Advisor
        Mutual Fund Advisor
```

Mixing groupings

If you stepped through the group-by-subject, group-by-task exercises we described in the preceding two sections and found that some stuff fit into one system and some into the other, you are not alone — that's often the case. You may find that the best way to go is to group some stuff by content. For example, you may group pages according to the products covered — that's subject grouping. Then, you may group other pages according to the tasks that the users do — for example, buy that product. Just find what works for you and your industry.

Grouping by utility

Here's another grouping to consider: Some stuff is going to appear on your site that you may want to keep in one place for your own convenience as the Webmaster. For example, all of the images are going to be easier for you to find if they're in one place. (Many folks call this category the *artbin*. Cute, eh?) You may not find that you have an obvious need for this sort of grouping just yet — it will probably come into play more when you get to the point of arranging directory structures. Just keep it in mind for now, and if you do find that you have some material you want to categorize separately in an artbin or some other category based on how you plan use it, go ahead and plop it right in that category.

Doing the grouping two-step

Now take out a fresh piece of paper and a pencil or launch your favorite word processor. With your content before you, finalize the organization of your content as follows:

1. **Jot down the major categories under which you think you can group your content.**

   If you aren't sure quite how to arrange the content, reread the last few sections of this chapter, and think things through a bit more. Your organizational scheme depends a great deal on how you organize information in your specific industry. (Or, if you work for a Web job shop and you're organizing content for a client, it depends on the client's industry. Interview your client to find out more about his or her industry if necessary.)

2. **Place subcategories under the major categories, if that seems appropriate, and within the subcategories, list the content that falls into place there.**

All of this is a lot easier if you consider that placing a piece of content in one category excludes it from consideration in another category. The whole point of Web content is that you can link it, so forget double placements. If you find that you've placed one document into more than one category, decide now where you think it should best fit — in which of those categories do you really want the document to be? (You can link to it from elsewhere.)

Establishing Hierarchies Where Once There Were None

Roll up your sleeves; now it's time to really plunge in. With your content organized into conceptual groupings, it's time to turn that information into a map of the site. A site map basically takes all of the site's content and arranges that material into a hierarchy.

First, consider why you need a hierarchy. When you read a book or magazine, you read from left to right (at least in English). (See Figure 6-4.) It's all very linear. When you "read" a Web site, by comparison, you may jump from this page to that, in an intuitive process that is anything but linear. (See Figure 6-5.) That may make it seem as though it doesn't matter where you put what.

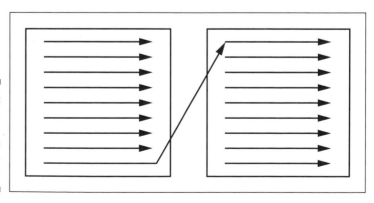

Figure 6-4:
People read books and magazines from left to right.

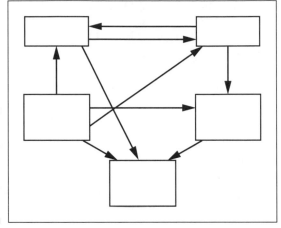

Figure 6-5:
Web sites
can be
"read" in
any
direction.

Visitors to the site hop around it, so what difference does it make how the thing is organized behind the scenes? There are two very important reasons to assemble a decent site map and keep it in order:

✔ It helps users find what they seek on your site if the structure is orderly, both because a site search engine works better then and because users may be able to intuitively follow the URLs.

✔ It helps you maintain your site if you know where everything is and how to write a link without having to dig around too much.

Your goal, then, in this section, is to organize your content a bit further, so that it fits into a hierarchy that goes from the general to the specific, as shown in Figure 6-6.

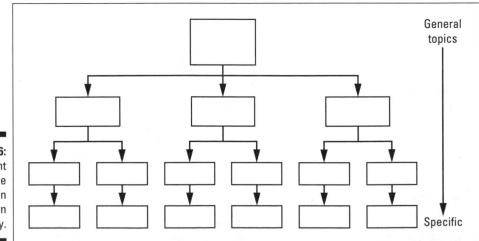

Figure 6-6:
Content
should be
organized in
a top-down
hierarchy.

Building the hierarchy

Before we move on, note that every piece of content you have must go someplace in the hierarchy. As you go along, if you come across a page that doesn't seem to fit anywhere, place it at the top level — just below your site's home page. Either you'll find others like it, or you'll find that it stands alone in some way.

Also, as a general rule, it's best not to make your site either too wide (with many top-level categories and fewer subcategories) or too deep (with few top-level categories and many subcategories). If you have to go one way or the other, though, err in the direction of making your site a little deeper than wide. It's a bit easier to organize links onto a home page that way.

If you find, as you move along, that a clear hierarchy for the material you are putting on your Web site is just not coming together, that may be a sign that your overall plan is weak — it's rare that a site just doesn't lend itself to some type of hierarchy. If this happens, you may find it wise to go back and review your overall plan and the groupings that you've created. Consider, too, whether the amount of content you've planned per Web page is appropriate.

The topic of page length is highly debated in the Web world — some say that a page should fit on a single screen with no scrolling necessary, while others think that a page can be any length. In practice, it's good if your pages address one point or issue apiece, whatever their length. If you find yourself unable to group pages constructively, take a look at the content you've planned, and consider whether you're including too much content on each page. If you break the pages down, perhaps they'll begin to form a more logical grouping.

Bunching pages into organized "types"

You've sorted out by subject, task, or some other system the general categories of stuff that's on your site. At this point, it's a good idea to consider the type of pages you are going to use on your site. Some types of pages lend themselves to one or another type of content or task, while some offer the user assistance in navigating. In these next sections we'll look at the types of Web pages that most commonly appear in sites. You're probably going to find that most of the pages that make up your site fall into one of these types.

Home page

The *home page* is the first page that a visitor sees on entering the site — it's the site's main page, index page, or "front door." The home page's purpose is to act as the site's table of contents in a sense, but that doesn't mean that everything on the site is linked directly from the home page. Only the most compelling or necessarily accessible items appear on the home page — these items then link to deeper areas of the site. Another purpose of the home page is to convey to visitors the personality of the site. All in all, the home page's purpose is to provide a quick and easily comprehensible overview of the site.

Note that there is often more than one home page in a site. In a site with several main sections, each section may have its own "home page." For example, a software company's site may include a home page for the entire site, a home page for the Products area of the site, a home page for the About the Company area, and a home page for the Technical Support area. For the sake of clarity, the custom is to name the files for home pages index.html, and so often people refer to the home page for the entire site as the *home page* while calling the home pages of sections of the site *index pages*. When we discuss creating the directory structure of a site later in this chapter, you see that home pages generally map to the index file in a directory.

Navigational pages and nav bars

Navigational pages in the strictest sense are pages that help users to navigate the site. Some examples are as follows:

✔ A table of contents page that lists all of the sections of the site

✔ An index listing all of the pages in the site

✔ A page containing common navigational elements — perhaps a link for each section of the site — that is displayed in a navigational frame that appears next to, above, or below a frame containing content

✔ A search page that lets users examine the site for items of interest

✔ A What's New page that lists new additions to the site

Including *some* navigational pages can be important to your site's navigability, but which of those listed you actually use depends on the style of your site. Just remember that navigational pages should not contain any content — their purpose is to facilitate navigation. Also, the last item in the list (a What's New page) is getting kind of passé — it's far better to pepper your home page with tag lines or very short blurbs telling them what's new on your site than to make them drill down to and through a What's New page.

Another way of handling navigation is to place links to the various areas of your site on a navigation bar (a *nav* bar) that appears on every page of the site, or at least on most pages. The nav bar can either be graphical or a set of simple text links.

Registration/user input page

Sometimes you want folks to register to use your site or a portion of it — maybe to get access to an area containing special content, maybe for a contest, maybe to set up an account with your online store, or maybe as a requirement for downloading some software. Registration pages work because they're driven by a CGI script (a special program that runs on the Web server). To the user, the page just looks like a form.

Search page and results page (s)

As your site blossoms, it may become harder for users to find what they seek, even if you are grand master champion of navigational planning. To give users a path straight to what interests them, you can include a site search engine. Including a search engine on your site is going to involve the creation of several specialized pages. The most obvious ones are those on which the search box and the primary list of search results appear, but you also probably want a help page that explains search techniques, an error page that lets folks know when they've made some boo-bette, and a template for the more specific results the user sees when he or she drills down in the preliminary list.

Most of the search engines that are available for use on individual Web sites include sample query and result pages. You should customize these before you add the search engine to your site. We've seen some otherwise really polished sites that start looking kind of lousy when the search engine goes to work. You don't want other companies' logos all over your site, for example, nor do you want the result pages to appear in dumpy old Courier font if the rest of the site uses Times Roman.

Help pages

Help pages are designed to . . . *help.* Some sites include only a single help page, while others provide a whole online help area with FAQs, tips, and bells and whistles galore.

Keep in mind as you put together your help pages that to document using a browser or a computer is both hopeless and outside the scope of your responsibility. Focus your help files on navigating your content — and using any special gizmos like your site search engine. It's always a good idea to include at least one help page on your site. Be sure to include links to the help page from your home page. You may also want to include links to the help page from any navigational pages or nav bars on your site.

Content pages

The content of your site is, presumably, the bulk of your site. Content pages can contain content of any number of types, but whatever the content is, it should be organized intelligently, and for the most part, all of the content pages should have a common look. If you produce content pages that look vastly different from each other, you may confuse the user.

The simplest way to accomplish a common look is to repeat elements from page to page — hey, what about the *nav bar?* Or maybe your logo? A color scheme you've chosen as the overall palette for your site can work, too. The point is that you should create a look for content pages that reinforces to users that they are on your site, not someone else's.

In some cases, you may want to limit the number of links going into or coming out of content pages. For some types of content, you may want the user to be led down the path you are placing before him or her, and to follow that path like the yellow brick road. This is often the case in promotional sites or purchase-support sites, for example. You may alternatively feel that your content lends itself to more free-for-all click paths. Perhaps your content is a humor column about the Web, and the surprise of the link is the point, or maybe you're providing users with a dynamic experience within in your site, and many internal links are the route you want go. You don't want to overwhelm or confuse the user with links, but remember that content and links are the point of the Web.

Company pages

If yours is a company site, as many are, you need to include some About the Company information on the site. Perhaps this is a corporate backgrounder, the company values or mission statement, press releases and a list of awards that the company has received, a list of the executive officers, and the company's location(s). In many cases, job listings and information about the company culture and the benefits of working for the company also fit in here.

Unless you're building a corporate image site, avoid splattering company information all over the site. Put that stuff in one area of the site so people who have an interest in the company can go there and easily find what they need, while those who came by to browse your content or purchase your merchandise don't have to trip over excessive amounts of company info.

Transaction pages

Transaction pages are those used to conduct financial transactions. This can include purchasing a single item from your site, purchasing a shopping cart full of items, transferring cash from one account to another at a banking site, and so on. We discuss transactions and what you should keep in mind in putting together transaction pages in Chapter 3.

It's crucial that the design of transaction pages be clear and easy to understand, and that navigation be a breeze. As we discuss in Chapter 3, the last thing you want is to place barriers in the way of completing a transaction — to sell, you must *remove* all the barriers. As you organize and oversee the design of transaction pages, make sure that there is no way a user could get confused or frustrated following your system. Put clear labels on any buttons that the user needs to click, and keep the number of pages he or she must traverse to complete the transaction to a minimum.

Drawing the site map

It's time to chart your site map. We like to use the symbols shown in the following table when we draw site maps, and we suggest that you use them as well:

Symbol	What It Looks Like	What It Stands For
	Square box	A page with links
	Small rectangle	A terminal page (one with no links)
	Cylinder	A script that works on a database
	Program symbol	Any other script
———————	Solid line	Link
....	Dotted line	Task path

The site map you're about to create can provide you with a logical overview of the site from which you can later work when it's time to create directories. The directories you create, by the way, may not exactly line up with the site map — there are other considerations to take into account in organizing directories — but the site map will, in any case, help you when you get around to creating directories.

Placing the home page and content pages

Grab a big piece of paper (or launch some nice graphing software, such as Visio). At the top center of the page, in big, bold letters, write **home page** and draw a box around that text. This box represents (guess what?) the home page of your site.

Then, under the box representing your home page, in a horizontal line, draw more boxes — one for each of the major subject groupings you've identified as part of your content. In each of these boxes, jot down the name you used for each grouping in your notes. From the box that represents the home page, draw a straight line to each of these new boxes. Figure 6-7 shows the top level of a site we built — yours is going to look somewhat different, but this can give you an idea of what it should look like. Each of the lines from the home page box to the other boxes represents a major link in the site as it is to appear later.

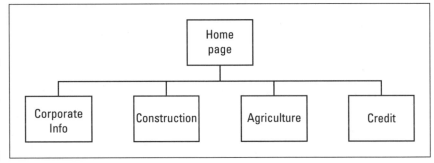

Figure 6-7:
The home page and top-level pages.

Now that you've done that, simply repeat the process, going farther down level by level into your site. Here and there you can connect content via a script instead of a link. For example, you may plan a guest book page and save the results to a file or perhaps a catalog page that's dynamically generated by pulling information out of a database. If so, use the special symbols that we showed you for scripts there. Figure 6-8 illustrates this idea.

You needn't map out every smidgen of your site just yet — not every single page has to appear. Just stick to the bigger picture. After you've pulled together a site map that includes all of your major content, all mapped out in a hierarchy with lines representing the links and cylinders showing the scripts that are going to make up the final site, it's time to turn your attention to task groupings.

Adding task paths

With all the related content on your site linked in the site map, you've represented ways for a user to find information. You may still have to lay out paths for a user to take to complete a given task on your site. Whether you

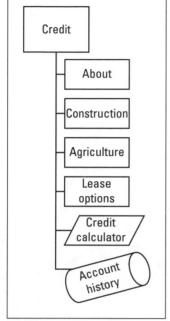

Figure 6-8:
This part of the site includes a number of scripts.

have to do this depends on whether users have to complete tasks when they move through certain areas of your site — for example, registration or downloading. This is where the task lists you made earlier in this chapter (in the section "Grouping by task") come in.

Pick up the notes you made when you read that material. On your map, draw dotted lines to represent tasks the user completes between the content pages where the tasks are done. Later, when you put your pages together, you may use scripts for parts of the underpinnings of these tasks — you can drop in cylinders now to represent scripts that you may use, or you can pop 'em in later. Figure 6-9 shows the example site map at this stage.

Revising your site map

As you chart your site, you may find that the map isn't working out quite as you imagined in one way or another. Don't worry. The purpose of mapping your site at this stage is to think things through as well as to provide yourself, your colleagues, and any outside contractors you may take on with information about how you envision the site. Stay flexible — if you find you need to modify your plan, that's no big deal. Similarly, if you find that your plan is not working out, it's okay to scrap the thing and start over. It's far better to discover a flaw in your logic now than to stumble on that flaw later,

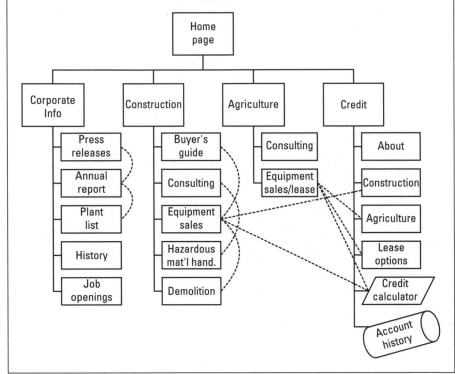

Figure 6-9:
Now the site map includes task paths and indications of scripts you may use.

when you're too invested and too close to launch to turn back. Your goal at this point is still planning. It's better to plan more than less — this saves you time when you get to implementing and even more time when you get to maintaining the site.

Structuring the Site's Directories

Having charted your site into a clear and understandable map, you've arrived at the moment for thinking about how to structure the site on the server. There are no hard-and-fast rules when it comes to creating a directory structure for your site. A number of practices have become customary, however (for example, creating special directories to hold files of certain types that you then use throughout the site). This includes scripts and images, for example. We recommend that you follow those customs. Other than this, the structure of directories on your Web server is mainly dictated by the flow of your site.

When you plan the directory structure for your site, it doesn't matter which Web-server software you're using or what platform it's running on.

The good of site-mapping software

You may wonder about all that wonderful site-mapping software you've heard about and why we're asking you in this chapter to draw the site map by hand. Site-mapping software falls into two categories: software that can read an existing site and build a map of it, and software that allows you to create a map as you build the site. Neither these helps much with planning — they map sites pretty much after the fact. They can be quite useful, though, in letting you see maps of existing sites for research purposes and in letting you see a map of your site after it's at least under way.

Look at this figure, and you see the IDG Books site as viewed in the form of a site map generated by Microsoft WebMapper. With WebMapper, you can specify an existing URL and select which of several optional views of the site you prefer; in a moment, the software reads all the pages comprising the site and produces a nifty site map. (You can then click on portions of the map to focus your view on a particular section of the site.) WebMapper also produces reports showing the number of files comprising the site and any bad links that may have cropped up. InContext's WebAnalyzer produces similar maps and reports; the look is different but the idea's the same.

Microsoft FrontPage is an example of the type of software that lets you see a site map as you build the site. Known primarily as an HTML editor and authoring tool, FrontPage offers site-building features including one that lets you view a site map as you build your site.

These tools can be very powerful in helping you maintain your site, but they don't substitute for solid planning. Preproduction planning is the bedrock of a successful site.

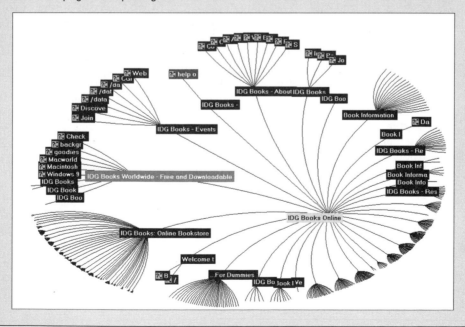

Some technical backstory

Before you delve into organizing files on your Web server, you should be familiar with a few technical details. These details are true regardless of which server you are using (with a couple of notable exceptions). There's nothing very heavy here — this stuff is background, but it's important background. Be sure to read it before you move on. (For more on choosing and running a server, turn to Chapter 10.)

The directory structure on your Web server is one and the same as the directory structure that appears in the URLs that a user sees when visiting your site. When a user accesses a URL either by going straight to it or by following a link, the directories and subdirectories within the file they are reaching for all appear in the URL. The actual document, whether it's an HTML file, a graphic, or other item, is a file that's located on the Web server within some directory or subdirectory. This is no different than what happens when you open a file on your hard disk, at least in the sense that your hard disk contains directories (folders) and subdirectories, and the document that you seek when you open one in a word processor is a file that lives somewhere in that structure.

The *root* of your Web site (the top of the hierarchy of directories and subdirectories) corresponds to a directory that exists somewhere on your server. The directory is called the *document root directory*. Where exactly on the server that directory exists depends partly on the type of server software you're using (Apache handles things differently than Netscape Enterprise Server, for example) and how the server was set up by whomever put it together. (Presumably this would be the tech Webmaster — maybe *you?*)

When a user loads a URL such as `http://www.acompany.com`, what is actually returned is the *index* file in the server's document root directory. The index file is the file the server uses when no other document is specified in the URL. In reality, the Web browser is assuming that the home page's filename appears at the end of the URL — it's just that everyone knows it's there, so there's no need to spell out the filename. Generally, most Web servers use the name `index.html` for the home page file; but Microsoft Internet Information Server (IIS) has to be different; it calls the file `default.htm`.

The following example, using `index.html` as the home page file, shows the relationship between URLs and the files they access. (We aren't showing you the path including the document root here because the root is handled differently by different servers, remember?)

This URL	*Accesses This File on the Server*
/index.html	index.html
/	index.html
/projects/index.html	projects/index.html
/projects/	projects/index.html
/projects/scientist.html	projects/scientist.html

Mirroring the site's structure

Perhaps the simplest way to structure files on your Web server is to mirror the hierarchy you've created. That is, you can use the same logical grouping of files when it comes to creating your directory structure that you used in creating your site map. It's always handy when this works out.

To use this method, place the files from the topmost page of the site (the home page) into the server's document root directory. Then create directories under the document root directory for each section of the site. When you follow this method, each of the square boxes you drew on your site map becomes a directory (which may well have an index file located in it). For now, ignore the dotted lines on your site map — those are the paths users may take when they are trying to do a particular task. But make sure the links — the solid lines — are logical.

Into each of the directories you've created, drop the files for that part of the site. If your site plan calls for finer groupings of files, create subdirectories as needed, and repeat the process for each of these subdirectories, dropping in content and creating more subdirectories until your Web server's directory structure matches your site's structure. Figure 6-10 shows the directory structure for the site we mapped out earlier in this chapter.

Figure 6-10:
It's very convenient when your directory structure can match the site map you created.

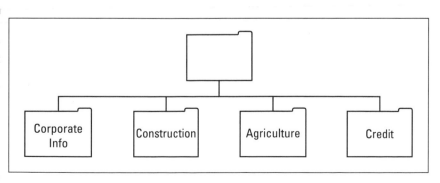

ISPs, IPPs, and the root directory egg hunt

When you run your own server, the location of the document root directory is pretty clear — it's wherever you put it when you installed your Web server. But what if you're using an Internet service provider (ISP) or an Internet presence provider (IPP) to host a virtual domain for you? (We talk about ISPs and IPPs in Chapter 11. A *virtual domain* is one that's housed on someone else's machine.) The server's document root directory usually holds the service provider's Web site, not yours. The document root for your site is then usually contained within a directory called `public_html`, which is located in your home directory on the service provider's Web server. When you open your account with the ISP or IPP, its personnel tell you exactly where this directory is located on its server and how you can place files in it.

Using a single directory

Some folks just forget about all this directory and structure stuff. They just plop all the files that make up their site onto their Web server in the document root directory. Regardless of which part of the site the files pertain to, they all reside in the same directory.

If you decide to use this structure — or *nonstructure* — for your site, it's important that you use filenames that will help you quickly identify the files. You can use a filenaming system that identifies each file as belonging to a certain portion of your site. For example, you can assign numbers to certain areas of the site (be sure to note these numbers on your site map) and name of the files that use those numbers. Or, you can name the files with the name of the area of the site they pertain to. If one area of the site is about Java, you can name the files javawriting, javacode, javafuture, javadecaf, and so on.

Generally, we don't advocate these methods. We think it's a lot easier to find your socks and undies if you declare one drawer the sock drawer and another the undie drawer, and put your socks where they belong. (Guess what? Our mothers turned out to be right.)

Special directories for special purposes

Some files deserve their own special, separate directories. These include resources that are commonly used throughout the site, such as images and graphic elements (hey, the nav bar, for example!), sound and video and other media files, CGI scripts, and data files (which contain data that the CGI scripts use when they're running). It's probably best to consider how you may categorize these items — you don't want to toss your art and scripts in

Avoiding the CGI security pitfall

It's not strictly necessary to keep CGI scripts in a special directory. Many servers, including Netscape's and Microsoft's recognize the file extension CGI, indicating that the file is a script. So technically, you can put scripts anywhere that you want.

In fact, you may prefer to store script files in the same location as the content to which they relate. For example, if you include a puzzle game on your site, that area of the site may include a page of instructions (a plain HTML file), a number of GIF images (GIF is a common file format for images on the Web) for the puzzle pieces, and the script that runs the puzzle. If you use the CGI file extension in naming those scripts, you can place the scripts in the same directory as the rest of the content for the puzzle. That entire section of the site is then self-contained in a single directory tree. Moving that section of the site or making a backup copy of it is a snap.

On the other hand, using the CGI extension opens a big security hole in your site. It opens the possibility that some unscrupulous person can execute a command on your server from his Web browser. You sure wouldn't want that person executing the command format.exe (which would reformat your hard drive); you also wouldn't want him to retrieve password files or the log file from one of your forms. After all, would you want to make a file that contains information for people that are interested in your products potentially available to your competition? We think not.

the same directory any more than your socks and undies (that is, unless you only expect to ever possess one piece of art and a couple of scripts). Lots of folks call these special directories *bins*. Cute, eh? They're bins for whatever you toss into them.

The CGI bin

Generally, CGI scripts should go into a special CGI directory. This directory is often named cgi-bin and is referred to by the URL /cgi-bin. It's commonly located either in the server's document root directory or one directory directly above the document root directory. Check your server's documentation to see where it should be located on your particular server.

Data directories

Data directories are those that hold data used in running CGI scripts. They can hold data the script uses to generate HTML, or they can hold data that's been gathered by the script. The data directory is usually called data and is often a subdirectory within the cgi-bin directory.

Some Webmasters like to separate the files that a CGI script reads from the files that it writes and place them into two separate directories. While this adds some complexity to the directory planning, it also adds an extra layer of warm and fuzzy security to the Web server. The security advantage is that

CGI scripts can then be set up so they have *write* access only to the directory that holds output from the script. The script clearly doesn't need write access to the directory that holds its data. And, as a general security rule, you want to minimize the amount of access allowed, so this is one handy way to limit access.

Images/media directories

Images are customarily placed in their own directory, which is often called images. Sometimes it's called art-bin. And, with the explosion of other forms of media — such as video and sound — many sites have renamed their images directory, calling it media. Into this directory go all of the non-HTML-content files. Alternatively, you may want to keep images in one directory and media in another — perhaps you're the sort to iron your socks before you put them in the drawer.

If you are mirroring the site's structure as you create your directory structure, each directory you create should have an images or media subdirectory within it. This directory should hold all of the media used by that section of the site.

Common resources directory

As in an office setting, it often works well to place commonly used resources into a common area where everyone can get to them — hey, maybe the copy room? You may find that some files should go in a location that's convenient to every area on your site. Perhaps you want the image files that contain your corporate logo, nav bars, or identifying banners in a special directory.

Why would you want to do this? Because when Ursula User visits your site, if that stuff is in an artbin or media directory, every time she accesses a page that includes that stuff, she has to wait for that file to download (again). If you put commonly used media files into their own directory, customarily called either common or resources (at the root level of your site), you can exploit the cache that's built into many Web browsers. It then appears to Ursula and all other visitors that your site is a tad faster to load. This is because, after they've downloaded a common image for one page, it's cached in their browser and it pops onto the screen quickly the next time the user comes across a page that includes that same image.

Mapping the directories

All your organizational prep work can now come to fruition, as you create the directory structure that you plan to use for your site. Go ahead and sketch this out, either on paper or in your favorite word processor or drawing program. Figure 6-11 shows the directory structure we created for the site whose content we mapped in Figure 6-9.

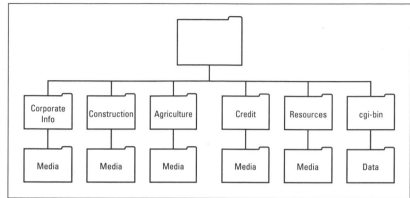

Figure 6-11:
The now-complete directory structure.

There's one more bit of your site structure that you should really consider at this point. If there is some huge pile of stuff — maybe all of the info in your product catalog or a list of resellers organized by ZIP code — you don't want to have to create individual HTML files for that material. In the next section we'll look at databases as a solution to that issue.

Database? I Don't Need a Stinking Database — Do I?

So far, we've been talking about where to put your static pages — Web pages that correspond to plain HTML files. What are you going to do with dynamically generated pages (that is pages that change in some way every time they are loaded)? These usually require that you have a database server as well as a Web server. They also require that you create a template into which the data can flow dynamically from the database to be viewed by the user. We talk about databases in some detail in Chapter 12. At this point, we'll briefly go over how you can determine, from the work you've done organizing your content and site, whether you would benefit from including one or more databases. Consider these points:

- ✔ If your site includes thousands or hundreds or even dozens of pages that look pretty much the same, then you need a database.

- ✔ If you need to change pages based on user input (maybe you have a set of pages that list something, and you want the user to be able to specify how many items are listed on a page), then you also need a database.

- ✔ If you plan to install a shopping-cart system that includes a catalog of products, then you need a database. (You may even wind up with two or three databases, if you count the database of customers and the one that tracks sales.)

Ten tips for creating smashing Web pages

✔ Give your site a title that's brief, descriptive, and easy to remember.

✔ Keep the title's promise, and provide any content you say you will.

✔ At the top of each page, offer clues about what's on the page. Don't assume that people are going to scroll unless you give them a reason to scroll. Break pages that are more than three screenfuls long into multiple pages.

✔ Make anything that looks like a button act like a button.

✔ Make links meaningful — avoid generic Click Here links, and decide whether you're going to link on the active phrase (Go To) or the destination phrase (Our Chat Archive).

✔ Use small image files that contain no more than 50 colors.

✔ Keep directory names and filenames short and consistent.

✔ Tell your users the size of any downloadable files — they need to know whether they can manage a file of this size.

✔ Provide an e-mail link to the Webmaster.

✔ Before you announce the site, test it until you can't stand to test it another minute. Get others to test it. Find all the bugs, and *squash* them. Then launch.

✔ If you're producing one set of content — say an About the Company area — that you plan to use on multiple sites and you want to minimize the time that you spend duplicating efforts as well as minimize errors that may occur in that material on one site or another, then you need a database.

Unless your site is small and your endeavor is not labor intensive, you probably need a database of some sort. Just how are you going to cope with this? Well, for now, look over your site plan and directory structure, and consider whether you are including a category that inclines you to need a database. If so, pencil that in on your plans, and turn to Chapter 12 to look further into the whole bag of database questions. You need to sketch out (at least preliminarily) the fields and queries you may use in your database as part of your overall site plan.

Putting Together a Rock-Solid Design Document

Whether you're jobbing the design of your site out to a Web shop in whole or in part, or just turning over pieces of the design process to members of your own staff, you must document all the planning you've done. Then you have to fork over that documentation to the people who are doing the work so they can all know and follow the plan. It will also help those who maintain the site in the months to come if you've created documentation. Even if you alone are responsible for the site, you can be sure that 3, 6, or 12 months from now, you are going to have only dim memories of just what you decided. You need notes regarding what you decided and how you thought you could expand it to handle future developments.

A typical design document includes the following items:

- ✔ The site map you created
- ✔ The directory tree, showing the structure you created along with notes associating pieces of the tree to pieces on the site map
- ✔ Descriptions of content and task pages
- ✔ A listing of buttons that appear on the nav bar that goes on every page of your site

The design document can also include information about the following topics, some of which we discuss in other chapters:

- ✔ The server software you plan to use (see Chapter 10)
- ✔ The server platform you are going to use (again, see Chapter 10)
- ✔ Any database requirements, including the fields, queries, and reports you hope for (see Chapter 12)
- ✔ Scripting requirements you know of at this point (discussed throughout this book)
- ✔ Any information about the transaction system you would like to use, or what you would like a transaction system to do for you (see Chapter 3)

The design document should also include the following items:

- ✔ Sketches showing your ideas for the look of various pages (this is called a *storyboard*)
- ✔ A listing of all the text elements your pages may include, such as titles and headings, lists (bulleted, numbered, simple, and multicolumn), text that's set off in boxes (called *sidebars*) or as special notes, any kind of special fonts that are used to indicate special text (bold, italic, or perhaps something indicating programming code on a software site), tabular information, text links, visited links, linked headlines, and so on.

With all this, though, remember that your design document is not carved in stone any more than any other aspect of your site. It's perfectly okay to make changes to it as your site develops. It's actually a good thing to update the design document; you may even want to place it online where everyone involved in the project can see it. (In that case, you should obviously alert the whole team if you make a change.) What's more, you can use the online design document as the basis of the style guide that you develop. (We discuss this in Chapter 9.)

Finally, make sure that you've shared this design document with everyone who designs, implements, or posts content on the site. It helps them to know where new content should go and generally makes the process of working with a group run much smoother.

Do I really need a domain name?

The short answer is: Yes, at least if your site is more than a personal Web page. If your site is more comprehensive (perhaps a company site), you need a simple address that people can find. For bonus content on this topic, including tips for selecting a winning domain name, visit `http://www.dummies.com` and use the convenient search feature to find *Webmastering For Dummies*. Or simply look for the Resources & Extras category and link to "Really Useful Extras."

Chapter 7

Beyond HTML and Son of HTML

• •

In This Chapter

▶ Understanding the ground rules of HTML

▶ Knowing when to implement live content

▶ Knowing your options for livening up your site

▶ Running your own discussion group

▶ Making a successful chat area

• •

*Y*ou've set your goals, planned your Web site's structure, and budgeted time and money. Now what are you going to put there? And how are you going to do it? Sadly, we can't cover *all* the nuts and bolts of making a Web page in this short space, but HTML is not hard — it's just a bunch of codes. With a few pointers and helpful hints, we trust you can start writing HTML if you haven't already, and you can even start looking at the ins and outs of what's beyond HTML. In this chapter, we spell out the theory behind writing HTML code and point you to some excellent reference sites that you can use to learn the rest. After that, we look at what's behind interactivity and point you toward adding live content of all kinds to your already-killer Web site. (After all, if your site isn't amazing without Java, it isn't going to be amazing *with* Java, either.)

The Basics of HTML (Just in Case)

Even with all the WYSIWYG HTML editors that are currently on the market (some of which are actually good), you need a firm grasp on HTML. You needn't know every obscure tag, but having a keen understanding of HTML issues can help you understand the whole business of production Webmastering. What's more, there is no single HTML editor that covers every detail of marking up a Web page well. They all add odd codes of their own to the HTML they produce, and not even the best programs handle advanced elements like frames or style sheets very well. In short, knowing your way around the code that makes up your Web pages can only help you in the long run, and the more you know, the better equipped you are to handle complex design issues and fix any errors that come up. Plenty of good books and Web sites include instructions for using the tags themselves; in this chapter we discuss the basic ground rules for writing good HTML. After that, you can go exploring.

The CNET people are experts at everything, and you can learn HTML from them by visiting their HTML for Beginners site at `http://www.cnet.com/Content/Features/Howto/Basics`.

Our very own HTML Master's Reference (`http:/www.htmlreference.com`) is a complete guide to HTML, including coverage of the Netscape and Internet Explorer tags, style sheets, and more.

What makes a Web page

A Web page is simply a text document that contains instructions for Web browsers. If you look at a Web page (a.k.a. an HTML document) in a regular text editor, you see a bunch of code in angle brackets and a bunch of text; it's not very exciting. When a Web browser "sees" a Web page, however, it uses these bits of code, called *tags,* to interpret how the document should look and what is to happen when certain things are clicked on. Technically speaking, any text document that begins with `<HTML>` and ends with `</HTML>` can be read as a Web page, although other elements are essential for making a Web page that meets the standards most Web browsers expect. An entire Web site is simply a collection of these text documents arranged in directories, possibly in combination with images and other media.

Whether you're a novice or a pro, you should fill your bookmarks file with many helpful HTML reference sites. A few of our favorites? Quadzilla (`http://www.quadzilla.com`) covers everything from software to style sheets. The Yale Web Style Guide (`http://info.med.yale.edu/caim/manual`) takes the case study approach, teaching you as you read along with their development. And the Davis HTML Guide (`http://www.dcn.davis.ca.us/~csandvig/ip/example.html`) shows you the source code and what it does, side by side.

The history of HTML in a paragraph

HTML is an acronym for Hypertext Markup Language. The original *specifications,* or rules, for HTML were based on SGML, a language used by publishers to designate text elements such as headings, boldface and italic characters, and so on. However, as you know, HTML is good for much more than just formatting the way that text looks. Hypertext is somewhat like Text Plus: It can include not only text but links to other documents and files anywhere on the Internet. The first Web browsers allowed you to click on links to download images, sounds, video, and other multimedia objects. Very quickly, Web software was designed to include *inline* images (images within Web pages), and now many other forms of media can be displayed or played directly in the browser window. As Web browsers became more multimedia-savvy, Web designers became more concerned with the look of their Web sites, and design elements, such as background colors and images, tables for laying out text, and more flexibility in the look and alignment of text, were added to the mix. As Web browsers and the people who designed for them have become more sophisticated (read demanding), other doodads have been added, such as multiple frames per window, the ability to en-hance multimedia capabilities by using plug-ins and other add-ons, and the capability of Web browsers to read scripting languages that are included within the HTML document.

HTML purists argue that the Web should never have progressed beyond the level of text and images, and that people should download the extra stuff if they want to see it. While it's true that the markup language was never intended to be either a formatting (design) language or a multimedia inter-pretation code, it has lent itself to those tasks despite groans of protest from both the old guard and their computers. Keep in mind, however, that few people have access to the kind of bandwidth or computing power the most graphics- and multimedia-intensive pages demand.

Listen to the rules

Every Web page has to follow a few basic rules (in terms of its HTML makeup) to be read by the majority of Web browsers on the market. Web geeks of all stripes gripe about bad, sloppy, or inconsistent code, and with good reason. Bad code sets a bad example for other new Webmasters, but perhaps more importantly, bad code simply doesn't work in some Web browsers, including newer versions of Netscape Navigator. Because some Web browsers (such as older versions of Navigator) are fairly lenient in overlooking mistakes or omissions, people who don't follow the standards of HTML can get away with designing pages that don't *always* break. But you can never be sure what software people are going to use to view your site, and if they're using a browser that, to them, is perfectly legitimate, but your code isn't, they can't see your site. We talk about how to optimize your site for various browsers later in this chapter. First, we look at some of the basic rules for writing good code.

NCSA's Beginner's Guide to HTML was one of the first of its kind, and it's still one of the best. You can find a reference to every basic tag that you could possibly want to use by visiting the Guide at `http://www.ncsa.uiuc.edu/General/Internet/WWW/HTMLPrimer.html`.

What's in a tag

Any element on a Web page that is surrounded by angle brackets `<like this>` is called a *tag*. Tags are pieces of code that Web browsers read as instructions. Images, links, and formatting are all instructions that the Web browser looks for within those angle brackets. If tags are formatted properly — that is, if there's an opening and closing angle bracket — the tags themselves are not displayed as text on the Web page. If you put an incorrect or fictional tag in your code, such as `<butter>`, it also doesn't show up on the page. Web browsers that don't understand nonstandard tags simply ignore them.

What's not in a tag

Any text that is placed between `<BODY>` and `</BODY>` on a Web page (see "The essential tags," later in this chapter), and is not included between angle brackets `<like this>`, has the potential to show up as regular text. This regular text can be modified by any number of tags that affect how and where the text is displayed, and whether the text is a link.

A fun way to learn about Web-page design and HTML code writing is to visit pages that do it utterly and completely *wrong*. Try Web Pages That Suck (see Figure 7-1), at `http://www.webpagesthatsuck.com`, or the Bad Style Page, at `http://www.earth.com/bad-style`, for pointers to lousy code.

In our examples, the words within the tags are printed in all uppercase characters. While HTML tags are not case sensitive, many HTML authors use all capital letters to make the tags stand out clearly from the rest of the document when they're editing Web pages.

Pairing your tags

Most tags come in pairs: an opening tag and a closing tag. The opening tag is generally a plain English word or abbreviation that describes what action the tag is to take; the tag may also include additional *attributes* that describe how the tag is to act. (You can think of the main work in a tag as the verb and the other attributes as adverbs.) Closing tags include the main action of the tag, which is preceded by a forward slash (/). For example, to make the word *new* boldface, the code would look like this:

```
<B>new</B>
```

Figure 7-1:
Look at
Web Pages
That Suck
to see how
not to
design a
Web page.

In this case, the first tag, `<B>`, indicates the start of boldface type, and the second tag, `</B>`, indicates that the Web browser should stop printing boldface type. On the other hand, while opening tags may include other attributes, closing tags merely need to close the main instruction in the tag. For instance, to make the word *green* appear in green text, you would use the following code:

```
<FONT COLOR="#04B222">green</FONT>
```

The main instruction in this set of tags is the word `FONT`, which indicates that this tag controls how the text is to be displayed. The `COLOR="#04B222"` portion of the tag indicates what color the text should be. The closing tag, `</FONT>`, indicates to stop displaying the previous font instructions, but it isn't necessary to tell it which other attributes you initially indicated.

There are exceptions to the rule that tags must come in pairs, most notably `<P>` (paragraph break), `<BR>` (line break), and `<IMG>` (image). For the most part, however, you need to close every tag that you open for your Web page to look and act the way that you want it to.

What is the correct order of tags?

Tags should be *nested;* that is, when you open a series of tags, you close them in reverse order. If you wanted to make a word boldface, italic, purple, and centered and act as a link, your code may look like this:

```
<CENTER><FONT COLOR="#99038F"><I><B>
        <A HREF="PURPLE.HTML">purple!</A></B></I></FONT>
        </CENTER>
```

Note that it doesn't matter in what order you place the elements to begin with, but they should be closed in the reverse order of how they were opened. The word *purple!,* in our example, is nested within a series of tags.

Do you want color? Take your pick, using ColorServe Pro, at the following URL: http://www.biola.edu/cgi-bin/colorpro/colorpro.cgi.

The essential tags

All Web pages, including yours, require a few essential tags to work consistently. When those tags are in place, you have a Web page. Please note that many HTML editors put these tags in place for you, and you don't need to repeat them. The following, in order, are the tags you need to make a basic Web page, along with a line or two of text:

```
<HTML>
<HEAD>
<TITLE>Your Title Goes Here</TITLE>
</HEAD>
<BODY>
Your content goes here.
</BODY>
</HTML>
```

The <HTML> tag tells the Web browser that it is reading an HTML document. The head of the document, which precedes the body of the document, includes information that doesn't show up in the Web browser window, such as the title and any META tags that you may want to include. (See Chapter 13 for more on META tags and how to use them.) The title of the document, which is included within the two HEAD tags, includes the text that is to appear in the title bar of the Web browser that loads the page. The <BODY> and </BODY> tags enclose the parts of the document that the Web browser shows in the document-viewing window. You can include any number of other tags within the body of the document. The last tag in any document is generally the </HTML> tag, which indicates that the Web browser can stop reading the document, because it's over.

Are you doing it correctly? How's your HTML? How can you tell? This list of HTML Validation Tools can help you check your HTML from top to bottom: http://www.cre.canon.co.uk/~neilb/Weblint/validation.html.

Looking Good in a Variety of Web Browsers

So you've learned every trick in every book that you could get your hands on, and you've implemented all of these tricks. You've promoted your site so that it's bigger than John Lennon, but the hits aren't so much of a flood as a trickle. What gives? Making a whiz-bang site that makes use of all the latest technology is only half a good idea — because the other half of the Internet population can't even see your pages if you don't make some effort to cater to the many different browsers, platforms, and levels of bandwidth available to the masses.

Who uses what?

You're probably aware that the Web browser you use to surf the Web is not the only browser on the market. Even if you've test-driven several different browsers, you probably have your opinions about which browser is the best. Not everyone may agree with your choice, however. There are plenty of reasons why people use different browsers. It's important to note that various browsers display the same page quite differently. What's more, various versions of the same browser — Navigator on a PC versus Navigator on a Mac, Internet Explorer 3.0 versus Internet Explorer 2.0, and so one — can all display the exact same document looking terribly different.

Netscape versus Microsoft

According to BrowserWatch (a site we describe in Chapter 2 that tracks and reports on usage of Web browsers and plug-ins), Netscape Navigator, in its various permutations and as of this writing, commands a whopping 65 percent of the market share. This may change, but if another browser takes over the number-one spot any time soon, it is most likely going to be Microsoft Internet Explorer, which now holds the number-two spot. Please note that these two browsers together hold *90 percent* of the market share — which is *not the same* as 100 percent.

While it's almost a given that the majority of folks who use your site are going to look at it using one of these two browsers (unless your site is about Amiga software), there are at least four different versions of each of these two browsers floating around on the Internet. And even though each company continually upgrades its software to make use of startling new features, not all of its customers feel like changing software every few months. As a result, many hold on to their old browsers, much to the chagrin of both the software companies and Webmasters everywhere. Many schools and libraries, for example, still run Netscape Navigator version 1. Although this is a Netscape product, it can't read frames, use plug-ins, or display such nifty things as animated GIFs.

BrowserWatch (Figure 7-2) tracks Web software usage at `http://browserwatch.iworld.com/`. It's *the* place to go for news, facts, and figures on Web browsers.

Figure 7-2:
Browser-
Watch lets
you know
who is
using what
software.

Get a (down)load of all the different browsers by looking at the Yahoo! browser listings at `http://www.yahoo.com/Computers_and_Internet/Software/Internet/World_Wide_Web/Browsers/`.

Before you start filling up your hard drive with new (and old) software, look at your pages in the Backward Compatibility Viewer, which you can tweak to emulate any combination of browser features. Bookmark it at `http://www.delorie.com/Web/wpbcv.html`.

Platforms galore

Many people who surf the Web do so on different platforms, on which they may not be able to run the more popular software like Netscape Navigator and Microsoft Internet Explorer. People surf the Web using Amiga, Atari, and OS/2; ancient Macs and PCs can run Web browsers but not the popular, new, robust ones.

Different browsers for different folks

Almost as many browsers litter the Internet as do Web sites. Okay, maybe we're exaggerating a little, but the last time we looked, Yahoo! listed more than 300 different browsers in use. What's the difference between Cyberdog and Albert, or Charlotte and Cello, or Mosaic, AirMosaic, and NetCruiser? To find out, you'd have to download a variety of browsers and fiddle a while. Forget that. To check out what most people use, our suggested shopping list for browsers is as follows:

✔ The latest version of Netscape Navigator and Microsoft Internet Explorer, and at least one obsolete version of one or the other

✔ Netcom's NetCruiser or AOL's old AOL Web browser

✔ At least one version of Mosaic (NCSA, AirMosaic, or Spyglass)

✔ At least one version of Lynx

✔ Access to copies of at least one browser in all three of the most popular platforms (Windows, Unix, and the Mac)

The point is not that you need to look at your pages in every browser ever manufactured but that you have access to a wide variety of browsers at least for the final beta test; this ensures that most people can see your site. We're not demanding that you use Amiga Voyager, just that you be aware that not everyone has Netscape Navigator 4 or whatever supersedes it.

Additionally, many people use ISPs or commercial online services that recommend or include the use of Web browsers you may never have heard of. Beside the fact that not all software runs on all platforms, there are some other considerations when designing a site, such as slight display differences between UNIX, Mac, and PC (the three most popular platforms for viewing the Web). These differences include both alignment on the screen and *color shift;* this means that on a PC, colors appear slightly lighter in tint than on a Mac or a UNIX/Linux machine.

Web designer David Siegel's Web Wonk (`http://www.dsiegel.com/tips`) is a collection of smart tips for erstwhile Web designers. He covers the image-alignment shift between platforms, typography, and white-space control, among other hot topics.

Bandwidth (and the lack of it)

One crucial mistake many Webmasters make is overestimating the amount of bandwidth their visitors have access to. Ma and Pa McGillicuddy in Mt. Aukum may look at your site using a 9600 bps modem and a Mac Classic. They don't want to wait half an hour for your pages to load, so they may turn off automatic image loading or use a text-only browser. Keep in mind, too, that the World Wide Web is, after all, worldwide, and if you want folks in Europe, Asia, and the rest of the planet to see your site, you should follow these guidelines:

- ✔ Make sure your site doesn't depend on images to be useful.

- ✔ Make your image sizes small enough to load quickly.

- ✔ Keep total page size (that is the sum of the size of the HTML file along with any graphics) below 50K. (Okay, you can go up to 70K if you really insist.)

- ✔ Check your pages with a version of Lynx to make sure that text-only browsers can still read your site.

GIFWizard is simple software whose purpose in life is to help you reduce the file sizes of your GIF images. Check it out at `http://www.gifwizard.com`.

Making a friendly site

There are several ways to make sure that everyone who wants to visit your site can do so. Keep in mind that many tags and formatting techniques can be read only by Netscape Navigator and Microsoft Internet Explorer. These high-tech gizmos include such seemingly basic formats as tables, frames, background images, different font colors, and centered text, not to mention plug-ins, Java, and JavaScript. There are several ways to make your site visitable to everyone:

- ✔ Check your site in every browser you can get your hands on.

- ✔ Make a text-only version of your site for people with low-end browsers, computers, or modems.

- ✔ Be sure to offer text equivalents for every image or image map that acts as a link.

- ✔ Use descriptive ALT attributes with all of your images so people can decide whether they want to download them.

- ✔ Offer a frames version and a nonframes version of your site, and leave all the high-tech stuff out of the nonframes version.

- ✔ Make your entire site low-end. It can still look *really* good.

You can find out about Lynx, where it came from, and how to use it by reading the Lynx Users Guide, which is found at `http://www.cc.ukans.edu/lynx_help/Lynx_users_guide.html`.

Clicking with Lynx

Lynx (sounds like *links*) is a both the name of a specific piece of software and a nearly generic name for text-only browsers. Just because they're text-only doesn't mean that they're not *hyper*text — Lynx browsers still allow you to follow links, copy e-mail addresses to an e-mail program, and download hypermedia files, including images. The images just don't happen to be inline. For a long time, plain-text Web browsers were the only kind available, and they're still much faster than surfing the Web with images. Many people use Lynx when they're in a hurry, or when they're limited to a slow connection or a lousy modem and a dumb terminal. Purists say that your site doesn't look good unless it looks good in Lynx. While we don't go that far, it's a good idea to remember that many people — including those whose only access is through a public library or Internet cafe — still rely on Lynx as their Web browser, and you don't want to leave them out in the cold.

Download instructions are included. To take a quick look at your pages from a Lynx point of view, load your URL into a Lynx viewer, such as Steve's Lynx View, which we found at `http://www.miranova.com/~steve/Lynx-View.html`.

Why Even Include Interactive Content?

Ye Olde Guarde of the Internet, that being the folks who have been dialing it up since there was nothing but text to see online, are a little disappointed in the Web. How can that be, you ask? Well, the Web is now beginning to resemble television, and the problem with TV is that all you have to do is sit there and watch it. If what you get out of a medium has to do with what you put into it, then you can see the problem: Television isn't interactive, and very few Web sites make much of an effort to engage their readers any more than an episode of *Cops* does.

In an age when e-mail, newsgroups, chat rooms, and BBSs ruled the earth, interactivity was key. You can't have a one-way discussion. You can lecture to the masses and hear crickets in return, or you can present what you have to say in a way that engages a response, although that response may be a barrage of e-mail, a thicket of flame-filled posts, or a fan letter or two from like-minded Netizens. When text was the medium and the medium was the message, everyone who wanted to join the fun engaged in what's called *many-to-many* communications. Many people posted their messages, and many people read them. E-mail can also include both many-to-many and one-to-one communications, depending on whether you're writing a letter to your friend Frank or posting a hot stock tip to a mailing list about Wall Street.

Enter the Web, which made it easier to broadcast your every thought to the countless millions — as long as they could find your site. Why do you think so many personal home pages have a giant, flashing sign that says, "I ♥ E-MAIL! PLEASE SEND ME FEEDBACK!"? It's because the Web, as a medium, can engage in one-to-many, many-to-many, or many-to-one communications, but there's absolutely no evidence that guarantees that anyone is listening. Even hit counts can only pad your ego so far if you never hear from anyone who is clicking.

That's why *interactivity* has been the buzzword on the Web for so long. When someone clicks on a link, he or she can get many different things in return: another page; a picture, sound file, or video clip; or a message composition window. When you complicate the equation, however, and make the click result in something that challenges, surprises, or exceeds the user's expectation, they become engaged in your site. The more a visitor is encouraged to contribute to a Web site — especially in a way that instantly changes his experience of a site — the more they are going to think of themselves as having fun. They are using the Internet instead of just being online.

Electric Minds (`http://www.minds.com`; see Figure 7-3), Howard Rheingold's brain child, is an excellent example of real community on the Web. Other examples worth exploring include the Doonesbury Electronic Town Hall, at `http://www.doonesbury.com`, and ParentsPlace, at `http://www.parentsplace.com`.

Figure 7-3: Howard Rheingold invites you to join him and other Electric Minds on the Web.

What's interactive content, Mom?

Interactive doesn't mean high-tech. It means that your visitors are able to get a different experience from each trip to your site, depending on what they access, what you've added, and what they can do to change their experience of your site while they're there. That's right, we said that *they're* going to change *your* Web site. They do this by clicking on stuff, thereby voting on preferences, but one hopes that you also provide avenues they can use to input feedback and create a unique experience they just can't get from watching TV or reading a magazine.

Content, our second key word, should be self-explanatory, but people often confuse *anything* with *content.* You have to start with good cucumbers to make pickles that people want to eat, and you have to start with ideas — ideas that are based on your site's goals and mission — to make good content.

Remember your goals?

Way back in Chapter 2, we talk about the goal-setting process for your site. Depending on the type of site you're creating, the audience you're trying to attract, and the goals that you chose, you're going to have different needs and options for interactive content. Again, there are six likely purposes that Web sites fulfill:

- ✔ Entertain
- ✔ Inform
- ✔ Sell
- ✔ Promote
- ✔ Distribute
- ✔ Research/report

Perhaps your site, The Social Climber, is a virtual storefront for an adventure travel company that sells climbing and camping gear, maps, and guided wilderness travel packages and caters to the singles market. Your goals are to sell your products, promote your company, and inform your clientele about your company and camping and climbing in general.

What purpose would be served, then, by a flashing Java marquee that says "Climbing is FUN!"? Whether these ubiquitous (and ugly) flashing banners serve a purpose at all, other than eating bandwidth, is moot. Our point is to remind you that you're getting ready to invest time, money, personnel, and computer resources in a Web site. You've probably heard the word *interactivity* so much that you're not sure what it is, but you know you have to have it — kind of like that other buzz phrase, *added value.*

Picking and Choosing Interactive Content

Interactive content doesn't just mean Java, just like it doesn't just mean chat, intelligent agents, or push technology. While it can and does generally mean that you've added something more than just the hypertext and images that you see on virtually every Web site, it's also important to remember what the two key words *interactive* and *content* mean.

The smart money

What can Joe and JoAnn, the proprietors of the Social Climber, do to make their site truly interactive and a truly good example of content?

There isn't a single right answer here, although there may be several wrong ones. There are many different technologies you can use to create an interactive feel to your content, and the ones you choose depend on your goals, strategies, and available resources. The following is a look at what Joe and JoAnn should and should not do to make their site interactive.

Right	*Wrong*
Host a weekly chat to talk about real trips Social Climber customers have taken.	Put up a guestbook, call it a chat page, and tell people to start talking.
Implement a clickable map that highlights all of the travel areas that the company covers, which leads customers to information about every site on the map.	Implement a clickable map of the world, and when people click on a place the company doesn't cover, tell them "We're working on that part."
Use JavaScript to update the table of contents and direct people to areas of the site they may like, depending on what they click on.	Use JavaScript to make the colors change arbitrarily every time a user clicks on anything.
Create a VRML representation of an adventure hike that includes VRML links to facts and figures, hotlists of other adventure sites, and photographs of places to visit.	Create a VRML representation of the company storefront. Nothing is clickable, users can't use it to shop, but those backpacks and tents sure look cool in 3-D!
Offer a Java "personal shopper" that recommends camping gear or tours based on the number of people in the group, the length of the stay, the preferred climate, and other customer input.	Offer a Java "personal shopper" that recommends camping gear based on the user's favorite color (red or blue).

Right	Wrong
Make a Shockwave mini-movie that lets users navigate their way through a tour from start to finish. Include video, film stills, maps, and an audio narrative of what the trip was like.	Make a Shockwave game that lets visitors scare away e-bears by throwing virtual rocks at them.
Sponsor a travel essay or photography contest, and give away camping gear as prizes. Post all of the best entries on the site.	Offer a free flashlight to anyone who is willing to design the Social Climber site.

We realize that many of the examples in the Wrong column are silly, but that doesn't mean that people don't waste quite a bit of time and money putting frighteningly similar material on their own companies' sites. With careful planning, any of the content-rich, informative, and entertaining ideas in the Right column wouldn't cost any more than the geegaws thrown around in the Wrong column.

So what are your options?

Here, next, we go through some of the most popular options for livening up your site. Keep in mind that if no one on your staff knows how to do these things, you can still outsource most of them. (Chapter 8 covers outsourcing.)

Intel and CNET collaborated to create the most high-tech site yet. If you want interactive, try the Mediadome, at http://www.mediadome.com.

Java

Java isn't a cure-all, a hit-getter, or even an attention grabber unless it's used wisely. Java is just a programming language, albeit a platform-independent, incredibly flexible one. People have written entire Web browsers in Java, and its potential capabilities increase every time the limits are pushed by an innovative programmer. Java's amazing uses certainly aren't limited to animated dancing bears and light-up tables of contents, although those are certainly popular gimmicks. Java is an incredibly efficient method of interface design, especially where databases and the Web intersect. You can create entire freestanding applications, make your advertisements automated, or simply spark up your pages using Java, although it generally requires someone good with programming to get anything remarkable or complex accomplished.

Johns Hopkins University's Java resources collection (`http://www.apl.jhu.edu/~hall/java`) is a great place to start learning about Java programming. If you would rather look at some existing applets, try SGI's Java Showcase at `http://www.sgi.com/Fun/free/java-apps.html`.

JavaScript

JavaScript, while not as robust a language as Java, nonetheless has several advantages; for one thing, it's not as difficult for nonprogrammers to learn to use. JavaScripts are generally placed within the HTML document for the Web page itself so that, after the page is loaded, the JavaScript is enabled. On the other hand, Java applets can take several minutes to load. JavaScript can be used for mini-applets, animations, navigation and interface tools, and all kinds of other functions, including error checking. JavaScript was developed by Netscape Communications, although Microsoft has added JavaScript capabilities to its Internet Explorer.

Netscape's own guide to JavaScript can be found at the following URL: `http://home.netscape.com/eng/mozilla/Gold/handbook/javascript/index.html`.

The JavaScript Tip of the Week site (`http://webreference.com/javascript/`) has a nice repository of useful and fun things you can accomplish with JavaScript.

VRML

Although VRML hasn't yet revolutionized the Internet the way its proponents suggested it would, it is an incredibly innovative way to present information. The Virtual Reality Modeling Language (VRML) is a programming and rendering language that's used to create three-dimensional environments that are navigable from within a Web browser, such as Netscape Navigator, or a VRML browser, such as V*Realm. Users can fly through imaginary landscapes, walk through a virtual storefront, or spin and even walk inside everyday objects. It's a fascinating development in the world of information architecture, although most VRML worlds now serve the realms of pure entertainment or pure science.

ActiveX/Active Platform

Microsoft's Active Platform language uses already-familiar Microsoft programming components, such as Visual Basic (for software authoring) and OLE (for interapplication compatibility), to extend its Internet Explorer Web browser's capabilities. Anyone who can write in Visual Basic can create an ActiveX control that can be added to Internet Explorer's repertoire. ActiveX is being used to create many cool games and animation effects, but it's also a gateway into real online collaboration. Using ActiveX, you can make

Microsoft Word and Excel documents accessible to an Internet or intranet community so that people can change the content of an online document in real time. Writing ActiveX controls can be useful for multimedia presentations, navigating a Web site, or creating an interface to a database.

Visit ActiveX.com to find demonstrations of Active Platform and links galore that can tell you how you can use it. The full URL is `http://www.activex.com/`.

Multimedia plug-ins

Some time ago, Netscape extended into infinity by opening its Navigator software to plug-ins, and the Web has never been the same. Plug-ins are external applications that, rather than launching as separate software from the browser, display a non-HTML media type within the browser window. In other words, the Web can include any media type you can digitize.

Companies such as Macromedia have made great use of plug-ins by making CD-ROM – quality multimedia movies and games accessible on the Web. Consequently, media designers have more flexibility with the kinds of content they can put online, and Macromedia sold a great deal of Director software so people could put Shockwave on their site.

Unless you're already a software company, it doesn't make much sense to write your own browser plug-in. There are over 300 plug-ins available for Netscape Navigator — choose a popular one that you've seen used a lot, and you could find the perfect conduit for your ideas, especially if they're ideas of sound, video, or multimedia.

Macromedia's Shockwave, which you can download and play with at `http://www.macromedia.com/shockwave`, is the best expression of what plug-ins are designed for.

Push media

Push is a big word in multimedia online communications. Until push came along, people "pulled" content to them, by choosing a page or clicking on a link, and thus loading a page or other media. Looked at another way, in the more traditional "pull" the user requests data from a server, while in "push" the server serves data without waiting to be asked for it.

Got that? Push technologies allow content providers (Webmasters like you) to push content to the user without the tired old business of waiting for the user to find you and request it. Of course, the user can refuse your oh-so-generous offering — and waste a lot of time and make many enemies if you go around pushing stuff at people who don't want it. (Hmmm . . . *push spamming*!) But this new concept even still turns the model of information delivery on the Web around 180 degrees.

Push technology is particularly useful for delivering real-time news, stock prices, or any other data that changes quickly and without notice. Some software companies are also looking into push as a way to deliver bug fixes or version updates to users.

PointCast, with its three-pronged approach, was one of the first to use content *channels* that were pushed to the user. PointCast not only used a Web browser plug-in to deliver content, but the plug-in was available as a screen saver and a standalone client, too. Today, other companies, including InterMind, Marimba, and Netscape Communications, are offering their takes on push media, which can be used to deliver news, entertainment, games, and reference material — in short, anything that *could* appear on a Web page but is instead being delivered through a filter, a proprietary information service, or a personal librarian.

Visit the PointCast Network at `http://www.pointcast.com`. Other push examples include InterMind Communicator (`http://www.intermind.com`), Marimba's Castanet tuner (`http://www.marimba.com`), and Netscape's Netcaster, at: `http://home.netscape.com/comprod/products/communicator/netcaster.html`.

Custom scripting

If you have access to a wily programmer (or several of them), you can get just about anything done. Smart folks online have written their own Web software that works within the HTML environment to accomplish many things. Here are some ideas that you may have already considered:

- A login system that offers perks to registered users

- Browser cookies (explained in Chapter 15) that track visitors and remember who they are and what they did the last time that they visited

- Shopping-cart systems (explained in Chapter 3) that keep a log of what people bought — and what they considered buying

- So-called intelligent agents, which compile sets of preferences and retrieve information based on customer preferences and profiles

- Randomization scripts that change the look of the site with every visit

- Advanced guestbook utilities that offer your users the chance to contribute something useful to the site

- Fun gadgets such as personality tests, recipe finders, or wine suggesters

Most of these things can be accomplished with some knowledge of PERL and a few CGI scripts, although the more complex the process is, the more time (and code) it involves.

An incredibly simple and creative use of CGI scripting can be experienced by visiting the Surrealism Server at: `http://pharmdec.wustl.edu/juju/surr/surrealism.html`.

What's Involved in Implementing Interactive Content

Most, if not all, really interesting live content involves some heavy-duty programming and possibly some multimedia editing skills. Having a programmer in-house may be advantageous if you're undertaking a huge project that needs constant maintenance. But in most cases, you can outsource much of the programming to independent contractors or consulting firms. (See Chapters 8 and 11.)

Whoever is put in charge of implementing your site's hardware should be intimately familiar with your plans to extend the site. You may need to consider security issues for media like RealAudio and Java, and there are disk space and bandwidth issues involved in broadcasting things other than text.

Make sure that, when you undertake making a large part of your site dependent on any sort of non-HTML programming, you have the staff or the contract to maintain the site after it's launched. Things break, new quirks arise, and the script that works fine today may not be able to meet your demands six months from now.

When you publicize your site, you shouldn't need to rely on the high-tech aspects of your site to get people to show up. But don't let the fact that you have some cool code to show off go unnoticed. Many sites that have complex CGI scripts running the show from behind the scenes don't make much out of it, and that's fine. But if you have some killer Shockwave animation, which you paid a lot for, that's hidden deep within your site, no one is going to find it unless you make it easy to find.

Talking about Discussion Groups

Discussion group is a broad term that's used to mean any type of online communication in which people communicate with people (versus computers, for example). The emphasis is on give-and-take rather than on broadcasting. There are several ways to implement a discussion group, the most popular being newsgroups and e-mail distribution lists. Both of these formats require very little in the way of initial setup, although the maintenance can be time-intensive if you're planning on moderating a discussion group.

Moderation is the key, or rather it may be. A nonmoderated discussion group is a free-for-all: Anyone can post anything at any time, and it's distributed to the entire group with no screening process in place. While this may be a good idea for some kinds of discussion, a moderator may be useful for groups in which a strong signal-to-noise ratio is important. In these cases, a person or team of people reads every post that comes into the discussion group before it's posted to the entire list. In this way, the moderator can screen out the spam, flames, misposts, and other irrelevant messages. While this generally gives the discussion group more content and less junk, it also makes life much harder for the moderating person, especially if he or she has other tasks to accomplish.

Making e-mail your friend

Running an e-mail distribution list can be an extremely cost-effective way to get the word out about your site, both initially and over time. Basically, there are two kinds of mailing lists you can run: an *announcement list* and a *discussion list.* An announcement list is fairly self-explanatory: Folks sign up to receive e-mail on a semiregular basis, and you send them what amounts to a newsletter, telling them what's new at the site and why they should come back for another visit.

On the other hand, a discussion list involves input from the readers themselves. This can be a great way to make your users feel like they're involved in your site; it can also be a real pain in the assets. Discussion lists can be either moderated or unmoderated, but generally you must put someone in charge of administrating the list to make sure no one abuses the list for advertising purposes or some other personal or political agenda. It's your list, remember? A moderator can also gently steer the conversation back to the topic at hand, whether it's comparison shopping or quantum physics.

Making news with newsgroups

Newsgroups are great forums in which (if it's seen as okay in that particular newsgroup) you can announce happenings in your company, your industry, or your Web site. They're discussion groups, too, so it's generally a good idea to have at least one person in your company who is committed to keeping up with newsgroups related to your field. This person, if he or she has the time to devote to it, can make posts to the newsgroup offering expert advice, not just advertisements. A discreet SIG file at the end of each post can signify to the online community that your company is devoted to being a part of that community, and to offering free advice. The better a member of the group your rep is, the more likely he or she is to gain respect — and bring visitors to your site.

The vice versa

Remember that you can join mailing lists as well as run them and that you can make your own newsgroups as well as join existing ones. Netscape Communicator's Collabra component, for example, makes it easy to create and moderate your own private newsgroup, and many e-mail programs offer filtering and forwarding options that simplify subscribing to and participating in mailing lists.

Can We Chat?

Chatting is still the most interactive form of content you can easily put online. It's people talking to people, only better: It's people talking to people they've never met in person. (Okay, they're really typing, not talking — why quibble?) Chat is incredibly addictive after people get past the fact that it's text-based, and it takes most people a few tries to enjoy it.

When you're considering what kind of chat to run, remember to consider your audience. Who do they want to talk to the most: a celebrity, an expert in the field, or each other? Does basing the chat on a specific topic help promote conversation? Would people prefer a Q&A session, an interview they can just follow, or a gab session? Is privacy important? Would they like to be able to meet privately with other chat members? Does your audience include children?

Implementing Web chat

Creating a successful Web chat area requires a bit more thought and effort than just slapping a guestbook onto your site, although from all the mediocre chat areas on the Web, you would hardly be able to tell that this is true. One site that has used the guestbook model of chat to great ends is Bianca's Smut Shack. Don't visit it unless you're open to seeing a lot of dirty words, but if you can deal with the high-octane sexual subject matter, it's an excellent case study in running a chat house on a Web site.

Wanna chat? Are you male or female? Bianca's Smut Shack (http:// www.bianca.com/) is one of the most successful chat areas that exists, although the content *is* adult oriented. Others to try are Chat Soup, at http://www.chatsoup.com/, and Chatting.com, at http://www.chatting .com/. For a list of popular Web-based chats, try Hot100's list, at : http:// www.hot100.com/chat.chtml.

One problem with using a guestbook format for a so-called chat space is that many implementations of this form require the users to press their browser's Reload button before they see new messages. However, using CGI scripts, it's a simple process to have the chat auto-reload every minute or so (or every time that the user posts his or her message to the page).

Another important issue to consider when implementing a chat space of any kind is the privacy of the users who use the space. You want to create a certain level of accountability so that people don't have complete impunity to harass or insult other users, particularly if you're creating an all-ages forum. However, many people don't use a chat space or bulletin board if their e-mail address is attached to every message. One popular compromise is requiring users to create a login ID to participate. In this way, you can track down and chastise (or remove) users who disregard your guidelines, but honest people don't have to expose their e-mail addresses if they don't want to. An excellent example of this type of system is HotWired's bulletin boards. Creating a login ID at HotWired or its chat site, Talk.com, is free, private, and instantaneous, and users can choose whether their e-mail address is made public.

Register with HotWired, or at least find out how to do it, by visiting `http://www.hotwired.com/reception/joi`. After you register, try your hand at Talk.com (`http://www.talk.com`), a Java chat system that's hip, stylish, *and* functional.

Running an IRC session

IRC (Internet Relay Chat) is an interesting member of the Internet family of tools. IRC has been around since the dinosaur days; that is, it's an all-text medium that's nonetheless engaging, addictive, and easier to use than it looks. IRC has the additional benefit of leaving issues of anonymity and findability up to the participants, which releases you from a lot of technical and legal headaches.

What IRC does

So what is it? Basically, like Usenet, IRC consists of many IRC servers that are together via the Internet. IRC uses the same type of client – server protocol most Internet media use. At various points around the globe, there are IRC servers that store the data sent to them by the clients. (The clients are both the software packages that send messages to the server.) The servers store information about the chat rooms themselves, the *channels*. This data includes the name of the room, the person or people in charge of it, the people who are in the room, and what they're saying. The people who join a room can be anywhere in the world, and their messages are sent directly to the server that they're logged into, which then *relays* it to the other IRC servers on the network — hence the name.

IRC is based on the old `talk` function that still exists in many Unix shell accounts. You can join a discussion that holds hundreds of people babbling at each other, you can be invited into a private chat room with just a few people holding meaningful conversation, you can create your own private or public room and invite people in, or you can "whisper" to just one other person who also happens to be in the same chat room with you.

Why IRC?

The benefit of running an IRC session rather than setting up a Web chat or using proprietary chat software is that it isn't absolutely essential to run your own server or even have much technical know-how beyond what it takes to participate in a chat. If you're planning on running a well-publicized chat with a rarely seen celebrity, setting up your own IRC server can have its benefits. But even then, some chat software companies, such as Quarterdeck (the company that makes GlobalChat) are more than willing to help you set up and publicize a chat if you recommend that your participants use that company's software. In short, running an IRC session can be basically free in terms of money, and it can cost you little in time as well.

What kind of chat is right for you?

No matter what technical form you use to set up a chat, you need to decide what sort of content it's going to include. Obviously, the quality of the chat depends on the people who participate, but different kinds of chats attract different people.

Hosting a special-event chat

One tried-and-true way to host a chat is to bill it as a special event. Book a celebrity, an expert in your field, or an author; schedule an event; or even pick a topic. Then advertise it. From there, you can choose to run it as an interview, in which anyone can "watch" the chat, but a host is the only one who can actually "speak" to your guest. Or you can make it a free-for-all, in which anyone with a connection can shout questions at the celebrity speaker. It's somewhat like the difference between a call-in radio talk show and a live Q&A session. Either way, you need a good moderator to hold your celebrity guest's hand through the whole thing, especially if he or she isn't particularly Net-savvy.

Regardless of what kind of chat you decide to run, make sure your Web site includes specific instructions on how to log in, how to participate, what the rules for discussion are (if any), and where and when the chat is to be held.

Running an open chat space

You can also make chat space available on your site that doesn't have any special attraction other than the fact that it exists. Some sites have chat spaces that are open 24/7. Not only do these sites require more technical maintenance and more disk space, they also require more in the way of moderation, especially if yours is not an age-restricted site. Although you may run into an infestation of obnoxious teenagers using swear words, a far more common dilemma is what happens when no one shows up at all.

Some sites have the clever idea of running special-event chats that take place within regular chat rooms that are open at all hours. Attracting people for a special chat session from 5 to 6 p.m. about bike safety in your neighborhood can be accomplished with the right level of publicity. After people have found your chat room and after they've attended a special event there, they're more likely to show up as participants — productive and attractive ones, you hope.

Chat and the other beyond-HTML options described in this chapter are really only a beginning. To stay abreast of what's happening in online content, stay in touch with your Webmaster compadres. Get hooked up with one of the groups mentioned at the end of Chapter 1; learn as you go, and pick up tips and insights into new, good stuff. That's the ticket.

Chapter 8

Jobbing Out to a Web-Publishing Shop

. . . .

In This Chapter

▶ Knowing and selecting from the various types of shops

▶ Judging experience, style, substance, and service

▶ Defining a project for all the players

▶ Managing costs

▶ Understanding contracts and nondisclosure agreements

▶ Maintaining good client – vendor relationships

. . . .

Maybe you have a staff, and maybe you don't. Maybe yours is a "virtual" organization, which pulls together skilled people from various venues depending on what type of projects you have going.

Whether it's for a short-term project or with a long-term understanding, or whether a whole site is under construction or just a bit of programming needs to be done, plenty of Webmasters work with lots of outside vendors. Knowing how to pick the right companies or individuals and knowing how to handle those oh-so-important contracts and relationships can be a big part of Webmastering.

Types of Shops You May Encounter

No two Web-publishing shops are alike in every aspect. Even two shops that seem on the surface to offer identical services have different slants on things — this is true in every field, right? Yet Web-publishing shops do fall into some general categories, and understanding what these are can be your first step in choosing among them.

A Web-shop success story

Web site coordinator Marcy Lyon says, "We contracted out for the development of our entire site, from HTML to graphics to database programming. The main advantage was that we got ten professionals in different areas working on our Web site: a database programmer, two types of designers, an HTML person, a technical writer, someone who specialized in Web-site navigation, and a slew of others whose roles I don't even know. They did a fantastic job, and the company provided all of the paperwork and managed another firm that provides quotes for our Web site. They had clearly defined goals and milestones and more documentation than most people would think you would need, although it's really paid off in the final analysis."

Internet presence providers

Internet presence providers, or IPPs, offer their clients Web hosting, design and implementation, and sometimes even consulting. An IPP's computers are usually connected directly to the Internet (see Chapter 11), and many businesses find storing or hosting their Web site at an IPP to be an economical or business-savvy alternative to purchasing and maintaining their own Web server.

In cases where the IPP provides only hosting but no content development, design, or implementation, you may end up hiring a second (or even third) company to take on those tasks. You may also have your own staff to handle all that. Matters to be taken into consideration in these situations are covered in Chapters 10 and 11.

In cases where the IPP claims to provide full service, including content development, design, and implementation, ask the IPP personnel (and yourself) whether the IPP has a fully staffed Web-publishing team that works independently of the Web-hosting team. Or (shudder), is the IPP's publishing staff just Tom in tech support who is going to be working on your site between calls?

Be sure to interview a potential IPP (or any other Web shop) carefully. Answers to these key questions may foreshadow your experience in working with a given IPP:

- ✔ How large is the IPP's Web-publishing staff? Who's on staff, what do they do, and what sort of background do they bring to the project?

- ✔ Is Web publishing the IPP's only function? If not, what else does it do? What percentage of its time is devoted to which functions?

> ✔ To have access to the Web-publishing staff, must one purchase Web-hosting services at the IPP? What sort of packages or short- or long-term deals are available for each?

Working with an IPP for both your hosting and Web-publishing needs can be an ideal solution for those who can't take on the responsibility of staff (equipment, hiring and training, benefits, insurance, and so on). No one knows the ins and outs of a specific Web server better than the people who own and run it, and if the IPP is a reputable one, it is presumably up on the latest technologies and techniques. The downside, however, may come if the IPP's Web-publishing group is poorly staffed or underdeveloped, or if Web production takes a back seat to urgent matters on the hosting side. IPP services are definitely not cheap. The end cost may be no higher than hiring your own staff or using the services of an ISP and a Web-publishing shop that does no hosting. But if the IPP is an ad agency (again, see Chapter 11), costs may soar.

Ad agencies

If yours is the type of company that retains an ad agency, having that agency create or oversee the creation of your Web site may not be a bad idea. The agency presumably knows the media message and style you feel are appropriate to your company's marketing mission, and it probably employs many creative and talented people. However, working on Web stuff is a new endeavor for most ad agencies, and they don't always understand the difference between creating ads or brochures and producing compelling content that brings in traffic.

Before you turn over responsibility for the development of your site to an ad agency — even a reputable, familiar one — make sure it has people on staff with real Web experience. If the agency you have on retainer or often work with doesn't have good, previous Web experience but you want to keep them in the loop for the sake of continuity in your overall media presence, we recommend that you have the agency work on the concept for the site and then review roughs developed by another, more Web-savvy company.

Either the ad agency or you can hire the Web shop. However, if the ad agency does the hiring, it is most likely going to feel it should control the Web developers. Perhaps a better strategy is to manage the project yourself, with the ad agency providing input and the Web shop also providing input into what can work (at least technically) on the Web.

If the ad agency you work with is genuinely Web-savvy, you're set. You may find having the agency do your site is the route to an overall media presence that sends just the right message to all fronts.

Design firms and publishing shops large and small

Design firms come in different sizes and configurations, from the big, famous type that charges high fees and accepts only those clients they see as cool to the small, independent operators (and even virtual organizations) that pull together talent from a pool of freelancers. Which type works for you (if any) is a big question that brings into play your budget, how much outsourcing you really want to do, and what your site's overall goals are.

Big, exclusive design firms

Big-name design firms (like Organic Online, Razorfish, and a host of slightly lesser-known shops) almost always have many people on staff who are skilled in all of the hip and happening Web-design techniques. You can expect their staffs to include marketing moguls; programmers and database developers; video and sound producers; public relations pros; dozens of artists, typographers, and other multimedia whizzes; and the usual crew of assorted production folks. In some cases, the key phrase describing these firms may be *design for design's sake*, but that's not always such a bad idea. This is much the way that big, famous ad agencies work — they establish a certain style that they market to their clients. If your audience responds well to first-class treatment with a touch of exclusivity, this may be the path to success. Your site is going to be stunning and probably also very navigable, with strong technical underpinnings. You should also plan to pay a hefty price for this service. Some of these houses are able to screen their clients and accept only a chosen few — their services often can be had for no less than a $100,000 commitment and then only if you, the client, seem as cool to them as they seem to others.

Boutique shops

A *boutique shop,* one that has between 5 and 20 employees on staff, also often specializes in a specific design style or type of client. Here, again, you find most design and implementation staff in-house, including those performing specialized jobs such as converting video and sound files to the appropriate Web formats and implementing cutting-edge programming and database techniques. When you sign up with a shop like this, a handful of people may be deployed as a team for producing your site. These folks may or may not be on staff; they may be pulled from a pool of freelancers. The team may include some or all of the following specialists:

- **A producer,** or project manager, who manages the design and production process
- **A designer,** who creates the site's look and feel, including the theme, metaphors, palette, typography, and special element placement

✔ **Artist(s),** who create and/or edit graphics to be included in the site (often with direction from the designer)

✔ **Programmer(s),** who implement the programming and scripts needed to make forms, Java applets, message boards, chat areas, or other specialized applications that run on the site

✔ **Production staff,** or coder(s), who translate the output of the designer and artists into HTML

The titles of Web-publishing staff vary among companies. You may be assigned any configuration of folks who have an array of titles. At a minimum, you should be assigned a producer or project manager who then acts as your primary contact throughout either the project or your entire relationship with this firm.

Boutique shops can be a great choice when you don't want to pay the big bucks to a big-name design firm but want and need the security of working with a proven team that can function like a well-oiled machine. Prices vary widely for these firms; our advice is to read through this chapter to get insight into the jobbing-out process and then get a few bids before you settle on finalists.

Small, independent operators

Small, independent operators in the Web-design business are popping up like video stores did in the early 1980s. Often, these outfits consist of an owner, and . . . well, that may be it. Or there may be a pool of freelancers backing that person up. If the owner of a small shop does have a pool of freelancers he or she works with on a regular basis, that again offers the advantage of working with a proven team. Keep in mind when you work with a small shop that the skills of the owner often define the primary skills of the shop. If yours is a project with a big database component, strong database skills are more important, while if you need more help with content, a content developer is important. In any case, when you investigate small shops, look into how relationships between the primary shop owner and any freelancers are defined, and whether the principals understand the processes they are subcontracting out.

Small Web-publishing shops may take on only one large project at a time. If so and if your site is that project, you have their full attention from beginning to end. On the downside, if a small shop is mid-project when you approach it, the shop may be unable to get started right away. In some cases, small shops can be a very economical alternative. They can also offer more personal service, and for small-to-midsize projects, they may be a good choice, especially if you find one with which you can maintain an ongoing and successful relationship.

Finding Qualified Web Shops

As is true in many other areas of life, word-of-mouth referrals are often the best source of information about Web-publishing shops. Contact the Webmasters of sites you admire; ask them who designed their sites and how to contact those firms. (Of course, you may run into some who do all of their development work in-house!)

You can also find referrals (though without personal references) through professional organizations such as those cited at the end of Chapter 1. In that case, you often find that members of the professional organization have posted samples of their work on the organization's site so that you can see what they do; the organization may also include an e-mail address so that you can make easy contact.

Yahoo! (`http://www.yahoo.com`), one of the most popular search tools on the Internet, devotes whole sections to the sites of Web-publishing shops. Do a quick search there, and see what turns up. You can try the Internet services area (Figure 9-1), which can be found at `http://www.yahoo.com/Business_and_Economy/Companies/Internet_Services/`.

Regional listings may be found at `http://www.yahoo.com/Regional/`.

As you seek a Web-publishing outfit or design firm, refer again to the mission statement you wrote at the end of Chapter 2. Keep those goals in mind as you review each shop's style, experience, skills, and references. If your primary mission is to provide technical support for your products, a shop that specializes in slick, mood-driven design and postmodern copy may not be the one for you.

How are you going to figure out who is worth working with when you have a few candidates in mind? You must judge their experience, style, and the depth of their abilities. We cover those topics next.

Judging experience

As with hiring an employee or contracting with another vendor, you have to evaluate the experience of potential Web-publishing shops before you hire one. Any shop with even basic public relations and marketing skills is more than happy to tell you what it does best. The following points are what you want to know:

> ✔ **Where did these folks come from?** With commercial development of the World Wide Web still in its relative infancy, most people who are employed in this field bring with them some background from another field. (We cover this in Chapter 1.) Some people have rich experience gleaned in related fields such as publishing, print design, marketing,

and programming; others were plumbers. We're great believers in the transferability of skills, and as we point out in Chapter 1, no one has a degree in any aspect of Web development yet. But you must make sure that the staff at your prospective Web-publishing shop actually has those transferable skills. You may want to review Chapter 1 to get the lowdown on the skills various Webmasters may have and what fields these folks may come from.

✔ **Does their background translate to ability?** Many skill sets lend themselves to Web publishing. (Again, see Chapter 1.) The catch here is to know how well those skills have been adapted to the unique requirements of the Web world. Artists in the Web world have to be concerned with the limitations of color depth and density that arise in Web design. Print publishers simply must relax the layout control they're used to having and come to grips with the flexible nature of HTML layout. Advertising and marketing pros are faced with a medium that combines some of the best — and the worst — of all the media they've previously worked with. Techies have to become more conversant in visual design issues than is generally needed in traditional programming and MIS fields.

✔ **Does their background and focus fit your goals?** Remember that mission statement that you drew up in Chapter 2? Pull it out again, and review it side by side with each prospective shop's offerings. A shop with a solid background in advertising or marketing may be a good match for a site whose purpose is to inform and excite. A technical shop should do well with a site that's geared toward user support for your new widget product line. Make sure their focus is compatible with yours.

Obviously, artistic talent is necessary in producing a site whose goals make a designerly look a requirement. If that talent isn't present in the prospective Web shop's principals, design can be subcontracted without a problem. But should the artist be required to have extended years of experience in *computer-created* graphics? Not necessarily. Designers and artists in the print and advertising worlds have skills required of all artists: an eye for color, a sense of placement, and knowledge of visual balance. Adaptability to the constraints of Web publishing is key to those people's success in the Web world. Knowing how to convert graphics that are deeply saturated with color into files small enough that they don't choke your modem separates the standard artist from the Web artist.

On the technical side, one may think any programming experience is acceptable, but again, programming for the Web takes many forms. Someone with experience developing spreadsheet applications or video games may not have the programming skills and experience mix necessary for Web programming. New languages (Java, JavaScript, ActiveX) and technologies (Marimba and more) are introduced to Web developers at breakneck speed. It takes a talented and impassioned technical staff to keep up the pace and to separate hype from real utility so they can focus on what's important.

Time and the Web

The Web has only been around for a few short years. Almost no one got into the industry right away, and anyone who tells you that he or she has ten years of Web experience is full of hogwash. If some shop does claim more than two or three years of experience, ask the personnel to define that experience. Do they simply mean that they had an e-mail connection for seven years? (That's not very impressive.) Were they actively publishing content on *gopher servers,* a forerunner of the Web, for the first six years of their eight-year history? Have they been on the graphics side of computer game development for four years before migrating to full-fledged multimedia CD-ROM production two years ago? "Years of experience" can mean many things, but more than two or three years of experience on the Web is well nigh impossible.

Quantifying experience and success

How many accounts a shop has handled doesn't necessarily indicate the quality of that shop's experience, but knowing this information can help you define the breadth of its experience — especially if the accounts have been for a widely diverse or an intensely focused client base.

In Chapter 2, you considered what would qualify your site as a success; you can get more information about that in Chapter 15. Get a clear picture of what will qualify as success for your site. Then ask the prospective shop to tell you how success was defined in each of the sites it feels most proud of, whether those success benchmarks were reached, and how long that took. If you're planning a site that is to include online sales, ask the prospective Web-shop personnel what sites they have done for online merchants and what impact their input had on that aspect of the project. Did sales increase as much as or more than predicted? Did the customer base grow into previously untapped markets? Has the client been satisfied with the process of delivering and handling those sales? Did the shop follow up or find out about success?

References are paramount

Prospective Web shops should provide you with at least three references from current or recent clients. Get the name of the decision-making contact, an address and phone number, and a URL for the Web site the shop created for that client. First, investigate the site that was created (more on this in the next section). Then, when you contact the reference, interview your contact with these questions in mind:

 ✔ Who was your primary contact at the Web shop? Was this person professional, and how did he or she handle any problems that arose? Did you deal with anyone else, and if so, what was that person like?

✔ Was the site delivered on schedule? How was the schedule organized? Were alpha and beta versions of the site delivered as expected?

✔ Was the site delivered within the allotted budget? What glitches or surprises occurred, and how did the shop handle that?

✔ Did the Web shop perform as expected? Did the quality of what it produced match its promised expertise?

✔ Would you do business with this shop again? If not, why? If so, what would you like to have done differently the next time?

Because vendor references are not nearly as legally sensitive as employee references have become, you should get good information from contacting a prospective Web shop's references. Ask specific questions, and make sure you take notes.

Judging style and substance

So you get those handy references in your mitts, and what do you do with the URLs? Fire up your browser, and go forth to look them over, that's what. Study them in detail, but don't stop there. Most Web-publishing shops maintain their own Web sites. Forget looking at the site itself, and head for a section on that site where links to client sites are provided. Review these sites as well as those you were given as references, remembering that these are the projects the shop is most proud of.

Can you clearly see what the mission or purpose of one site or another may be? What did the Web shop do (or not do) in designing and implementing the site to further that mission? On reviewing the site, have you learned something about the company that owns the site? Does its products or services interest you? Have you been persuaded to make a purchase or request more information? Your own responses to other sites can be a valuable indicator of the response others may have to this shop's work.

Plays well with others

How vendors — including your Web shop — interact with in-house staff and even other vendors has a big effect on the success of your endeavors. Points to ponder as you think this over include not just how often but *how* (in what style) they communicate, how willing they are to maintain communications with others, what office hours they keep, and what client-to-producer ratio they maintain. (Is your Web endeavor going be put on hold for another deadline?) Avoid the arrogant, crabby, or blaming Web shop in favor of one that is respectful, communicative, and responsible.

View awards with caution

Awards can indicate experience and quality, but only if the awards are recognized and respected, and if they are based on clearly defined criteria. See Chapter 15, where we talk about measures of Web-site success in general. When you're judging Web shops, consider with caution any awards they've received. You may want to review the awarding organization's methods for selection and judging, as well as its credibility, before you decide that an award validates the shop's capabilities.

Ask specific questions, including (as applicable) whether the shop is going to work directly with your ISP or in-house IS group to coordinate installation and future updates. Does the shop expect you to handle all of those communications? It's okay if you're going to handle it as long as you know this up front and the shop provides you with all the information you need. This is something you can explore during an early interview with a shop; pay attention to whether its personnel respond completely or only offer half comments.

We saw a recent case where a Web shop A was hired to revamp an existing site, and before the contracts were signed, it became clear the shop was going to have to work with another shop B to coordinate the sharing of a big database with a sister site. Shop A visibly balked when this was mentioned, while shop B responded cooperatively. Shop A was hired and did the site revamping, while shop B worked on the database. Throughout the whole project, shop A balked and complained about many matters large and small, while shop B kept a very calm and cooperative attitude. The project was finished, and one vendor was retained to maintain both sites. Guess which one?

Here are some more questions to keep in mind:

- How proactive are the shop people in coordinating with your marketing, public relations, and other staff?
- Do the personnel expect perfectly complete and final copy to be delivered to them, or can they reach out and ask questions and accept a few last-minute alterations?
- How are the people going to be about delivering the site and getting your final approval?
- How is the site actually going to get onto your server?
- Can they install the site for you?
- Can the site be delivered on a zip drive or other portable storage media?

✔ If you plan to use a virtual server, can the shop gain full access to upload the files and set permissions for the programmed functions to operate?

They listen, but do they hear?

During your conversations with Web-shop candidates, beware of these red flags that should inspire you to consider another choice:

✔ Are you presented only with predefined templates to choose from rather than having a considered and carefully constructed plan for your site based on information you gave these folks? (Chapter 6 describes making a site plan and writing a design document.)

✔ Do the shop personnel try to shoehorn your site into addressing just one goal — even if your mission statement covers several? (Chapter 2 covers setting goals for your site.)

✔ Do the personnel try to copy a competitor's site with the intent of mimicking that success rather than taking an original approach?

✔ Do the people quote prices or present a proposal without first discussing your site with you in detail?

If any of these flags pop up during conversations with a prospective Web shop, don't immediately exclude that firm from consideration, but investigate the area that makes you pause in much more detail by asking more questions and by making clear the intentions for your site. Do your best to get your answers in writing.

The day after: now what?

It's easy to focus your attention on launching the site while forgetting what's going to happen the next day and thereafter. This is a pitfall both for the in-house Webmaster and for many Web shops. You may actually have a sterling plan for site maintenance and need no help with it, or you may be planning to job some or all of that out to the Web shop that's building the site. What, in that case, happens after launch?

In a "cash-and-carry" situation, the Web shop may be interested only in producing the site, and it may plan to hand all other concerns thereafter back over to you. If you and your staff have the skills for dealing with this, that's fine. Just be sure you write into your contract some criteria for acceptance and approval. Make it clear that you require a warranty or time period during which the shop is required to fix any problems that occur.

Some shops offer basic training to your staff, agreeing to deliver the site and then spend time training you or your team to make minor changes and handle small maintenance tasks on your own. The shop may provide templates, written instructions, or even on-site, hands-on training. Insist on receiving thorough instructions before this objective is considered complete. Also, be sure to define how requests for assistance are to be handled after basic training.

In a full-service setting, the Web shop delivers the site, provides some announcement or other site marketing services, and remains involved in the day-to-day maintenance of the site. The shop may provide daily updates if the site calls for it, perform scheduled maintenance, provide detailed analysis of the site's performance, and more. This type of ongoing relationship requires that a clear maintenance contract or retainer agreement be put in place. We discuss more on this in an upcoming section on contracts.

Defining the Project

As you go about selecting the Web shop you plan to work with, it may help to have a clear picture of what various shops do and don't do as a matter of course. Remember, part of your job as Webmaster is to manage expectations (see Chapter 1); in this context, that means clearly knowing what you expect, what the shop expects, and which aspects of those expectations are negotiable. Poorly defined or undefined expectations can easily lead to disappointment in the final product (your Web site).

So, how can the intrepid Webmaster make sure that what's expected by both sides is clearly defined? *Put it in writing!* This sounds simple, but it's amazing how much people assume and how much folks don't seem to know about what needs to be put in writing. In your conversations (and written communications) with the Web shop of choice, make sure you cover these points:

✔ **Clearly define the deliverable product.** Be as descriptive as possible. Instead of writing a basic work order, express how you expect the site to look and perform. Be very specific about your needs, referring to the design document you wrote in Chapter 6. In fact, you wrote that design document so you could communicate to whomever was going to work on the site what it was supposed to be and what it should accomplish; attach that document to a brief summary and fork 'em over.

✔ **Lay out each step in the production process.** Each Web-publishing shop is likely to have its own version of the production process; this is information you need to get from the shop. Review the process with its personnel, inserting any additional approval points or benchmarks may be required on your end — for example, sign-offs from executives, your marketing department, the sales or human resources folks, and so on. (Don't forget legal reviews.) In Chapter 9, we talk about the review process. Make sure you understand how this particular shop defines various stages (alpha, beta, and final) in the site-building process (see Chapter 6 for more on that).

✔ **Agree on timelines.** With your outline of the production process in hand, set a timeline that marks out when each step must occur. Make sure both sides understand whether the timeline represents goals or true deadlines. Establish what the consequences of missed deadlines are for either side.

✔ **Consider potential "gotchas."** Don't forget to assign responsibility for the incidentals that come with launching a new Web site. What happens if something goes wrong somewhere along the way? Figure out just who must do what. One doesn't want to think of the worst, but as Webmaster, you have to.

✔ **Decide who is going to announce and promote the site.** Can the Web-publishing shop announce your site and submit its URL to search engines and indexes or is it your responsibility? If the shop is to handle this, which search engines are they to target? Are there specialty directories in your field of business that the shop may not know about? Is your public relations staff going to make announcements to appropriate newsgroups, mailing lists, or print publications, or is that expected of the Web shop?

✔ **Understand when and how payment is expected.** Payment to the Web shop is often tied closely to the timeline. You must agree on whether payment is due upon delivery of a given step or upon *approval* of the component delivered in that step. If it's on approval, whose approval is needed? If yours is a company that cuts checks just once a month, let the Web shop know that, especially if you're dealing with an independent operator.

✔ **Come to terms with what may happen after launch.** How is the end of your relationship defined — or is it defined? Many contracts neglect provisions for maintenance, updates, or a warranty of services and functionality. Make sure you put these matters in writing.

What You Are Going to Pay

Pricing within the Web-publishing industry can be very fickle. Because standards are not yet set, many shops use pricing structures modeled on those used in the industry from which the principals came. Former ad execs who are now Web-shop entrepreneurs often use a pricing model like an ad agency's, while those who come from a publishing or multimedia background may approach things quite differently. Overall, assigning value to the production of a Web site can be a tricky and arbitrary business.

Use a one-stop shop or specific vendors?

In general, we recommend that most projects involve only one Web shop. Using multiple vendors often means that management overhead increases exponentially on all sides, sometimes driving your costs (and maybe your blood pressure) through the roof.

However, you may find yourself in a spot where the most practical route is to outsource one highly technical portion of your site to a shop that has great programmers, then contract the rest of the development to a firm with a more artistic flair. Or, you may find the best firm, the one that meets all your other goals, is lacking a database developer. If you go with multiple vendors, make sure your control of the situation is from the top down. Get the executives of the various vendors on board,

make sure they understand the scope of the project(s), and make sure these are the type of people who work well with others.

Remember, in this situation, you or someone on your team may have to act as project manager, coordinating the efforts of the various vendors. You may also have to establish, at least implicitly, who among the vendors is top dog. It generally makes sense to assign this spot to the vendor with the largest or most important role in the project. That may mean the vendor that controls the layout and overall design of the site, or in a highly database driven shopping site with a complex transaction system, those who would normally work more behind the scenes.

What drives rates

Other than the scope of a project, how many person-hours it may take, and what the real costs are, five major factors drive a shop's prices:

- ✔ **Experience and accomplishment.** Your review of the shop's skills and the breadth of their accomplishments can help you evaluate its fees. Has it had clients in a wide variety of industries? Has it been able to produce successful sites for businesses of all sizes? Are the small-business sites that it has done as clean and professional-looking as sites that it's done for big, international corporations? Has it captured the essence of each company within that company's site? High marks in these areas allow a shop to command higher fees than its less-accomplished peers. However, an impressive portfolio shouldn't always translate into high fees. Make sure the quality of the work justifies the quantity of the bill, and get the best you can for your budgeted dollars.

- ✔ **Level of service.** Review the information you gathered earlier in this chapter regarding what a shop can and cannot provide for you. Does it produce the original site and then turn everything else over to you? Is it going to be training any of your staff? Is it going to be an ongoing partner in the development and success of your site? Shops providing more services for longer stretches of time may merit higher fees.

✔ **Geographic location.** In any industry, the country, state, city, or neighborhood a business is in can inspire higher or lower fees. You pay more to go to the theater in New York than in Seattle, and you pay less for tomatoes in January in Texas than in New Jersey. In the Web-publishing industry, the costs of doing business (commercial rentals, state and local taxes, availability of enterprise zones, the cost of utilities, and the overall cost of living) contribute to setting base fees. Web-publishing shops located within high-tech centers, such as California's Silicon Valley, San Francisco's Multimedia Gulch, and New York City's Silicon Alley, may also charge a premium simply for being where the action is. (Then again, because they are where the action is, they may be the savvyest of them all.)

✔ **Human overhead.** Having a large and accomplished staff is expensive. Compare a prospective Web shop's staffing with its experience and current client list. Is there enough work in that shop to keep specialty employees such as sound and video editors, Java programmers, and 3-D modeling artists busy? On the other hand, is the shop understaffed? Hiring many contractors can be very expensive, too, but it's less costly than having many folks standing around. Look for a good balance between workload and employee assignments. You don't want to pay for someone else's unnecessary or underdeveloped staff.

✔ **Status, fame, and positioning.** Has the firm positioned itself as one of the cyber elite, or is it marketing itself as an affordable alternative? If it's the former, is the shop worthy of being included, and do you want that status enough to pay for it? To find out if a prospective Web shop is truly high-profile, ask other Web professionals who they would include on a short list of premier Web shops. Does your candidate show up on those lists? If the shop you're considering promotes the value of its services rather than its status or fame, do you agree after your evaluations that it offers a great value?

If you find that a shop's prices are either higher or lower than those of its local competitors and peers, consider that to be a red flag. A high price may indicate that the shop holds an inflated opinion of its worth. A low price may indicate inexperience or naiveté, or that the shop is in financial trouble. Look for a shop whose fees are in your acceptable range, and consider that your best bet.

Negotiating fees

While the Web world is no flea market, mostly everything you contract out is flexible. There's often a bit of room in an estimate to get a discount when it's justified. At the very least, you can request that the project be priced in pieces (*x* dollars for this portion and *y* dollars for that) so that you can scale back your plans, if necessary, to stay within your budget. We've had our best successes, though, in staying within budget by fully specifying projects and providing adequate information to the vendor. Making the vendor's job easier avoids increased billable hours.

If you receive an estimate that's seriously beyond your budget but you really want to work with that vendor, you may want to review the production to see which (if any) preproduction or approval steps can be reduced or eliminated. You may be able, for example, to scan your own art or rely on a simpler two-step approval process instead of endless rounds of review by a variety of players.

While we don't recommend low-balling a prospective vendor, you can and should ask if the price quoted is its best price. Offer what you consider to be a reasonable alternative amount in response. Feel free to negotiate, but don't get silly about it. A counteroffer of perhaps 30 percent less than the shop's bid is reasonable. The shop will obviously come back to you with its own counteroffer, and off you go, negotiating 'til you reach an agreement.

"Feature creep" can really cost you

So you make up your mind that you're going to buy a new car and head to the dealer that offers a great price on a cute little sedan. When you get there, you find that the sedan has no stereo. You decide you really want one, and then the pal who's with you suggests a moonroof. The sales rep walks by, and you ask about performance. You learn that the car has a four-cylinder engine, while you were hoping for more power on hills. A moment later, you find yourself looking instead at the red convertible with the leather interior and V-6 engine. That's called *feature creep*.

Feature creep drives up costs. That cute little sedan is a lot cheaper than the red convertible, and that's no accident. As you add bells and whistles to your site, costs go up, and it's a rare Web shop that halts its work to give you a new estimate based on all the stuff you or your higher-ups have started thinking would really make the site special since the contract was signed.

Don't be pressured by your Web shop to include features that aren't in the best interests of the site. Don't let your higher-ups think that they can add Shockwave and push marketing without consequences, either. Get estimates for any additional features, and consider those estimates in the context of whether that stuff is going to contribute to the success of your site. Find out what alternatives exist for accomplishing the same goal without the added cost. The price your Web shop quoted at the outset of your project was based on the specifications you provided and on the shop's understanding of the scope of things. While most shops budget for the minor changes and corrections that almost always occur in the approval phase, major changes or feature enhancements increase costs. It's your job to keep them in line.

Deciphering Contracts and NDAs

The fact that you need a signed contract in hand before the project begins is probably clear by this point. The contract must outline what you expect from the vendor and what the vendor expects from you. It must also establish what occurs if those expectations aren't met. At the time the contract is signed, no important questions should remain unanswered.

It's always prudent to have your company's legal staff or corporate counsel review contracts prior to signing. They see things you don't — ambiguities and opportunities for misunderstanding — and they can clarify the language.

Nothing is carved in stone (until it is)

A contract is a document of mutual understanding and agreement. Up to the point when it's signed, much of what's in the contract may be negotiable, but contract negotiations can slow progress in any project. At the outset, define which terms are non-negotiable to you and have these deal-breakers in mind when you're wheeling and dealing. Remember that the prospective Web shop will also have deal-breakers on its side. You can start the contract process by putting forth your standard contract or by letting the shop put forth its contract. Yours is probably written to your benefit, but the shop's contract may provide you with clues to its business practices. Most Web shops have a standard contract from which they operate. Have your legal counsel review this at the outset for any clauses contrary to your company's standard policies. Find out what points you can and cannot, in your company's view, negotiate on, and whether you use the vendor's contract as a starting point or use yours.

Intellectual property and copyrights

Just who owns the final product? If you aren't experienced at hiring someone to create intellectual value for your company, this may sound like a preposterous question. However, it is one that lands many Web shops and their clients in plenty of hot water. Review Chapter 5 to find out more about these important matters.

Nondisclosure agreements: covering yourself

A *nondisclosure agreement* (NDA) is meant to protect confidentiality — NDAs are a standard feature of many modern contracts, even employment agreements. They can also appear as stand-alone documents to be signed before a particularly confidential project is described. When a vendor signs an NDA, he or she is agreeing not to disclose whatever is labeled through the NDA to be confidential. If your site is to feature an as-yet-unannounced product or service, keeping that under wraps may be a priority, and you must be sure NDAs are signed and filed. Web shops are often also interested in keeping their design and bidding processes confidential. You may be asked to sign an NDA before the bidding or contract negotiation phase begins. As with the overall contract, the NDA is an explicit statement of expectations. Decide what can be disclosed to whom and at what time or under which circumstances, and that shapes your NDA.

Maintaining Vendor Relationships

Finishing a project and ending the contract on a positive note is great for both parties. When it's all over, you may well have established a business relationship that continues, and the Web shop can add you to its roster of happy clients who can tell others of their good experience.

Working with a shop you know — one that has done good work for you and now knows your site inside and out — can be a huge time and energy saver. The Web shop that knows you can immediately pick up a follow-up project with little prep time, and you know what to expect in working with their people again.

This type of good relationship is definitely a two-way street. It's up to the Web shop to deliver as promised, but it's up to you to make the scope of the project clear, to manage expectations, to keep the budget in line, and to resolve any misunderstandings or glitches as quickly and professionally as possible. Do these things, and you are at least in the right; you may also (if the Web shop keeps its end of the deal) end up with a valued partner.

Chapter 9

QA, Document Control, and the Style Constables Who Love Them

●●●

In This Chapter

▶ What makes up a style guide, and why you need one

▶ Style standards for the site's look and HTML

▶ Establishing standards for page length, links, and graphics

▶ Learning to love editorial standards

▶ Setting up and maintaining a style guide

▶ Shepherding pages through an effective review process

●●●

*M*ore and more frequently, Web sites are seen as legitimate representations of credible companies, companies that care intensely about how they look in print and are coming to realize the importance of looking good on the Web. This chapter's all about that — about setting guidelines and sticking to them. This is all about QA — *quality assurance*. It's also about production standards and editorial standards — how to set them and how to maintain them.

Why You Need a Style Guide

Have you ever thought about why people give so much credence to what appears in print? ("It must be true; I saw it in the paper.") The print media has worked very hard for hundreds of years to establish and maintain credibility. They consider credibility to be the cornerstone of their industry. Behind every inch of print media you see is often a whole team of editors, writers, fact checkers, and proofreaders, all checking and double-checking to make sure the reader's experience is smooth and that the material presented is accurate and understandable. As a group, these people check that both layout standards and editorial standards are maintained.

This is not to say that you must have a whole cadre of people keeping your Web site pure, but keep in mind that, to establish credibility and provide users of your site with a smooth experience, you should maintain visual, editorial, and navigational standards.

The Elements of a Style Guide

You may already have a corporate style guide. Perhaps it's not etched in stone or even readily available, but you probably have some conventions set for what printed matter should look like, how and where to use logos, and what tone to use in written communications. If you as the Webmaster don't know these parameters, check your marketing, marketing communications, public relations, and packaging or design departments to find out what you can in advance of setting your own styles.

Your style guide should cover the following points:

- ✔ Look, including font and color choices, as well as layout and page size
- ✔ HTML conventions used, including those that affect which browsers you support
- ✔ Linking and crosslinking policies
- ✔ Editorial tone and conventions
- ✔ Navigation and architecture, including directory structure along with instructions about where to store what type of content
- ✔ Legal matters, such as how to use the company logo and which copyright notices to place where
- ✔ Review processes and procedures

Above all, the point of a style guide is to provide *consistency.* Your site should have an identity that is recognizable; every page should not have a different look. Editorial conventions should be decided on and stuck to — this is a tough one, so we dwell on it a bit in this chapter. Navigation should be consistent. Items should be placed into sections and directories according to a consistent system so that you and your team can find them easily (see Chapter 6 for information about organizing your site). Your logo and copyright policies, as well as your linking policies, should be consistent to provide you with legal standing in defending against any infringement.

You'll present a far better Web site if you give these matters consideration during its planning phase and build according to the style guide. However, if you find that you've created a site without the benefit of a style guide, by all means pause now and put this tool in place. It can help you immeasurably in maintaining the site.

FIELD NOTES

A corporate Web editor says . . .

Multimedia writer and producer Debra Goldentyer says, "More and more, corporations are looking to editors to help with their Web sites. People are beginning to expect content on the Web to be as professional as the content in print. Besides [fixing] typos and copyediting, Web editors do 'Webification,' which can include everything from breaking down paragraphs to suggesting graphics and links."

If yours is like most Web teams, it consists of several people working on the site, and keeping a written record of the standards that you use is a time saver. This can be as simple as a list (preferably online) that you add to and change as the site develops, or as complex as the style site that Sun keeps (`http://www.sun.com/styleguide`). The goal of most Web pages, whatever the purpose of the site, is to communicate ideas and information as powerfully as possible. In the sections that follow we look at some of the commonly accepted style standards for getting the most out of HTML. Later, we look at editorial standards.

Style Standards for the Site's Look and HTML

Reading text on a computer screen is *not* like reading text on a book page. The special nature of presenting material on-screen, along with the limitations of Web design, have led to the creation of some guidelines for using headings, text, graphics, links, and other file types (which together make *content* on the Web). A few areas that come under careful scrutiny are page length, the use of links, and the choice of graphics, sound, and video. As you consider how to handle these elements, refer to our discussion in Chapter 2 about the importance of defining your goals and identifying your audience. A site that sells Web-order flowers, for example, is going to have a different take on page length than one that posts updates for a society of medieval scholars.

TIP

Think about your standards early and often. If you've ever had the task of imposing consistency on a project after it's in place, you know that it can be like trying to put toothpaste back in the tube. Most people are so busy they don't have time to go back and make changes to a document that's already been posted — and you get more professional results by setting the ground rules early.

Your site's visual style

When you design your site or job out its design, think through what different types of pages are to be included and what those pages should generally look like. (Chapters 7 and 8 talk about these issues.) In general, you'll come up with a visual style — a design personality for your site. You'll also often design *template pages* (a generic page that includes samples of all the elements you'll use on your site). You may have a template for an index page (a home page), one for content pages, one for special content pages of a certain type, one for an events calendar, one for a transaction page, and so on. Having these template pages provides you with a basis for laying out new content on your site.

Include in your style guide:

- ✔ A listing of the template pages your site uses along with descriptions of what each template should be used for, and any exceptions to the overall style that any particular page template may require. Of course, if your style guide is online, you can also link from each type of template page to the portion of your style guide that discusses HTML conventions or other matters that may affect it.

- ✔ Notes about why certain decisions were reached regarding the look of the site — perhaps even who approved the look. These are pieces of information that shouldn't just be kept as verbal lore; if you don't write this info in your style guide, make sure it's on file somewhere.

- ✔ A corporate identity guide that specifies how the company should be identified and represented in public. These guidelines may include how and where the company logo should be used. They may even specify in which font and what color the company name or slogans should appear. You may find that you have to interpret company guidelines to fit into what the Web can do. There are some technical limitations; for example, your company's exact shade of red may not be available on the Web.

- ✔ A record of who designed specific elements of the site (which artists or production people). This can help you or your successors in the event that some new art is needed. You can go back to the designer who created other elements on that page and thus maintain a consistent look.

Managing style standards in HTML

Your HTML style guide can help anyone who works on the site to know how to lay out and maintain the site's pages. Keep track of any decisions you make about tags to use, dimensions of design elements, and so on, and track those details in your style guide.

What to include

When you set your style guide for HTML, consider every detail of page layout. Your HTML style guide should cover, at a minimum, the following points:

- ✔ The screen size for which you'll design — this is generally 640 x 480 pixels or the less common 800 x 600 pixels

- ✔ Treatment of headings, including whether you use the heading tags for all headings, a graphic for some, or just bold text for others

- ✔ Use of bold, italics, and any special fonts that indicate specific types of text

- ✔ Typography, including which fonts are used on the site and what size they are

- ✔ Paragraph spacing

- ✔ How tables are used in the site, including specifics such as table dimensions, cell widths, and other attributes

- ✔ Specifics regarding the use of frames

- ✔ Reminders not to use smart quotes, em dashes, en dashes, bullets, or other special characters that aren't supported by HTML

- ✔ How to handle art, captions, tabular matter, sidebars, pull quotes, and so on

- ✔ Treatment of footers, including any that identify the site, provide a navigational option, or specify the site's stand on copyright issues

For each of these items and every other design element of your site, provide the HTML specifications — that is, which tags to use — along with any special considerations (like whether to insert an invisible GIF between paragraphs to maintain spacing).

Headings

Headings divide pages into logical sections, helping the reader to navigate the page's content. There are three basic ways to handle headings. You can use HEAD tags (H1, H2, H3, and so on, discussed in Chapter 7), use graphics you've had designed for the headings, or use bold text or even italics. Remember that higher-level headings should be larger or otherwise more prominent than lower-level headings.

The first heading on the page should tell the reader what the page is about. In fact, many Web developers use the same text for the title of a page and the level 1 head that appears at the top of the page. (Again, see Chapter 7.)

Font and color choice

Everyone knows that Web browsers don't afford many choices in fonts and colors. You're basically restricted to the few fonts available to most browsers (Courier, Times Roman, and Helvetica) and the 216 colors that are similarly available. Since Netscape Navigator 3, it's become possible, via the FONT tag, to specify more fonts. Versions 4 of Navigator and Internet Explorer improve on this, but there are still limits; remember that not everyone who views your site has a full range of font and color capabilities.

You need to decide how to handle color and fonts and specify it in your style guide. Remember that fonts of the same specifications appear 2 to 3 points larger on a PC than on a Mac. More than 70 percent of those viewing your site will do so on a PC, while many designers create on Macs. Be sure to view your site design and any later modifications on a variety of machines and browsers.

Remember, too, that Netscape Navigator and Microsoft Internet Explorer both allow the user to override any specification of font, size, and color. This has been true for some time, and it's a controversial matter between Web developers and some Web-user advocates. The growing consensus is that users should be able to override choices made by the site designer. Why? Because this gives users with special needs — those who are color blind or visually impaired, for example — the ability to customize pages so they can see the text more easily.

Page layout and length

Many Webmasters believe that short pages are most effective because of the size and nature of the computer screens used to look at them. Readers are unlikely to make the effort to scroll beyond the first page, the argument goes, so you'd better say what needs to be said in very little space. Where have we heard this before? It's the idea behind display ads, television commercials, billboards, and just about anything else that tries to grab our attention.

Short pages minimize the likelihood that important material falls below the bottom of the screen, where it may not be seen. As we've said, the variety of Web browsers on the market ensures that no one can control exactly how a page appears on each computer; however, many computer screens are 640 by 480 pixels in size. This means that many people see only the first four inches of your Web page — make 'em count. Don't think in pages but rather in screens, keeping the most important material in the top screenful of your pages. And don't make the page wider than your users' screens will be; nothing drives users away faster than forcing them to use horizontal scroll bars. The most effective pages may arguably be those that offer the user maximum info and options in those first four precious inches.

Of course, the wisdom of keeping your pages short also depends on the nature of your site's mission. Online magazines, such as Salon (http://www.salon1999.com) and The Red Herring (http://www.redherring.com), use pages that must be scrolled. Their offerings are based on the old magazine model and assume that visitors to their pages are text-hungry readers who don't mind using the scroll button or a mouse.

Shorter Web pages are more appropriate for the following items:

✔ Pages that (presumably) include little text, especially home pages and navigational pages

✔ Pages that include very large graphics

✔ Pages that are meant to be read only online

You may, however, want to use longer pages when these conditions apply:

✔ It's important for the user to be able to search the page using the browser's Find feature

✔ The page must be easy to maintain

✔ The page is meant to be downloaded and printed

✔ The page is highly designerly and scrolling is no problem

Your style guide should include some guidelines for when and how to break up pages. Let folks who'll be working on your site know what size the chunks should be as well as how to handle links and navigation between various types of pages.

The (next to) last word on HTML

HTML has caused plenty of head-scratching. Exactly how should a page designer decide what to link to? Should we change the way that we write to accommodate the unconventional nature of hypertext? How large should a document be? The inventor of the Web, Tim Berners-Lee, addresses those questions and more in his online style guide at http://www.w3.org/pub/WWW/Provider/Style/All.html. For more on HTML, see Chapter 7.

Designing for different browsers

One of the keys to using HTML effectively is to remember that you need to focus on what you want to communicate rather than trying to control exactly how it appears on screen. This is one way a Web page differs drastically from a traditional printed document. As previously mentioned, because of the many browsers in use and the differences in how they interpret HTML, you may want to indicate the function of a portion of text — such as a heading — rather than trying to pin down exactly what it looks like when viewed on the screen of a PC running Netscape Navigator. A document that uses HTML consistently throughout has the best chance of looking good in any number of settings, whether the viewer is using Netscape Navigator, Microsoft Explorer, or some other nifty browser.

This helps to explain the difference between the two types of highlighting you can use for characters in HTML: *physical* and *logical*. If you're still attached to the old desktop-publishing way of looking at things, you may be tempted to go the physical route and label text as italic or boldface. Seasoned Webmasters often recommend using logical labels instead to indicate that the text should appear in a distinctive style. This means that you may mark the text with the STRONG tag (`<STRONG>`) rather than the BOLD tag (`<BOLD>`). The argument behind this approach is that it gives better results in the multibrowser climate of the Web.

A good online resource for information about everything from HTML tags to graphic formats is the HyperNews Forums Web Mastery Resource Lists (`http://union.ncsa.uiuc.edu/HyperNews/get/www/html/guides.html`). Despite its formidable name, this site is very friendly, and it invites visitors to pose their questions, which are answered by forum participants.

Always test your pages on several different types of machines, using multiple browsers. You have little hope of controlling the exact look across the browser board, but you can at least pinpoint specific problems and address them before you launch the page. Earlier sections in this chapter address additional concerns about designing for multiple browsers; you may want to review those sections for more information.

Avoiding graphics pitfalls

Put a bunch of Web-page designers in a room and open the floor to the topic of graphics, and you're likely to get an earful. Everyone seems to have an opinion on this one. Graphics have been a hot topic for as long as the Web has been around. They really add to a page, and a big part of the Web's potential is the forum that it provides for visual expression. But graphics are memory intensive and can take an excruciatingly long time to appear on screen. During this time, a user can easily have second thoughts about whether the wait is worthwhile. He or she can make a quick choice to cancel the request, and there goes another potential visitor who never sees your document.

Be ruthless about weeding out images that aren't crucial to the content and message of your document, even if you aren't concerned about how long it takes for images to appear on screen. When outlining your style guidelines, set limits for the use of images. Of course it's not that these rules can't be bent in case of an especially worthy graphic; the rules simply provide a buffer against the "image bloat" that can be an inevitable part of maintaining a Web site. Here are some suggestions for managing graphics:

- Don't use too many colors. Most people use the garden-variety 256-color screen. There's no need to try to impress them with colors that aren't available on their screens. In fact, it's probably best to stick to the 216-color Netscape palette (`ftp://luna.bearnet.com/pub/lynda/CLUTS/`). In some cases, you may even want to consider using gray scale. (Just look at what Ansel Adams could do with black and white.)

- Use big blocks of solid colors in your GIF files. GIF files compress solid blocks of colors very well. Avoid dithering.

- Use the JPEG format for photographic images. JPEGs compress the same photographic image much more than GIFs.

- Use interlaced files that load in several passes. They allow the viewer to see the image as it is loading, and they're much more satisfying than large graphics that load slowly from the top.

- Avoid linking to a large graphic that takes a long time to download, unless you warn the user in advance. This introduces the element of choice (hmmm, maybe it's time for pizza . . .) into the long pause while downloading.

- Be kind to viewers who can't load images. Keep in mind that some browsers can't load all types of images and that users can choose not to view graphics. Be sure to provide a path through the site that does not depend on clicking on images. Also, be sure to use the ALT attribute to describe all images.

- Put a limit on the size (in bytes) of all the files that make up a page. This may sound harsh, but it's the best way to keep your page files slim and your pages loadable. Table 9-1 shows the amount of time it takes to transfer pages of different sizes with connections of different speeds. (Note that this table shows only the amount of time it takes to move the data over the connection. Delays may be introduced along the way, for example, by the Web server or the browser.)

Table 9-1	Transfer Times (In Seconds) for Various Page Sizes and Modem Speeds					
Page Size	14.4 Kbps Modem	28.8 Kbps Modem	56 Kbps Modem	ISDN 1 B Channel	ISDN 2 B Channels	Cable Modem
40K	22.2	11.1	5.8	5.0	2.5	0.06
80K	44.4	22.2	11.4	10.0	5.0	0.14
160K	88.9	44.4	22.9	20.0	10.0	0.30
320K	177.8	88.9	45.8	40.0	20.0	0.62

Linking Smartly

It just wouldn't be the Web without links. They give the whole shebang its wonderful character. You'll want to decide what types of words or phrases to link on and how many links leading outside of your site are acceptable as well as what types of outlinks are okay, when and where to crosslink within your site, what types of other sites you are going to trade links with, and more.

How many links is too many links?

Like so many other good things, links — those underlined or highlighted bits of text that whiz you to another page, image, or site — shouldn't be over-done. A link invites the reader to leave what he or she is currently looking at and take off for another alluring destination.

How many is too many? It's hard to say, but it's important to think about this. And again, it depends on the goals of your site. If your site is meant to act as a source or if you are writing about stuff on the Web, you may want to pepper the page with more links. If you are providing plenty for your users to do on your site and want to keep 'em there, stick to links within your site and link more sparingly.

Linking on just the right word or phrase

Put some thought into choosing the words you use for a link. We've all seen too many Web sites with the words *Click Here* underlined in several places. Don't fall prey to that lack of creativity.

Perhaps you've finally cashed in your 401(k) plan and bought that scuba resort that you've been dreaming of. A friend offers to provide a link to your document about scuba diving in Micronesia from an article about adventure travel. You would probably be happy to see something like this:

> <u>The Micronesian Scuba Association</u> provides rates and booking information along with mind-blowing descriptions of reefs and walls at <u>Micronesia Online</u>, the definitive resource for scuba in the region.

That's much better than the all-too-common approach of letting the reader guess what's at the other end of the link, as follows:

> For information about scuba in Micronesia, <u>click here</u>.

Worse yet are links like the following, which seems designed to leave you clicking around in thin air:

> For <u>more</u> about this, click here.

Think carefully about whether you plan to link on the verb in a sentence or on the noun or phrase that describes the link destination. (We recommend the latter in most cases.)

More linking tips

Text links have introduced a whole new element into the art of reading. What was once a linear process that started at the top of the page, went from left to right, and continued across to the next page is now an experience where you can zip from document to document to image to video and back again without ever reaching the end of a sentence. Keep this in mind when you're composing a Web document. As you incorporate links into your Web pages, you may find the following tips to be handy:

✔ Never allow links to dominate your document. Some Webmasters recommend composing the text as you would any piece of writing — as if there were no links in it — and then add links later. Others say that you should be especially careful to include plenty of context on each page, because people may enter your work from any of many different places on the Web.

✔ Choose your words carefully. Make certain the words you underline as the link are meaningful for the subject to which you're linking. Choose, as your linked word or phrase, text that is similar in context to the Web page you're linking to.

✔ Help the reader understand what the link does. Text that accompanies the link should make the subject of the link clear. That way, users aren't disappointed by what they find when they click.

✔ Select as links those words or phrases that emphasize the important concept in a sentence. Don't link on words that are generic or secondary to the point.

✔ Be meticulous about applying style rules to the linked text. If your style is *not* to underline punctuation that follows linked words (as we recommend), make certain you don't underline any periods, commas, quotation marks, or other potential culprits. To do so inconsistently looks just plain sloppy.

Remember, words that are chosen as the text for links sometimes show up as explanatory text when the user adds the site to a list of bookmarks or a hotlist. This is another good reason not to use the tired old *Click Here* as link text.

Getting to Know and Love Editorial Standards

Editorial standards is one of those terms that can easily inspire glazed eyes and a vanishing audience. Along with junior high health class and orthodontia, editorial standards definitely have the whiff of obligation rather than fun about them. That's one reason why hands-on editors are sometimes considered quirky cranks: These people (note that one of your friendly authors is among them) actually *enjoy* figuring out whether to use *which* or *that* in a sentence, and they get a kick out of applying arcane rules of grammar to sentences that otherwise run in circles.

Why this matters

All publications (including the ever iconoclastic *Wired* and even the lowbrow *Mad* magazine) probably have house style guides, and if they're really good at adhering to them, you'll probably never know they're in use.

In the broadest sense, these editorial standards help determine the personality of a publication or a Web site. They act as a unifying force, governing matters of taste and style. Standards at a family publication would almost certainly rule out the use of obscenity or nudity, while a magazine aimed at twenty-somethings would have looser standards — but standards just the same — that specify how *much* skin can be shown. Most editorial shops have legal standards designed to keep them out of hot water by making sure they don't violate copyright law (see Chapter 5) or defame someone.

Style guidelines allow editors and Webmasters to impose consistency by resolving questions that go beyond mere grammatical correctness. At their most mundane, for example, these rules determine whether you'll use Arabic numerals or cardinal numbers to discuss quantities. Is it *10 maniacal Webmasters* or *ten maniacal Webmasters?* (If you see the difference, you have the soul of an editor, and we salute you.) Maybe you prefer to always use numerals — that's fine, it's your call. Just make a decision and stick to it. Otherwise readers think that you can't make up your mind — or that you don't know what you're doing.

You need editorial standards on a Web site not because you can't live without them, but because they bolster your position as a professional publication.

Creating your editorial style guide

By creating style guidelines and making them available to everyone working on your Web project, you'll save a lot of time. *Consistency* is the watchword when applying style rules. Even if the rules you develop are unconventional, they should be applied consistently throughout your site. Switching from one style to another is jarring to the reader.

References for editorial style

Before setting out to create your own style guide, take a look at some style manuals that have stood the test of time. The two reference books you hear cited most often in discussions about style are *The AP Stylebook* and *The Chicago Manual of Style*. Most publications take one or the other as their bible and then develop their own in-house style guide as needed. Newspaper editors usually depend on *The AP Stylebook,* which was developed by the Associated Press as a handy reference for time-challenged wire service reporters.

Magazine and book editors keep *The Chicago Manual of Style* at their elbows. Its index alone stretches for dozens of pages. (The University of Chicago Web site at http://www.press.uchicago.edu/News/manual_of_style.html lists the manual's table of contents and information about purchasing it.)

If you're going to be handling words at all, you want to purchase one or both of these reference books along with a good, definitive dictionary that's no more than five years old. (We like *Webster's Tenth New Collegiate Dictionary.*) You should probably also take a look at *Wired Style,* the book we mentioned earlier in the chapter that was compiled for what the editors of *Wired* magazine call "the post-Gutenberg era." *Wired Style* is an interesting read, as much for the information it contains as for the glimpse it offers into the minds of the editors at *Wired.*

Web-editing questions and answers

Grace Allison, who works on a Web site that's affiliated with a major computer publishing company and its 20 or so magazines, answered our questions about what's best in Web editing.

What specific differences do you see in editing for the Web?

Surfing the Internet is a short-attention-span experience. Users skim and click through Web pages, so you need to break information into small, easily digested bits, and you need to make sure that the writing is clear and concise; otherwise you lose the reader and lose the clickthroughs.

Also, it's very difficult to read long columns of text on a monitor, so brevity matters all the more. I try to break long articles into smaller chunks or to give people the option of reading a short teaser and clicking through to the full-text article. This way, they can get the gist of what's available at a glance and then decide what merits further investigation.

Linked text should be considered very carefully, because it's always highlighted or underlined. In fact, I try to think about my links like pull quotes. I think it works really well to have strong verbs or eye-catching phrases in the linked text — good copy makes people want to click to the next page.

When you look at Web pages (other than the site that you work on), what do you see that, as an editor, either strikes you as good or appalling?

When I look at other Web pages, the things that bother me the most are:

✔ Whole paragraphs of linked, underlined text.

✔ Sites where it's obvious that someone spent hours on the graphics but didn't bother to spell-check the page.

✔ Sites that lack stylistic consistency. This is a hard one, because there's no *AP Stylebook* or *Strunk & White* for the Web. (I guess Wired made an attempt, but I haven't used it and haven't heard good things about it.) At least people should be consistent within their own pages.

✔ Pages that have a 2,000-word article flowed into one l-o-n-g column so that I have to scroll forever to get to the end of the thing. (I do think that there's a balance to be struck here, though. Some sites break up the text too much and make you jump from page to page; that gets annoying as well.)

The main thing that I would say about editing for the Web is this: Keep it short and simple. Use strong verbs, check spelling, and don't overwhelm users with endless screens of unbroken text.

Note that all dictionaries are not created equal. Have you ever wondered why there are so many different dictionaries at your local bookstore? They differ from each other in subtle and not-so-subtle ways. You can save yourself time by deciding that one dictionary rules for all of your spelling questions. Make sure that everyone on your team is using the same edition of the same dictionary.

Decoding editorial titles

Pickiness may not be a trait most of us look for in a spouse or partner, but even the testiest author admits that there's nothing better than an eagle-eyed editor. (We love our editors and pretty much think we couldn't live without them.) It's simply not possible to edit yourself. You need a fresh pair of eyes to look at what you write and to point out where it could be improved. An editor's job, in a nutshell, is to step in for the many readers that (one hopes) are going to follow, making sure the writer has conveyed what was meant to be conveyed in a manner that reads smoothly and accurately.

There are many types of editors in the world of publishing and news, from high-profile *acquisitions editors,* like the late Jackie Onassis, who sign authors to book deals, to the *wire service editors* at small-town papers, who sift through mounds of foreign dispatches to cull the day's top stories. *Development editors* in the book business work with authors to transform an idea into a book. *Managing editors,* true to their title, manage the day-to-day operations of a publication or of editorial business. What specific editorial titles mean may vary from company to company, but the last line of defense in just about every editorial setting is someone called the *copy editor.* That person checks the text for spelling, grammar, style, and general all-around appropriateness.

You probably don't need to fill all of these positions on your Web project; the most important one, if you have to choose (which you almost certainly do), may be the copy editor. A good copy editor can work very quickly to check content for consistency and adherence to your style as well as legal matters and, on Web projects, some navigational matters. You can often make arrangements with a freelance copy editor to check material on your site for a very reasonable fee. Copy editors use a set of traditional, standardized markings to indicate what corrections should be made on text — and for a great introduction to these marks, see Karen Judd's *Copyediting: A Practical Guide* (Crisp Publications, 1992).

Even if it seems that there isn't a minute to spare for a quick edit — make one. Newspaper people have been doing this for years under tight deadlines. Just about every rookie reporter has had his or her neck saved by the critical eye of a copy editor who pointed out an embarrassing mistake right before a story went to press. It's better to take a few extra minutes for editing than to log onto your Web site and be embarrassed by a glaring mistake. Our list of the most egregious oversights on the Web includes incidents where companies misspelled their own names or announced product releases for the wrong year. How's that for inspiring confidence in your credibility?

What editorial style matters to cover

Putting together an editorial style guide is best done as a collaborative process. But then you could say the same thing about putting up a Web page. You want to tap people with different types of experience and various perspectives to provide input about what sort of style fits the bill for your purposes. An editor whose expertise lies in sharpening text may have one perspective, while a graphic artist who creates icons and bitmaps has another, and your legal manager may have a third. Creating a style guide can be a good opportunity to get people with different ideas to exchange them. After all, one of your main goals is to create Web pages that integrate the talents of everyone on your team.

You also want to establish procedures and a deadline for reaching style decisions. Unstructured discussions of picky points of style have been known to drag on for months and to develop into feuds. That's why we recommend that you put a limit on free-floating democracy. Appoint someone as "style czar." (Feel free to give this person a more palatable title. We often suggest the gentler "style constable.") Then everyone can go back to creating the best possible prose and graphics, rather than arguing about how many angels can dance on the black space of an umlaut.

Tales from the trenches

Web editors draw much of their inspiration from the long tradition of editorial standards in print publishing. At the same time, they're intent on carving out a niche for themselves in a whole new industry: the online world of the Web. This means developing a whole set of skills that weren't even thought about a few years ago. Whenever they get together, these editors are likely to talk about the excitement — and the frustration — of working in this new medium.

Editors are usually pretty vocal about what they bring to the process of creating and maintaining a site. "Web editing is a unique skill. It is not exactly like print editing. I think a good Web editor needs a really deep familiarity with the Web," said freelance Web editor Claudia L'Amoreaux. "A good Web editor can edit more than just copy. She can look at the architecture and flow of information (both text and image data) and point out how it could be organized better, just as a developmental editor can critique and improve the structure of a book."

It may not be the most popular thing to do, but a good editor can put the brakes on a seemingly exciting idea that isn't going to fly on the Web. "An editor can get you good copy, but their real strength is ensuring that the purpose of the site is carried through in each area," said Barbara Bruxvoort, who has edited a corporate Web site for three years. She said that the editor acts as "a sort of user advocate, if you will, who continually brings the 'Does it make sense?' response to the 'Let's do it; it's cool' side of the business."

Doing something "by the seat of your pants" is an accepted approach among a lot of software developers and Web enthusiasts. "You have to be careful to distinguish between creativity and chaos," said Diane Rowett Castro, who helps clients market their products and services on the Internet. "There are many, many Web sites out there that have three or four columns of cluttered information," she said. "My philosophy in Web writing is to keep it simple. We have enough clutter in our lives."

Examples are essential to a good style guide. Asking someone to use a style guide with no examples is like telling him or her to study the chemical ingredients of a cake and then describe how it tastes. Including plenty of examples makes your style manual user-friendly, for lack of a better phrase.

The Yale C/AIM Web Style Guide at `http://info.med.yale.edu/caim/manual/index.html` is both an excellent model of organization and a great example of a style guide that includes a mision statement.

Include these items in your editorial style guide:

- The *publishing mission* or philosophy and goals behind whatever you're publishing on the Web. Talk about who your audience is and what you hope to offer them, the importance of overall quality to your endeavor, and legal concerns, such as libel and copyright infringement.

- *Capitalization,* whether to use lowercase or uppercase characters in a word has always been a key style question. Be especially careful to set up rules for using capital letters in headings. Also, choose whether to follow the way companies and products are named (like NeXT, CNET, and dBase) or impose an arbitrary rule about using an initial uppercase letter for company names. If you're going to try to observe spelling preferences, include a list of frequently cited companies and products in your style guide.

- *Punctuation* separates the gawkers from the serious style mavens. Take time to make sure that everyone knows the difference between an en dash (a dash that's as long as an *n*) and an em dash (one that's as long as an *m*). Watch out for an overpopulation of quotation marks — they multiply rapidly if not checked. Another punctuation mark with a behavior problem is the hyphen. It's easy for writers to toss in a hyphen if they're not sure whether words are supposed to be connected. Our pet peeve is the exclamation mark! We believe that excessive exclamation marks are a sign of very weak writing! We once had an English instructor who allowed us to use only one per semester. Try not to use them at all. No matter how fresh and hip your documents may be, if you're using a style guide, you're concerned about communicating clearly with your audience. That's what punctuation is all about. It's one of those elements of language that usually goes unnoticed but becomes jarring when used inconsistently.

- *Compound words* are tricky. The trend is toward closing up words that are frequently used together and have a single meaning. That's how *Web master* became *Webmaster*. And *electronic mail* has become *e-mail*, which has become *email* (although it remains *e-mail* at IDG Books Worldwide). Your dictionary is a good source on which words are now accepted as compounds. Your style guide is the place to answer questions about when to use the closed-up form.

✔ Use of *special elements,* such as how long figure captions should be and where they should appear, the limit you've set for the size of images and their files, the use of color in your documents, and the format for tables so that headings and text within them are consistent. The size and use of headings should also be covered. As we mentioned earlier, consistent headings are essential for creating a unified, professional appearance on a Web page.

✔ *Commonly used terms and unusual spellings* can appear in an alphabetically organized list of terms that have proved to be problematic and have come up often. It can include specialized terminology for the subject you're covering. You may want to include a statement about when the use of acronyms is okay and a list of which ones have gained wide acceptance with your audience.

✔ *Frequently asked questions,* a FAQ section like the one you may read when you join an online newsgroup, can be especially helpful for new people or freelancers who join the group and are trying to get up to speed quickly.

Jutta Degener has compiled a list of her pet peeves — little things that Web writers do that make her grind her teeth. Take a look at What Is Good Hypertext Writing? at `http://kbs.cs.tu-berlin.de/~jutta/ht/writing.html`. (We may tell you to "Check it out!" but that's one of her no-nos, and one of ours, too.)

Maintaining the editorial style guide

You were probably hoping we'd say the job was over after the guide was completed, but style guides have a life of their own. They are living, breathing entities. (That's why *The Chicago Manual of Style* is in its 14th edition, at last count.) Just when you think you've pinned down usage of a certain term, the language takes a detour or a new technology hits the market, and you must be ready to make a change. If you doubt this, think about the way social change has affected how we describe certain groups. Women can now elect to use the title *Ms.* and some publications have switched fairly painlessly from the term *black* to *African-American.* Then there are all the new words that spring up to describe things that were the stuff of science fiction a few years earlier. It wasn't long ago that people mailed each other letters rather than sending them by fax or e-mail. For that matter, just about everyone can probably remember a time when the words *World Wide Web* would cause people to draw a blank.

That's "copy editor" (two words) to you

For a look into the mind of a seasoned (and opinionated) copy editor, visit The Slot at `http://www.theslot.com`. Copy editors are famous for standing their ground on matters of grammatical minutiae, and *Washington Post* copy editor Bill Walsh is no exception. The site enumerates style points large and small, giving Walsh's well-reasoned arguments for why he chooses one usage over another. When he's just being arbitrary, he admits it. Not all copy editors are so honest. The heart of the site is The Curmudgeon's Stylebook, an alphabetized listing covering matters such as the difference between a lawyer and an attorney and how to create the plural form of names such as *Denny's*. (The last is a trick question. Don't try it, says Walsh; just recast the sentence.) The Curmudgeon's Stylebook is a good place to get inspiration for your own work in progress. Not only is Walsh a solid copy editor, he's a good writer with a wicked sense of humor. Walsh says both of his brothers are also copy editors. That must have made for some interesting conversation around the family dinner table.

By the way, the verb *copyedit* is one word — isn't language fun?

Again, consider giving one person the authority to make final decisions and changes. This is where having a style czar saves time. Try to maintain a single, sacrosanct copy of the style guide, where changes are made from time to time, either by the style constable or by a single appointee advised by others. You should virtually need a secret code to get into the inner sanctum of the great style guide document to change it. Okay, we're exaggerating here, but remember that there are exceptions to every rule, and you must be firm after you've decided on a particular style point.

Maintaining a single authoritative copy of your style guide is crucial. We've seen insidious examples of "style guide creep," where editors and writers began appending their own rules to the style guide without passing them through the proper channels. Chaos ensues. Ampersands proliferate. Exclamation marks multiply!!! Don't let this happen to you.

Noting Navigation, Architecture, and Directory Structures

As you organized your content and navigational schemes and then created a site map and directory structure (see Chapter 6), you kept careful records, right? Now you can easily pop the final versions of your plans into your style guide so others can get to know and appreciate (and follow) your carefully conceived brainchild.

Be sure to include the site map, the directory structure, and notes about how to place content into this master plan. If exceptions are acceptable, note what and where they are allowed.

Formalizing Legal Matters

Your style guide should include some references to basic legal matters. You needn't reinterpret the whole of the copyright and trademark laws, but be sure to cover your company's specific policies on matters related to the Web site. What standard legalese must appear on the site, and where and how should it appear? If you run a contest, what are the rules and where do you post them? If you license portions of your content, cover the ins and outs of that. And describe how to use logos and other identifying marks from a legal perspective. Chapter 5 discusses legal matters.

For a great example of how to discuss the use of logos (and other elements) in a style guide, look into the Lincoln University's University Outreach style guide at http://outreach.missouri.edu/Webteam/style/index.html.

Formatting Your Style Guide

Contrast the organization of the Yale C/AIM Web Style Guide (http://info.med.yale.edu/caim/manual/index.html) with that of Ball State (http://www.bsu.edu/handbook/) and you'll see that one can just as easily apply lessons of navigation and organization of content to a style guide as to the Web site itself. The Yale C/AIM guide not only sports a lovely home page but also categorizes its contents into an easy-to-read list of links. You can just zip to what concerns you. The Ball State guide, on the other hand, is a single page of text that users must scroll down to find what's of interest. One advantage to the Ball State format is that it allows readers to use their Web browser's Find feature to search the page, but the Yale C/AIM guide is set up so that much more information can be presented neatly.

We recommend setting up an index page for your style guide. The only real flaw that we see in the Yale C/AIM example and the Sun style guide is that they appear to include precious little on editorial style matters — an oversight, for sure.

The style guide from West Virginia University at http://www.wvu.edu/~telecom/wwwinit/guidelines.html does mention editorial matters, specifying when to use *AP* and when to use *Chicago*. However, it again is a single page that must be scrolled and contains relatively little info.

A note for closet Luddites, who still like to feel paper between thumb and forefinger: If you use or distribute a print version of the style guide, it's a good idea to use a loose-leaf notebook format to make updating easy.

Reviewing Processes for the Few and the Many

So you've taken an idea and made it a reality. You've carefully planned your Web site, and now you're ready to live with it. But hang on a minute; you need to take one more detour before you introduce your new offspring to the world. It's time to ask some impartial reviewers to take a look before you leap.

Alphas and betas: building prototypes

One does not wave one's hands or even a magic wand and — poof! — there's a Web site, all set to launch. Developing a site takes time and involves moving through a number of stages. You must test your site before you make it public, and to do so, you have to put it somewhere where the public can't get to it but your testers can.

After the site is pasted together and ready for its first review — probably by a closed group of trusted testers — you're in the *alpha* stage. Pages on an alpha site can be in any state of development — from nonexistent to fully tested and ready to deploy. That's up to you. If you're contracting out your site's development, the development folks are probably going to host the alpha site on their server — the one where they do their work. They probably don't want you to make changes on the alpha site, and they may even restrict your ability to look at it, for fear that you may see something that's not done and express undue anxiety.

At a later stage, the site can be placed on a *beta* server. Again, what marks this stage is up to you and your developers. Usually, all of the content and graphics are done. The links should all work. Beyond that, who knows? At the beta stage, you open the site to a wider range of testing, although you probably don't make it available to the public. Beta sites are usually housed on a different server (or at least a different part of the server) than the alpha site.

All this talk of multiple servers may sound intimidating, but it's not so bad. You can quite reasonably run your alpha, beta, and even your publicly accessible Web server all on the same physical machine. (See Chapter 10.) The point is to keep these three versions of your site separate.

It's wise to assemble a group of people to really bang away at your beta site to test it. What may seem like an obvious click path to you may never cross someone else's mind. Likewise, having a representative sample of your expected users test the site can help you identify problems that arise from the use of different browsers, operating systems, and connection speeds. The more diverse and representative of your final user base your beta testing group is, the better it is for your site and for you.

Presenting staging servers

When your site is operational, you'll presumably keep freshening up and adding to its content. You need a *staging server* to act as the beta server for new material. In a sense, your alpha and beta sites are actually on staging servers; the point here, though, is that you need a staging server on a continual basis as long as you have a site.

A staging server provides you with a place to work and try out new things without making them public. (Just imagine what it would look like if some hapless user started accessing a page while you were working on it.) You should enforce security on the staging server so that access to it is limited only to those who need it. You don't want the public looking around your staging server. You also don't want just anyone inside of your company to look at it.

Who reviews documents and content?

Depending on the policies that rule at your company, you may simply want to run individual pages or whole sections of your site by a single person in the marketing department, or you may want to get a number of people involved. A review squad of this type often includes representatives of the editorial, marketing, finance, and legal departments. Even if your company isn't large enough to have an in-house attorney, you may want a qualified legal mind to examine your content for potential libel and copyright infringement problems. The review process is a good time to clear up issues that are potential legal land mines. Especially if you publish news stories, reviews, or feature pieces, you may want to consult a lawyer before sending out your proverbial message in a bottle.

Libelous statements have a way of creeping into publications through carelessness or ignorance. If you injure someone's reputation, you libel them and can be taken to court for doing so. While the U.S. judicial system has upheld the right of free speech as essential to a democracy, that in no way gives you permission to commit libel. A critical comment that looks witty and sly when quoted may easily be libelous.

Before you approach the people you hope are going to participate as a Web site review team, decide on the most efficient way to conduct the review. You may want to simply send each person a copy of the documents and have him or her respond by e-mail. Or, you may choose to put your pride and joy on a staging server and have everyone you've chosen take a look.

Whatever your approach, set a firm closing date by which everyone must send feedback to you. With all the excitement that you've generated about your new site or fresh, new content, you don't want any delays. Besides, some office joker has probably set up an office pool to predict the date you'll finally launch. Go ahead and surprise them all by meeting your own deadlines.

Part III
Under the Hood: Server, Database, and Search Engine Strategies

The 5th Wave — By Rich Tennant

"IT'S ALL HERE, WARDEN. ROUTERS, HUBS, SWITCHES, ALL PIECED TOGETHER FROM SCRAPS FOUND IN THE MACHINE SHOP. I GUESS THE PROSPECT OF BEING HIS OWN INTERNET SERVICE PROVIDER WAS JUST TOO SWEET TO PASS UP."

In this part . . .

This part was written not just for the tech head, but also for Webmasters of all likes who really need a background in tech matters. It isn't so heavy as it may sound — generally, we try to give you enough backstory to demystify servers and databases and search engines (oh my!). This part will help newly minted tech types get their footing, but it will also help the more technically challenged to be conversant in all that tech talk you just have to engage in sometimes.

Part III talks about servers, firewalls, and dealing with internal IS dilemmas. It also offers pointers for dealing with Internet Service Providers and Internet Presence Providers (and even describes the difference). Here, too, you find out about flat-file and relational database back ends, various products you may consider, and how to talk to database developers. You also learn about implementing a search engine on your Web site so users can find what they seek within your site in no time flat.

Chapter 10

Under the Hoods of a Few Good Server Options

In This Chapter

▶ Selecting a server platform

▶ Looking into server software options

▶ Deciding whether you or your ISP should run your server

▶ Considering your administrative, hardware, and connection-speed needs

▶ Dealing with the firewall

▶ Running your own server effectively 24/7

*W*hich server software you select and how you handle your server in general has a big impact on your Web site. It affects the technologies you can use to create active pages, how easily you can integrate databases and other servers into your site, how robust and reliable the site is, and more. Whether you plan to run your own server or have an ISP or IPP host your site (see Chapter 11), you need to know a bit about Web-server software — the actual software that you run on your server machine to turn it into a Web server. A number of Web servers are now popular, and each offers its own set of strengths and weaknesses. In this chapter, we walk you through what makes each of the popular server options good as well as discuss their relative weaknesses. Then we look at what's involved in running your own server, why you may want to do that, and what it's all about.

Servers and Platforms and Software — Oh My!

Your "server" actually consists of server hardware — it can be a machine as simple as a desktop PC or as complex as a Sun workstation — an operating system (the platform on which the server software runs) and the server software. Note that you can run several types of servers on a single machine — perhaps a Web server, an FTP server, and a database server. Each of those servers would have its own server software running on the machine, although they would all be running on the same platform.

Here, we concern ourselves with the Web server. For information about databases, turn to Chapter 12. For information about FTP servers, you need to turn to bigger books on the topic — there are plenty of good books available on the topic of server software. Our goal here is to help you through the maze of information about Web servers and how to choose one.

The purpose of a Web server is to respond to requests from Web browsers. This usually means locating a file on the server based on the URL that's provided by the browser and then returning the contents of that page to the browser. It can also mean executing CGI scripts that run on the server or directing to the database server and executing database queries. Basically, a server serves what the client software (the Web browser) requests.

Some really big sites actually split the load among a bunch of Web servers. In this case, requests that come into the site via its main URL are automatically redirected by a main server to one of the many other servers. This scheme allows a big site to handle much more traffic than one with a single Web server.

We said before that a server can run on a machine as simple as your desktop PC — this is true. Many smaller sites are run on Web servers under Linux (a UNIX-like operating system) on relatively simple PCs. However, Web-server software usually runs on a computer that's quite a bit more powerful than the one that's on your desk. You'll often find server machines running on platforms like Windows NT or UNIX, and in this chapter, we talk mainly about those server options — these are really the only viable options for a company Web site that gets reasonable traffic.

You may wonder why the more popular desktop operating systems, like Windows 95 and Macintosh OS, are unsuitable for running your public Web server. Those operating systems, for all their other capabilities, aren't really up to the job of staying online 24 hours a day and 7 days a week (often referred to as _24/7_).

When you are making server selections, one big question is whether you should first determine the operating system you will use or the Web-server software. (Obviously, specific Web-server software packages run under specific operating systems.) If you've already chosen a Web server, you may be locked into an operating system. If so, your Web-server software choices are limited to those that run under that operating system. If you have a specific reason for selecting one type of Web-server software, that may dictate your choice of platform. If all of your options are open, read on in this chapter, and you should be able to make a choice based on your situation and what you learn here.

If you have an ISP or IPP maintain your server, the provider is probably going to pick the Web-server software you use. Nonetheless, you should be able to have informed discussions on the topic, and you may even go with one or another ISP based on your preferences about your server setup.

Selecting a Server Platform: NT or UNIX?

People get religious when it comes to operating systems. We don't want to step on anyone's intensely held beliefs, and anyway, we believe that both Windows NT and UNIX are great choices for your Web server's operating system. Each has solid strengths as well as weaknesses. So we aren't going to pick one and recommend it; we're going to tell you what's what so you can choose.

When looking at which operating system you should run on your Web server, ask yourself the following questions:

- ✔ Does the server that you want to use run under a specific operating system? If so, your choice may be clear.

- ✔ Are your system administrators already familiar with Windows NT or UNIX? If so, you may want to stay with that one. (Of course, you should weigh other factors.)

- ✔ Will you have physical access to the server, or will it be housed in an offsite location? If so, your choice may be made for you.

In the sections that follow we'll look at the pluses and minuses of those two ever-popular operating systems, Windows NT and UNIX. (For info on the UNIX-like Linux, turn to the UNIX section.)

Windows NT

Before Microsoft launched the Windows NT operating system, it launched a marketing campaign using the slogan "Windows Everywhere." While Windows isn't your only choice for everything, you do have several Microsoft operating systems from which to choose for most of what you want to do with computers. The Windows option for running a Web site is Microsoft Windows NT, that powerhouse that builds on the overwhelming success of Microsoft Windows. NT comes in two flavors: NT Workstation and NT Server. NT Workstation can be used as a server platform; however, it lacks some features that NT Server has. In either flavor, NT is a robust and reliable operating system that's often used to run handy servers such as database, file, and Web servers. NT Server comes with Microsoft Internet Information Server (IIS) — Microsoft's Web-server software — bundled with it.

Both versions of NT come with the now ubiquitous Windows interface. This means that most people can sit down in front of an NT machine and know at least how to do basic functions — for things like saving files and other familiar tasks, using NT is a lot like using Windows 95. Many companies have chosen Windows NT as the operating system for their local area networks. If yours has done so, this makes adding another NT machine to act as your Web server a logical choice. Because Windows NT is a Windows product, machines running NT integrate easily into existing Microsoft networks. You can usually just plug the new NT machine into your corporate network, and the machine will appear in the Network Neighborhood on your desktop machine as a resource or a server (or whatever you've designated it). If you set up an NT machine as a server on a Windows network, it's a snap to access the survey's document root directory (see Chapter 7) right from your Windows 95 desktop machine.

The Windows NT Server home page is at `http://www.microsoft.com/ntserver/`, while the NT Workstation home page is at `http://www.microsoft.com/ntworkstation/`. Finally, another good site that's chock-full of NT information is the Windows NT Resource Center at `http://www.bhs.com/`.

As previously mentioned, the guts of NT Server and NT Workstation are the same. The two OSs differ in some of their features, however. NT Server is designed to act like a file and workgroup server for a large group of people. NT Workstation is designed to be a desktop operating system — it can take the place of Windows 95 on your desktop computer. Don't let the name Workstation fool you, though — NT Workstation is still a capable operating system for servers. It can act as a file server for a small workgroup of people, or it can be used to run server software such as Netscape FastTrack or Enterprise Web Server.

Microsoft's Web server software — Internet Information Server (IIS) — runs only under Windows NT Server, not NT Workstation. Why's that? Seems to be just a decision Microsoft made about how to differentiate NT Server and NT Workstation.

The two biggest drawbacks in using Windows NT are that its hardware requirements are kind of hefty and that its remote administration capabilities are limited. Our experience is that, to run a Web server on NT, you need a much more heavy weight machine than you would to handle the same amount of traffic running a Web server on one of the versions of UNIX for PCs. The bigger machine is going to cost you more moolah, too.

When it comes to remote administration, Microsoft says that it's working to improve those features in NT, and indeed you can buy third-party software that lets you do some remote administration. But on the whole you still have to be sitting in front of the machine to do plenty of the tasks you could handle remotely if you were using a UNIX machine. While this may not sound like a problem at first, it can become a real headache if your site is hosted at an ISP or IPP that uses an NT box — you're going to be traipsing down there all the time. Likewise, if you need to do maintenance on the Web server when no one is accessing your site — maybe at 4 a.m.? — you'll end up driving to where the machine is instead of sitting at home in your jammies sipping cocoa and taking care of business remotely.

That said, the convenience of setting up an NT machine as a server may make the choice plenty attractive.

UNIX

UNIX has always been a popular operating system for running server and other mission-critical software such as Web servers — in fact, the Web was originally built on UNIX machines. Until recently, running a Web server basically meant having to have a machine running UNIX. Many Webmasters still think that UNIX is the one and only operating system to use for Web servers.

Among the advantages is that Web-server software for UNIX has been around a while. It's more stable and better developed than that for Windows NT. Likewise, UNIX itself is felt to be very robust and reliable as an operating system. It's common that a machine running UNIX can run for months nonstop; this is more than can be said of just about any version of Windows, although NT is no slouch.

What's more, a vast collection of freely available software exists for use with UNIX. This software ranges from tools you can use to develop your Web site to Web-server software, such as the highly popular Apache. Even entire UNIX-like operating systems — Linux and FreeBSD — are available (for free!). Whatever you want to do, you can usually find software that's ready for your purpose — or at least ready to be modified for your needs — freely available (*and* at no cost) for UNIX.

Remotely administering UNIX machines is a breeze (if you know UNIX). Sitting in Santa Monica or Altoona, you can install software and make changes to a machine in Oswego, Bala Cynwyd, or Spokane without trouble. This can make installing software on your machine at an ISP or IPP a simple process. It also makes it easy for you to maintain your Web server at odd hours — when the machine is not being heavily trafficked and you just can't bear to pop on your parka and brave the storm outside.

The sad but true limitations of Windows 95 or Macintosh servers

We're sorry to say that the popular operating systems for desktop computers — Windows 95 and the Macintosh OS — just can't cut it as an operating system for your Web server.

Although these two offer many features that make them ideal for end users, they just weren't designed to provide the reliability that's required for running a Web server.

Unlike Windows NT, however, when you talk about UNIX, you are talking about a specific version of it, and we don't just mean Workstation or Server. There are many versions of UNIX, and each version is designed essentially to work with one particular brand or type of computer. Hardware companies like Sun and Silicon Graphics customize UNIX for the machines they develop and sell. Likewise, a number of companies make versions of UNIX that run on PCs. (Those versions can run on basically the same types of machines Windows NT can run on.) Some of the more popular versions of UNIX available for PCs include Sun Solaris, Novell UNIXWare, BSDI, and the free and easy to find Linux and Free BSD.

Should you choose to use UNIX as your OS, you have at your disposal the conveniences of remote administration and freely available software. On the other hand, you (or your system administrator) have to learn the ways of UNIX, a text-based OS with its own ins and outs. You also have to do some work to configure your machine. However, you get a robust and reliable operating system — like most things in life, it's a mixed bag.

All of the Best Server Software

Plenty of programs exist to turn a computer into a Web server, but they aren't all gemlike wonders, so here we concentrate on the more popular and robust packages. You are most likely going to end up using one of these to run your Web server.

Find out all about recent versions of popular Web servers, along with information about other add-ins and tools you can use to maintain you site, from Server Watch at `http://www.serverwatch.com`. A feature-by-feature comparison of Web-server software can be found at `http://webcompare.iworld.com`.

Netscape server software

Netscape is pretty close to synonymous with the Web in many people's minds. Netscape (the company) was founded by the good people who wrote the first graphical Web browser (Mosaic), and the company launched its newer Web browser, Netscape Navigator (often just called Netscape), before anyone else had written a commercial Web browser. So, it's no surprise that Netscape also makes very popular Web-server software. Netscape was one of the first companies to sell a Web server, and its servers are generally considered to be some of the best. Netscape makes two versions of its server software: FastTrack and Enterprise. In the next sections, we'll look briefly at each.

You can find out about Netscape's full line of server and other developer products at the Netscape DevEdge site (http://developer.netscape.com). For specific information about Netscape's FastTrack server, see: http://home.netscape.com/inf/comprod/server_central/product/fast_track/.

Likewise, you can learn all about Enterprise server at: http://home.netscape.com/inf/comprod/server_central/product/enterprise/.

FastTrack

FastTrack server is Netscape's entry-level Web server. It includes all of the features you need to host a basic Web site. It can serve up HTML pages and execute CGI scripts just fine, thank you. With FastTrack, you can administer the entire server right from a Web browser (such as . . . Navigator, for example). FastTrack server also includes Netscape's HTML editing tool. You can use it to create Web pages and upload them to the server.

Netscape offers versions of FastTrack server for Windows NT (it can run under either NT Workstation or NT Server) and for various versions of UNIX, including Sun Solaris, HP-UX, and IRIX. Features are the same for all of these versions of FastTrack. They all do just about the same thing and look practically identical. FastTrack server is also available for Windows 95, although we don't think that this is a viable option for running your public Web site.

FastTrack server does not include SSL security, so you can't create secure connections to Web browsers with it. This makes this server a poor choice for building online commerce sites. If you plan a transaction system, get Netscape Enterprise server instead. However, if you plan to go to transactions next year, don't feel that you have to get Enterprise server now. It's very easy to upgrade a FastTrack server to an Enterprise server.

Enterprise

Enterprise server offers all the features of FastTrack server, with the addition of SSL security. With Enterprise server, you can safely and securely send information over the Web. For a more detailed discussion of SSL and how it is used in online commerce (along with info about other security options than SSL), see Chapter 3.

Enterprise server has the advantage of being the most commonly used secure server on the Internet. If you plan to do secure transactions on your site, consider Enterprise server seriously. Many folks have experience administering it, and it's very robust. Also, if you're using an ISP or IPP (see Chapter 11) to host your Web site, this is the secure server that they most likely have installed on their computers, so you may wind up with it by default.

Through the Netcraft What's That Site Running page (http://www.netcraft.com/cgi-bin/Survey/whats), you can find out what server software any site on the Internet is running. Just type the URL for the site of interest into the text box provided, and watch what happens. Netcraft also maintains a Web-server survey (http://www.netcraft.com/Survey/), where you can find out which server is most popular at the moment.

Microsoft server software

Microsoft is also in the server software game and calls its entry Microsoft Internet Information Server (IIS for short). IIS is included with Windows NT Server and is only available in the Windows NT Server version. You cannot run IIS under Windows NT Workstation or any flavor of UNIX. Internet Information Server includes a graphical configuration utility, which — much like the one for Netscape servers — lets you configure the server via a Web browser that's running on your desktop machine.

Because IIS runs under Windows NT, when you use it, you get all the advantages NT offers. For example, if yours is an existing Windows network, it's incredibly easy to access your Web server's directories from other computers on the network using the Network Neighborhood. On the downside, and like NT in general, IIS can be a royal pain to administer remotely. You say you need to reboot your NT machine so those changes that you made to the server can take effect? Great. Hike over to where the machine is located and do it. You say it's 1 a.m. and the ISP hosting the machine is closed for the night? Tough luck, compadre.

All of the Microsoft products work well together. IIS integrates nicely with other Microsoft BackOffice products, for example. (BackOffice is a suite of server products.) It can use the same security features that are found in Windows to secure transactions on the Web, so you're set there. In addition, it's easy to create Web applications that use BackOffice servers such as the highly popular SQL Server, Microsoft's database server, along with IIS.

Find out all about the Microsoft Web development tools, along with much information on building Web sites around IIS, at the Microsoft Site Builder Network site at http://www.microsoft.com/sitebuilder/. Your best source of information about IIS is the Microsoft IIS page, which can be found at: http://www.microsoft.com/ntserver/info/iis.htm.

Microsoft offers a number of other components that you can add to IIS to expand its functionality. You can build an online storefront using Microsoft Merchant Server (which runs in conjunction with IIS — see Chapter 3). You can quickly and easily build data-centric Web pages using a component called Active Server. And the highly anticipated suite of new servers, known in advance of their release as Normandy, are expected to bring all types of functionality to IIS. To use any of these components from Microsoft, you need to be running IIS. They do not work with other Web servers.

Apache server software

According to Netcraft's Web server survey, Apache is the most widely used Web server in the commercial world. More .com Web sites use Apache than any other server. Apache has gained this status despite — or maybe because of — its freely available and unmarketed nature. Like Linux, Apache was developed by a large group of volunteers who were mainly interested in making it good.

Apache is primarily a UNIX-based server. (It's also available in an OS2 version, but that's beyond our scope here.) You can find downloadable versions of Apache suitable for most versions of UNIX at http://www.apache.org. You can also find extensive documentation about Apache there.

Unlike Netscape's and Microsoft's servers, Apache does not include any graphical utilities to help you set it up. You have to edit the Apache configuration files using a text editor, and you're clearly going to need to be a UNIX head to get this done. If you're already a system administrator and are familiar with maintaining UNIX machines, it isn't going to be much of a challenge, but if most of your experience has been in administering Windows networks — Windows NT and 95 — then you may want to set aside a good chunk of time to work through what you need to do. In this context, the cost of one of Netscape's servers may seem more worthwhile to you compared to the free and useful but technically challenging Apache.

One more yummy aspect of Apache is that you can use all of that good UNIX stuff with Apache. Much of that stuff is free, but again, if you aren't UNIX-adept, it may be challenging.

Running It Yourself versus Having Your ISP Run It

Now that you know about your options in choosing a server, you need to consider who is going to run the thing and where it is to be located. The answer is not automatically you and in your own cramped cubicle. Basically, the server can be located at your site — that is, attached to your corporate network, which is in turn attached to the Internet — or it can be located at an ISP or IPP. If your server is located at an ISP or IPP, your site can be housed either on one of its servers — in which case yours may be one of hundreds hosted on that same machine — or on your machine (or a leased one) at the ISP's or IPP's locale.

Chapter 11 talks about the ins and outs of having an ISP or IPP host your site for you, so to find out more about that subject, turn to that part of the book. As in most matters, there are pros and cons — enough so that we gave it its own chapter. Here we talk more about the ins and outs of hosting your site yourself.

If you plan to go the ISP or IPP route, read on in this chapter anyway to get a small mountain of information that can help you in talking to your ISP or IPP about your server.

Running Your Own Server

To some people, the very nature of being a Webmaster is one and the same as running a Web server. Some folks think that a Webmaster is primarily a server administrator. (We don't think that way, and if you do, turn to Chapter 1 for more on all that a Webmaster is and does.) Running your own server does, however, offer some distinct advantages over entrusting it to the care and handling of an ISP or IPP. On the other hand, it can be a bit of a pain. We'll start with the upside.

Why bother?

The first question to ask yourself in assessing whether to run your own server is *why bother?* With so many companies now offering Web-hosting services, the need to run your own server may seem less compelling now than in years gone by, when you basically had to maintain your own Web server to have a site at all.

Your own server = Total control

Running your own server in-house gives you total control over the machine. (Okay, so you may experience budgetary constraints, but that's life.) You, the Webmaster, can decide what software is used, when the machine needs to be upgraded, and when a second server is required. Some ISPs and IPPs that host sites or servers allow you to run only server-side scripts that they have approved, while others don't let you run any server-side scripts (for fear of security holes and a drag on server performance). When you own the box, you don't have to worry about these restrictions.

Running your own Web server also means that you can install additional servers as you need them. Many of the more technologically compelling forms of content — RealAudio, RealVideo, Castanet presentations, and so on — require special server software. If you're using an ISP or IPP to house your site, you may have to persuade or even bug the provider to install the additional servers that you need. It's hard to find an ISP or IPP that offers such a broad and inclusive mix of servers that everyone who wants something special is pleased. When you're running your site from your own server, you can install additional, specialized servers as you need them.

But (and this is a big but): Having full control of the box also makes you fully responsible for the thing. You, not the ISP or IPP, have to keep the box and the Internet connection running all of the time — 24 hours a day, 7 days a week — come fire, flood, or pestilence. You will be the one to rise at 3 a.m. when the boss (who is in London, where it's a decent hour) notices that the site has gone down and calls, and you must figure out what to do. (Turn to "Keeping Your Server Running 24/7," later in this chapter, for clues.)

Connecting to existing systems is easier

Running your own server at your own location (maybe right under your desk) makes it much easier to connect with any existing back-end systems you may have. This can include database servers that you're using for an online storefront or your existing in-house fulfillment system.

What's more, you don't want scripts that are hosted on an ISP's or IPP's machine accessing resources that are on your network (like your database or fulfillment back ends). This poses many technical and policy problems. From a technical point of view, it's hard to do. Many things can go wrong, and the connection between your ISP and your corporate LAN usually doesn't have enough bandwidth to handle data transfer.

Likewise, you don't want the security hole involved in letting scripts running on a machine owned by your ISP or IPP access some of your internal machines. It's much more secure to run your own server and allow your own, well-controlled server to access your existing machines. If you work for a company with a network security committee, the committee probably isn't going to let pass a plan that involves any type of back-and-forth communication between in-house systems and an ISP's or IPP's out-of-house scripts.

If your company already has a Web server as part of its intranet, you probably already have the technical expertise to run your Web site in-house. The technical demands of running a Web server for an intranet and for a public site are about the same.

The hardware you need

You can run a Web server on any of several hardware choices. We have seen Web servers running on computers ranging from 486 PCs that cost about $1000 to a cluster of Sun workstations that cost upwards of $20,000 each. Of course, the $1000 PC can handle a lot less traffic than the $20,000 workstation, yet everyone would rather use the $1000 PC if it could do the job. So on what basis can you decide where you fall in the continuum?

A big determining factor is the type of content that comprises your site. If your site is almost exclusively static HTML files, you can get away with a less powerful machine. If you're going to be running lots of CGI scripts that take up processing time on the Web server, you need more juice. Connecting databases and fulfillment systems, or running cool stuff like RealAudio or Castanet treats, is going to up the ante even more.

Take into account these matters:

✔ Do you plan to generate dynamic Web pages, or are you using static HTML pages? The more dynamic your content, the more powerful your hardware needs to be. Static HTML pages can run on less robust machines, like that basic $1000 PC.

✔ Do you plan on running many CGI scripts? You need a Pentium or Sun machine with a great deal of memory to do this.

✔ Do you plan to run additional servers — say a database server or a RealAudio server? You can run a Web server and a database server on the same machine if it has a powerful processor or more than one processor. It needs plenty of memory for multiple servers, too. You may even need multiple machines for this one — and the more traffic that you expect, the more machines it's going to take.

✔ Do you plan to serve thousands of visitors per day? Every simultaneous user takes up memory on the machine. A simple PC can handle a few at a time, but for a commercial site that may have even just hundreds of users simultaneously, you need 128MB of memory, and for thousands, you need multiple machines.

We've seen all types of machines used to host Web sites, ranging from the small I-can't believe-it-works type to the huge I-can't-believe-they-can-afford-that type. Here are some examples:

✔ A 486-based PC running Linux (a freeware version of UNIX) with 32MB of RAM and a 1GB IDE hard disk. This site consisted of mostly static HTML pages and used only one CGI script. The sturdy but homely machine that housed this site served thousands of pages per day without taxing its abilities, and it never crashed once.

✔ A Pentium 200 – based PC running Windows NT Server with 128MB of RAM and an 8GB SCSI hard disk. This machine served a site consisting of static HTML pages, a catalog database, and a secure but simple ordering system. It had thousands of visitors per day but just hundreds using the transaction system.

✔ A cluster of three Sun workstations, each with 96MB of RAM and an 8GB hard disk. One of the Suns ran a Web server that served static HTML pages, while a second executed CGI scripts and a third ran a database server. This site successfully handled hundreds of visitors per day doing complex database searches.

Keep in mind that you get more bang for the buck (or for the CPU) using computers running UNIX than computers running NT. This means that the same machine running UNIX can handle more hits than one running NT.

Also, don't skimp on hard disk requirements. There are two types of hard disks: IDE and SCSI. IDE is cheaper, and SCSI is more robust. Most desktop machines come with IDE drives (the 486 PC in our previous example had an

IDE hard drive). IDE drives are fine for desktop PCs, but they slow to a crawl under the burden of a server's load. Get a SCSI drive, even if you use the stodgy $1000 PC option. The extra cost of the SCSI drive is well worth it.

Finally, the same software-is-a-memory-hog rule applies here as well as on your desktop PC. Get memory — lots of it. No matter what hardware you choose, load your machine with all of the memory it can handle. More traffic is a heavier load. More scripts represent a heavier load. You don't want slow loading of your pages — you lose traffic that way.

All about administration

Running a Web server is not a matter of setting up the machine and heading for Hawaii while the thing hums nicely along. Keeping a Web server up and running all the time takes a unique set of system administration and networking skills. To keep your server running, you need to have someone on board who can keep the Internet connection going all the time — someone who knows about TCP/IP networking, and more specifically about the type of leased line that you have. (TCP/IP, by the way, is the networking protocol that holds together the Internet.)

This person can monitor your connection to the Internet, and if and when it goes down, they're on the case with your ISP. (You need an ISP even if you run your own server — right?) This person may also have to coordinate visits from the phone company to maintain the leased line. The administrator can also review the system's log files, looking for anything out of the norm and keeping an eye on disk usage and security.

These are matters that need vigilant attention — don't relegate them to an overworked techie whose first priority is fixing the CEO's computer. (Most system administrators opt for the CEO's computer if forced by time constraints to choose.)

To keep your server in top, reliable condition, you need to attend to its maintenance as if it were a fine car. Don't assign this to the dog groomer or your hair stylist. Get a knowledgeable, diligent administrator with both system and network administration skills.

What about connecting to the Internet?

Running a Web server is not like hooking up your desktop PC to the Internet. When you run a Web server, many people (you hope) are going to be accessing the machine at once. You need a *permanent* (that means a 24-hours-a-day, 7 days-a-week) connection to the Internet that can handle some traffic. And even if you run your own server, you need some kind of ISP account, so you need a good ISP and a good relationship with that provider.

Your ISP can help you determine the best option for connecting your corporate LAN to the Internet. Whatever technology you wind up using, it's important that your ISP is already familiar with that option. You don't want to be its first customer using a new technology that your ISP is just getting the hang of.

Tackling the question of what type of connection you need means considering bandwidth and speed and how to cope with your firewall, if you have one.

Bandwidth and more bandwidth

Different types of connections afford you more or less bandwidth. You want as much bandwidth as you can afford. (This is kind of like memory in that way.) *Bandwidth* is a measure of the amount of data that can travel over your connection to the Internet. Bandwidth is usually measured in *kilobits* (1024 bits) per second or *megabits* (1024 kilobits, or 1,048,576 bits) per second. The abbreviation for these measurements are *Kbps* (kilobits per second) and *Mbps* (megabits per second).

Bandwidth usage usually comes in bursts — it isn't spread neatly around the clock. It's common knowledge that most folks use the Net during lunchtime, so there's a big surge in bandwidth then, for example.

What do you connect to?

So what exactly does your dedicated Internet connection connect to? Well, it usually connects you to an ISP's network — often the same sort of ISP that you may use for dial-up Internet access at home. (Much as the phone company offers both residential and business usage at different pricing structures, so too does an ISP.) Your ISP's network, in turn, uses dedicated lines to connect to the Internet backbone. This figure shows the typical relationship between a local network, an ISP's network, and an Internet backbone.

In interviewing potential ISPs (see Chapter 12), check what type of bandwidth the ISP has and how many other customers it has using that bandwidth. The ISP should have more bandwidth than it's using. In a perfect world, there would be more bandwidth between the ISP and the Internet than between all of the ISP's customers and the ISP. (If you find an ISP like this, please . . . let us know. They're rarer than honest politicians.) You can use the ratio of the ISP's bandwidth to all of the ISP's customers' bandwidths to compare one ISP to another. Pick the one with the lowest ratio. Again, Chapter 11 is all about dealing with ISPs.

Yes, Virginia, you really need a T1 line (or better)

Having done the math to figure out how much bandwidth you're going to need, you can now turn your attention to how to get that bandwidth into your building. All of the options (with the exception of one — cable modem — which is not much of an option yet) are based on using telephone technology. Check with your local phone company's business office to see what's available in your area. Pacific Bell, the telephone company that operates in most of California, dedicates a section of its Web site to describing the digital services it offers. You can check into Pacific Bell's offerings at `http://www.pacbell.com` and Nynex's (for the greater New York area) at `http://www.nynex.com`.

The first question that you may have is: What is a T1 (also called a DS1)? A *T1* is just a big phone line (big in the sense of having large capacity). If your company has a PBX and multiple phone lines, it probably already leases one or more T1s from the local phone company to simply handle telephone calls. This same phone line technology (that is, a T1 line) is used to make a dedicated connection between your corporate LAN and the Internet. Table 10-1 shows the various types of connections that are available and the amount of bandwidth that each of them offers.

Table 10-1	Connection Types	
These Connections	*Offer This Much Bandwidth*	*Suitable for Hosting a Site?*
Frame relay	56 Kbps – 1.5 Mbps	Yes, but only at higher speeds
ISDN	56 Kbps – 128 Kbps	Yes, if traffic is low
T1 (a.k.a. DS1)	1.54 Mbps	Yes
Cable modem	10 Mbps	No, because Internet protocol for cable is not tweaked for publishing information
T3 (a.k.a. DS3)	45 Mbps	Yes

All about bits and kilobits

It may surprise you that 2 Kbps is not 2000 bps. That's because 1K (one kilo) is actually 1024 — 2K then, is 2048. Likewise, 1M (mega) equals 1024K, and 1G (giga) equals 1024M. Going backwards, 1G = 1024M = 1024 x 1024K = 1024 x 1024 x 1024, which equals 1,073,741,824. In other words, 1024Kbps equals 1,048,576 bits. (Did you really want to know all that?)

About ISDN

To run your own server, ISDN is really only an option if you expect very low traffic, say in the dozens of users. It's often not economically feasible to keep an ISDN line running 24/7. This is because usage on an ISDN line is metered. For a company Web site, ISDN is really not practical.

About T1s and T3s

The two most commonly used connections — T1 and T3 lines — warrant a few notes:

- ✔ T1s (also known as DS1s) are commonly used to hook up office PBXs to the phone system. You may already have a T1 line.

- ✔ When a T1 is used to connect to the Internet, the T1 is routed to your ISP instead of to the phone company's central office. The entire capacity of the T1 is used to handle Internet data. A T1 is the slowest connection that you should have to the Internet if you're going to host your own Web server.

- ✔ Some big sites use multiple T1s when then need more capacity than a single T1 but less capacity than that provided by a T3. (Use of T3s is pretty rare; usually only very large Internet software companies and huge ISPs use T3s. In some cases you can lease part of a T3.)

- ✔ Although the T1 is leased from a phone company, your ISP can often handle all the details of ordering it and scheduling its installation. We've been involved in ordering a number of T1 and other fast connections to the Internet in California, and the only contact that we had with the phone company was when its people arrived to install its equipment. Our ISP placed the order and arranged the installation.

- ✔ A T1 is the slowest connection that you should consider if you are planning to host your own Web site. Unless yours is a really big organization number-ing in the hundreds of Internet users, the bandwidth of a T1 is capable of handling all your Internet traffic.

- ✔ A T3 (also known as a DS3) is like a bunch of T1s tied together. A T3 can be used for telephone traffic or for connecting your corporate LAN to the Internet. The only difference between a T1 and T3 is that, with the T3, you get gobs more bandwidth — sometimes 40 times as much.

- ✔ For both T1 and T3 lines, the phone company charges by the length of the run of the line. The farther away your ISP, the more the phone company charges.

- ✔ In addition to the fee that you pay to the phone company for having a T1 or T3, you also pay your ISP for the privilege of accessing the Internet via the T1 or T3. This costs more than the twenty smackers per month that you pay for your personal Internet account.

Be sure that your ISP has enough bandwidth to handle your connection. Having a 45 Mbps connection to your ISP does not help you much if your ISP actually has only 3 Mbps of bandwidth to the Internet.

About cable modem connections

Cable modem connections aren't the best for hosting your Web site. First, outside of a few test markets, no one actually offers this option. Second, while a cable modem connection is faster than a T1, the bandwidth it offers is not divided evenly between data going into the cable modem and that going out of it. Basically, you gets lots of bandwidth to browse and only a little bandwidth to publish. When cable modem systems were designed, the idea was that the only thing you would be sending back upstream was e-mail — not big ol' Web pages. The @Home Network (http://www.home.net) and Time Warner's Road Runner (http://www.rdrun.com) are both very involved in developing cable modem access to the Internet. If you want more info, check 'em out.

Getting around the firewall

A *firewall* is usually a combination of hardware and software that's designed to isolate your corporate network from the Internet. If you're setting up your Web server on a network that has a firewall (and if your corporate network is connected to the Internet, it *should* have a firewall), you have to do some special configuring to make everything work. The basic challenge is where to locate the Web server — inside or outside the firewall. Refer to the following section for details.

Many companies have a security committee. These good people are responsible for network security. If your company has such a group, you may have to get their approval for the way that your Web site is set up. This is especially true if your site is to interface to your back-end systems or if your server must house confidential information. Remember that it's this august group's job to keep the company's data and resources safe. It is not their job to keep your Web site jumping with cutting-edge technologies.

Looking into firewalls

The point of a firewall is to allow people on the corporate network to access the Internet (perhaps with restrictions as to who can do so or what they can access) while not allowing people on the public Internet to access resources on your corporate LAN. Basically, a firewall acts as a gateway through which all your Internet traffic must flow. The firewall's job is to allow and disallow traffic on a case-by-case basis, obeying rules that are set up by the network administrator.

Firewalls work well in limiting access from the Internet to your corporate LAN. They do not always work well when you want to run a Web server, want everyone in the world to be able to access the server, and want people on your corporate LAN to access the Web server, too. If, on top of all that, if you also want your Web server to be able to execute queries against databases that are behind the firewall, things get very interesting. And given that those are all perfectly usual things to want if you're a Webmaster, the firewall is likely to be the subject of much of your attention.

A firewall can exist at some point or another in the configuration of your network. Everything on your network that's directly connected to the Internet is said to be outside of the firewall, even if it's in the building, while everything that has to go through the firewall to get to the Net is considered to be inside the firewall. A firewall treats any computer outside of it as an unknown machine. Figure 10-1 shows a typical firewall setup.

Where you place your Web server is one of the bigger choices you get to make (unless your network administrator or security administrator makes the choice for you). Technically, you can place your Web server inside or outside the firewall. Each choice has its pros and cons, as with most things in life.

The work of configuring the firewall usually falls to the network administrator. We hope to give you enough information here so that you can talk to that person about your options and work together to place your Web server in the best location for your particular network and Web-site requirements.

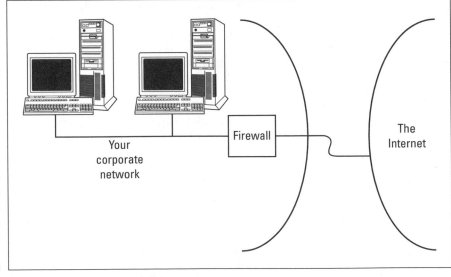

Figure 10-1:
The firewall marks the line between the corporate LAN (inside the firewall) and the public Internet.

Placing the Web server outside the firewall

Putting the Web server outside the firewall is at first blush the easiest and most secure way to go. Figure 10-2 shows a conceptual diagram of this setup. Please note that the locations of the pieces in Figure 10-3 indicate their conceptual positioning, which is not necessarily the same as their physical positioning on the network.

This option makes it easy for folks outside the firewall to access your site, but it's harder for those within the firewall to gain access. To get around this, the network administrator must set up the firewall to allow people within it to access the Web server. Be forewarned, though, that doing this can introduce a problem if people on the local network are not usually allowed to access material on the public Internet. Likewise, if your Web server needs to access resources inside the firewall — say a database server for example — the firewall must be configured to allow this access. You may have to negotiate with your network administrator to get the access that you need.

It is possible to place not only the Web server but any other servers that it requires — say, a database server — outside the firewall. You can even replicate data between a database server inside the firewall and one outside the firewall. These options introduce many security concerns, however, which your network administrator has to address.

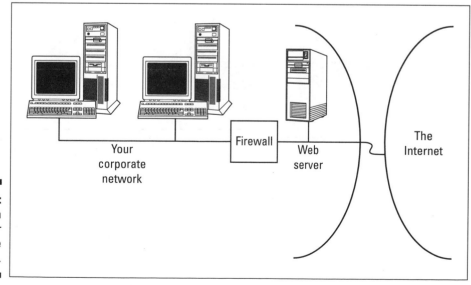

Figure 10-2:
Here is a Web server outside the firewall.

Placing the Web server inside the firewall

If you place the Web server inside the firewall, your network administrator must configure the firewall to allow people on the Internet to access the machine — otherwise you'll have a Web server that only people on your corporate network can access. (Hmmm, isn't that an *intranet?*) Figure 10-3 shows a typical setup with the Web server inside the firewall. Most network administrators frown upon putting the Web server inside of the firewall, because this means that they have to open a hole in the firewall to allow outsiders to access the Web server. The more holes that you put in your firewall, the more it resembles the Jarlsberg cheese of security.

Placing the Web server inside and outside at the same time

You can have it both ways — maybe not always, but about this topic. Figure 10-4 shows a setup consisting of two Web servers, one inside the firewall and the other outside.

The advantage of this is that users on both the corporate LAN and the public Internet can access the Web server. The network administrator does not have to compromise the security of the firewall, either by letting people on the public Internet access the Web server or by letting people on the corporate network access the public Internet. This keeps the security committee happier and more cooperative, too.

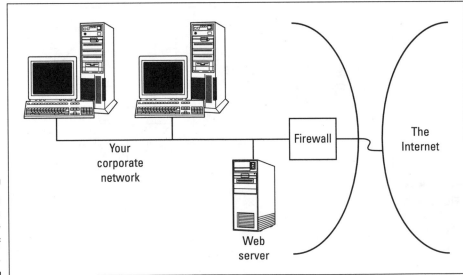

Figure 10-3:
Here the
Web server
is inside of
the firewall.

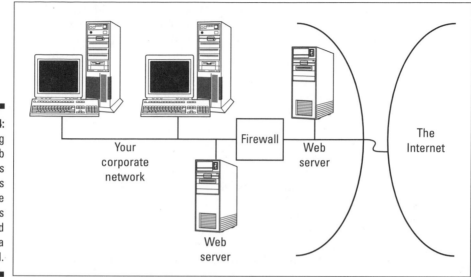

Figure 10-4:
Having
two Web
servers
addresses
some of the
problems
associated
with a
firewall.

The drawback to this scheme, though, is that you have to keep two Web servers running and in sync. This is no picnic. Often, an updated piece of content that's posted to one server does not make it to the other server. This can cause quite a bit of confusion, as employees look at the site and see something different than what people on the public Internet see. This is sloppy, but it's also the result of highly understandable human error. Whether the pros and cons of this option are acceptable for you is your choice.

Keeping Your Server Running 24/7

Running your own server means keeping it running 24 hours a day and 7 days a week. Someone must be available at all hours to fix the server if something goes wrong. Weekends, holidays, you name it — someone has to be responsible. Servers don't take vacations. However, this is not as daunting as it seems. Paying attention to the server during your working hours goes a long way toward your confidence that the server can run smoothly after hours.

Backup hardware also helps. Have a second machine ready to take over the duties of your Web server at a moment's notice, and you can quickly get your site back up when a hard disk crashes or another major hardware problem occurs. Just remember that your backup machine must have the same updated content as the original machine. This means double-posting, which opens the door to human error, but it is a viable choice if you want to make sure that you're up 24/7.

Computers — like children and puppies — don't think about your schedule much when they act up, and you need someone on call to reboot and fix things 24/7. But that person needn't sit by the machine around the clock — the server may never crash.

We once ran a Web server that hummed along 24/7 for nine months with no crashes. Routine maintenance for this machine consisted of about 15 minutes every weekday reviewing log files, and then random remote checking of the machine on occasional nights and weekends. When the server finally went down, it was because of a county-wide power failure. (The box, by the way, was running on Linux.)

Even a power failure can be sidestepped with adequate investment of resources. We know one IPP that not only uses a UPS (uninterrupted power supply) to fend off the effects of a power failure but also has diesel generators and direct multiple connections to different Internet backbones available so that its clients' sites and servers continue to run, even in the event of a long-term power failure. (These folks are in earthquake country.)

A good compromise measure that can get you both the benefits of running your own server and some nice 24/7 support is to colocate your server at an ISP or IPP. In this scheme, you usually lease a computer and place it at your ISP. It plugs into your ISP's backbone — giving it full access to all of the provider's bandwidth — and because the ISP usually has a system administrator on site 24/7 to do emergency maintenance, you're covered. Chapter 11 (hey, that's the next one!) covers dealing with ISPs and IPPs.

Chapter 11

Dealing with ISPs and IPPs

● ●

In This Chapter

▶ Choosing an Internet service provider (ISP)

▶ Considering an Internet presence provider

▶ Determining what it's going to cost

▶ Growing your Web site gracefully

▶ Avoiding painful mistakes

▶ Changing ISPs smoothly and carefully

● ●

*T*he most important decision you may make for the future of your Web site is choosing the company that serves your data to the world. You want your visitors to be able to get into your Web site on the first try — if this doesn't happen, they may never try again. You also want to relax and not have to worry about whether your pages are available so that you can focus on the content and promotion of your site. The ISP you use should be flexible, competent, and trustworthy, as any vendor should. We tell you this up front: *Comparison shopping is essential* when choosing an Internet service provider. This chapter focuses on the Web-hosting aspects of Internet service rather than exploring every connection option for Internet access in general. (For information on types of connections and how you can run your own in-house server, turn to Chapter 10.)

ISPs and the Services They Offer

Different ISPs (*Internet service providers*) offer different services, although the basic idea behind all of them is to offer data transfer to and from the Internet, and to offer additional services to allow you to access online information and to create, implement, and distribute your own data over the Internet. In contrast, IPPs (*Internet presence providers*) are in the business of hosting sites but not necessarily providing Internet access to you, and they may do all or some of the creation and production on your behalf. Most ISPs offer packages that include a combination of services for a fixed monthly fee, a metered rate based on traffic, or both. Companies that run Web sites or ftp servers with high traffic may pay more per month depending on the amount of data that is transferred or stored.

Choosing a service for hosting your Web site is somewhat different than choosing an ISP for providing Internet access. You may use one company for hosting your Web site and a different company for basic access, or you may find one company that fits the bill all around. When choosing an ISP for Internet access for your company and its staff, you want to know how fast it can serve data to you, but when you're choosing a provider to host your Web site, your main concern is how fast it can serve data to your customers. Ideally, your site is going to have more visitors than your company has employees, so the ISP that hosts your Web site should have much more bandwidth and hardware than is needed to serve you personally (or serve you and all your work buddies with access to the Internet).

You have the following options:

✔ Maintaining a direct connection and an in-house Web server (we talk about this in Chapter 10)

✔ Hosting your Web site remotely with the company that you use for Internet access

✔ Hosting your Web site remotely, but using another company for access

✔ Colocating your site by placing it on a dedicated server that's located at an Internet service provider, in which case you may either lease or purchase the physical machine

✔ Using an IPP for hosting and possibly for content and maintenance

Recommended reading: Rick Adams, founder and CEO of national ISP UUNet, has written an enlightening article, "How To Select an Internet Service Provider." You can find it at `http://www.cnam.fr/Network/Internet-access/how_to_select.html`.

Using your existing network

If your office is already set up with a corporate intranet that's connected to the outside world, or if you have company-wide Internet access, you may not have to choose an ISP, because you're already connected to the Net. Two options are available if your company already has a direct network connection: (a) maintain your own Web server on-site (as described in Chapter 10) or (b) colocate a server with your ISP (we talk a bit about this in Chapter 10 and cover it further in "Server Colocation: The Best of Both Worlds," later in this chapter). It's also possible to do both by setting up a router to transfer traffic (depending on flow) either your way or to your ISP. Contact your existing ISP to discuss colocation or mirroring options such as these.

The Webmaster's role in setting up a network

While setting up an entire office intranet is not exactly within the scope of the Webmaster's usual duties, you need to make sure that you're in on the decision-making process about what route to take when installing a network. If you are not the company's systems administrator (sysadmin), make sure that you befriend this person and keep each other informed on decisions involving the Web site's connection to the world. Decisions such as where the servers are to be located (on-site or at the ISP), how much server space and bandwidth is to be reserved for the Web site, and who has password access to the servers can certainly affect the Webmaster's daily routine. Be sure to use the checklist in "Questions to ask an ISP," later in this chapter, when discussing server and network options with your sysadmin or with a network consultant. Owning and operating a Web server that's directly connected to the Internet is the best way to have a site that's easily accessed by company employees and is quickly updated, but make sure that your administration and support staff is up to such a task. Be sure to consider security, maintenance, and human resources issues as well as those involving bandwidth and budget.

If you are lucky enough to be in on the decision-making process about what ISP is to supply direct access, your first priorities should be proximity to your server's physical location (for speed of access), reliability, reputation, and budget. Before you sign on with any company for direct Internet access, ask its personnel for the names and URLs of clients who are running sites on a similar scale and budget. If you're considering T1 or T3 access, talk to T1 customers. If you're considering ISDN, contact ISDN customers. (In Chapter 11 we discuss connection options.) The same consideration is valid with other bandwidth options. Talking to the administrators and Webmasters who use a particular ISP to run their sites is the best way to make a decision about which company to use.

If you or your systems administrator is looking into ISDN, cable modems, or other fast and furious data transfer options, take a gander at High Bandwidth, a Web page that organizes useful links about all of the hot data transfer technologies. You can find it at http://www.specially.com/hiband/.

Web hosting doesn't mean full-time access

Some companies, particularly smaller businesses, may have no need for full and constant Internet access. Examples of businesses that may want Web sites but probably don't need their own networks include coffee shops, comic book stores, art galleries, clothing and record stores, automobile dealers, restaurants, building contractors, and other small retailers and service-oriented businesses. In other words, if you serve most of your customers in person rather than from a distance, you probably don't need direct access unless you're planning to develop an online sales division.

In these cases, the premises may not even have a computer, or there may be a few computers located in the business office. You, the Webmaster, may or may not be an employee of the business, and you may do most of your work from home. Each person or workgroup is probably going to want his or her own dial-up account for purposes of keeping e-mail separate, but most people in the company are probably only going to use these accounts for e-mail and Web surfing.

As the Webmaster, you need to consider additional features when choosing an ISP. Unless the owner of the business is married to the idea of using a specific company, you should probably choose the ISP first and then help the other employees that are connected with the Web site set up e-mail accounts with the same company or through the Web site itself.

Questions to ask an ISP

Consider what you want, and then choose an ISP that offers those features. Choosing an ISP based on price alone is probably not your best bet, because many ISPs offer similarly competitive prices for slightly different sets of features. What's more, changing ISPs later, whether you are registering a domain name or not, is a hassle that you want to avoid, if possible. You need to find a company that responds to questions quickly, that's easy to work with, that can help you make decisions confidently, and that offers specifically what you need. Ask for customer testimonials (and corresponding e-mail and Web addresses). Ask your friends or business contacts in the trade who they recommend — and (perhaps more importantly) who to steer clear of.

Make a checklist of the following questions, and compare the features of the ISPs that you're considering to your answers. Your priorities and budget both affect the weight of each question when you're making your decision. Consider these points:

We look at each of these items in turn.

- ✔ **How reliable is the service?** Your most important concern when choosing an ISP is its reliability. How much downtime a week (in hours) does it suffer, and how is that going to affect your business? How often does it back up the data on its servers? Does it have a contingency plan for power outages, storms, and natural disasters? Does it have strong customer service, return phone calls and e-mail quickly (say, within 30 minutes), and follow up on the tough questions?

- ✔ **How much disk space on the server do you need for the site?** The amount of disk space that your site needs depends on the kind of site that you're running. If you plan to include large files, such as QuickTime movies or downloadable software products, you're going to need a lot more space. Don't forget that databases and large e-mail archives are often counted differently from HTML documents; discuss these storage options with the ISP before you sign on.

✔ **Do you need a UNIX shell account for maintenance?** Shell access, in a nutshell (yuk, yuk), means that you can telnet into a server to conduct remote operations such as scripting, editing, and site administration. Some sites offer shell access or shell accounts routinely, while others avoid handing out telnet access to the servers for security reasons. You may not need shell access, depending on your abilities and your site management methods. Many Webmasters are able to manage their sites just fine using routine ftp operations; it follows that full ftp access to your files is essential.

✔ **Do you need the capability to install and execute CGI scripts?** A lot of interactivity, randomization, redirection of traffic from page to page, and other nifty site features are accomplished with the use of CGI scripts. If you predict the need to run CGIs, make sure that you choose a company that offers you that option.

✔ **Do you want prepackaged Web-page services?** Many ISPs, including a lot of companies that don't offer the option of custom CGI scripts, offer their customers predesigned Web-page functions such as forms processing, site-specific search engines, guest books or bulletin boards, and chat capability. Some companies go as far as offering templates that you can use to design extremely simple Web pages. Make sure that these tools (or toys) are up to snuff. Find out how customizable they are before you get too excited about them.

✔ **Do you need an automated mailing list package?** If part of the plans for your site include running your own mailing list, you may want to consider using Majordomo, Listserv, or another automated mailing list package. Some ISPs offer use of this software routinely as part of their standard Internet package, while others charge a modest fee for use. Mailing list software, however, is one Internet option that you can add easily from another company if your own ISP doesn't offer it.

✔ **Are you considering implementing live content?** *Live content* is a buzzword that stands for a lot of other Internet buzzwords: Java, Shockwave, RealAudio, CUSeeMe, push media, and so on. Live content basically involves interaction between the user and the computer server, beyond the level of simple requests for data. Some live content, such as RealAudio, involves operating specific server software. Other live content involves other issues you should discuss with your ISP.

✔ **Do you plan to run a high-traffic Web site?** While everyone wants his site to be popular, you need to acknowledge the minimum and maximum goals for the size of your audience when you're considering a Web-hosting service. Running a site that has mass appeal for a specific niche of people (like gardeners or teenagers) is quite different than creating the next Yahoo! competitor. Talk to your ISP about how many clients it has and how much Web traffic it handles each month.

✔ **Are you using the site to sell a product? Do you need to provide secure transactions?** Security in things like e-mail messages is important to everyone on the Internet, but protecting things such as customer records and credit-card numbers can make or break your company if you sell online. When online transactions are part of a site, the ISP must support popular transaction systems. (See Chapter 3 for more on security and selling online.)

✔ **Is a database part of your site?** There are basically two kinds of Internet databases: the kind that stores data that your customers submit and the kind that serves archived data to your visitors. These can, of course, exist in the same package, but not all sites need both features. Customer surveys and online transactions are examples of the first type, while search engines and reference directories are examples of the second. You may not need a separate database server for certain data, but you certainly need software. If you have an existing database, find out whether your ISP can accommodate the software you use in ways that are useful to the Web — converting data from package to package is tedious at best. On the other hand, if you're building the database at the same time as the Web site, your needs may be more flexible.

There are ISPs that market themselves as gay-friendly, Christian, family-oriented, chic, intelligent, or ultra-hip, and if image is a key factor to you, you may consider whether your image is compatible with theirs. One publishing firm we know chose the Well as its ISP to make the firm appear to be "wired." A right-wing banking firm in California changed providers immediately when it discovered that its ISP also served some outspoken pro-choice coalitions as pro-bono work. (Chapter 8 talks more about jobbing out the creation of your site.)

✔ **Are you going to be registering a domain name?** Registering a domain name should be relatively painless. Make sure that your ISP has experience in doing this quickly and well; ask the provider for the domain names of several other clients that you can speak to so you can make sure that this is the case. While a one-time setup fee for registering a domain name is common, it's also avoidable, and the fee shouldn't be exorbitant. On the other hand, if you're pretty sure that you don't need a domain name, make sure that the pathname that's to be assigned to your home page isn't too unwieldy.

✔ **Are you counting on using your ISP for consulting as well as hosting?** Some Internet service providers offer routing consulting on networking, administration, scripting, HTML, and other aspects of a site. Others simply do not, and they ignore all requests to that end. Make sure you establish at the beginning of your relationship with the ISP what its position is, to avoid any misunderstandings. Often, if the ISP doesn't do consulting work itself, it can recommend one of its own clients who does.

> ✔ **Do you have any use for additional offerings?** These bonus features or extra packages can include things such as Web-page design, Internet marketing support, business partner connections, custom advertising servers, catalog servers, or database packages. Look at the descriptions of what the ISP offers, and decide if any of it looks essential.

You can find out a lot about thousands of ISPs by searching The List of Internet Service Providers, a.k.a. The List. You can search the List, or you can browse it by state, region, area code, and even country code. The List resides at `http://thelist.iworld.com/`.

In general, it's best to choose a local ISP with a solid background and reputation. Occasionally, investing in the new kid on the block can be a great move and the best inroad to innovation, but unless your gut says otherwise in a resounding voice, go with a more established or a widely recommended local provider.

Types of ISPs

Internet service providers essentially fall into three basic types, any of which is perfectly capable of hosting a Web site: commercial online services, national Internet service providers, and local Internet service providers.

Commercial online services

Commercial online services include America Online, CompuServe, Prodigy, and NetComplete (from Netcom). These companies provide content and interactivity to their subscribers, with Internet access offered as part of their services; most of them also host Web pages. Notice that we said *pages,* not *sites.* Unless you have a strong commitment to using such a service for your site, it's probably better to look elsewhere. Many online services don't support domain name registration, but more importantly, they're notorious for slow response times and busy signals on their Web servers, and they just don't offer the power that a company site — even a smaller one — usually warrants. (P.S. Commercial online services are not considered hip, cool, or groovy; if your e-mail address or domain name includes `aol.com`, for example, others even slightly in the know may take you far less seriously.)

National and local ISPs

National Internet service providers and local Internet service providers vary widely in terms of who their clients are. A local ISP may host Web pages or sites from all over, rather than from its little corner of the world, and it may offer quite a lot of bandwidth. One distinction, however, is that national ISPs, such as UUNet, BBN Planet, Netcom, or AT&T, often own and maintain a piece of Internet backbone, and that makes their service *theoretically* quicker and more reliable than others. In practice, however, you can serve just as many customers via a healthy local ISP as you can via a company that is set up as a nationwide provider. Keep in mind, too, that physical location of a server means little to surfers of the Web. You can host your Web pages anywhere in the physical universe and they will still be accessible to the whole world, as long as the ISP's Internet connections are stable and reliable.

CNET's Ultimate Guide to Internet Service Providers (http://www.cnet.com/Content/Reviews/Compare/ISP/) offers reviews of both national and local services. Not only do the experts rate the companies on what features they offer, but you can read comments about the best and the worst ISPs that are written by users like yourself.

Internet bandwidth: the condensed version

You've probably heard the much-told fable of how the Department of Defense first set up the Internet in the form of ARPAnet, a computer network that was conceived 25 years ago to be able to survive a nuclear attack. If one node on the system went down or even if part of the network was taken out in the blast, the rest of the network was supposed to be capable of surviving and transmitting data by circumventing the point that no longer existed.

Today's Internet isn't a military project (nor is it a centralized, government-run network), but the principle is the same: Each piece of data that's sent over the Net must be able to get from point A, the origin, to point Z, the destination, without relying on another network station in between. Each piece of data, divided into packets, finds the most expedient way to reach its terminal. If a few packets get into a traffic jam outside of Chicago and the rest of the packets divert themselves south to Chapel Hill, they all get reassembled and delivered as a whole, wherever they're supposed to wind up.

To make the best use of the existing Internet, the fewest possible number of "hops" should occur along the way. Each time data is routed through a computer, that's a hop. It's kind of like riding the bus: The more stops the bus makes, the longer it takes you to get there. Additionally, you get across the country faster

in a 747 than in a Pinto, so the quality of the machinery involved, both computers and cables, contributes to the speed of the transfer.

The original Internet had a single *backbone*, but now there are several major backbones — thick pipes of telephone cable bundled together — that all other networks on the Net are connected to. The original groundwork ARPAnet laid is still there, while other backbones have been built more recently by the major telephone companies (AT&T, MCI, and Sprint) and by national Internet service providers such as Netcom, BBN Planet, and UUNet. The closer an Internet service provider is to a major backbone, the faster its transfer rate is. Additionally, a good Internet service provider is connected to more than one brand of backbone that's operated by a different carrier, so if, for example, Netcom's service fritzes out at a central location, its MCINet lines can pick up the slack.

Ask your prospective ISP which carriers it uses, how close it is to major backbones (also called *pipelines*), and what its contingency plan is in case of connectivity outages from the major carrier. Ideally, you want to choose an ISP who has multiple T1 or T3 lines that are linked to different major carriers, all in relatively proximate paths.

What IPPs Do That's Different

While ISPs are primarily in the business of providing connectivity but usually provide no content either to users or to the sites that the ISP may host, IPPs are in the business of securing for clients an online "presence." They can host your site, but this is often a sideline to their main consulting business. In other words, these types of companies often focus on creating, maintaining, or revamping your online image, reputation, and available online services — they want to help you present your content to the world. This often involves reselling or subcontracting Web-hosting services to you that are actually provided by an ISP, which may or may not work out well for everyone involved.

With all this, the term *presence provider* actually has myriad definitions. Some Web-page design firms call themselves IPPs, while other companies in the presence business focus on supplying clients with multimedia and live content solutions. AN IPP may get your site rolling and teach you how to maintain it, or you may contract certain aspects of your site's production to the provider. Some IPPs focus on consulting, letting you do the implementation, while others prefer to tackle projects from soup to nuts within their own creative group.

You may decide to use one company for access and one or more different companies for presence. For example, you may get your access through Pacific Bell Internet Services, retain the terribly famous Organic Online to do your Web-page design, and use Site Specific to accomplish advertising and marketing. (Whew! Do you ever have a *big* budget.) Many IPPs do less comprehensive consulting in specific fields as varied as networking, CGI scripting, copy writing, and live broadcasting. The main thing to consider when choosing an IPP, however, is the same thing as choosing a vanilla ISP: Can the provider serve your data well, consistently, and quickly?

Look at Web sites whose design and features you enjoy. Although some sites have extensive in-house programming and design staff, many others use IPPs for at least a portion of their look and feel, publicity, or interactive content. Look for a link marked <u>Staff</u>, <u>Credits</u>, <u>About Our Site</u>, or something similar, or check the bottom of the home page for a "Designed by" link. This can help you find out who does what, and where to find a company that does what you seek.

Some Internet service providers, such as Best Communications, also offer some presence options, while others, such as Sirius Connections, offer access and delivery options but not presence per se. While it makes sense to get a good deal on the access package that you need and then consider a different firm for presentation and content services, you're better off to limit your company's outsourcing to a single company. If you decide to retain an IPP, choose a company that has adequate staff to help you redesign your pages, undertake your advertising campaign, and write killer CGI scripts for your site — rather than having to locate three consultants or firms for these projects. Even if you don't have big plans for your site right now (but who doesn't have big plans?), consider your IPP's *potential* so that your company can grow with its company.

You can use Yahoo! to find an ISP, a Web-hosting company, or an IPP in your area. For general Internet services of all kinds, try http://www.yahoo.com/ Business_and_Economy/Companies/Internet_Services/. To find Web-only stuff, click on <u>Web Services</u>. To find companies in your area, in the Yahoo! search box, type **[Your City] ISP** or something similar and then click on the Search button.

What Internet Service Costs

Prices for Internet services are as varied as the companies that offer them. A single dial-up account with an e-mail address, 5MB of Web-server space, and access to the Web, Usenet, and ftp may cost less than $20 a month. Add extras like mailing list hosting, domain name maintenance, and server colocation, and your bill can increase to more than $500 per month. If you're running a site with a direct Internet connection and data transfer rates of more than 1GB per month, the numbers get even higher, ranging toward $2,000 per month or more. What's the difference? We talk about that next.

Your physical location may be important

Whether or not it benefits you in other ways, the more Internet services are offered in your area, the more competitive their rates are going to be. If your company is located near the San Francisco Bay area, a region that includes San Jose and Silicon Valley and thus many high-tech companies, you can find extremely competitive rates. Almost any company you sign on with offers the latest new services as fast as it can make them available. Other Internet-savvy cities, including Austin, London, Berlin, Los Angeles, Portland, New York, Richmond, Dallas, Seattle, Denver, and Washington, D.C., are close behind San Francisco in terms of competition and timeliness.

Smaller and less tech-savvy cities have fewer connectivity options and thus may charge more per month or per service, although cities that host universities often have more choices than cities without them — the university itself may often be one of the local ISPs to consider. It's no longer impossible to get Internet access in rural areas as it was just a year or two ago, but rurally located companies may not have the years of experience that Net geeks in bigger cities do. If you're way deep in the country or even in a small rural town, you may want to have your site hosted at an ISP or IPP in the nearest metropolis instead of in your charming hamlet.

What's the contingency plan?

Storms, earthquakes, fires, a guy tripping over the power cord, telephone outages, tornadoes, rains of frogs, and other emergencies are hard to prevent. When they do happen, what's Plan B? The more prepared an ISP is to cover your Web site in such an emergency, the more it may cost. At the very least, your ISP should incrementally back up all data at least once a day. Backup generators, multiple backbone access through different carriers, and multiple site storage for backup servers can help transcend physical breakdowns of electrical and phone equipment, and those become more important to you as your site grows. Some companies go beyond that, providing multiple backup generators and storage facilities that are nuke-proof. However, you pay a pretty penny for goods like these, so make sure a little downtime really is going to be a crisis before you shell out huge sums of money.

Direct-access costs

Direct Internet access through ISDN or a T1 or T3 line costs you the most money. (See Chapter 10 for a comparison of types of connections and their speeds.) Setting up a direct line costs a certain amount of money, depending on who's doing the installation and how experienced he or she is. Direct access for you and your users is generally based on monthly rates, as is a dial-up account. Using a T1 line basically starts at $500 per month and goes up from there, depending on the company providing it, where it's located, and how much it charges you per megabyte of data transfer. Most companies offer a base rate that covers up to a gigabyte of data transferred per month; you are charged additional fees for exceeding these basic limits. Some ISPs operate more like the telephone company, charging you a basic monthly maintenance fee and then metering data transfer and charging as you go.

Long-distance Web hosting

If local companies offer expensive or inferior Web services, consider using one company for access and another to host your Web site. Many companies, particularly in Net-savvy cities, offer simple Web-space packages for as little as $10 per month. You can then dial in to your local ISP for e-mail, and once logged in to the Internet, use ftp and telnet to transfer and maintain your Web site without paying long-distance charges. Be sure to look at companies in other cities when you compare pricing. Using a Web server in an area such as San Francisco or Washington, D.C., may end up speeding your customers' download times, because Net traffic is often routed through these areas anyway; it may cost less, too.

Long-distance Web hosting may be exactly what you need if you're setting up a mirror site, that is, an exact duplicate of your Web site that's located in a different part of the world. This option can offer much improved access to users who live outside your geographic region; if you're not in a tech-savvy area with good ISPs available to you, consider this option seriously.

Leasing a server

When you create a site that offers enough data and experiences enough traffic to warrant living on its own server, you may want to lease that server instead of buying one. Sometimes you can lease a server through an ISP that you're colocating with; otherwise, you may be able to lease a server through a reseller or computer rental company.

A handy site called Leasing a Server spills the beans — and _lots_ of them — about leasing a server to host your site. You can get good general info and many links to low-cost Web-hosting services at: `http://union.ncsa.uiuc.edu/ HyperNews/get/www/leasing.html`.

Haggling

Basic prices are almost always listed on the Web sites of the ISPs you're considering. (Would you really consider an ISP that _didn't_ have a Web site?) Generally, the prices that you see posted are for the most popular packages that company offers. These packages may not be exactly what you want. If the monthly services you need differ from what is advertised, call the ISP's business office and talk to a representative. Tell this person what you want and how much you're willing to pay — and get ready to haggle. In particular, if you're considering direct access, that makes you a high-paying customer, and you may be able to wheedle some extras out of the ISP, especially if you mention what its competitors are offering. The more money you're spending with an ISP, the more benefit you may get from persuading, bargaining, and badgering.

The I-Net Access FAQ, at `http://www.amazing.com/internet/faq.html`, is primarily a guide for people considering setting up their own ISP, but it can be useful to you in two ways. One is that, by reading this FAQ, you can get insight into how ISPs work, and that may help you in bargaining with them or selecting one.

Server Colocation: The Best of Both Worlds

Colocation, a relatively new option that you may consider for your site, entails your company purchasing or leasing a physical Web server, which you then keep at the Internet service provider's location. You take care of maintaining the content on the server (from your desk at your office, using ftp and telnet), while the ISP worries about security issues, mechanical failure, and other physical networking concerns. The basic idea is that you and the ISP split the administration duties; the specifics of this arrangement are determined by you and your provider.

You can't just pop any machine over to your ISP and expect those nice people to host the machine or colocate it. Many ISPs (the smarter ones) have rules about what machines they support. This is not an arbitrary matter — the ISP has to have the right people with the right skills on staff.

Even if you are able to run your own server in-house (because your company has a direct link to the ISP), there are direct advantages in colocation. For one thing, an ISP usually offers 24/7 service. And presumably, the ISP's connections are much stronger than yours could ever be — the access potential (bandwidth) of most ISPs is much higher than that in a standard office building. ISPs are equipped to handle the visitors of dozens or thousands of Web sites at once. Having the Web server serve data from the ISP's office can minimize risks such as service failure from network crashes. Most of the time, server colocation dramatically increases the speed at which visitors can access your data.

In particular, you may want to consider server colocation if you expect a lot of traffic, if you want to set up a mirror site in another part of the country or the world, or if you want to dramatically increase your access speed. Colocating a server in Silicon Valley when you're in Montana, for example, may speed *all* of your access. Colocating a server may involve either purchasing or leasing the physical machine, although it also entails choosing a machine that falls within the guidelines that are set by the ISP. Which software is to be run on the machine can be determined by you and the ISP.

Painful Pitfalls and How to Avoid Them

When choosing an ISP or an IPP to host your Web site, consider your decision to be a permanent one. Changing providers in midstream is a huge hassle at best. Such a move could involve not only relocating the contents of the Web site but reassigning domain names, redirecting customers to a new site address, changing e-mail addresses, and possibly losing visitors at every step in the whole annoying process.

When you select an ISP or IPP, think not only of the site's immediate needs but of any needs that potential growth of your site may incur. If you cut a few corners now, you may regret it six months down the road. In short, make sure the ISP you choose now will still be the ISP you would choose six months or a year from now. Think of the choice as a marriage — divorcing from an ISP is messy, expensive, frustrating, and no fun for any of the parties involved. the sections that follow will help you look at several problems that could crop up.

"Finding an ISP That You'll Really Enjoy Using," a series of articles offered by Web surfer Dawn McGatney about finding and keeping a good ISP, includes how-to advice and recommendations (as well as cautions). Find this handy guide at `http://www.mindspring.com/~mcgatney/isp.html`, or visit ISPs Folks Like and Dislike at `http://www.mindspring.com/~mcgatney/isprate.html` for other firsthand reviews.

The bandwidth follies

You want your site to grow. Ideally, you want your site to be terrifically popular. In the case of a small business, you may not be reaching for worldwide notoriety and a cadre of devoted daily visitors, but you surely want as much traffic as you can get. What happens if you achieve Net fame and your ISP isn't prepared to handle the traffic? Repeated Internet "busy signals" drive visitors away from your site in droves.

If your ISP offers fast, dedicated connections to the Internet — say T1 lines — that's a good sign that the ISP can handle a lot of traffic. Even ISPs that don't offer T1 lines, however, can still have an impressive set of connections to Internet backbones. Ask prospective ISPs about their proximity to major Internet backbones and (just as importantly) whether they're connected through multiple routes, so that if one segment of the network crashes, they can keep your site up and running.

Similarly, ask prospective ISPs about their plans for growth — in terms of bandwidth, equipment, and staff. The physical servers and routers need to have excellent response time, even during peak hours like lunchtime and happy hour, to guarantee that traffic flows smoothly. You're in good hands with an ISP that is already stable and efficient and has a strong commitment to growing and helping you grow with it.

Counting the clock ticks

Your ISP is composed of both people and machines. The people are an important element in that they plug things in, fix problems, input data, register domain names, set up your account, and bill you. They're both the man behind the curtain in the Wizard of Oz and the folks who handle every question you ask them, from account setup to questions about adding or improving services. Some ISPs go the distance, setting up mailing lists and newsgroups that their staff then monitor for questions and concerns. Make sure your ISP has a reputation for timely customer service at every level, from billing to tech support. You don't want to be sitting in your office biting your nails, wondering when that domain name registration is going to go through. You want to be confident that the folks at your ISP are on top of things and that they care and take action when glitches occur.

Doing the ISP shuffle

We've cautioned you that changing ISPs after your site is up and running can be a big headache that you're better off without. Occasionally, however, what seemed like a good company is unable to fulfill its promises for some reason. Sometimes, too, ISPs, like other new businesses, can't meet the financial strain, and they fold or get sold. Sometimes the one employee who really held things together with organizational or technical expertise leaves the company, and the ISP is never the same. And sometimes new companies just take on more than they can handle, lose sight of their goals, or simply burn out.

There really isn't any way to predict these kinds of human weaknesses — they happen to the best of us occasionally. And, of course, some ISPs don't go downhill but rather present themselves to be much more competent or responsive than they really are. If your ISP goes belly up or falls asleep on the job, or if you get overly frustrated with your ISP's level of technical support or customer service, you may have no choice but to change ISPs and hope that your second choice outdoes your first. What is involved in changing ISPs and how to make the move as painless as possible are the subjects of the next sections.

Physical movement

When you've located a new ISP who has at least the same level of bandwidth as your initial provider and that meets your criteria for service quality and options, you need to move both your data and any equipment the ISP currently holds from ISP A to ISP B. If you own or lease a server, the process may be as simple as picking up a box (the computer) and driving it across town. There is a possible trap here, however: Just because you own the machine, don't assume that you own all of the software that's on it. Make sure you know who owns the Web-server software as well as any essential extras such as database packages and servers, multimedia transmission software, CGI scripts, and security software *before* you tell the ISP that it's over and you're leaving.

Whenever you move your server, don't forget to back up your data beforehand! In fact, make backups often anyway—you know you're going to need to restore from a backup one of these days for some reason or another.

FIELD NOTES

Take your time: a moving story

Wendy Van Wazer was involved in two ISP moves while working as system administrator at a big publishing company. Her advice? "Don't rush into it. Take the time to ask all the right questions. If you find at the beginning that the ISP does not return phone calls regularly, that indicates what it may be like to work with later on." One ISP was being bought out at the time of the move, so it couldn't help much, and Wendy's horror story even includes transporting a server in her car and having the brakes fail!

Another pitfall that Wendy ran into at the time of the move was finding out that her company didn't own either the Web-server software or the database package that they had been relying on. "The ISP stopped responding to our tech requests, it stopped returning our calls, and it had been the ones doing the administration. The system software hadn't been updated, and we discovered that we didn't own any of the database software. We had to update the system and redo the entire database." You can avoid these problems by talking to the ISP about these issues from the beginning. "Communicate with the ISP about who owns the hardware, who owns the software, and what software it is using for its servers," Wendy advises.

She also recommends owning your own hardware and having a hand in keeping the DNS records, as well as maintaining at least one DNS server at all times to aid in the process of propagation (see "Changing names and propagation of the records," later in this chapter). "The old ISP needs to guarantee the rerouting of your domain name," says Wendy, "but you must be explicit about what recaching information is included in your DNS records."

Virtual movement

Moving a physical server box can be easy compared to transferring all of the data that's involved in a Web site. This is like packing your entire house and making its contents fit in your car. What's more, you're sure to forget something, but you may not know what it is until you're finished unpacking. Make an agreement with the old ISP not to completely erase your data until an agreed-on period of time after the move — try for 90 days. Here are some other things to deal with during the move:

- Transfer of domain name administration from one host to another
- Password files and username records
- E-mail archives for both users and mailing lists
- Ownership of unique newsgroups or IRC channels
- Any CGI scripts, agent programs, or other executables
- Software and licenses that you own

So you want more?

To find out all about choosing and registering a domain name or implementing a search engine on your site, visit `http://www.dummies.com` and go to the link Really Useful Extras (in the category Resources & Extras).

- ✔ Anything that's archived on the ftp site
- ✔ All of the HTML files, the images, the sounds, and the multimedia files
- ✔ A copy of all of the access and referrer logs you may have stored on its servers

Don't take no for an answer. Unless you signed a particularly poor contract with the ISP, you own your data.

Changing names and propagation of the records

While registering a domain name is easy enough, transferring it can be a nasty headache unless all parties involved cooperate smoothly and quickly. If a certain reticence in customer service is one of the reasons you're leaving an ISP, you may have to hound the provider until it submits and does what's needed.

InterNIC records of domain name ownership involve an administrative contact, a technical contact, and a billing contact. Because your administrative contact is most likely someone in-house, the person taking on that role may not be changing when all else is. (Then again, he or she may, which complicates matters.) InterNIC e-mails all parties involved in a name transfer — that can be as many as six people, all of whom must respond to InterNIC's e-mail requests before the name transfer is finalized. Do this quickly, and allow time for everyone to answer, because part two of the change begins only after the name is transferred.

The primary record that declares that a site exists and where it's located is stored on a *nameserver*. This nameserver is responsible for tooting loudly to the rest of the Internet, including InterNIC, that your site is out there. It works like this:

1. **InterNIC maintains a nameserver; in it is a record for every registered domain, including, of course,** `yourdomain.com` **(your domain).**

    Along with the record for `yourdomain.com`, there is a pointer to your ISP's nameserver.

2. **Your ISP's nameserver includes a record for your Web server, again including a pointer that goes to your Web server, wherever it may be physically located.**

3. **When a user tries to access** www.yourdomain.com, **his computer first checks with his ISP's nameserver to see if it has a record for** www.yourdomain.com.

   (It caches records of sites that the ISP users have visited recently.)

4. **If no record is cached for** www.yourdomain.com, **the user's ISP's nameserver contacts InterNIC's nameserver in its quest for the machine hosting** www.yourdomain.com.

5. **At InterNIC, the nameserver returns to the user's ISP a pointer to your ISP's nameserver — the one for** www.yourdomain.com.

   (Remember, this information is stored in the records mentioned in Step 1.)

6. **The user's ISP's nameserver follows the pointer, retrieves the record from your ISP's nameserver, and then both caches the record and sends it back to the user's computer so that the machine can access** www.yourdomain.com.

You can see that if you change the record — even if the change is posted both at your ISP and at InterNIC — it can take a while for all of those cached records to be updated. Until they are, some people can't reach your site. This insinuation through all of the pipes, nooks, and crannies of the Internet is called _propagation_. Propagation should take only a day or so to occur; however, not all ISPs are well set up for this, so it can in fact take a week or more.

If you are changing ISPs, make sure the old ISP updates the record on its nameserver to point to your Web server at the new ISP. This helps speed things along. You may also want to arrange for overlapping time so your old account with the outgoing ISP does not expire until a month or so after the new account with the new ISP goes live.

Data does its little dance

There's a another piece to the propagation puzzle, a piece that occurs in everyday Internet use (and not just in moving your site). Many large Internet servers cache the Web pages that their users request. Even if you're not aware that you're using a proxy server, you are often requesting a copy of the page from your own Internet service provider rather than directly from the site that made it in the first place. This is true of all commercial online services, whose caches are bigger and last longer than your run-of-the-mill ISPs. Even small corporate intranets often cache requested pages to speed access to the Internet for the entire network, because requesting a page that's down the hall takes much less time and energy than requesting the same page from Japan. What's unique to moving (or even drastically changing) a Web site is that it may take a while for all of the caches in the world to be overwritten, and until they are, some people don't realize that you've moved.

Testing your newly moved site for errors

Any time you create or move all or part of a Web site, you need to get a bunch of people, preferably in different locations and using different Internet services, to surf the site looking for errors. (See Chapter 9 for info on review processes.) These folks may discover that the reproduction of the directory structure that occurred in your move wasn't flawless or that you forgot to reinstall some of your data, or they may uncover something more at the infrastructure or problems with your CGI scripts on the Web server. Make sure you test the site extensively as soon as it goes back online. Get as many different people as you can in on the testing process.

Expanding your universe

Initially, you may set up a simple Web site consisting of a few HTML pages with text, links, and graphics included. Then someday, you may decide that's just not enough. Now you want to add online transactions, live content, increased interactivity, and RealVideo, and who knows what. Can your ISP keep up?

For instance, suppose you decide you want to start selling ad space on your site. You think it would be really cool if a user could register his or her interests with your site. Wanda Webuser can register, and the next time she visits, she'll see her areas of interest in bigger letters, the ads on the page will reflect her tastes in music (or books or cars), she'll have the opportunity to hear a RealAudio interview with her favorite hockey player — and then she can even purchase a copy of a Great Moments in Hockey video using a Java ordering form.

This type of setup, depending on how you execute it, could require a customer database. It would demand several sophisticated CGI scripts, a RealAudio server, and enhanced site security for both online ordering and Java applets. It may also capitalize on an automated mailing program and a site-wide search engine, and it certainly requires a lot of storage space on the Web server.

So you call your ISP. The news isn't good: No nonstandard CGI scripts are allowed, no RealAudio is available, and no secure transactions are accepted. You cajole and you threaten, but it's no go. Then you simmer down and consider whether it's worth the effort to drop the ISP like a handful of boiling oil.

Head this type of thing off at the pass. If there's any chance that you may want to implement interactive content on your site, see if your ISP offers such things or if there are plans in the works to do so. And if you're considering making your site a technical wonder, consider whether you or the provider has the staff to write the programs. If not, you may be in the market for an IPP as well.

In the end, you do far better in selecting and working with an ISP or IPP if you know as much as you can about servers and connection options. Our final bit of advice in this chapter: Read Chapter 8 for tips on dealing with any vendor. Then take a look at Chapter 10 to familiarize yourself with server and connection basics. ISP folks, just like car mechanics, take you more seriously and listen more if you can speak their language.

Chapter 12

Databases for the Masses

● ●

In This Chapter

▶ Defining databases and their components

▶ Looking behind the Web site database scene

▶ Comparing flat-file and relational databases

▶ Distinguishing between Oracle, Microsoft, Sybase, and Informix database products

▶ Talking to database designers

▶ Maintaining your database

● ●

*J*ust what is it about the Web that inclines users to put up with slow transfer speeds and inspires companies to fork over the big bucks? Underneath the glitz and hype, the Web is all about *content* — information. It's about organized, accessible information, and lots of it. As you add content to your Web site and it grows and grows, keeping things current and helping users find what they seek becomes an increasing challenge. What's a Webmaster to do? Behind many Web sites big and small — whether their goals are sales, information delivery, product distribution, purchase support, or whatever — lies a solid solution — a *database*.

What Exactly Is a Database?

It's really pretty simple. You could keep your clothes in a heap in the corner and sort through the whole thing every time you wanted to find a pair of blue socks, or you could buy a dresser, make one drawer the sock drawer, and look there when you want your blue socks. Knowing that this was the *sock* drawer, you'd just search for the color *blue*.

A *database* is a system that lets you organize and store pieces of information in a file so they're easier to find and use. It's more complicated to arrange than your dresser, but it operates on fundamental principles that are as simple as organizing drawers.

The difference between data and information

There's a big difference between data and information, so we should clarify here. Basically, *information* is useful and meaningful, while *data* is broken down information — just pieces of stuff that can be manipulated and that, when compiled in some organized way, becomes information. For example, a list of first names (not the first names of actual people, just *first names*) is data. When the first names are combined with last names, so they describe actual people (or when you can imagine faces that go with the first names), those two pieces of data — the first name and the last name become *information*.

Consider another example: Joe keeps the names and phone numbers of his friends and associates on scraps of paper in his wallet. One scrap to a person, each has a name, phone number, and maybe an address on it.

Each of these scraps is what's called (in database lingo) a *record. Data* is what is scribbled on the scraps. If Joe organized all that data in alphabetical order into an address book with a-b-c tabs along the side, he'd have a *database*. (But not an electronic one.) A database is just a bunch of information broken down into discrete pieces and organized in a way that's easy to use. An encyclopedia is a database. So are recipes on index cards in a box. A magazine is *not* a database, because, while it is full of information, the material is not broken down and organized around a reference point (it's not arranged alphabetically, or by number, or by any other system that makes it easy to look things up).

Joe, with his wallet full of loose "records," can write information down on the papers in his wallet in any order; it doesn't matter. When he wants to call up Lana Cartwheel, he looks at every scrap of paper to find the one with Lana's number on it.

If Joe used an address book, he could instead turn to "C" for Cartwheel, and there he'd find some boxes on the page, including one where he'd written Lana's name on one line, her address on another, and her phone number on a third. In database lingo, each of these lines of data is called a *field*. Every record in a database includes the same set of fields. When Joe gets a new address book, all the boxes, which are *records* on the page, have identical fields — and that, along with the alphabetical tabs on the edge, makes it easy for Joe to look up his friends' addresses and phone numbers. Asking a question of a database is a *query*.

A *table* is just a collection of records with the same structure: all the records in the table contain the same kind of information. A database can consist of one table, or of many tables. There are two basic types of databases:

✔ A *flat-file* database allows you only a single table in which you store all your information.

✔ A *relational* database allows you to create multiple tables that can then be linked via shared fields, making it possible to create complex relationships between data in the tables.

Regardless of whether you are storing your data in a flat-file or relational database system, to make your database system work, you also need ways to work with and manipulate the data, including ways to:

✔ Add an entry (say, for example, a record for a new customer)

✔ Delete an entry (if, for example, you lose a customer)

✔ Update the data in an entry (if the customer moves or changes phone numbers, for example)

✔ Find, sort, and display the data

All the database products you can use in conjuction with your Web site that we describe in this chapter are programmable and customizable. A big part of actually deploying them involves creating special programs or *scripts* that pull data out of the database, slap some HTML around it, and display it via a page template or form that appears on the user's Web browser screen. The user does not see the database, but only the Web pages generated using the data in it.

A database, then, typically includes a *back end* (the database itself and any other pieces of it that live behind the scenes), and a front end (the interface to the database). Often a database has more than one interface — for example, there may be an interface (usually quite utilitarian looking) that's used by those who enter data into the database and another interface (with nice grpahics and an attractive on screen layout) that's seen by those the database serves. In a Web site setting, the front end that's seen by the public appears in the form of Web pages.

A Good Database May Be the Backbone of Your Site

A good, sturdy database can easily become a Webmaster's best friend (next to a humming, never-fails Web server). Whether your role as Webmaster is content, production, tech, or exec, you're likely to find that a database eases your load and makes maintaining content as well as the whole site a far simpler matter. If your content consists of a lot of related information — as is so often the case — that's a good indication that organizing the data that makes up that information in a handy database is the way to go.

What your Web site database contains can vary widely. In the case of the big search engine Web sites (AltaVista, HotBot, and the rest), the database contains data about other sites on the Web. In the case of a site like Amazon.com, which sells books, the data in the database is all about the books that are available. For your site, the data might be product specifications for all the products that make up your catalog. This data may already exist in some nice database within your company, or it may have to be entered into the database you have developed for the Web site.

Take a quick look at these examples of successfully implemented Web site databases:

✔ Microsoft Expedia travel server (http://expedia.msn.com) places tremendous information at users' fingertips, including worldwide availability of air flights and more. Expedia uses a quick, robust database to bring up flight information and track the folks who register and use the service.

✔ Ticketmaster Online (http://www.ticketmaster.com) also has an impressive online system, built around a huge entertainment database that covers every city in the United States.

✔ On a smaller scale, Foothill College, a community college in the heart of Silicon Valley, posts its course schedule at http://wwwfh.fhda.edu/FMDB/FHSummer.html. Of course, Foothill College could have simply created one or several static Web pages listing each course's name, number, description, and meeting times, but offering a searchable database and a nifty fill-out form makes things a *lot* easier for users . . . er, students.

How to Do a Searchable Database, at http://www2.ncsu.edu/bae/people/faculty/walker/hotlist/isindex.html, examines a number of different options for hooking a database up to a Web site. Web-Database Gateways (http://gdbdoc.gdb.org/letovsky/genera/dbgw.html) is a hotlist of software options for putting database access on the Web. Accessing a Database Server via the World Wide Web (http://cscsun1.larc.nasa.gov/~beowulf/db/web_access.html) includes articles and tutorials describing not just how-tos, but pros and cons of putting a database online. Databases and the Internet (http://w3c2.com.au/steve/is3.html) is a short report written by Steve Moore, a student at the University of Canberra.

Pros and Cons of Flat File and Relational Databases

The term *database,* then, can refer to a single, stand-alone table of data or to a group or system of many related tables. Databases can be simple or extremely complex; which is appropriate when depends on what the data is and what sort of information it's meant to convey. Of the many database products available, some are relatively simple and inexpensive while others are more sophisticated and (of course) more expensive.

About flat file databases

The table that actually comprises a flat-file database is very commonly stored in a plain text file (although this is not a strict requirement). If you were to open up a customer information file using a word processor, you may see something like this:

```
Lori Grant          456 Elm St.    Clanton     OH 55556 #3378887
Jessica Buehrle     285 Oak St.    Bayshore    FL 09876 #7787447
Kevin Cunningham    83 First St.   Palo Alto   CA 98474 #8976235
```

As you can see, the table is a collection of records, one record per line. Each record contains several fields, or items of data, and in the example shown, each record is simply a collection of data about one person. The records shown aren't even organized alphabetically, but rather in the order they were entered into the database.

Basically, if you have a very simple list of data to work with, a flat-file database will probably work for you and may keep things quite simple. For quick and simple jobs, a flat-file database has some advantages:

✔ **Development is easy.** Anyone who's familiar with a programming language like Perl or C can probably build a flat-file database in just a few days. This suggests that a flat-file database may be the ticket if you're running a contest on your Web site for three weeks and need a way to collect, organize, and retrieve contest entrant data. Beware of this quick-fix temptation, however — what may seem to save you time now can come back to haunt you later, especially if you plan to use your new database for a more than a short time or more than a limited number of records.

✔ **Access time is quick.** If your flat-file database is small, you can generally add, alter, and retrieve data very quickly. (If it's big, you've got a problem.) Some factors that affect speed include how many people are accessing the database at once (many flat-file databases cannot handle more than a handful of users) and how experienced and conscientious your programmer is (a number of programming tricks that enhance speed are known to database pros).

There are distinct reasons to go the flat-file route:

✔ If you have only a single table of data, it may be easier to manage the data in a flat-file database then a relational database.

✔ If you have no existing database from which to start, getting a database up and running using a flat-file system is a quick and dirty option.

Remember, however, that these advantages are true only if you have a single table of data to manage. Here are some disadvantages of going the flat-file route:

✔ **A flat-file database is rigid in its structure.** A list is a list and a flat-file database, once implemented, is very rigid. It's just not able to expand its capabilities to handle future requirements as they arise. Even the simple process of adding a new field to the database can involve excessive programming and testing time. It may also involve converting the existing data over to a whole new flat-file database that includes the new field.

✔ **The database can quite easily grow bloated.** A flat-file is okay for lists, and it may seem that's no big deal, but there are plenty of cases where keeping a simple list is not a good idea. For example, look at a simple sales system. If a single customer places two or more orders, the same data — the customer's name, address, and other identifying info — has to be repeated in each order. Each individual record has to be larger (to include all that customer info), so excessive data is being stored. What's more, each record has to be entered separately, so there's plenty of room for mistakes (for example, the spelling of a customer's name may not be repeated consistently).

✔ **As your database grows, it will slow down.** Over time, your database may grow to be pretty big. And, as it grows, the slowly it will perform. In a typical flat-file database, a search must look through every line of every record — that's just the nature of the thing. If, for example, you conduct a search of a customers database looking for everyone with the last name of *Smith,* the search has to sift every line of data in every record to find all the Smiths. Searching through 100 lines of data is clearly a lot faster than searching through 10,000 lines; a bloated flat-file database is going to be very, very slow.

If you have complex needs in using a database — for example, for a product catalog or sales system — the relational database solution quickly gains appeal.

About relational databases

A relational database, as described in earlier sections, allows you to set up tables of data and *link* them to other tables of data. Think of tables as the building blocks of your relational database.

It's like this: Priscilla maintains a database for her small business (in the real world, not online). In her database, she has one table that functions as her *customer address* book. It's pretty basic, a lot like Joe's address book, which we described earlier in this chapter. Then she's got another table that functions as her *invoice* book, in which each record contains the particulars of an order. The Customer Address table in her database, then, which tells her *who* placed the order, is linked to the Invoice table, which tells her *what* was ordered. (In Priscilla's order-entry system, every invoice is linked to a customer, but not every customer is linked to an invoice.)

Remember that all the records in a table contain the same fields. (In other words, each record in the Invoice database contains lines for Date of Order, Product Ordered, Quantity Ordered, Price, and so on.) Figure 12-1 shows a set of related tables that are linked to form one big relational database.

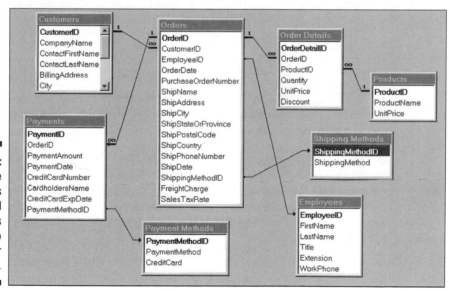

Figure 12-1:
Each table
in this
relational
database is
linked to
other
tables.

In a relational database, the data in several tables is linked through one or more fields they have in common. For example, the names, addresses, and phone numbers in Priscilla's client list are the same as those that appear in her invoice list. When Priscilla writes invoices with her Invoice table, the database automatically pulls the customer's name and address from her Customers table. It's probably easy to see that Priscilla's relational database system could translate into a Web site operation, and that if she went that way, using her relational database system would me a big advantage over using a flat-file system.

Relational databases are very powerful tools — they are robust, expandable, and there are many to choose from. Here are some of the advantages they offer:

✔ **If you can dish it out, a relational database can take it.** Relational databases are expandable; you can add as many tables of related data as you need, ad infinitum (well, almost). For a Web site that handles a medium-to-large amount of related data, a relational database is the way to go. Both the Expedia and Ticketmaster examples described at the beginning of this chapter use relational databases.

✔ **A relational database can be customized to do all sorts of tricks.** Because relational databases have their own standard programming language — Structured Query Language, or SQL — they can be programmed to manipulate data and display it in all sorts of nifty ways. The more powerful, expensive packages (see later sections in this chapter) can really do some cool things.

✔ **Just about everybody offers a relational database product.** From Microsoft Access to Filemaker Pro to the big guns like Oracle and Informix, relational database products are available for purchase for many platforms, including Windows NT and UNIX platforms, and for many prices.

On the other hand, those powerful and robust relational databases are not usually so simple or cheap to implement. Here are some of their disadvantages:

✔ **Relational databases are expensive and tough to install/design/maintain.** A few of the relational database products available today won't cost you a small fortune, but most are far from cheap, and some are *very* expensive. Plus, you'll probably need a consultant or two on hand to help you install the system, to customize it to interface with your Web site, and to correctly structure your data in a way that makes sense for today and for your future needs. Finally, depending on the scope of your database and the relational database software you choose, you may need to a DBA (database administrator) on staff.

✔ **Relational databases are system resource hogs.** These are big programs with big jobs to do, and that means they take up a hefty chunk of your hard disk and need plenty of RAM to chew on while they work. What's more, because they can be used by many visitors to your Web site at once, they'll also hog your Web server's processor time and make your site run more slowly. If they get rolling enough to really sap processor's power, everything else happening on that machine (including the serving of your overall Web site) can slow considerably or even grind to a near halt. If you expect big time traffic, consider putting the database server on a separate machine to alleviate this problem.

A Light-Duty Relational Database Product: mSQL

Mini SQL, or simply mSQL, is a light-duty relational database from Hughes Technologies, a company in Australia. The current version of mSQL is available for download from `http://hughes.com.au`. mSQL ships with a database-to-Web module called w3-msql, as well as a simple-to-use interface programming language called Lite. Using w3-msql and Lite, you can link mSQL to your current Web server. (This is particularly easy if you happen to be running the Apache Web server, which is described in Chapter 10.)

The mSQL database server runs on UNIX platforms and requires about 8MB of disk space. While mSQL is another one of those UNIX applications that you must *compile* — that is, you must build the program from the programmers' code — it is certainly among the easiest of programs to compile. It simply figures out for itself what kind of UNIX you're running and installs itself appropriately, allowing you to sip coffee all the while. mSQL comes with a tool called mSQLexport that will take data out of the mSQL format and turn it into a *comma-delimited file* (a text file that uses commas to separate fields) that can be imported easily into any other database. mSQL version 2.0 costs about $250. If your organization is an educational institution or a registered nonprofit, mSQL is available at no cost.

mSQL's great overall strength is its ease of use. If you know how to write simple Perl programs and you know the bare basics of SQL, you can quickly learn to create simple database applications using mSQL, w3-msql, and Lite.

Specifically because mSQL is not particularly hard to manipulate, you can get away with asking a Perl or C programmer who wants to read a few chapters in a beginning SQL book to administer your database and create the database-to-Web interfaces.

mSQL is a great product for small databases because its simple to set up and use. It does, however, have its drawbacks. mSQL cannot cope with large fields. We tried using it for a recent project, and had major problems placing text that was longer than 4,000 characters (4K of data) into any given field. This can be a drawback if you're dealing with large chunks of data, as we were.

Also, while mSQL uses standard SQL query commands, it does not support the full set of SQL specifications. Again, this may be fine if your database application is small, but if you need to do more complicated data entry and retrieval it will become a serious drawback.

mSQL is a good product to choose if yours is a small, simple set of data that you expect to remain small for a good long while. It's also a great choice for database dabblers and novices, or companies that really need a relational database but just can't afford one of the bigger relational database servers.

The Information Systems Meta-List, at `http://www.cait.wustl.edu/cait/infosys.html`, offers annotated pointers to all aspects of information systems, including client-server databases and data warehousing. Meanwhile, the Free Database List (`http://iamwww.unibe.ch/~scg/FreeDB`) includes a searchable index of all free databases known to the editors.

The Big Bruisers and What They're Good For

If you need a little more bang than a database like mSQL can give you, investigate the next big step up — there are several larger, more functional relational databases. In the sections that follow, we give you a quick rundown of the heavy weight champs of the relational database world. All the products we describe can be used for Web site back ends as well as other database applications; which one is right for you is a pretty big question we hope you'll be better prepared to address after reading this material.

As you consider these products, keep in mind that your organization may already have one or more databases in place. You may want to check which products those databases run on, because using them in your Web endeavor will afford benefits including that a skilled in-house staff person is probably in place, and perhaps even the data you need to get started is there and in the correct format.

For online advice, Ask the SQL Pro (`http://www.inquiry.com/techtips/thesqlpro`) and get answers to questions about SQL and relational databases.

Keep in mind, too, that to implement any of these products you'll need a professional database developer (unless you are a professional database developer). Don't imagine you can skimp on this; if your database is important enough to your Web endeavor to consider these impressive options, get a pro to put your database together.

Oracle

When it comes to heavyweight champion databases, none is heftier than Oracle (`http://www.oracle.com`). In the real world, every time you use a credit card or an ATM machine, odds are that you're interacting with an Oracle database (without even knowing it). Oracle is quite famous for producing high performance databases that can handle hundreds of thousands of transactions per second. If your site must be driven by a really big, powerful database, look into Oracle.

The latest version of Oracle ships with Oracle's database-enabled Web server, aptly named . . . WebServer. WebServer is fully functional and supports both static Web pages and dynamic Web pages (which combine the usual static text and graphics with information that's queried from an Oracle database). In addition to working with Oracle's WebServer, Oracle will work as a database back end for almost any of the third-party tools we discuss in the "Middleware: The Glue that Binds" section later in this chapter.

Oracle is available for UNIX and Windows NT. More detailed information on individual system requirements can be found at `http://www.oracle.com/platforms` or by speaking with an Oracle sales rep. Oracle will cost you somewhere in the neighborhood of $8000 just for the software; there are additional development and staffing costs to consider, however. You'll need someone who has worked with Oracle before to help you install and build your database. For normal, day-to-day operations (such as adding new records, retrieving data, updating data) you will probably not need a DBA, but it is a good idea to have one on call just in case. When you want to add new kinds of information — the kind that would require you to add another table — you will need to call on a DBA or database developer.

Hiring a database developer

Cordell Sloan, a systems architect and database specialist, advises, "In database development, bet on experience. Getting the job done quickly and correctly requires that. It may cost you more per hour to hire a pro, but it will cost a lot more in the long run if you don't. You want someone who will hit the target in one shot; you don't want to pay for someone else's learning curve."

Microsoft SQL Server

Microsoft SQL Server is a relational database designed specifically for Windows NT. Unlike other database products we discuss in this section, SQL Server comes with easy-to-use Windows-based tools for maintaining and monitoring your SQL Server database. Like all Microsoft products, it works well with other Microsoft products, such as IIS (Internet Information Server). You can investigate SQL Server and the requirements for using it in detail at http://www.microsoft.com/sql. SQL Server is fairly simple to install and provides a powerful relational database application for Web sites. According to Microsoft, it will process over 10 million transactions per day at the best price-to-performance ratio in the industry. While it may not be the fastest database or be able to handle the most data, when it comes to ease of installation and use, SQL Server is a clear contender. SQL Server also will work as a database back end for almost any of the third-party tools we discuss in the "Middleware: The Glue that Binds" section later in this chapter.

Microsoft offers a SQL Server license specifically for folks who plan to use the database for their Web site. This Microsoft SQL Server Internet Connector license is currently available for approximately $3,000 and allows unlimited access from the Web to a single Microsoft SQL Server. Of course, actually implementing a SQL Server solution will cost more because you'll need to hire pros to get the thing set up.

All in all, consider choosing SQL Server as your database back end if you already use or plan to use predominantly Microsoft technology for your Web site. The folks at Microsoft have worked to make SQL Server tightly integrated with other Microsoft Internet technologies including Active Server Pages, Microsoft Transaction Server, Visual InterDev, FrontPage, Microsoft Office, and BackOffice.

Sybase SQL Server

Sybase SQL Server *sounds* like Microsoft SQL Server, but they are not the same. Microsoft SQL Server started life as a spin-off of Sybase SQL Server but the two companies took quite different directions and now present quite separate products. Sybase SQL Server comes in various versions, the most appropriate of which (for a Web site) is Sybase SQL Server Professional for Windows NT.

Sybase SQL Server Professional for Windows NT costs about $1000. You can download an evaluation copy from http://www.sybase.com/products/system11/workplace/ntpromofrm.html. You'll probably need a DBA or someone else who is experienced with designing databases to actually design your Sybase SQL Server database and to create scripts and other interfaces between it and the Web.

Informix

Informix (http://www.informix.com) produces several different versions of their relational database. The INFORMIX-SE database server is suited for small to medium-size databases, the INFORMIX-Online Dynamic Server accommodates larger databases than the SE server, and the INFORMIX-Universal Server is designed for large multimedia databases. INFORMIX-SE in particular is marketed as a low-maintenance, high-reliability solution for folks who need a relational database but don't have the IS support needed to administer a complicated database. To run INFORMIX database servers, you must have a UNIX system. For other requirements and capabilities, consult an INFORMIX rep or http:www.informix.com/products/new/plo/plol.htm.

INFORMIX Universal Web Connect software is one option for integrating your Web server and an INFORMIX database server. If you run the Universal server, you'll want to use the Web DataBlade instead of the Universal Web Connect for communication between your Web server and the database back end.

The INFORMIX-Online Dynamic Server can accommodate larger databases than the SE server. It can also take advantage of machines with single or multiple processor chips, and it runs efficiently on a cluster of machines.

FIELD NOTES

One copy of a database is enough; two is too many

We once found ourselves managing a situation in which a company that had two Web sites wanted its online catalog database to appear on both sites. This may sound like a piece of cake, but a strange hardware setup (one site was run on a UNIX machine, the other on a Windows NT machine) combined with custom database configuration on one made it difficult for both sites to physically access the data. As a result, the company decided to keep one copy of the database on the UNIX server, and replicate a second copy on the Windows NT server. This was a recipe for disaster! The data in one database was always a day behind the data in the other, and the company always had to worry that customers at one site were getting less (or incorrect) data if they were coming in from the "secondhand" site. Luckily, this company was actually updating only one database and then making a copy; had they also decided to allow their staff to make changes in both databases, their data would have been out of sync then and forever. What a mess! We strongly advise you that a basic principle in database design is that you must never, ever imagine that you can keep up two copies of a single database. Both human errors and machine glitches will creep into both systems and they will never be right. Trust us, and don't try it.

The Universal Server, in conjunction with the Web DataBlade and its associated Web page creation and maintenance tools can allow your Web team to build and administer your entire Web site as a database. With this exciting software, the database will take care of maintaining the links between your Web pages. The Web DataBlade works with any existing Web server. If you happen to be running a Netscape or Microsoft Web server, the Web DataBlade will also speed up the performance of your CGI applications. For more information on the Web DataBlade technology, visit `http://www.informix.com/informix/products/techbrfs/dblade/datasht/webdb.htm`.

As with Oracle, you'll want to have someone familiar with Informix to help you install the software and set up your database. How much help you'll need from a database administrator after your initial setup depends on which version of INFORMIX you've selected.

If you need a hefty relational database but require simple (relatively speaking) setup and maintenance, the INFORMIX-SE server may be for you. At the other end of the spectrum, if you need a high-powered database for generating Web pages on the fly, including graphics, video, or sound, you'll want to take a serious look at INFORMIX Universal Server and Web DataBlade.

If your information management requirements change in the future, INFORMIX-SE applications can be easily migrated to INFORMIX-OnLine Dynamic Server. Migration to non-INFORMIX systems may require first exporting all your data to a text file.

Middleware: The Glue that Binds

Your database, your Web server, and the user's Web browser don't automatically and seamlessly work together — they need introductions, they need lines of communication, they need *middleware*. Middleware is software that allows Web pages to be created from the data in a database. These pages can be created dynamically on the fly or based on user input. (For example, when a user visits a site, he or she can fill out a form and that information is used to query the database. The user then sees the result in the form of a Web page.) In any case, it's middleware that does the work.

In general, middleware falls into two categories:

✔ Drivers that allow CGI scripts to access the database. The addition of the proper middleware driver for a specific database allows a programmer to write scripts that query the database. Drivers exist for most databases that work with C, C++, Java, or Perl.

✔ Special HTML autoring tools that allow you to integrate data from the database into the pages you create. Generally, you don't have to be a programmer to use these tools.

Some database products come with middleware. This is perfectly good stuff and can be used to publish many types of information and content on the Web. But using what a database product comes with isn't your only option. You can also get and use third-party middleware. Fusion from NetObjects (http://www.netobjects.com), for example, is a full scale WYSIWYG (What You See Is What You Get) HTML editing system that also includes the ability to publish the contents of a database as part of your Web site. Fusion is not simply middleware, but can be used as middleware with many popular database products.

Middleware is somewhat like an authoring tool, except that it allows you to create templates for dynamic Web pages — pages that combine static text and graphics with data pulled from the database. It allows you to create one "page" that becomes thousands of pages based on various combinations of data from the database.

How to Talk to Database Developers

Databases offer a powerful way to organize data and maintain the information offered on a Web site. Database design is a specialized skill that is different from programming or Webmastering. The job of a database designer or developer is to create and implement an orderly definition of the data you'll be incorporating into your Web site. To be successful, the database developer has to understand your site's objectives, know which database product or solution to use given your purpose and any time or budget constraints, how to translate your needs into a database design, and how the database needs to evolve in the future. To enable the database developer to do his or her job well, you need to provide this person with a clear picture of your content and your resources.

Give your database developer a copy of the design document you created in Chapter 7; highlight those portions of it that particularly concern the database issues, and perhaps provide a special summary as a cover sheet. Prepare the answers to these questions, which you are sure to be asked:

✔ What platform does your server run on? UNIX or Windows NT?

✔ What kind of Web server software are you using or planning to use?

✔ Where is the data right now? Is it already stored in a company-run database? If so, what kind of database? (Provide as many details as possible.)

✔ How do you plan to allow users access the data? Will you want them to register or otherwise fill out forms in the course of accessing the data? Will you want text links to the database data?

✔ How do you expect users to query the database? What kind of data or information do you want them to be able to get? Which fields do you want them to be able to search on? Are there any they should not see?

✔ Will users be entering data into contest or site registration forms?

✔ Will this database be used in conjunction with any others? With an online transaction system? Again, provide all details.

✔ How do you expect your database needs to change in the next six months? In the next year? In the next two years?

Finally, you should know and be able to describe or even sketch out what kind of data your database will hold. It will help you (and your database developer) to see things more clearly if you put together a chart that lists the specific fields that will make up a record, as well as how you imagine tables will work together.

When you sketch out the records, estimate how many characters or words you expect each field to contain, describe what sort of data (text, numeric, other?) it will be in each field, and note any peculiarities that may help the database developer anticipate problems. Here's an example:

Field	Size	Type	Notes
Last name	20 characters	Text	
First name	20 characters	Text	
E-mail address	25 characters	Text	
Phone number	10 characters	Text	Place hyphens after area code and prefix; use text because this won't be a number on which math will be performed
Amount of most recent purchase	Varies	Numeric	Math may be performed on this number, so it should be numeric
Opinion of electronic commerce	40 words/ about 200 characters	Text	Some people may write more; should we cut them off at 40 words, or allow for the potential of more data than we expect?

Keep in mind as you talk to database developers that while they know databases, they don't know your business or your needs. It's up to you to communicate this information to them, and to iron out any wrinkles that appear along the way. Offering them clear information up front is the best way to avoid confusion later.

A Few Words on Database Maintenance

You needn't be a database developer or DBA to do most database maintenance. In fact, in the course of setting up your database, systems and processes should be put into place such that you or someone on your Web team (even someone who isn't necessarily a database whiz kid) can take care of these operations:

- **Adding new records.** You should be able to add new records and the data they contain to your database whenever necessary.

- **Editing records.** You must be able to make corrections in existing records at will.

- **Deleting records.** You should be able to delete records at will. Furthermore, if you expect records to expire on a regular basis, you should have a feature in place that automatically removes expired records for you.

- **Making regular backups.** Backups are *very* important. Depending on which type of database you implement, your data may be backed up automatically when your Web site is backed up, or it may require a separate backup procedure. Arrange a backup plan with your Web site administrator and/or database developer at the outset of your database project.

- **Keeping an eye on performance.** Make a point of using your new database application regularly, and when you first launch it, pound on the thing mercilessly. This is the best way to detect and correct problems with the database itself. It's also a good way for you to determine if your database is getting so much use that it's slowing down the machine it lives on.

From time to time, you'll also probably want to make minor or major improvements to your database. Unlike routine maintenance issues, which you can usually handle yourself, you may quite likely need to bring in a DBA or consultant to help you implement improvements. Improvements you may want to make include:

- **Creating new kinds of queries.** As you and visitors to your site use your database back end, you may discover ways you or they want to access the data that you didn't anticipate in the beginning of the project.

What's it going to cost?

A database solution may well represent a major piece of your site budget. In planning for the costs associated with creating and especially maintaining your database, you'll need to remember to factor in:

✔ The estimated cost of day-to-day maintenance, including not just the big ticket maintenance but simple data entry and the deletion of dead records.

✔ The cost of bringing in a DBA or developer to accomplish the improvements you've planned.

✔ The cost of occasionally bringing in a DBA or developer to troubleshoot. (Don't imagine you'll never need a DBA; plan at least a few visits per year.)

✔ The cost of upgrading software and hardware.

✔ The cost of creating backups and (preferably) storing them off-site.

Remember that last one especially — don't let cost stop you from protecting your valuable data by making and storing backups off-site.

✔ **Adding new types of data.** Say, for example, you've launched an online catalog of your company's t-shirts in the form of a database. Six months later, the hard-copy catalog starts printing both U.S. prices and Canadian prices. Now you need to add the Canadian prices to the online version of the catalog.

✔ **Upgrading the software.** Software developers love to release new and improved versions of their product, usually about once a year or so. At some point in your database's lifetime, you'll probably want to upgrade to a newer version of database software — there's bound to be a new feature you'll decide you need. Sometimes upgrading is a snap; sometimes it isn't.

✔ **Upgrading your hardware.** With luck, your Web site will become so successful that the hardware you've set it up on will become bogged down. At that point (or whenever you get the opportunity), you may want to upgrade to a more powerful server.

All these tasks signal the time to call in a DBA or developer. Make sure when you do that you both have a current backup of your data socked away and that you call in someone with professional experience with the specific database product you use.

Part IV
Winning: Promoting and Assessing Your Site's Success

In this part . . .

1 f you build it will they come? Only if you let them know your site is there! You have to go out and push the thing to get visitors; you have to do some genuine site promotion. Luckily, these days, information is available to tell you how most people find Web sites of interest. In this part, we tell you what works in site promotion and how to carry out your promotional efforts. We also let you in on what winning looks like — that's not such an obvious matter on the Web, after all.

Part IV describes techniques you can easily use to get noticed by search engines like AltaVista and indexes like Yahoo!. It also describes buying ad space, and a wide variety of promotional techniques you can put into practice for cheap or free. Finally, in this part, you learn to recognize, define, and measure the sort of success you may specifically expect given the goals you've set for your site.

Chapter 13

Maximum Exposure via Search Engines and Directories

In This Chapter

▶ Discovering search engines and directories

▶ Placing the right tags in your Web pages

▶ Making sure that search engines can find you

▶ Maximizing your search-engine mileage

▶ Excluding parts of your site from search engines

*L*et's face it. Even if your whiz-bang beauty of a Web site tells folks the meaning of life, if no one knows it's there, no one is going to see it. You want people to visit your site, and you want *lots* of people. There are a number of ways to get attention on the Web; the first is to make your site as wonderful as possible. The stronger your content, the punchier your design, and the fresher you keep the thing, the more people are going to tell their associates and the more people are going to return. But first you have to attract the attention of the first wave of those folks, and the big question is *how* to do this.

As Figure 13-1 shows, one of the most common ways people find out about sites is through online search tools (AltaVista, Yahoo!, and so on). You can take advantage of this by getting your site listed and by maximizing your site's standing within all of the major search engines.

You can implement a special sort of search engine on your site that will help users find their way around the site itself. (We cover that topic in a bonus chapter on the Dummies Web site at http://www.dummies.com. Look for "Search Engines for Visiting Your Site" from the link Really Useful Extras.) Here we're talking about those big bruiser search engines and directories that help people find what's on the Web. If you want to know all about getting max exposure via the search engines and directories that people use to navigate the whole Web, read on, bucko.

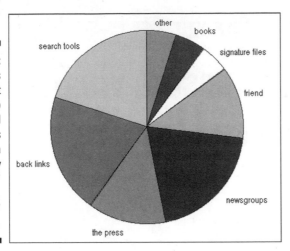

Figure 13-1:
How users find out about Web sites (based on findings of Georgia Tech survey at http://www.cc.gatech.edu/user_surveys).

What's the Big Deal about Search Engines?

Finding your way around the Web can be a very big challenge — so much so that the search-tool industry was born. *Search tools,* as you know, are gigantic, automatically built catalogs of Web pages. They're usually comprised of a Web crawler, spider, or robot that scours the Web for new pages; a huge database of 30 to 40 million individual Web pages all cataloged and indexed; and the search engine itself, which allows users to query the database. When a user does query the database, the results that are returned by the search tool appear in a list. The list is usually ranked by *relevancy,* with the Web sites that are the most relevant at the top of the list. Your goal is to create a situation that puts your site at the top of the list whenever a user searches for a site on a topic like yours.

The trick here is that relevancy is kind of, well . . . *relative.* You see, relevancy is generally calculated by some simple means — like counting how many times the word or phrase that you searched appears in a given Web page, its URL, its title, and so on. This way to calculate relevancy is both a weakness of the whole search-engine business and something that you can capitalize on. You can make this bug into a feature by simply including specific tags or repeated word patterns in your page so that a specific search tool can catalog your site correctly and give it a truly relevant relevancy ranking. What's not quite so simple is that all of the search tools do things a little differently, and you want your site to shine on each tool to maximize the number of visits that you get. Later in this chapter, we show you how to tweak a Web page so that it gets a high ranking across the board. First, though, you need to take a look at search tools in general.

Search Engines and Directories: What's the Diff?

There are basically two kinds of Web search tools:

- ✔ A *directory* is a large database that's filled with references to Internet sites; the organization of this database is overseen by human beings who (presumably) keep it intelligently organized and who often add some kind of categorization or editorializing (like site reviews) to the mix. Excite includes a directory among its features; Yahoo! is a directory, too, although it's more the *index* type of a directory.

- ✔ A *search engine* differs from a directory in that it is not categorized by the hands of human beings and it offers no editorial content; instead, it is a huge database that has been compiled through the use of a Web crawler or spider that went out, got a lot of stuff, and put the stuff in the database in no particular order. (Seeming order is "imposed" when a user searches the database and the results appear in a list based on . . . dare we say it? . . . *relevancy*.)

Keep this in mind when trying to get your page listed with a search engine or a directory: Directories are usually only interested in listing the top (home) page of the Web site or maybe a few other selected pages that have knockout content. Search engines, on the other hand, send their web-crawling robots out to gather *everything*. These 'bots start with a link to your site (which may be a link that you submit to them) and follow all of the other links on that page through your site until they've indexed everything they can. Then they follow all of the links that leave your site. Although many people often find your site by following links on other pages, the corollary is that robots can also find your site more often if there are more links to it from other sites.

What a search engine really is

In actuality, a *search engine* is the software that conducts a search, whether that search occurs in the context of a big database of Web sites, in the context of your Web site alone, or even in the context of a database that has nothing to do with the Web. (There is a search engine in Microsoft Access and in other database programs, for example.) Use of the term *search engine* to refer to a tool for searching the Internet has come into play just recently. In this chapter, we use the term *search engine* generically to refer to all Internet search tools.

Both directories and search engines include search capabilities in their offerings, and they all work in more or less the same way — user types topic of interest into text box, user clicks on Search button — you know the routine. The search is executed, and the results are returned in a list that's been sorted based on criteria that were set up by the search-engine producers. (Whew!) Your goal, then, is to manipulate matters to your advantage. You can do this by cleverly using META tags, TITLE tags, and HEAD tags — yep, that's HTML we're talking about. (The section that follows this one talks about these special tags, while Chapter 7 discusses HTML in general.)

 Search Engines Watch, by Calafia Consulting, includes backgrounders and tips for most of the major search engines. There is an associated mailing list that posts announcements about major changes in the world of search sites. Visit http://searchenginewatch.com.

HEAD Tags, TITLE Tags, and META Tags — What They Mean to You

As an Internet pro, you know that the whole web of Web pages hangs on HTML. Everything you see on a Web page is the result of HTML and therefore of HTML tags. Some tags create text, some create links, some create images — and some convey information about the document as a whole. These are the tags that perk up the interest of search tools. Knowing how to use these tags well can help you to produce content that the search engines and directories can then correctly catalog.

HEAD tags

The *HEAD tag* defines a special area of the HTML document that contains information about the document. That information often includes the document's title and perhaps some other coding that describes the document. For example, in the following snippet of HTML, the head section contains the title of the Web page along with a META tag that specifies a description of the page:

```
<HEAD>
<TITLE>World-Class Ping-Pong for Dummies</TITLE>
<META NAME="description" CONTENT="world-class ping-pong">
</HEAD>
```

Most search engines pay very close attention to the contents of the head section, so you should, too.

TITLE tags

Every document on the Web has a title. That title usually appears in the title bar at the top of your Web browser window when you're looking at the document. So — where did that title come from? The *TITLE tag!* The following is an example:

```
<TITLE>World-Class Ping-Pong for Dummies</TITLE>
```

Remember, the TITLE tag appears within the all-important head section of the page.

"Welcome to XYZ Home Page" is a poor title for a Web page — it's too long, it's full of irrelevant words, and it will appear in alphabetically organized bookmark lists under *W* for *Welcome.* A better title would be short and pithy — it would include those two words that you thought up and jotted down for this occasion.

When you're naming your page, keep in mind that the title that appears in the TITLE tag is also the title of the page in a list of hits produced by a search engine. It's also the title that the directory and index people use to refer to your page, not to mention all of the random Webmasters who link to you. So if the title is just Ping-Pong, it isn't going to stand out from the herd. However, Killer Ping-Pong Tips certainly would, because it gives some idea about the kind of content to be found on the page (Ping-Pong *tips,* rather than photographs or a rule book).

META tags

A *META tag* is a special tag that contains meta information about the page — that is, overview information about the stuff that's contained in the page. An example of a META tag is as follows:

```
<META NAME="description" CONTENT="world-class ping-pong">
```

This META tag says that the page it is embedded in is about *world-class Ping-Pong.* You can specify any META tag that you like. For example, rather than specifying that the tag is a *description,* you may spec it as a *title,* as follows:

```
<META NAME="title" CONTENT="World-Class Ping-Pong for Dummies">
```

The overall, agreed-upon specs for HTML allow you to include just about any name and content descriptors in META tags, with a few exceptions. (For example, the name *refresh* is reserved for forcing a browser to reload the document.) Some search engines look specifically for a META tag with the name *keywords,* and then those search engines catalog the page based on the keywords that are included in the META tag. Such a tag would look like this:

```
<META NAME="keywords" CONTENT="ping-pong, table tennis,
        world-class, ping pong, tournament, champion,
        pingpong, book, world-class ping-pong for
        dummies">
```

Notice that this list includes *ping-pong*, *table tennis*, and *ping pong*. Synonyms and common misspellings are important when you're trying to get your page in circulation — whether the intrepid searcher looking for a page like yours types *ping-pong*, *table tennis*, *or ping pong* in the search box, your page ostensibly should show up in the search if you use synonyms carefully. Meta tags also appear in the head section of an HTML document. Notice, too, that all of the keywords are lowercase. Some search engines exclude *Ping-Pong* (the correct name of the game, written with initial caps because the game is trademarked that way) if a user types *ping-pong*.

Now, remembering that search engines focus on the head section of a given Web page, and noting that you can use META tags in a number of ways, here's the kicker: You can embed multiple META tags in your page, directing the attention of search engines to suit your purposes. However, META tags are not the magic bullets that so many people think they are. Some search engines ignore them, and others recognize some META tags but not others.

It is better, to list your keywords one time each in a META tag than it is to do the clever thing that a lot of beginning webmasters try. You may have seen a page that has a bunch of blank space (
 tags, actually) after the content is finished on the page. If you scroll down far enough, you see a bunch of words, sometimes not-so-cleverly hidden, that look like this:

```
PING-PONG TABLE TENNIS WORLD-CLASS DUMMIES BOOK WINNING
        STRATEGY
PING-PONG TABLE TENNIS WORLD-CLASS DUMMIES BOOK WINNING
        STRATEGY
PING-PONG TABLE TENNIS WORLD-CLASS DUMMIES BOOK WINNING
        STRATEGY
PING-PONG TABLE TENNIS WORLD-CLASS DUMMIES BOOK WINNING
        STRATEGY
PING-PONG TABLE TENNIS WORLD-CLASS DUMMIES BOOK WINNING
        STRATEGY
```

ad nauseam.

This may look like a good way to force your page to the top of the heap, because *Ping-Pong* certainly appears several times. Generally, however, a page's relevancy rating is based not only on frequency but on weight. That is, a page that mentions Ping-Pong several times within the body of a page has more weight than a page that mentions Ping-Pong only once, but some search engines discount lists of words with no context.

Search-Tool Backgrounders

To make the most of META tags and other tricks of the trade, you need to know a thing or two about the how the various search engines work. The best way to get your site indexed by the major search engines is to submit a link — your home page, generally — to the Add Your Site section of the search engine's Web page. But before you do, make sure that your Web page is in top shape for each of the biggie's search methods.

When you're getting ready to submit your page to the major search engines, take a few minutes to read the help files. If there's a help file about submitting the page, it's generally useful, but some Web sites include information about relevancy and META tags within their general help files as well. Infoseek, for example, offers a help file that explains how to increase your relevancy rating, while AltaVista's Add Your Site page includes many tips for Webmasters. In any case, reading the help files is often the only way to find out what ranking strategies and extra doodads the various search engines have available.

AltaVista

AltaVista, considered by many to be the premier search engine, was developed by Digital Equipment Corp. to demonstrate the company's ability to manipulate enormous databases. AltaVista, which has now completely outgrown its beginning as a relatively humble demo of technology, is actually the sum of several parts. First, a robot (called Scooter) automatically searches the Web for new pages. Then a cataloging program takes the pages that are found by Scooter, indexes them, and plops them into a database. Finally, there is the AltaVista database itself, which is filled with those cataloged Web pages. The AltaVista database has more than 30 million Web pages. Your job is to make sure that Scooter finds your Web pages and that the indexing program properly files them in that big whoppin' database.

Scooter streaks through the Web continuously, but you may have to issue an invitation to Scooter to have it stop by your site. To submit your URL to AltaVista, fill out the form at `http://www.altavista.digital.com/cgi-bin/query?pg=tmpl&v=addurl.html`. After you've submitted your URL, two days may pass before Scooter visits. Then it is another two to four weeks before your pages appear in AltaVista.

Select your site's central page, and submit it to AltaVista manually. AltaVista asks that you submit only *one page* (generally the top or home page) to its Add-URL page. As long as all of your pages are linked to from at least one of your pages, the spider finds the rest automatically — that's what search-engine robots do. You can have your site stricken from the database by *spamming* the index, that is, submitting your page multiple times in hopes of making your page show up multiple times.

AltaVista is a full-text search engine, meaning that it searches the entire contents of a Web page. Whether it's right or wrong, AltaVista uses the following criteria to determine ranking:

- Keywords that appear near the beginning of the Web page are given more weight than those that appear toward the end of the page.

- Keywords that repeat throughout the page are given more weight than keywords that do not repeat. What's more, if a word is repeated a number of times in the same region of the page (say the top), that document gets a higher relevancy ranking than a document that doesn't use this trick.

- A page in which a keyword appears 20 times, for example, is given a higher relevancy ranking than a page that contains that keyword 15 times.

Note that AltaVista pays attention to your use of the description META tag — but not to many other tags.

AltaVista ignores punctuation (*ping-pong* and *ping pong* are all the same to AltaVista) and is a little fussy about capitalization. For example, if you repeat the phrase *Ping-Pong for Dummies* throughout your site, and a user types *ping-pong for dummies* into the AltaVista Search box, that attempt shows up as a match. However, if *you* repeat *ping-pong for dummies* in the site and the user (who was obviously paying attention in high school English) types *Ping-Pong for Dummies,* no match occurs. Go figure.

Excite

Like AltaVista, Excite is really the sum of (a) a robot that searches the Web for new pages, (b) an indexing program, and (c) a resulting database of all the Web pages that Excite has encountered. Unlike AltaVista, and in fact unlike any other search tool on the Web, Excite uses *concept searching;* this basically means that it includes a thesaurus against which it compares any and all search strings. A search for *Ping-Pong* may turn up . . . hmmm, what's a synonym for *Ping-Pong?*

To submit your site to Excite, use the form found at `http://www.excite.com/add_url.html`. You should find your site in the database within about three weeks.

Spamming gets you nixed

Registering your Web site with many search engines is a very good idea. Registering your site many times with the same search engine is a very bad idea — this is the search-engine version of *spamming.* Other forms of search-engine spamming include repeating a keyword several times in a META tag or in a Web page. Our favorite example is when Joe Schmoe gets the clever idea of placing a repeated keyword in white text on a page with a white background so that no one but the search engine can see the keyword. This, folks, is a kind of spamming, too.

When search engines come across these nasty, spammy pages, they impose penalties. Some search engines simply delete spammy pages. Others push those pages to the bottom of a relevancy ranking so that no one is likely to see them. Still others have been known to eliminate an entire domain from the search engine's database if that domain included even one spammy page!

Use the information in this chapter to increase your site's representation within search engines. Don't use it to try to trick or spam search engines — they're on to that sort of thing.

Excite keeps most of the criteria that it uses in relevancy rankings under its hat. However, we do know this:

- ✔ Keywords that appear in the title of a Web page are given more weight than those in the body of the page.
- ✔ Keywords that are repeated are given more weight than those that appear only once.
- ✔ Keywords that appear in the TITLE tag and are then repeated get even more weight.

Note that Excite penalizes spammers and does not support META tags.

A *search engine for your site*

Excite also provides search-engine software you can implement on your own site to help users find what they seek within your site's content. To find out more about this, visit http://www.dummies.com and link to Really Useful Extras (in the Resources & Extras category). Look for the bonus chapter, "Search Engines for Visiting Your Site."

HotBot

HotBot, by Wired Ventures, is powered by the Inktomi search engine, which was first developed by a group of computer scientists at the University of California at Berkeley as a research experiment in distributed computing.

HotBot constantly prowls the Web for new pages to add to its database. If you don't feel like waiting for it to get to your site (and with the way the Web keeps on growing, yours could be a long wait), you can submit your URL to HotBot via a form at `http://www.hotbot.com/addurl.html`.

HotBot uses the following criteria in determining relevancy ranking:

- ✔ When a keyword appears in the document's title, that document appears before documents that do not have the keyword in the title.

- ✔ When a keyword appears within the contents of a META tag, the document appears after documents that have the keyword in the title, but before documents that have the keyword only in the body of the document.

- ✔ The rest of the documents are listed in the order in which the keyword appears in the rest of the document. The more times that the keyword appears in the document, the closer to the top of the list it appears.

HotBot ignores certain very common words such as *and, or,* and *web.* HotBot also holds a very big grudge against spamming — especially spoofing and word stacking.

Infoseek

Infoseek, like Excite, is a combination of a search engine and a directory. The Infoseek search engine catalogs sites in a database, while the directory offers a more subject-oriented listing. The search engine is full-text, like many others.

You can submit your URL to Infoseek by using the form found at `http://www.infoseek.com/AddUrl?pg=DCaddurl.html`.

Infoseek uses the following criteria to determine ranking in search results:

- ✔ The closer to the top of the page a keyword appears (including the title), the more weight that page is given.

- ✔ The more often a keyword appears, the more weight the document is given.

- ✔ The more unusual the keyword is, the more likely the search engine is to notice it.

For example, searching for *loquacious bodacious babes* makes any page that includes loquacious *and* the other two words bounce right to the top; documents that contain loquacious and not babes are more likely to show up than pages about babes who aren't loquacious.

Another interesting thing about Infoseek is its case-sensitive searching. As is true of AltaVista, capping excludes lowercase words. Also, if you enter two initial-capped words in a row (whether they're *Bill Gates* or *Brown Shoes*), Infoseek searches for instances of those two words as a *name,* including both *Bill Gates* and *Gates, Bill.* This would work in your favor for *Ping-Pong* but probably not for *brown shoes.*

Infoseek also indexes words that are used in image ALT attributes to index the page. When you place an image in your page, the ALT attributes is what people see if they're not autoloading images. This tag also shows up as a tool tip when you drag the cursor over an image in browsers like Netscape Navigator and Microsoft Internet Explorer (versions 3 and later).

Infoseek does support META tags, and it penalizes spammers by removing their pages from the database. You cannot submit your site to Infoseek's directory; only submissions to the search engine are accepted. However, all sites that are submitted to the search engine are potential candidates for inclusion in the directory.

Lycos

Lycos is not a full-text search engine. Instead, it uses the seemingly odd method of building its own abstracts based on the headers, titles, links, and the first few words it finds in what it considers key paragraphs on any given Web page. The abstracts are supposed to describe the page, and the searches occur against the abstracts.

Lycos ranks pages in this order:

- ✔ Keywords in a document title get the most weight.
- ✔ Keywords that are repeated in the first part of the document are considered next.

To make sure that your Web pages appear in Lycos, place those all important keywords in the title section. Lycos recommends then repeating the keywords near the top of the document. On the other hand, Lycos penalizes word stacking — yet they don't tell you how much is too much. Go figure.

Lycos is unique among search engines in that it can catalog sites that require a password for entry. If yours is such a site, when you submit it to Lycos, be sure to provide a password; you may want to set up a special password for this purpose.

Yahoo!

Okay, strictly speaking, Yahoo! is not a search engine. While all the rest send some kind of crawler out to find new stuff on the Web, Yahoo! sits back and waits for Webmasters to submit their pages to Yahoo! — and they do, in droves. Yahoo! is the granddaddy of Web indexes and a very prestigious placement. Yahoo! pays absolutely no attention to the title of your page, any special META tags, or the position of words within your page. Inclusion in Yahoo! is up to the discretion (whim, we could say) of real human beings sitting in a room in Silicon Valley.

You can submit your pages to Yahoo! by using the form found at `http://add.yahoo.com/fast/add` (see Figure 13-2). You have control over a title and a description that's used to describe the site — you can enter them as you like. You can also select the exact category — and even secondary categories — that your site may appear in when you register. Plus, if your site has regional appeal, you can suggest that it be included in any of the Yahoo! regional directories that seem appropriate.

Think about those keywords. A real person reviews every site that's submitted to determine its worthiness, and if the description doesn't seem right, they are known to snap that site right out of their sight.

Figure 13-2:
To submit
your site to
Yahoo!, go
to the
category
that it
belongs in
and then
click on
Add Site to
type a
descrip-
tion and
your URL.

Category:	
Title:	
URL:	`http://`

Our site uses Java: ○ yes ◉ no
Our site uses VRML: ○ yes ◉ no

Optional Info:

Additional Categories:

Geographical Location of Resource (if applicable):

City: State/Province:
Country:

Comments: (no HTML tags please)

Should I submit my pages manually?

Dozens of announcement services are available (Yahoo! lists over 100) to submit your site automatically to a number of different search tools, leaving you free to handle other details of the site. Many of these search-engine submission sites, like Submit-It offer a free version of their services and a professional version for which you pay. Whether you want to pay for one of these upscale versions depends a lot on both your time and budget. Before you sign up, keep a couple of things in mind:

✔ Don't worry about getting your site listed by every search tool in existence. There are plenty of search tools out there that have such a limited audience that it may not affect you at all.

✔ You may want to submit your site manually to some of your favorite search tools, and to several of the big search engines, just to make sure that your site gets in there quickly and the way that you want it to appear.

✔ Using more than one submission service doesn't do you much good, because there's little variation in the lists of search engines to which they submit. (The only great differences are in volume and price.)

✔ When deciding where to submit your site, you may want to see if the announcement services offer lists of search tools that you can peruse for free.

✔ Some search tools suffer such a backlog of submitted URLs that you'll be in queue for a long time (weeks or months!). If your site is submitted with a batch of sites from an announcement service, it may sit on the waiting list even longer.

That said, if you have more money than time to get your Web page announced to the world, you may want to consider some of these tools. Keep in mind that their offerings (and their prices) can change at any time.

✔ **Submit-It** (http://www.submit-it.com) offers a free 20-engine service. Other services include software that you can use to submit your URLs and submission packages ranging from $60 to $400.

✔ **The PostMaster** (http://www.netcreations.com/postmaster/) submits your site to about 400 directories for $75. The free trial version includes about 25 sites. PostMaster offers other services, such as direct mail and advertising, for more money.

✔ **AAA Web Site Promotions** (http://websitepromote.com/) starts at $110 for 50 directories and goes to $345 for 200 directories.

✔ **Pointers to Pointers** (http://www.homecom.com/global/pointers.html) can list your site in 50 search tools for $10.

✔ **Easy Submit** (http://www.the-vault.com/easy-submit/) lists add-your-site links to over 100 search tools. This is still a manual process, but it's a good starting point for doing things by hand.

✔ **Yahoo!** (http://www.yahoo.com/ComputersandInternet/Internet/World_Wide_Web/Announcement_Services/) lists promotional services, search-engine submission tools, and other announcement services.

Maximizing a Web Page for All of the Popular Search Tools

Obviously, you want to take into consideration all the ins and outs of getting listed and indexed correctly in all of the search engines. At best, you want your page to come up at the top of a relevancy ranking in all of the major search engines each and every time a user searches for the topic of your page. The following is a look at how to modify the HTML for a Web page to accomplish this noble task.

To start, identify a few items that describe your page and jot them down:

✔ One or two words that precisely match your topic and that can appear in the page's title

✔ A broader set of keywords (perhaps a dozen) that relate to the page's topic

✔ A sentence that describes your page clearly and simply

With these items in hand, you're ready to make your Web page search-engine friendly. For best results, make these tweaks *before* you register the page with search engines. It may be a long time before they come back around to check for any changes, so you want to have all your ducks in a row the first time. Follow these steps:

1. **Open the page in your favorite HTML editor.**

2. **Incorporate the two "title" words into the title section.**

   These need not be the only words in the title section, but they must be there. (The title should still make sense as a title, by the way.) Imagine that your site is about the following:

   ```
   <TITLE>A Classic Camera for Classic Photography</TITLE>
   ```

3. **Repeat those two words (*camera* and *photography* in our example) in the page's text, somewhere near the top of the page.**

   It also doesn't hurt to scatter them throughout the page so that they appear every few sentences.

4. **In the head section of your page, insert a META tag listing the keywords that you've developed for the page.**

   For example, use this META tag in the example page about cameras:

   ```
   <META NAME="keywords" VALUE="camera, photography, photographer,
   photograph, print, photo, film, 35mm, view camera, single
   lens reflex, slr, kodak, leica, nikon, ilford, picture">
   ```

Remember: Use lowercase letters in the keywords META tag, even for titles and proper nouns. Note the use of synonyms here — and make sure that you throw an occasional synonym into the text of the page itself. Also, avoid word stacking — don't say *camera, camera, camera.* You get penalized for it.

5. Add a description META tag.

The following is an example:

```
<META NAME="description" VALUE="Professional photographer
demonstrates classic cameras for use in fine photography.">
```

Note that in the description one should not use first person references ("I") but rather third person references ("professional photographer"). This is because using a third person reference, which is ultimately more descriptive, also allows you another chance to fit a keyword (of sorts) into your HTML.

These tidbits can give a Web page extra oomph in search engines and can help users who are interested in the topic of the site go straight to it.

The Northern Webs Search Engine Tutorial is a first-person look at how one Web team learned (through frustration) the hows and whys of getting its page to show up in the major search engines. Read what they have to say at `http://www.digital-cafe.com/~webmaster/set01.html`.

Another Webmaster, perusing his referrer logs, was amused to find that people found his page when looking for adult videos. Read A Brief Word About Search Engines at `http://manor.york.ac.uk/htdocs/ search.html`.

Excluding Areas of Your Site from Searches

Maybe you don't want every blasted search engine in the universe beating a path to your door and listing your site so that others can drop in. If you run a big corporate Web site, like one of the 6,000-page whoppers, you may find a visit from a search engine conducting a complete search of your site to be too CPU and I/O intensive. It could slow your site to a pitiful crawl for a while. If you feel this price is too high for the privilege of inclusion in the search engines, you can mark pages or your entire site as being off-limits.

You can exclude specific pages from indexing by a robot by placing a META tag within the document head (see "Head Tags, Title Tags, and Meta Tags — What They Mean to You," earlier in this chapter for instructions on using META tags). The name of the META tag in this case is *robots,* while the possible instructions are *index* (or *noindex*) and *follow* (or *nofollow*). *Index* means that robots record the page's contents for use in a database or search engine. *Follow* means that the robot follows all of the links on that page to collect more data.

To invite a robot to index and follow this page, the tag would look like this:

```
<meta name="robots" content="index,follow">
```

To instruct a robot not to index follow the links on a page, the tag would look like this:

```
<meta name="robots" content="noindex,nofollow">
```

You can use any combination of these tags (index,nofollow or noindex,follow), but be sure not to use conflicting instructions (such as noindex,index).

You can also control robots by placing a special file ¹/ₘ called robots.txt ¹/ₘ in your Web server's document root directory (which is discussed in Chapter 7). To find out, see `http:// www.webcrawler.com/mak/projects/ norobots.html`.

Webcrawler maintains an excellent resource about robots called The Web Robots Page. It includes a FAQ, a guide to the protocol, and an archive of the Web Robots mailing list. The URL is as follows: `http://info.webcrawler.com/ mak/projects/robots/robots.html`

Many of the files are old, but because the standard hasn't changed and isn't enforced, it's still the most helpful page around.

System administrators may be interested in perusing Webcrawler's Robots Mailing List archive or joining the list itself. The URL for the archive is `http://info.webcrawler.com/mailing-lists/robots`

There you have it. Now read on to find out about promoting your site.

Chapter 14

Promoting Your Site

● ●

In This Chapter

▶ Making your site a source

▶ Getting backlinks to your site

▶ Optimizing your promotional resources

▶ Using mailing lists and newsgroups to spread the word

▶ Popping your URL into print venues

▶ Purchasing and trading banner ads

● ●

*I*f you build it, will they come? Unfortunately, on the Web, as well as elsewhere, it isn't enough just to have built a site and made it available — you have to go out and let people know that your site exists. In fact, you have to put some substantial energy into this if you don't want to turn into a Web wallflower.

Advertising and promoting your site, both online and offline, is key to the success of any Web site. Although your site's purpose may be largely to promote your company's other products and services, people aren't going to be lured to your online ventures if they don't know that you're online to begin with. Additionally, if you have a product to sell online, you may need to seek traffic aggressively to justify the expense. What methods you undertake to promote your site may depend as much on your budget as anything else — it's true that big bucks can buy big-time attention — but you can do plenty to promote your site on a small budget. Many promotional venues explored in this chapter are cheap or free or promote your Web site by piggybacking on those marketing ventures for which you may already have a budget.

Keep in mind, though, the best thing you can do to build traffic to your site is to make your site so compelling that (a) people come back repeatedly and (b) they tell their friends. Turn back to Figure 13-1 in Chapter 13. It shows that word of mouth is a very important means by which people learn of Web sites. It also shows the proportionate importance of other means of learning about specific Web sites. The Georgia Tech study cited in Figure 13-1 shows that, in descending order, most people learn about Web sites from the following sources:

- Search tools like AltaVista, Yahoo!, Excite, Infoseek, and other more focused online search gizmos (we cover this in Chapter 13)
- Backlinks from other Web sites
- Newsgroups, where Web sites are mentioned in postings
- The press, where Web sites can be mentioned in articles or news pieces
- Friends who've recommended or described the site
- Signature files at the ends of e-mail messages
- Books (like this one) that include URLs
- Other sources of small measure that aren't specified

In this chapter, we describe how you can use these venues to get traffic hopping to your site.

Making Your Site Worth Visiting

We've talked throughout this book about how to organize your content so people are comfortable clicking around in your site for an extended visit. Making a good Web site means making a site that offers something useful or entertaining that people want to interact with, making the site look good, and making it one that's easy to navigate. In terms of promotion, if your site offers a unique or valuable resource to your customers, they'll not only visit — they will come back for more. Plus, they're going to tell their friends, and your fan club will spread. There's no better way to engineer word-of-mouth advertising than by offering a quality product — and that's what your Web site should be.

Giving something to people

People love getting free stuff, and although most Web sites are free to visit, some successful sites offer their visitors content that makes the users feel like they've come away with something more than just a visit to another Web site. Some types of online content are sure-fire winners; try these ideas:

- Offer free site membership with members-only benefits like chat rooms or exclusive, sought-after areas of the site.
- Give away free goodies in the form of software, screen savers, games, or Internet postcards.

✔ Host online events like chats, giveaways, contests, and games.

✔ Feature "Internet premiers," such as previews of magazine or book content, music or movie clips, demos of games and software, or sneak previews of new car or clothing lines.

✔ Announce "Internet exclusives" that customers can't get anywhere else.

✔ Throw in relevant celebrity endorsements or celebrity contributions to the site.

The more users find to do or see on your site, the more they are going to enjoy it. (Of course, everything that you offer should be relevant to the goals that you set for your site, as described in Chapter 2.) Note, however, that none of these suggestions mandates eye-popping graphics, high-bandwidth multimedia toys, a hard sell, or even a necessarily huge budget. SonicNet, an alternative music and entertainment site (see Figure 14-1) is a perfect example of a site that gives the customer things to come back for: celebrity chats, bulletin boards, live music broadcasts, contests, a mailing list, and a resource for other live events and links related to alternative music — all that in addition to their music reviews and articles! (SonicNet is located at `http://www.sonicnet.com/`.) If you're a large company, people are going to visit because of the brand name, but even then, you must give your customer a site worth appreciating and returning to, or a million dollar promotion budget doesn't do you a bit of good.

Figure 14-1:
SonicNet offers so much stuff to its visitors they can't help but return.

Making your site a source

The more your site has to offer and the more often you update and improve it, the more your visitors are going to think of your site as a source. Whether it's a source of entertainment, news, information, or bargains, you want visitors to think of your site as *the* place to go for that type of content. And it isn't enough to *tell* your readers that your site is number one — you have to *earn* the reputation. To do so, make your site smart, and as the Webmaster, be available for feedback. Listen to what your visitors have to say. (Chapter 15 discusses dealing with user e-mail, among other things.) You can make your content fresh without having to rethink your entire site every week by doing these things:

- Distribute an e-mail mailing list that informs your customers about news in the business or on your site.

- Maintain a quality index or directory of Web resources that are related to the topic of your site.

- Write a FAQ (frequently asked questions) list with answers about your business, a hot topic in your field, or both.

- Give visitors a chance to offer feedback and contribute to the site.

- Offer expert advice in the form of a column that's related to your business.

- Update material that appears on your site (Web indexes, online magazines, or news stories) frequently and on a predictable schedule.

When visitors come to expect new material and fresh ideas and information from your site, you've earned their loyalty, and that's worth maintaining. *The Wall Street Journal,* at `http://www.wsj.com/` (see Figure 14-2), for instance, is regarded as *the* source for financial news, and its Web site adds content such as customized business news, resources for business owners, and briefing books on publicly held companies. You can scale your services to your business and the size of your endeavor — you needn't fulfill the whole ambition of being *The Wall Street Journal* of your industry — but make your site a credible source of information, entertainment, or whatever you've decided to provide that can lure traffic in your direction.

Just in case you think you may not be up to comparing yourself to the venerable *Wall Street Journal,* consider Women's Wire (`http://www.women.com`), the premier resource for women's issues and entertainment on the Web. This beauty was started by a small group of women who found financial backing and used it to create a killer Web site. Their content is diverse enough to appeal to both high-powered businesswomen and housewives surfing at home. It's one of those sites that is so darned good that everyone links to them, and they're the first place that many people recommend when looking for women's resources online.

Figure 14-2:
The Wall Street Journal is a great example of a respected source both in print and online.

As another example, Studio B is a fresh computer publishing agency; to expand its image and reputation, Studio B created a Web site (http://www.studiob.com) and a mailing list, both widely popular in the computer book publishing industry. But more than that, Studio B created a community and a valuable information resource for the computer book publishing industry — a group of people who, for the most part, have never met in person. By finding a unique niche that had gone unexplored online and by filling it with information, Studio B now has a loyal following of both clients and visitors.

Creating Backlinks, Link Trades, and Net Alliances

For your site to be successful, a general rule is to make sure that you have many entry points, plenty to do there, and few exit points. Now, where are you going to get all of those entry points? In Chapter 13, we discuss how to optimize placement in search engines and directories to get traffic flowing into your site. These avenues initiate traffic to your site from people who are searching for something specific that's related to what you do. But many Web surfers float from site to site with no particular goal, following links that Webmasters of all stripes put up to point the way to other sites that are worth visiting. This is called *surfing* . . . you may have heard of it(!). How do you get a share of this random traffic? Getting link placement on other sites is often free, and soliciting it usually requires little more investment from you than a bunch of e-mail messages and perhaps providing a hotlist on your own site.

Getting backlinks

Obviously, other people are going to want to link to your page if it's good. If users find your site through search engines, other sites, or other media, they may just decide to place a link to your site on their site. These placements are called *backlinks*. The more backlinks you have to your site, the more traffic your site is likely to get.

Checking your backlinks

Perhaps you want to check out how many backlinks your site already has. Some online search engines, in particular AltaVista and HotBot, offer a way that you can search for links to your site. To try this out using AltaVista, follow these steps:

1. **Using your favorite browser, open AltaVista** (`http://www.altavista.digital.com`).

2. **In the text box, where you would usually type the subject of interest to conduct a search of AltaVista's database of Web sites, instead type the following (all in lowercase characters):**

   link:http://www.*yoursite.com*/ -host:*yoursite.com*

   where - is a hyphen and the host and URL are your own.

3. **Click on the Search button.**

   The hit list that appears shows the URLs of all the Web pages in the enormous AltaVista database that link to your site. (It doesn't show backlinks to pages within your own site, however; you have to repeat this process for important internal pages on your site to get information about backlinks to them.)

To try a similar search using HotBot, follow these steps:

1. **Using your favorite Web browser, open HotBot** (`http://www.hotbot.com`).

   The HotBot home page appears.

2. **In the text box, where you would usually type the subject of interest to conduct a search of HotBot's database of Web sites, instead type your URL. (Be sure to type the full URL, including the `http://` part).**

3. **Click on the menu box marked All the Words, and then select Links to this URL.**

4. **Click on the Search button, and HotBot returns a hit list consisting of Web pages that link back to your site.**

Trading links

Your backlink campaign should start by contacting Webmasters whose sites cover topics that are related to yours and simply asking them to link to you. If your company is part of a large corporation that includes sister companies, ask them to link to you. (You will probably be asked to link to them in exchange, so why not offer that up front?) If you have a list of Webmaster compadres — say if you belong to a group of Webmasters such as those described at the end of Chapter 1 — you may lean a bit on those friendly colleagues to trade links.

If part of your site consists of a hotlist or directory of Web sites or pages that are related to your own, let the people that you link to know that you've listed them on your site. Often, the Webmasters of these other pages visit your site and add it to their own hotlists. Many sites also incorporate publicity pages or Friends of Our Site pages that link to magazines, award sites, or individual Web reviewers who have given them recognition. If you've reviewed or applauded any Web site on your own pages, e-mail that Webmaster and let him or her know that you've done so.

If you have a reasonable excuse for providing people with an award, you can offer them a nice logo or button that announces that award to the world and provides you with a backlink to your site. Don't do this in a cheap-shot way, though — if you don't have a good excuse for offering awards, you end up looking silly. For ideas about how others do this, flip to the section "Submitting your site to awards pages," later in this chapter, and read up on the topic from another angle in Chapter 15.

Similarly, if you simply have a nice logo you can make available to Webmasters as a button, that can help your link stand out on their page. However, don't try to force someone to use your logo as a link — you may find that they balk, and rightfully so, in many cases. There's no real incentive for them to disrupt the look of their site with your logo unless, of course, you provide an incentive. For example, if you can offer some nifty software for download from your site, you can provide a logo for that software as a button that links to the download page. But again, don't cheapen this idea — if you don't have a good benefit attached to it, don't imagine that your logo alone is worth the trouble to other Webmasters.

Forming Net alliances

Sometimes trading links, e-mail, or information can lead to Net alliances that can have good effects for both parties. This isn't too different from the hotlist exchange that we just described, but in this case, you make more of an effort to make the other party feel recognized and involved. You may find that your company has some leverage with the big search-engine companies or some other Net bigwigs. If so, be sure to trade on that for linking and more.

But don't think that you can't form an alliance because yours is a smaller company. Be creative. For instance, if your company, Olaf's Solar Cells, maintains a really good solar energy factsheet, e-mail the Webmasters of some environmentally related sites, not just sites about solar energy per se. Mention your company's devotion to environmental matters, compliment their Web site, and tell them that you've added it to your hotlist. You may even mention a couple of other interesting environmental sites you've found online that they may find useful. Chances are, the Webmaster is going to appreciate your positive feedback and your suggestions. Not only may you hear back from your new friend in kind, but you may land a link to your site and maybe even a glowing review. Keeping up this sort of contact requires only an occasional e-mail message, but maintaining these Net alliances and virtual friendships pays off in terms of exposure and recognition.

Joining link free-for-alls

Some sites offer free-for-all hotlists that list anyone's page for free. Exposure on this sort of page is often short-lived, but it takes only a minute or so to submit your link to be listed. When you run across one, submit your link and move on.

Placing online classified ads

A number of sites offer free or cheap classified ads. People browse through these ads either when they're looking for a specific product or service or when they're bored. Either way, your site could benefit from placement of a brief classified ad. Be sure that, if you're selling something, you mention in your ad that visitors can buy it online. And don't forget that you may be able to trade a link from your site for the ad.

Be sure to trade at the rate of the real value of exposure on your site. For example, if your site gets four times the traffic of the site you're trading with, you should get four times the exposure on their site compared to the exposure it gets on yours. Remember to negotiate the best deal you can.

Submitting your site to awards pages

Multitudes of venues present clever or not-so-clever awards for various kinds of Web sites — design awards, content and presentation awards, Best of the Web awards, and general awards for cool or notable links. The type of awards offered range from big hit-getters like Cool Site of the Day, at `http://cool.infi.net` (see Figure 14-3), to the Best Financial Resource Pages or the Best Christian Web Sites.

Figure 14-3:
Awards like
Cool Site of
the Day can
garner
you both
prestige
and hits.

 Be frugal in submitting your site for consideration to these pages. If it isn't
particularly graphically stunning, don't bother with sites that present
graphical awards, and if you aren't a Texan Web site, you can skip the Best
of Texas awards. Look for niche awards that recognize excellence in your
particular field. Many of these niche awards are presented by individual
Webmasters or designers, so depending on that individual's status, the
award may carry more or less prestige. Whatever its prestige, an award may
still grab you some hits. And the more prestige, the more hits!

Optimizing Your Existing Promotional Budget

So maybe your company already has an advertising department or publicity
budget. Maybe it pumps out ads, announcements, and promotional materials as a matter of course. If so, adding your URL to these items is a simple
matter that can pay off handsomely in the long run. Without spending any
more money than usual, you can leverage your existing efforts to gain
exposure to pull people into your Web site as well.

Putting your URL everywhere

Make sure that any print ads your company runs include your URL. Whether these ads are for products, services, job openings, or new store locations, make sure that your URL appears somewhere in the ad. (And make sure you've proofread the URL before you go to print!)

If you print new letterhead, stationery, envelopes, or business cards, make sure they include the full, correct URL. Does your company regularly distribute freebies like bookmarks, pens, mouse pads, or T-shirts? That URL should be there — get it under as many people's noses as you can. You want to make your URL a part of the regular address block on any printed item; get people so used to seeing it that it becomes an integral part of your brand and your image.

Using your URL casually

Whenever an opportunity for publicity arises — an interview, a TV appearance, a guest lecture, a community outreach activity — mention your Web site, and mention it in a way that suggests that *everyone* should know about it and visit it. Get everyone in your organization to do the same. Talk the thing up; confidence about your Web site, as though it's as important as your other projects (and it is!), compels people to see what it is that you have to show off.

Cashing in at trade shows

Trade shows, conventions, and expos, no matter what your business, can be a great place to get your site some exposure. Whether your business is software, toupees, or comic books, have your URL printed on the banner at your booth. Hand out fliers, pens, or at least business cards that feature the address of your Web site along with any other message that you deem important. If possible, have a computer set up in your booth at which people can explore your site — right there, right when you mention it to them.

Seeing Your URL in Print

Web surfers don't just find new links to visit online through the psychic airwaves — they read magazines, newspapers, computer books, and fliers, too. Again, making your site a notable or popular one is going to make it attractive to publishers, editors, and writers of various kinds looking for links to add to columns or Internet guides. You can do things to make getting your URL in print more likely.

What should my URL look like?

How can you print a URL and still make it look good? There are two basic ways to "spell" your Web address to make it easy to spot. If your company has its own domain name and if yours is a Web-savvy audience, you can print your URL like this:

`www.company.com`

That sort of simple address is catchy, and the format is standard enough to make people realize that it's a Web-site address.

On the other hand, if your URL has a longer pathname or if yours is a less-Web-savvy audience, you may want to use this format:

`http://www.provider.com/`
`oursite/oursite.html`

Using the `http://` in the address indicates that it's a Web-site URL; many Web modern browsers don't need the `http://` spelled out for them, though, so the slick and savvy leave it off. However, not all people understand that, and some use older browsers. You must decide which method works for your part of the public. One more thing to keep in mind: When printing a tagline, such as *Visit our Web site,* remember that *Web site* is two words, and avoid redundancies like *Our online Web site* or *Our digital electronic page.*

Getting into magazines and newspapers

Earlier in this chapter, we talk about making your site a source and giving your customers something that they are going to remember. Again, this is probably the best way to attract attention: *Be a quality site.* Unless your company has a nationally known name, it isn't likely to get heaps of attention simply because it exists. And by the way, the sites of larger companies often undergo exceptionally close (and sometimes unflattering) scrutiny, because they're held to very high standards.

Getting your site listed and reviewed

Making sure that your site is indexed by sites like Yahoo! and listed with AltaVista, HotBot, and other major search tools (see Chapter 13) is a big step toward becoming visible to journalists and computer book authors. Posting to newsgroups and mailing lists, particularly with messages that contain information and insight rather than simple announcements, can also make your site visible to arbiters of what's worth visiting. In general, playing the publicity game, and playing it well, encourages writers to give your site a look. Many Internet writers consider a few specific things, however, when considering whether your site is going to be around long enough to make it into a magazine article or book:

- ✔ Has the site been around for longer than a month or two, and does it promise to be around when whatever's being written is on the shelves?

- ✔ Is the site updated or refreshed often?

✔ Does it deliver what the home page promises?

✔ Is contact information provided and easy to locate?

✔ Do all the links work?

✔ Do all the gadgets and gizmos have purposes that serve the goals of the site (rather than simply exist gratuitously)?

✔ Do the pages and graphics load quickly?

✔ Is it easy to navigate the site?

If you can answer yes to all of those questions, your site should generally get good reviews. Now all you have to do is promote it enough to attract all of the press that you deserve. Some magazines, such as *The Net, Yahoo! Internet Life* (`http://www.zdnet.com/yil`), and *NetGuide* (`http://www.netguidemag.com`), devote page real estate to reviewing Web sites. You may want to send them a simple press release (see the next section) to let them know about your site. But don't focus only on Internet magazines. Magazines about your area of expertise or your area may be good choices. If you own a catering company in Denver, Colorado, you can send a press release about what your site offers to Internet magazines, food magazines, catering and hospitality publications, and magazines about Denver, Colorado, and even the Rocky Mountains, as well as the daily and weekly local newsrags and entertainment listings, depending on what kind of information you have to offer.

If a magazine that you think would be interested in reviewing your site has a Web site of its own, see if its contact information includes an e-mail address or form you can use to submit a link. You may get a link on its site, a mention in print, or both. For more on contacting the press, read on.

Sending a press release

Getting listed in newspapers and magazines involves making your site worthy of notice and then actually *getting* their notice. We'd love to tell you that this is as simple as writing a snappy press release, but magazines and newspapers get thousands of unsolicited press releases. How often they get those releases depends on the status of the magazine or newspaper. If they get them often, lots go in the trash. Your company could act like those with big publicity departments, whose sole job is persuasion, schmoozing, and sending cute little gifts and fruit baskets. Oops, but you say you don't have that kind of budget?

You can and should send press releases anyway; just don't expect a fast call from your favorite columnist the next morning. To get the best bang for your buck, first target some good venues — magazines that cover Web sites, maybe? Take a look at their *mastheads* (the listing of who works at the magazine), zero in on some likely person whose title is *editor* but who's not *too* important, and send your press release directly to that person. (Unless the staff shown on the masthead is very, very small, don't send a release to the editor-in-chief, associate publisher, or managing editor; these are very busy people who are quite likely to toss your carefully composed press release into the circular file.) To find out how to write a great press release, mosey on over to your local book store and pick up a book on that topic. Be sure to follow the standard formatting, too.

These online magazines show folks what to see or how to see it on the Web:

- ✔ Yahoo! Internet Life (`http://www.yil.com`)
- ✔ NetGuide (`http://www.netguidemag.com`)
- ✔ Internet World (`http://www.iw.com`)
- ✔ Internet User (`http://www.internetuser.com`)
- ✔ The Web (`http://www.Webmagazine.com`)
- ✔ The Net (`http://www.thenet-usa.com`)
- ✔ Websight (`http://www.Websight.com`)

When you launch your site, send out a press release. When your site sponsors a chat hosted by a well known person or covers a hot topic, send out a press release. When you launch online transactions or some other nifty new feature that's sure to rock the industry, by all means, send out a press release. Create a list of local newspapers, trade publications, radio talk shows, and business and marketing publications to which you can send your announcements. (You can send to some via e-mail, but some are only able to manage printed pieces via snail mail.)

How many press releases and to what publications you send depend a great deal on how well known your company is. Small businesses may want to stick to local newspapers; larger, nationally known companies can extend the scope of their endeavors to bigger publications and a broader range of media. In the press release, make sure to include some type of contact information for your company, including an e-mail address; folks who contact your publicity department by e-mail may be more Net savvy and possibly more willing to give press to an online venture.

Whatever your budget, you should be able to manage at least a small, highly targeted press list and occasional press releases. If you can devote the time of a staff person to following up on releases and schmoozing your press contacts, that's even better. But remember, make sure that your site is worthy of notice, or you just end up annoying these folks, and you do *not* want bad press relations. Give them something worth writing about, and you may just get the good notice you hope for.

Placing a free or cheap print ad

We've already mentioned that any print ads your company places should include your URL. But you can advertise in some other print forums that incur little or no cost. If your city has a free computer publication like Computer Currents (http://www.currents.net, see Figure 14-4) or MicroTimes, check to see if it offers a free classified ad to first-time advertisers, or juts plain free listings for Web sites — some do! Similarly, check advertising rates for the Internet sections of free print weeklies like the *San Francisco Bay Guardian* or the *Village Voice.* Some of these "Webvertising" sections offer reasonable rates for back-page advertising sections, which may be particularly appropriate if your site offers an Internet service or online sales.

Posting fliers in the real world

Small, locally run businesses, local ISPs, and other service providers, and online magazines with local coverage, all may benefit from littering their home cities with fliers. An inexpensive but eye-catching flier tacked up on every legal wall or phone pole may get you some cheap notice — if door hangings of printed pieces work for pizza places, why shouldn't they work for local Web sites? (On the other hand, we absolutely despise finding door hangings on our house and fliers on our car windshields. Use discretion.)

Figure 14-4:
Computer
Currents
and other
local or
regional
free
computer
magazines
may list
Web sites
for free.

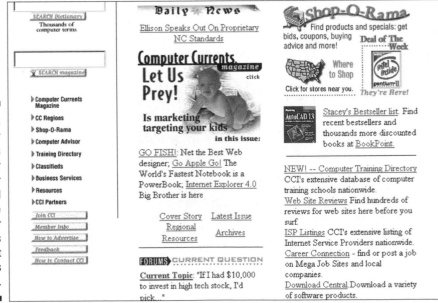

Enticing new visitors with gifts

Postcards, bookmarks, and stickers are a great way to make people visit your site. Many companies of all shapes and sizes leave stacks of postcards or other goodies in coffee shops and bars — people pick up this stuff because it's attractive, small, or useful. When they get home and find your nonvirtual bookmark (saying to bookmark your site) in the book they're reading, you're in! Look for coffee shops or other local hangouts in your city that have free postcard racks, and check the back to see who manufactures the cards. Some companies, such as Max Racks, can print bulk postcards and distribute them, free to the consumer, in major cities to which you may not otherwise have easy access.

Max Racks distributes eye-grabbing postcards for many companies, publications, and events in cities nationwide, and it offers free digital postcards on its Web site. Check it out at http://www.maxracks.com/. Odyssey Stickers, at http://www.generix.com/odyssey/, offers reasonable rates for printing vinyl decals.

Talk Is Cheap

Free speech is part of the Internet tradition, and you can trade on that tradition (within reason) to talk up your Web site. Talk, talk, talk — along the way, you can pepper your comments with references to your site.

Making and using a SIG file

Make sure that every employee in your company who interacts with the outside world via e-mail uses an attractive, brief, and standardized signature (SIG) file that mentions your Web site. Most popular e-mail programs, including Eudora, PINE, Netscape Mail or Messenger, and Microsoft Exchange, all include a signature file option. If you can't find this option in your e-mail program at a glance, look in the help files under *signature* or *sig*.

A signature file touting a Web site may look like one of the following:

```
Jennifer K. Jones <jkjones@applianceco.com>
Associate Director of Marketing
The Appliance Company
http://www.applianceco.com/
```

As a general rule, signature files should be short and to the point. A SIG file that's more than six lines long annoys and even offends some Netizens. Be sure to use the *full* URL, including the `http://` part, in your SIG file — in many popular e-mail programs, users can click on full, correct URLs, opening them automatically in a Web-browser window.

Participating in discussion groups

Many disciplines, trades, geographical areas, and hobbies inspire online discussion groups. There are three widely used types of discussion groups — mailing lists, newsgroups, and bulletin board systems (BBSs). The latter may be a bit tricky to track down, unless you already know of a BBS in your field or area. Mailing lists and discussion groups, on the other hand, are free, easy to find, and easy to use. Not only can you publicize your site with every message you post to an online discussion (got that SIG file ready?), but you and your company can become acknowledged experts in your field, just by participating intelligently.

Scout around for discussion groups that are relevant to the topic of your site, hang out there for a while, and every so often, spout off about the site. Be careful, though. As a savvy Internet user, you probably know that not every newsgroup, discussion group, forum, or mailing list is open to blatant plugging or advertising. Make sure that you get to know the group culture before you alienate the very people that you want to attract.

Yakking it up on mailing lists

Mailing lists seem to fall into three groups: announcement lists, digests, and discussion lists. Announcement lists are generally sent weekly or less often to a group of users interested in a particular subject. The author of these lists is generally an individual, company, or Web site that is offering news about a given field or the site itself. These are similar to company newsletters, and it may be worthwhile for your site to offer an announcement-style mailing list to visitors to your site.

To get people to provide their e-mail addresses for such a list, have them register on your site. To get them to register, offer them something in exchange — access to special content, a chance to win a contest, and so on. (Don't forget to offer them a way to unsubscribe, too, though, in each message you send — it's a turnoff to get junk mail, remember?)

Discussion lists and digests, on the other hand, solicit contributions from their general readership. Discussion lists are ongoing, whereas digest lists often compile the best or most typical questions and answers about a certain topic and then distribute a batch of several messages at a time to the readers of the list. Discussion lists may deliver several (or several dozen) messages a day about a given topic, to which anyone can respond and contribute. Some discussion lists are also available in digest format.

Find mailing lists in discussion or digest format, target the right ones for you, and assign someone who is involved in your company's Web site or publicity department to read and contribute to them. These folks may then be privy to Internet rumors and breaking news on the topic of the lists, which is always handy, and their thoughtful or informative contributions to the discussions can make your company well regarded as experts in your field.

An easy way to find a mailing list that's related to your field is to search a mailing-list directory such as Liszt, whose URL is `http://www.liszt.com/` (Figure 14-5). Just type a keyword into the search box, and Liszt finds you a mailing list about that topic. Liszt also features fact sheets and help files about using mailing lists.

Figure 14-5:
You can search Lizst for a mailing list that's related to your field.

Liszt, the mailing list directory

our sponsor! --> The Cool Place to Shop | PowerBook 1400 | for Computer Products

About Liszt | Newsgroup Directory | What's New at Liszt? | Tips for Newcomers | What Are Mailing Lists?

I. **Search Liszt's main directory** of **71,618 mailing lists:** *Junk Filtering:* ○ none ⦿ some ○ lots [go] [help]

II. **...or click on any topic to browse** *Liszt Select*:

Arts (135 lists)
Literature, Television, Movies ...

Business (68 lists)
Finance, Jobs, Marketing ...

Computers (148 lists)
Internet, Database, Programming ...

Culture (134 lists)
Gay, Jewish, Parenting ...

Education (48 lists)
Distance Education, Academia, Internet ...

Health (123 lists)
Medicine, Allergy, Support ...

Humanities (188 lists)
Philosophy, History, Psychology ...

Music (141 lists)

Nature (69 lists)

Navigating newsgroups

Usenet newsgroups cover almost every topic under the sun — from Java programming to collecting baseball cards to hating Wesley Crusher (and maybe even worshipping Whack-a-Mole). Some newsgroups experience extremely high traffic, while others have a small but devoted readership. It may be impossible to read every message that passes through some newsgroups, but on the other hand, high-traffic newsgroups are also read by a wider and larger audience. Here, again, the opportunities include assigning someone to haunt the mailing list, seeking and seizing openings in the thread that allow for mentions of your Web initiative, or even just yakking it up and flaunting a SIG file that promotes the site on each message that person posts.

Where can you find the right newsgroups? Deja News is a Web site that archives every post that spools through Usenet. You can search by keyword, by date, by author, and by newsgroup for messages on certain topics. You can also use Deja News to post messages to Usenet without having to use newsreader software. Visit `http://www.dejanews.com/`, and if you're still puzzled, click on Help.

When your Web site is ready for prime time, send an announcement to the appropriate newsgroups. As always, notice that we said *appropriate*. Sending the same message frivolously and redundantly to multiple, unrelated newsgroups is known as *spamming* — this offense can ruin your company's image faster than bad coffee. (What's more, some newsgroups specifically prohibit announcements and posting there will backfire by getting you a bad reputation.) Instead of taking that risk, hand-pick newsgroups that are directly related to your topic, and send your concise, typo-free announce-ment to a few select newsgroups at the right moment instead of tossing it like spaghetti toward the wall. As an example, an announcement of a new Web site about an online vintage video store would be appropriate to post to some newsgroups about movies and collecting, but it would be unwelcome spam in newsgroups about cooking or baseball — even if you think that those readers also watch movies.

Many newsgroups periodically post FAQs, a description, or an etiquette guide. Reading these documents is the best way to find out whether the newsgroup would be interested in your announcements — and whether the threads there are worth reading. An index of Usenet FAQs, including a FAQ about Usenet itself, is available at `http://www.cis.ohio-state.edu/hypertext/faq/usenet/FAQ-List.html`.

The PHOAKS (People Helping One Another Know Stuff) Report is run by the Web division of AT&T. Those nice phoaks scan every Usenet post (incredibly enough), looking for URLs. Those that are found are then compiled on a Web page that's searchable. You can save hours of tedious sifting through newsgroups if you use this resource; it can be found at `http://www.phoaks.com/`.

Buying Ad Space — Why, How, and When

Whatever the size of your advertising budget, you can place ads on other Web sites. Yes, we're saying that this can be done cheaply or for free — of course it can also cost mucho smackeroos, and spending money on advertising can buy you bigger traffic. But you don't necessarily have to spend a lot to get ad space.

Ad rates depend on how much traffic the site gets (that's the site you advertise on, not the one that you advertise for). You need to know a bit about this before you go forth. We cover that in upcoming sections of this chapter, and delve into it in Chapter 15, too. First, we'll talk about banner ad ins and outs.

Banner ad basics

Nearly every commercial Web site features banner ads — you've no doubt seen them on most corporate sites. A typical banner ad is a long rectangle that's about 468 pixels by 60 pixels, although many sites are featuring multiple, smaller ads in custom sizes, which are incorporated into the total look of the page rather than sticking out like a . . . *banner ad*. Banner ads can incorporate many print ad design elements, albeit in a much smaller space, and they can also be animated. A typical banner ad is shown in Figure 14-6.

On a site's home page, you generally find a link like <u>Advertise With Us</u> or <u>About Our Site</u>; clicking on it leads you to information about how the site takes advertisements. Few sites actually display rate cards online, but you can almost always find a contact phone number or e-mail address for advertising queries.

Figure 14-6:
A typical banner ad displays the name of the site and the reason to click on the ad.

Banner ads are sold in large batches, generally one thousand (or more) *impressions* (see the following section) at a time. Pricing can range from less than a penny per impression to several thousand dollars for the same number of ads, depending on the popularity of the site. Netscape, for example, charges over a million smackers for some of its more prominent slots, with the prices dropping to less extravagant sums, depending on the relative number of hits a certain section gets. Then again, the Netscape site gets more hits than any other site on the Web, so buying even a small number of impressions from Netscape could increase your audience dramatically.

You don't have to go to the big guns to buy ad space, but they're the folks who set the standards, so they're good examples and important to watch. To find out more about getting ad space on less-heavy hitters, read through this info and then turn to later sections in this chapter for tips on getting ad space at more accessible prices.

Impressions vs. clickthroughs

Ads are generally sold per *impression,* but sometimes they are sold per *clickthrough.* An impression is generated every time an ad appears on a Web site, while a clickthrough happens when someone who sees the ad clicks on it to visit the advertiser's site. Note that we do not mention hits here. A *hit* is generated for each file that's included when a page is loaded; a single Web page can include a few, dozens, or even hundreds of hits — just how many is hard to tell. That makes counting hits and drawing a correlation to the number of people who have seen an ad problematic. (See Chapter 15 for more detail.)

Another dilemma comes up, though, in accounting for the number of impressions that are served. There is no good way for advertisers to verify that the number of impressions the advertising venue has guaranteed have actually occurred. In print media (magazines and newspapers), ad space is sold based on the circulation of the publication. The publication tells advertisers its circulation, but that number is also verified by recognized companies that specialize in auditing and verifying circulation of print publications. Every legitimate publication is audited regularly, so potential advertisers can be assured that they're going to get the ad traffic they think they are going to get when they pay for the ad space.

In the Web business, though, there is no such standard system — at least not yet. Sites that charge for ad space often do so based on a guaranteed number of impressions and then basically give you their word that that number of impressions occurred. How do you know that they have? Well, you can't really check the log files for that site. There are some third-party companies that compile site-traffic statistics for the purpose of verifying traffic, but no industry standard or system has yet emerged. (Again, see Chapter 15 for more on this, from another perspective.) If and when you buy ad space, look carefully at how the company from which you're buying can verify that you've received what you paid for.

Among those companies that address the traffic-verifying problem are Nielsen I-Pro, which for a fee, provides a summary of your site's activity based on a census analysis of raw log files provided by the site. This is probably as close to an independent audit as you can get and is recognized as credible in the business. It's not cheap, however.

Note that, as of this writing, Yahoo! has just dropped I-Pro in favor of Audit Bureau of Verification Services as its measurement service and retained Ernst & Young to audit its self-measurement systems. Because Yahoo! is a big player, this could be an indicator of some shifts in the way measurement takes place.

Another option (also not cheap) is NetGravity, which provides an ad server you can run on your site, allowing you to target ads to individuals or groups and providing you with site activity reports including traffic analysis. This, of course, is not an independent audit, but it is a recognized way of verifying your traffic.

Going back to the clickthrough rate, this scheme came into vogue when some large companies demanded it from Internet advertising space providers. Their claim was that this was measurable and verifiable to them, and clickthroughs were what they wanted in the first place. The clickthrough rate from most sites is pretty low, however, so most sites prefer to base their advertising rates on impressions (where you pay for each time that your ad appears on any part of the site) rather than clickthroughs (in which you only pay for successful referrals to your site). The debate on this point is not over.

When you're looking into and buying ad space, remember that Internet ad sales reps can find a million excuses to reduce their stated rates. This is a soft market — they want your money, and the whole scene is set up such that you can haggle. Try offering them a third of what they've asked for, and then negotiate from there. You can also try to trade ad space, trade your product for ad space, and generally think up creative deals.

Context-sensitive and other new advertising ideas

The most highly trafficked site on the Net is Netscape's; other than that, the big traffic hits the search engines and online directories, and more specifically, a handful of top names in Web searching. Some of these companies offer advertising based on selling you a keyword or an appearance "in the rotation"; they may sell you a whole category in the directory (perhaps *computers: Internet: books*). Some also offer *context-sensitive* advertising, although the accuracy of that term depends on the methods that are used.

For example, suppose your site is an online book store. Visitors to a famous but unnamed Internet directory who look for the word *book* are treated to one of your ads, the appearance of which was triggered by a search for the word *book*. That's known as *keyword* advertising.

If you bought a spot in the *rotation,* your ad would appear *x* number of times in a random rotation with others until your ad reached the number of impressions you were guaranteed for the specified period of time. If you bought a *category,* your ad would appear each time someone browsed or searched that category until your time was up.

Truly context-sensitive advertising branches out and learns the relationships between words. For example, using the previous computer book example, when a user searches for a computer-related topic, like *programming,* or a book-related topic, like *Stephen King* or *romance novels,* that user sees your ad, although he or she did not search for computer books. Therefore, you may want to specify whether you want the context to be *computers* or *books*. Features like this that target specific ads to specific users are the hot thing in Internet advertising. If yours is a big budget with room to pay for search-engine and directory appearances, it may be worth the extra cost to get the targeted exposure you seek.

Building a successful banner ad

Banner ads have become ubiquitous — a couple of years ago, only heavy-traffic sites, like Netscape and HotWired, featured banner ads. The companies that pioneered the use of this advertising medium came from seemingly unlikely sources: Saturn cars, Zima malt beverages, Duracell batteries, and Sony's various endeavors all pioneered the banner-ad medium with innovative, eye-catching graphics and taglines that made users curious about the Web site that was hidden behind the ad.

Think of a banner ad as a sign in a shop window — if the sign is well de-signed, easy to read, evocative, and announces a special or discount, people come into your store to look at your wares. Stores that use hand-scrawled words that are hard to read often depend on customer loyalty rather than presentation for their living, but the Web is *about* presentation, so make your banner the type of sign that lures people in.

If you're buying (or even trading) ad space, your goal is to get folks to click through the ad to go to your site. Have your ad designed professionally. This may cost you a few hundred dollars, but it's important to provide a clean image that looks good. Specify to designers that they use the Netscape color palette so that your ad looks sharp. If the designer asks you what you mean, he or she probably hasn't designed for the Web before. Also, make sure that you have the correct dimensions in pixels for the ad space that you're buying. Unfortunately, there are no standard sizes for this yet, so you may want to specify that your ad design be scaleable to several different banner ad sizes. Also, make sure that the file size for your ad is small — it should load fast, and it stays before the user's eyes longer if it's quick to load. A maximum file size may be specified by the site you'll be advertising with, and in some cases the max may be as big as 40K. But for flexibility, try to keep the file size within 10K. Finally, include a call to action on your ad. Even the otherwise discouraged Click Here is okay, but try to include some clever phrase in the copy on your ad instead.

Here are more tips for designing and using your ad:

- ✔ Recognizable brand names and familiar company names attract their loyal following and the curious.

- ✔ Mysterious banner ads that offer suggestive images and taglines may or may not tempt curiosity clicks.

- ✔ Using several ads with different looks in rotation keeps people from getting tired of seeing the same image repeatedly.

- ✔ Changing the content of your ad to promote events and new features keeps people coming back.

- ✔ Shaping ads to appeal to demographically different audiences on various Web sites can work in your favor.

- ✔ Contests, events, live chats, and other timely content may make people click now, rather than later.

- ✔ As corny as it may seem and expensive as it may be, time-limited Today Only offers can be very compelling, as can tasty discounts or sales.

In the same way that companies like Nike and Guess? run different ads in different magazines, you may want to tailor your advertising strategy to different audiences, different Web sites, and different times of day. For more on advertising on the Internet, investigate the Adweek site at http://www.adweek.com. These are the folks who report on advertising news to the ad industry itself; they also often sponsor excellent seminars at Internet industry shows and conferences such as Internet World.

Getting ad space on less-big-gun Web sites

Depending on your budget, you may want to place banner ads on a handful of niche sites, on a few high-traffic Web pages, or on a wide variety of sites that are seen by different kinds of folks. Here, again, just as when you defined your site's goals in Chapter 2, you have to decide whether to go wide or deep. It's not always true, though, that going deep (niche oriented) in your site goals means that you go deep in your ad campaign.

Had iGolf (http://www.igolf.com) stuck to advertising only on sports-related sites, for example, it wouldn't have the high profile that it does today — its strategy involved purchasing ad space on both upscale Internet magazines and widely used search engines and pointer pages. Similarly, AutoByTel (http://www.autobytel.com), a telephone-and-Internet car sales and leasing company, achieved exposure not just by advertising on car dealers' pages but on a number of popular sites that are visited by millions of users each day. (And as of this writing, AutoByTel is also advertising on television!)

You may find that the best way to go is to advertise not with the big, highly trafficked sites but instead with less expensive venues, or with venues that reach highly targeted audiences. These sites are often willing to negotiate their ad rates, trade ad space or otherwise barter, and provide you with some verification that you received what you paid for. Many of the smaller sites, however, set their rates on a per-month or other time-based system. Find out how many impressions they expect to get in that month and how they can verify that number. (See Chapter 15 for more on how numbers are verified.)

If you choose to sell ads for your site as an in-house operation — which you are indeed doing if you trade ad space, by the way — you may need at least one staff member who deals with advertising and/or marketing on a full-time basis. Again, such considerations depend on both your budget itself and how you budget the time of staff members.

Exchanging ads — it's free!

Offering another company an advertisement on your site in exchange for a similar ad on its site can be one way to approach getting banner ad space. That may net you some traffic but certainly no revenue from ad sales, so whether this is of interest depends on your goals. (Remember, though, that building traffic leads to other good things, such as ad sales, if your traffic gets big enough.) If your company has strategic partners or alliances, the ad people from both companies may be able to work out a deal. You also may want to put some energy into contacting various venues with whom you don't have partnerships to strike a deal.

Another kind of advertising exchange involves signing up with a company such as Link Exchange (`http://www.linkexchange.com`) or The Commonwealth Network (`http://commonwealth.riddler.com`). These sites collect ads, which are stored on a central server that then places ads in a random order on the sites of other members. In some cases, you and your site receive a small commission for the number of impressions or clickthroughs your ad achieves. Link Exchange lets you trade banner ads for free, while The Commonwealth Network distributes ads for free and then pays royalties.

Contracting to ad agencies

Ad agencies do it all — they design the campaign and the ads, target place-ment, and place the ads. The big advantages here are that they are pros and not only do professional, slick treatments but can also maximize your exposure by including ad venues you didn't even know existed. And you don't always have to buy the full package of services from an ad agency. You may have a great in-house design team to design the ads and contract an ad agency to give you tips about what works best. A bigger ad budget allows you to retain a more high-profile ad agency. Some new ad companies that specialize in the Internet, however, have Net-savvy staff who can spice up your online image with banner ads.

Before you retain an ad agency, you probably should know what type of experience it has with the Net and who its Internet clients have been. Just as you would do when hiring other Internet vendors, take a look at the agency's client URLs. For more on hiring outside vendors, turn to Chapter 8.

If your company already retains an ad agency (or a creative agency, as they're sometimes known) and you have the budget for it, you may want to stay with that agency for the sake of message cohesion. Note in any case, however that most agencies job out Web design to some subcontractor. One way that you may go is to retain the ad agency for concept while having your own, more Web-savvy (and less expensive) design people do the execution. (Again, see Chapter 8.)

Keep in mind that an ad agency charges every dime of its outlay to the client. If it subcontracts to a designer, it charges you for both the designer's fees and the time it spends managing the designer. If the agency purchases materials, you pay for both the materials and the time spent purchasing them. If you exchange e-mail with the agency, it charges you for the time to handle the e-mail. If agency personnel fly to see you, it's at your expense, and the agency probably won't buy the ticket at advance-purchase economy rates. If agency personnel take you to lunch, they may well fold that time and expense into your bill. Its goal is to be profitable — you pay for that profit. It's up to you whether the expense is within your budget.

Sponsoring a Web site other than your own

Some Web sites (which may or may not sell banner ads) work on a sponsorship model, in which one or several corporations donate a flat fee and, in exchange, have their name, link, and logo featured on an Our Sponsors page. (We cover this in Chapter 2, along with a number of other revenue models.) In particular, nonprofits and small businesses that run Web sites may get a good deal of their Web budget from sponsoring companies. Sponsoring a nonprofit or charitable organization's Web site offers the same type of image-enhancing benefits that usually come with underwriting arts, public service, or charitable organizations.

If you already contribute a significant sum to a particular organization, contact the organization's donation committee to ask if you can be listed as a sponsor on its Web page as part of the recognition you receive. If you do want to sponsor a site, you may find that there's no easy way to find one that's seeking sponsorship. As of this writing, there aren't any central indices like Yahoo! or Excite that list sites in search of sponsors or sponsors in search of sites. But if you see a site whose work you respect, look at the background links to see if sponsors are listed or if it has a notice posted on its advertising page about potential sponsorship. It never hurts to ask.

The *Advertising Age* Sponsor Quest lists organizations in search of a sponsor — but the price tags can be hefty. Find Sponsor Quest online at `htp://adage.com/news_and_features/sponsorquest/index.html`.

Similarly, if there's a worthy organization on your radar whose Web initiative you would like to sponsor, you can contact its public relations or development person to investigate that. And finally, if you find, as many executives do, that nonprofits are calling on you to ask for corporate sponsorship or support, you also may find them open to the idea of your company supporting them in launching a Web endeavor. (Psst! You nonprofits out there may want to look into this from your end.)

Chapter 15

Measuring Success

. . . .

In This Chapter

▶ Looking at the five general types of success

▶ Measuring traffic and how that happens

▶ Reading log files (made simple)

▶ Understanding hits, impressions, visitors, and clickpaths

▶ Tracking page popularity with site statistic tools

▶ Auditing, and why and when it matters

▶ Handling feedback and assessing your own success

. . . .

Success in a Web site can be measured in traffic, in sales, in acceptance by the public of an online transaction system, in savings that occur elsewhere (for example, in a drop in the cost of customer support because the site is doing that job), and even in media presence (how much attention the site is getting from the press, for example). How you and your company perceive success depends a lot on the company's values and on the goals of the site. (Chapter 2 covers setting goals for your site.)

In any case, the most important factor is that the measurement of success be in line with your goals and be attainable. Your success benchmarks should be within reasonable expectations — and, as Webmaster, part of your role (see Chapter 1) is to manage those expectations. Later sections of this chapter describe specific tools you can use for measuring success; we start here with a quick overview of the types of success.

Types of Success

How you measure success depends a great deal on which goals you've set for your site. Of course, the goals you set will depend on what you imagine success to be — so to some extent, this is a chicken-and-the-egg question. However, your best bet is to set your goals early and realistically, and then consider how you plan to measure success within the context of those goals. If you don't do this, you're likely to fall victim to someone else setting your goals for you. It's all too easy for management to hear about the millions of visitors sites like Yahoo! or CNN Interactive get daily and decide that your site should get just as much traffic. For your site, that may not be the correct goal — or even an accurate measure of success. Consider how types of success correspond to the types of goals we outline in Chapter 2.

Hits, impressions, and traffic reports

You can track success through the popularity of the site, which is measurable in a number of ways. The three most popular ways to count are through *hits, impressions,* and *visits.* (For the technical lowdown on this, see "How Traffic Measurements Are Calculated," later in this chapter.) *Hits* are the number of *files* that are accessed on your Web site. Notice that this is not the number of visitors to the site, nor is it the number of pages they've viewed. You often hear people talk about the number of hits their site gets, and to be honest, that's a poor measure of popularity. A hit is generated for every page of text, every tiny graphic, and every scrap of video that appears on every Web page on the site. A single page (your home page, for example) may generate a bunch of hits every time it's loaded. Most of the time, without extensive research, you don't know how many hits make your home page or any other page on the site. People tend to use the number of hits to describe a site's popularity anyway, especially when they are talking in public, because these numbers are usually huge and easy to measure, even if they don't mean anything. A site with a great deal of graphics may get 100,000 hits per week, even though it gets only a few dozen actual visitors.

An *impression* occurs each time a single page on your site is loaded. This is a far better measure of popularity, because the number of images and other items appearing on the page does not affect the count. When sites sell ad space, they often base their rates on a guaranteed number of impressions. (See the sidebar "Setting ad rates based on impressions," later in this chapter.) However, as we note throughout this chapter, impressions are not easy to measure accurately.

One of the best ways to measure traffic (and success, if traffic is your benchmark) is through counting *visitors* — the number of visits that have occurred in a given time. Another is through counting *unique users,* or the number of individuals who have visited. However, figuring the number of visitors or unique users that you get is really no picnic. Remember all that business about hits? The problems with measuring traffic include the fact that you have to decide how to measure it and that the easiest measure — hits — is also the most meaningless measure. A number of handy software packages can give you a hand; we talk about them later in this chapter.

Measuring traffic and having good traffic are urgent matters regardless of your site's main mission; however, if your site is meant to generate ad revenue, big-time traffic is crucial.

The important thing to remember is that the goals you and your company set for your site define the benchmarks of your success. If you surpass your goals, you are succeeding. See Chapter 2 for more on setting goals. See "Measuring Traffic" and "Reading Log Files for the Few and the Many," later in this chapter for more on specific traffic-measuring tools and techniques.

Media presence

Yet another method for measuring popularity is less measurable but can be used; that measurement is *media attention*. If the goal of the site is promotion, you may find that media attention is the best measure of success. Did you get a notice in *Forbes* or a feature in *The New York Times?* For some smaller sites, even a blurb in the local alternative newspaper would count. Of course, it's easier to get attention after you've *had* attention — so big companies are generally more likely to get press attention than smaller ones. But here is where the Web can become the great leveler. Recently, we noticed that *People* magazine was covering the Web site that was created by the people who invented the game Six Degrees of Kevin Bacon. Media attention flocks to what's hot, so if this is how you're going to measure success, make your site really outstanding.

Popularity — measured through impressions, visitors, or media attention — is an appropriate way to measure sites whose primary purpose is to promote, inform, or entertain.

Sales, distribution, and revenue produced

If the overriding purpose of your site is to sell (or even just distribute) a product, you can probably measure your success in sales rather than traffic. How many wonderwidgets you need to sell is a tricky matter — the specifics are up to you.

As a cautionary note, you should not start with absurdly high expectations and base your revenue model on this alone. We know of one case where an online shopping system for a *hard-deliverable product* (a product that is tangible, like wine) was installed, and sales on the first day were four units — the system was considered a success! In that case, the expectation was that sales would build and that slow sales in the beginning would allow time to refine the shopping system and test *fulfillment* (the shipping of the items). Because the company is not relying on this shopping system as its primary method of distribution — at least not yet — it has the luxury of considering opening sales of four units a success.

Similarly, if your site's goal is to produce revenue through ad sales, sponsorship, paid placement, and so on, the amount of revenue that's produced can be a benchmark of success. If this is the case, make sure that your content is incredibly compelling. Even the highly trafficked search-engine and directory sites, many of which get upwards of 10 million hits *per day,* are not yet, as of this writing, producing a reliable profit through ad sales, sponsorship, or licensing.

Sales and distribution — measured in quantity — are reasonable ways to measure success for sites whose primary purpose is, well, to sell or distribute but are inappropriate for sites that are primarily meant to promote or inform. Revenue produced — measured in dollars — is a good way to measure success in a site that has producing revenue (perhaps through ad sales) as its primary purpose. This would have to be a *very* high-traffic site. Chapter 2 discusses the issues involved in relying on various revenue models to drive your site, including ad sales.

Information gathered and reported

You may find that, for your purposes, the best measure of success is the quantity and quality of information that's gathered. Think again about the Georgia Tech survey we mention in Chapter 2 — in that case, the information was gathered via a survey presented as a form on a Web site. The success of the venture can be seen in the number of respondents and the quality of the report that came from the study. Similarly, in the case of the BrowserWatch site also mentioned in Chapter 2, the quality of the gathered information can be considered a benchmark of success. Of course, quality of information also probably translates into popularity of the site, but why quibble over which is more important when the goal of the site is to gather quality info and disseminate it?

The quantity and quality of information that is gathered and reported may be a good measure of success for sites whose primary purpose is to gather information — as in a survey that's conducted for either public interest or marketing research purposes.

Subjective response: "We like it!"

This may seem odd, but a subjective response — a plain and ordinary "we like it" — can be a measure of success. This is most likely in a scenario where a company has jobbed out the design and implementation of a site to an outside firm, and the firm, on delivering the site, has no other means of measuring success. It's unlikely that you, as Webmaster for the company, have worked out a contract that lets you measure success before paying up, so you need to be sure that the site fits your specifications; one of those requirements is likely to be as simple as a "we like it" spoken by the right folks in your organization. In corporate speak, this is known as a *buyoff.*

Internal buyoff is very important, but it usually doesn't pay the bills. So make sure that you've specified other measurements for success, and that through the design and implementation process, you've continually sought buyoff. Furthermore, monitor the site as it shapes up to meet your goals and measurements of success.

Measuring Traffic

Whether you're a lone Webmaster who is charged with running a simple site or one responsible for a big-time corporate or commercial site, knowing how to measuring traffic is crucial. You can track not just how much traffic your site gets but also how much traffic individual areas of your site get; this helps you identify places where your site's navigation is less than easy and needs fixing.

To measure traffic, you can read the log files your server generates, you can rely on reports put out by any of a number of site-statistic packages, or you can hand the whole matter to an external auditor. Each of these options presents different advantages; for many, some combination is best. If, for example, yours is a relatively small site and you, a techie, are the sole Webmaster responsible for it, you may find log files to be all you need. They're free, and you probably know how to read them. (In fact, you must read them to do server maintenance.) If you work with others or want to know more readily about which pages on your site are most popular or where the clickpaths are going, you need to use some site-statistic software. This software generates reports based on your log files, making that data into useful information that's more accessible to nontechies. If yours is a site that is funded by ad sales, you should probably contract an external auditor to verify to outsiders the amount of traffic that you get. That's not cheap, but it's necessary if you sell ads or rely on other revenue based on your big-time traffic. (See "Revenue models we know and love" in Chapter 2 for more on what makes ad sales tick.)

Reading Log Files for the Few and the Many

Log files are generated by your Web server to record everything that happens while the server is running. Log files exist so that system administrators (like tech-type Webmasters) can track and resolve issues. Most Web servers generate a variety of log files, including an *access log* and an *error log.* The access log file contains a record for every hit the site gets. Remember, a hit is a request for a file, and a single document can be made up of many small and large files. The error log file contains information about every error that occurs while the server is running. It's a good idea to peek into both of these files on a regular basis to track how your server is doing. (This is a routine part of doing server maintenance.)

Looking into the access log file is our focus here, because this file contains information that you can use to determine how popular your site is. (To find out more about error log files, refer to server administration books.) Most Web servers produce log files in a standard format — called (sensibly enough) the *common log file format.* You can read a definition of the common log file format at the URL `http://www.w3.org/pub/WWW/Daemon/User/Config/Logging.html`.

A typical access log file entry looks like this:

```
www.dnai.com aneth-12.execpc.com - - [24/Apr/1997:18:56:15
-0700] "GET /~vox/news/welcome2.html HTTP/1.0" 200 1253
```

Like a database record, an access log file record appears in *fields,* or chunks, of data. The data in the first field in our sample log file, `www.dnai.com`, contains the name of the Web server that served the specific Web file that this entry discusses. While this information may seem redundant when you first start looking at log files — of course it's *your* Web server that served your document — it can be very useful to those who run multiple Web servers and have piles of log files from different servers to read.

The data in the second field of our sample, `aneth-12.execpc.com`, is from the machine that requested that this document be served. If the actual name of that machine is not available, its IP address appears instead. (You'll recall that every computer with an Internet connection has a unique number assigned to it as an identifier — that's the IP address.)

In the third field of our sample, a single dash appears. This shows that the field is empty, as this particular field usually is. Some Web servers place a username — the username of whomever is requesting the document from the server — in this field. But this data is usually available only if the Web server has been configured to retrieve that information *and* the person running the Web browser is using a UNIX-based computer running a special server (called an *identd* server). The combination of these two events is quite rare, so for the most part, don't expect to see any information in this field.

The fourth field in our example is also blank. It would contain the user's authenticated username if it were filled in. If you were to set up your Web server to require a username and password to access particular parts of your site, the username of the person requesting and accessing the file would appear here. (Note that this is different from the username that may have appeared just before it — *that* username is described in the preceding paragraph.)

The fifth field shows the date and time the file was served. In our case, this is `24/Apr/1997:18:56:15 -0700`, meaning that the requested item was served on April 24, 1997, at 18:56:15 GMT (Greenwich Mean Time). Servers log time in Greenwich-Mean-Time format, the international standard of expressing time that disregards the time zone that you are in. The last part of the time notation in the field, –0700, indicates that the local time (where the server is located) is seven hours behind GMT. Therefore, the local time when this file was served was 11:56:15 a.m.

The sixth field shows the request that was made by the Web browser. This indicates what the server was asked to serve. The request usually appears in the form of a command followed by a directory and filename. In a log file, you usually see the `get` command, which is the one that Web browsers send to fetch files from Web servers. The `get` command is followed by the full path and filename for the file that the server is expected to return. In this case, the Web browser is getting the file `/~vox/news/welcome2.html` from the Web server. Other commands that you may see in your log file are the `put` and `post` commands; these are used by Web browsers to send the contents of a form.

The seventh field contains a status code. This code indicates whether the command resulted in success (serving of the file) or failure (and if so, why that failure occurred). Your Web server can generate many status codes (a list of them should appear in your server's documentation). The common ones are as follows:

Code	Description
200	Success
201	File not found
202	Permission to access file denied
401	Unauthorized: The file requested is protected by a password that was not correctly supplied
500	Internal server error: A problem may have occurred with a CGI script on the server

The eighth and final field in our sample log file record shows the number of bytes of data that were sent to the Web browser when the requested item was served.

A single Web page is usually made up of many files — graphics, HTML files, and so on. Keep in mind that the access log file includes a record for each hit (each file that's requested). Therefore, a seemingly simple request to the server for a document can generate dozens of records in the access log file.

You may then wonder why you should care about log files. For one thing, as a Webmaster, you should know how to read them as part of your skill set. For another, these are really the only statistics that are recorded by the server; any other statistics (such as how many impressions you get) are based on these. Site-statistic software relies on your access log files to work up the information it delivers to you. External audits, by the way, don't always use your access log files as the basis of their information. We cover that later in this chapter.

How Traffic Measurements Are Calculated

Now we'll take a closer look at hits, impressions, visitors, unique visitors, and clickpaths. These are really the building blocks of measuring success. Each is a measure of something that's a little different; understanding those differences can help you judge your site's success and determine which success-measuring tools are best for you.

Hits

A *hit* occurs every time your Web server serves a file. This file can be HTML, a graphic, or any other piece of media that's stored on the server. A user who is accessing a single Web page can generate *many* hits, because loading that page may generate a hit for the HTML file followed by a hit for each graphic and every other bit of media that makes up the page. Every hit that occurs is recorded in the server's access log file, which we describe in an earlier section.

When a hit is not a hit

Guess what? Not every viewing of a page on your site results in a hit being produced. This is because cache systems, like the ones that Web browsers and proxy servers use, throw the whole thing off. Caching exists to facilitate fast loading of pages, but it does so by loading saved copies of the pages rather than by loading fresh copies. Depending on how an individual user's Web browser is set up to use the cache, that user's view of a particular page at a particular moment may or may not be a fresh view. If it's a cached view, it produces no hits in your log files. Similarly, many corporations and most commercial online services (such as America Online) use proxy servers to cache Web pages so users can access them more quickly. In this case, many users may access the same cached Web page, which has been stored on the caching proxy server. There's nothing you can do about this — just keep it in mind when you think about the accuracy of counting hits.

Impressions

An *impression* (sometimes also referred to as a *page view*) is the serving of an entire Web page, no matter how many hits make up that page. While a user who is loading a single page from your Web server may generate many hits, the user generates only one impression. Figuring out the number of impressions that occurs is more complicated than figuring out the number of hits because, while Web servers track hits in an access log file, they don't have a way to track impressions. However, it is possible to calculate the number of impressions that occur based on the hit data that's stored in the access log file, and a number of handy software packages can do this for you. We cover this in an upcoming section.

Visitors

A *visitor* in this context is simply a person who visits your site. A single visitor may visit your site many times and may view one page (causing one impression) or many pages (causing many impressions). Of course, each of these impressions can also generate many hits, each of which appears in the log file.

Visitors are harder to track than impressions — some software packages try to determine the number of visitors from analyzing the access log file. This file does not include specific information about visitors, but it does contain some information which, in conjunction with some basic assumptions, can be used to *guess* at the number of visitors. This is how it works: Using the access log file, the software assumes some time-out for a single visit — 15 minutes is common — and any two impressions that are sent by the server to the same Web browser within the given time period are assumed to be part of the same visit.

That's obviously not the most accurate way to go. But counting visitors, if it were highly accurate, would be a highly desirable way to measure traffic.

Unique users

A visitor may come to your site repeatedly. (In fact, you probably hope this happens.) Each time a new visitor comes to your site, he or she is known as a *unique user,* at least in theory. In actuality, it's hard to know whether a unique user is a new person visiting the site. One can track down a specific Web browser running on a particular PC, but if a person moves from one PC to another — or even uses more than one Web browser on the same PC — most software counts that person as a different unique user in each circumstance. Similarly, two people that share a single browser on a single machine count as one unique user.

Unique users can be tracked through special software you run on your server. This software typically uses cookie technology to assign a unique identification number to each user who visits your site (see the sidebar "Gotta cookie?" later in this chapter). When a user visits the site, the software checks the cookies to see whether the ID number is there, assigns one if it isn't, and thereafter logs in the user and tracks which pages are being viewed by that user. This is cool, but again, remember that these are unique users only in theory. This is close enough for many purposes, but it's not exact science.

Clickpaths

Everyone wants to know — but hardly anyone *can* know — which way, when a user clicks around the site, he is going. This is known as a *clickpath.* Clickpaths are useful to know about in determining which of your navigational gizmos are working and which are not. Does the user start here and head there, or there, or *there?* Clickpaths — the order in which various users click through a set of pages — are really tough to track. A simple example of the complicating factors that are involved is when a user clicks on the browser's Back button to return to pages that were previously viewed. Usually no record for this is generated in the access log file, so the clickpath trail is lost.

Gotta cookie?

When a user visits a Web site that uses cookies, the site's Web server creates and passes to the user's browser a kind of a note to itself, called a *cookie*, which is then stored among the browser's files. Forever after, when that user visits the same site, the site's server checks (just as it did the first time) to see if a cookie is there. On finding the cookie, the server can automatically identify the user and pick up any information (a password, online shopping preferences, or whatever) that's been stored in the cookie. Marketing people and many Web developers love cookies; some users, however, hate them. To the marketing people, this is a terrific method for not just counting users, but even tracking what they like and don't like. To the Web developers, this is a good way to track passwords and what's in a shopping cart. To some users, however, all this is too much like an invasion of privacy. Some users even go so far as to disable cookies, which many Web browsers will allow them to do. If a cookie-hating user visits your site with cookies disabled, all bets are off in terms of counting that user as a visitor to your site through cookie technology.

Some software packages attempt to extract clickpath information from the server's access log file, while other packages include special software that you can run on your Web server to track clickpaths. Again, this is no exact science, and determining clickpaths is a matter of sorting all of the records in the access log file and trying to work through where a person went at a given time. Forget trying to do this yourself; you really need the right software to do it for you. We discuss that software later in the following sections.

Tracking Popularity and Clickpaths with Site-Statistic Packages

As mentioned throughout this chapter, various software packages are available for your use in measuring and tracking the popularity of your Web site. These packages range from low-cost programs that run under UNIX to thousand-dollar graphical interface packages that run on Windows-based PCs or Macs. Which package is right for you depends on a number of factors. You need a fairly simple tool if yours is a small company site but a more sophisticated setup if you plan to sell ad space on your site. In upcoming sections, we look at each of the more popular packages. Here is a quick summary of what the packages measure:

Package	Hits	Impressions	Visitors	Unique Users	Clickpaths	Independent Auditing
Wusage	✔	✔	✔		✔	
Intersé Market Focus	✔	✔	✔	✔	✔	
NetCount		✔	✔		✔	✔

Wusage

Wusage, one of the most popular log-analysis tools available, runs under UNIX as well as Windows 95 and NT. It creates reports based on your Web server's access log file; these reports include the number of hits that occur for each file on the server, the number of impressions for each page, and the number of visitors the site receives. All of this handy information can be shown based on the time of day that it occurs, so you can see when certain parts of your site are busiest. Wusage reports appear in a series of attractive graphs that you can view and print via a Web browser. Wusage cannot track individual users of your site, and that's a downside for some. What's more, because you run the Wusage software, the reports are not seen by those purchasing ad space as objective and entirely reliable. Nonetheless, for many, this is a good choice.

You can learn more about Wusage — and download an evaluation copy of the software — from http://www.boutell.com/wusage. A license to run Wusage on a single server costs $75. Special educational, government, and site license pricing is available.

Market Focus

Market Focus is a package that runs on Windows 95 – and NT-based computers. However, while the software runs only on these platforms, it can analyze log files that are generated by Web servers running under UNIX as well. This means that you can run the software on an NT machine, for example, to examine records on another Web server, running under UNIX, and then generate traffic reports for that server. Market Focus produces reports that are quite similar to those produced by Wusage, and Market Focus is known for its robustness in dealing with very heavily trafficked Web sites. Therefore, you may want to use Market Focus for a big site, although it may not be your best choice if you need to provide objective, external verification of traffic.

Market Focus is available from the Intersé Web site at http://www. interse.com. Market Focus requires a machine running Windows 95 or NT with a minimum of 16MB of RAM (although 32MB is recommended), a Pentium processor, and 15MB of disk space beyond the space required to hold all your log files. Prices range from $695 for a single Web server version to $6,995 for a developer version.

NetCount

NetCount is a subscription-based service, not software that you run on your own server. The software itself runs on NetCount's server, and NetCount generates reports about the amount of activity on your site. Therein lies the perceived value of this service. Because the reports involved are generated by NetCount and not you, they are less vulnerable to tampering (let's face it — some people may tamper with their own site statistics), and for this reason, potential advertisers take NetCount traffic reports more seriously than any that you may self-generate. NetCount also has partnered with the recognized auditors Price Waterhouse (the company that compiles and guards the Academy Award votes), which gives people added confidence in the objectivity and integrity of NetCount's reports.

You can find out all about NetCount at http://www.netcount.com. Because the NetCount software does not run on your site, it doesn't have hardware requirements per se. It is available as a subscription service, and costs range from $195 startup and $98/month to $1395 startup and $698/month, plus additional charges for sites with more than one million hits per day. (Whew!) The cost you incur basically depends on your site's traffic.

Counting Backlinks

Counting *backlinks* — links on other sites that go to your site — is another way to measure your site's popularity. What's more, this is not just a matter of popularity; each backlink provides users with a doorway to your site, so counting your backlinks and beefing up those numbers are good ways to build traffic. Chapter 14 talks more about this and describes exactly how you can count the backlinks to your site using either the AltaVista or HotBot search engine.

Verifying Traffic Counts through Outside Audits

As the Web continues to take its place as the most important communication medium since the advent of television (or perhaps even the telephone), advertisers are looking at it more seriously as a medium for their message. Big-name advertisers pay big ad rates for big traffic, but they also want credible, third-party verification of that traffic.

This is nothing new; in the worlds of print and television, established auditors exist and provide reliable, trusted information that boosts credibility in the industry. Similarly, in the magazine and newspaper world, well known third-party auditors verify a publication's circulation at least annually, and that verified number is seen by advertisers as being credible enough to warrant paying the publication for ad space.

In the Web world, the same logic prevails: If you want to sell ad space, the ad space buyers (especially the big-name ones) are going to want to know what they're getting for their dollar. They want to know how many people are going to see the ad at what frequency, and they want that number verified by a disinterested but respected third party.

What do third-party auditors actually offer? For the most part, they offer an objective report. The information they gather and the reports they produce are actually very similar to those you can generate or have generated using the site-statistic tools discussed earlier in this chapter. Some third-party auditors even use that exact software! However, reports generated by third-party auditors carry more weight with potential advertisers, because it is assumed that if an auditor created the report, you could not have fudged the numbers. (For a perspective on this from the viewpoint of the advertiser, see Chapter 14.)

Unfortunately, reports that are generated by your ISP or IPP are not seen as having been generated by a disinterested third party. That's because third-party auditors set as a specific kind of professional reputation based on a kind of objectivity that others believe in. Simply put, ad space buyers won't see your ISP or IPP's word as being credible enough to suit them.

Generally speaking, third-party auditors may require you to run some special software on your Web server or to make some minor change to your Web pages to enable their tracking system to work. In some cases, they may conduct their audits based solely on copies of your access log file. The procedures that are used vary from one auditor to another — as mentioned in Chapter 14. Yahoo!, for example, uses one company to measure and another to audit its self-measurement systems. Some auditors want to come to your site — your physical site, not your Web site — and kick the tires by examining how you run your server and how log files are generated. They may want to investigate for signs of tampering or odd procedures.

In the end, third-party auditors produce reports that are based on the usage of your site; these reports are verified and signed off by them. Again, the big advantage here is that ad space buyers find auditors eminently believable. However, audit services from third-party auditors are not cheap. Prices vary tremendously and depend on the type of relationship that you establish with the company providing the audit. It's best to check various auditor Web sites and contact the companies offering these services to get up-to-date information.

Third-party auditing of Web sites is a new business. As time goes on, an industry leader is sure to emerge; in the meantime, look into the Audit Bureau of Circulations (`http://www.accessabc.com`), BPA International (`http://www.bpai.com`), and Nielsen Media Research (`http://www.nielsenmedia.com`). (This last one may sound familiar — Nielsen is known for doing television ratings.)

Keep in mind that these companies do not all produce the same reports, nor do their reports contain standard information. As of this writing, organizations representing those who buy ad space on Web sites are pushing for standardization, which these organizations want for the sake of easy comparison. Debate rages about whether to make the standard reports similar to those of some other industry — TV, perhaps, or print — but in the end, we believe a standard will emerge that's based on the Web's unique qualities.

To find out more about efforts to standardize Web-site success statistics, visit the following URL: `http://www.commercepark.com/AAAA/bc/casie/guide.html`.

On Subjective Assessments and Feedback E-mail

Everyone has an opinion. Some are smart, objective, and even informed; some are based on personal preference, guesswork, and something heard while standing in line at the grocery store.

Setting ad rates based on impressions

In the nonvirtual, print world, ad rates are based on circulation. Basically, one pays an ad rate per *CPM,* where CPM stands for cost per thousand. (*M* is the Roman numeral for 1,000.) In the Web world, the phrase CPM is also tossed around, but the "thousand" generally refers to impressions rather than readers, and the CPM for advertising ranges from $0.02 to $0.15, and sometimes more.

Sites with highly targeted readership tend to charge higher rates, because they can offer those who advertise there a direct line to an exact type of customer. For example, a golf equipment advertiser, who may advertise on a search-engine site like Excite (`http://`

`www.excite.com`), would get a great deal of impressions for its advertising dollar, but only a small percentage of those would very likely be golfers. The same golf equipment advertiser, advertising on iGolf (`http://www.igolf.com`), would get fewer impressions for its dollar. But the advertiser could assume that most, if not all, of those impressions would be falling on the eyes of golf enthusiasts — the venue is more targeted.

Thus, the ability to set a high CPM for ad space on your site and actually get that rate is a sign of success both in the sense of the traffic that you get and the number of users you reach that are interested in the topic of your site.

Before the advent of the Internet, market researchers had to spend beaucoup bucks to conduct what they call *focus groups;* the researchers would get people in a room to give them feedback about the company's product or services. Sometimes they conducted surveys, too. The point is that they had to work hard to get that information. You, as chief marketer of your Web site, can get immediate and cost-free feedback at any time simply by offering users a link to an easy-to-use e-mail form. This is a very powerful tool in that it lets your users talk to you whenever they have an opinion or request.

The downside of this is that some users are going to express opinions that are smart and well informed, some express opinions that are articulate and respectful, and some are going to write e-mails that are filled with rants and gobbledygook. You *must* treat each of these users with respect, and you must answer each one. These are people, and they are the keys to your success — they are your *audience.*

You may want to establish a set of stock, polite responses to commonly received feedback e-mail. We know of one search-engine company that (just like a big magazine) maintains a Letters department of four people. Their main job is to respond to user e-mail; these folks have a whole portfolio of responses they can use or modify depending on the situation.

Also, be sure to keep at least one file (electronic or printed) of user responses so you can compile similar pieces of feedback and get a sense from these e-mails of what is and is not working on your site. When you redesign your nav bar or overall look, you can refer to those files and find out what people have been saying.

The bottom line is this: Listen to your audience, and respond to them. Your response may take the form of sending a simple thank-you for the feedback, or it may take the form of acting on the specific feedback that someone offered. Don't ignore your audience, and don't send them automated responses. Take care of your audience — that's rule number one in Web-site success.

Take a Look at Yourself

As much as it's important to listen to your audience and respond to them, it's also important to remain objective. First, when you listen to feedback e-mail, don't take everything that everyone says as gospel. That can drive you nuts, and more importantly, you soon learn that you can't make everyone happy.

A word on awards

Awards can be, well, rewarding. They boost a person's ego, and to many members of your audience (and even to advertisers and others), they look like external validation of your success. (Bravo! You won an award!) There is, however, a tendency on the Web to fabricate awards and offer them to others as a means for getting backlinks to the award-giver's site. Awards can be so ego-gratifying they're hard to resist, and this is a notoriously successful tactic.

Having too many award-like logos on your home page heralding your success is a bit like having touristy bumper stickers pasted all over your car. The first issue is: No one can see the site for the stickers. The second: Who cares?

Awards are a sign of success only if they have been given by a respected entity for a specific accomplishment. Which awards are going to be the Oscars or Grammies of the Internet has not yet been determined. Until then, if someone offers you an award, you may want to look that gift horse in the mouth. If it seems truly prestigious, by all means, let others know about it. Issue a press release, tell your advertisers, and plaster that award wherever you like. Just remember how many times you've heard the phrase "award-winning" in marketing hype and not really known what that award was given for.

Similarly, it's important not to fall prey to personal attachment. You may love that fluorescent fuchsia and want it for your nav bar color, but does it suit your button-down audience? In writing classes, wise teachers often tell their students that to write well, one must be willing to "murder your precious darlings." This is as true in creating and maintaining a Web site as it is in writing a novel. If something that you absolutely adore does not fit into the scheme of things and if it does not serve the user and the site's mission, you simply must ax it.

Remember who you are and what you do (see Chapter 1), and keep in mind your site's overall mission and specific goals (see Chapter 2). You are it: the Webmaster. This is your site. Its success depends on you, your vision, and your ability to make that vision a reality through your (or your team's) skill in technical development, design, content creation, marketing, and management. You have the coolest job in the world, and part of doing that job is to stay clear about where your site is headed, how to get there, and what success is going to look like to you and to others. You're the *Webmaster*. Good luck to you.

Part V
The Part of Tens

The 5th Wave   **By Rich Tennant**

"THE IMAGE IS GETTING CLEARER NOW... I CAN ALMOST SEE IT...
YES! THERE IT IS — THE GLITCH IS IN A FAULTY CABLE AT YOUR
OFFICE IN DENVER."

In this part . . .

In the world famous Part of Tens, we offer you lifesaving treats and quick tricks. You'll want to bookmark this part. It includes (more than) ten Web sites a Webmaster can't live without, (more than) ten tools for jazzing up HTML, and (more than) ten types of live content you can implement today — in many cases, with no programming skills whatsoever!

Chapter 16

Ten Web Sites That'll Save Your Life

In This Chapter

▶ The ultimate directory of search sites

▶ Guides to Webmastering for the beginning, intermediate, and advanced

▶ A tech news and techniques resource

▶ Sites for learning HTML, designing pages, and testing your code

▶ An entry point to editorial information

▶ A comprehensive source of legal information

▶ An online marketing oracle

Suppose you were trapped on a desert island, but you still had to get that Web site launched. To make things worse, you could take only ten bookmarks with you. In this chapter, we make suggestions for those ten bookmarks. Okay, we couldn't narrow it down to *exactly* ten, so we sneaked in a few more.

Search.com

At some point, you're going to need to do some online research, whether it's to test the market waters or to find the e-mail address of that guy you networked with at last month's meeting. You can use C|Net's Search.com as a launching point for any and all searches that you could possibly do.

Gentle Webmasters, start your search engines at `http://www.search.com`.

Webmonkey

One of many spawns of HotWired, Webmonkey is a how-to guide for beginning-to-intermediate Webmasters. The site doesn't cover everything, so looking for something specific in these pages may not be the way to go. On the other hand, if you're learning HTML from scratch, following the colorful Webmonkey tutorials can be a great way to learn the basics.

Give your site (and yourself) a quick lesson in Web mechanics with Webmonkey, which lives in the trees at `http://www.webmonkey.com`.

Webreference.com: The Webmaster's Reference Library

The table of contents alone at The Webmaster's Reference Library is daunting — luckily, this site is searchable. It's also packed with know-how, both in the form of links and original content.

You can find a bookshelf-full of ideas and how-tos at `http://www.webreference.com`.

iWORLD

Mecklermedia's iWORLD covers buzzwords when they start buzzing, stocks when they jump or fall, and just about any new Internet software package or development tool that comes down the pike. Not only is this one of the newsiest of sites, but its impressive catalog of Web resources includes The List of Internet Service Providers, BrowserWatch, The Internet Product Site, and The Electronic Commerce Guide. It's well-organized to boot; this is a winner.

Learn everything from the basics to what happened three minutes ago by visiting Mecklermedia's iWORLD at `http://www.iworld.com`.

NCSA's Style Guide and Beginner's Guide

NCSA's Beginner's Guide to HTML is a legendary reference that includes everything that you need to know about basic HTML. The Style Guide goes beyond basic code to discuss how to organize information, how to present your pages to search engines, and how to create your own sense of HTML style.

Learn from the experts at NCSA by visiting `http://www.ncsa.uiuc.edu/General/Internet/WWW/styleguide.html`.

The Beginner's Guide to HTML is at `http://www.ncsa.uiuc.edu/General/Internet/WWW/HTMLPrimer.html`.

Web Page Design For Designers

As the author, Joe Gillespie, of Pixel Productions says, this is not an HTML reference site. Instead, his articles, tutorials, and tips focus on teaching visual Web design to people who have some experience creating visual impact in print media. If you want your pages to look good, take a look at this site. You can also learn a lot by looking at High Five, a showcase of well-designed Web pages selected by guru David Siegel.

Joe Gillespie's Web Page Design For Designers can be found at the URL `http://ds.dial.pipex.com/pixelp/wpdesign/wpdintro.htm`.

Visit the High Five archives to view dozens of sites that got the visuals right. The URL is `http://www.highfive.com`.

Doctor HTML

Wouldn't it be handy if a Web site could check your code, your spelling, your image locations, and all of the links on your page? Well, that's what Doctor HTML does — it's a Web "lint" program that really goes the distance. You can check the code, links, and spelling on one Web page at a time for free. Webmasters of larger sites may want to purchase a Site Doctor License so that they can use Doctor HTML to expedite revising an entire site at once.

Have your Web pages been in for a checkup recently? Pay a visit to Doctor HTML at `http://www2.imagiware.com/RxHTML`.

Links for Copy Editors

There's nothing like a good set of reference books on your desk for checking rules about writing style and grammar usage. You should be as picky about your grammar as you are about your HTML, and the sites listed on Links for Copy Editors can help you take pride in the words on your Web pages.

Pick those nits! Read Links for Copy Editors to find the nits in the first place. The URL is: `http://www.copyeditor.com/Links.html`.

Another favorite is The Slot, at `http://www.theslot.com`, while Wired Style, defined at the following URL, defines, well, Wired style: `http://www.hardwired.com/hardwired/wiredstyle/index.html`.

FindLaw and The Cyberspace Law Center

FindLaw is the Yahoo! of legal information on the Internet. This searchable index links to general legal resources as well as particular articles about current hot topics and frequently queried cases. The site has an entire category called Cyberspace Law that includes articles on everything from domain name conflicts to the Scientology vs. Usenet case.

You can find most legal sites on the Web with FindLaw (`http://www.findlaw.com`), or you can skip directly to the Cyberspace Law category at `http://www.findlaw.com/01topics/10cyberspace`.

You should also pay attention to the Cyberspace Law Center, at the URL `http://www.cybersquirrel.com/clc`.

Who's Marketing Online

Who's Marketing Online reveals marketing techniques and reviews other sites that specialize in marketing or simply present themselves well. This is a good place to begin learning the twists and turns of online advertising and image creation; it's an even better place to keep up with the latest news — including reviews of relevant mailing lists.

Read the news about who's making the news at Who's Marketing Online, which can be found at `http://www.wmo.com`.

Chapter 17

Ten Tools for Jazzing Up HTML

In This Chapter

▶ HTML editors

▶ Image editors

▶ Java authoring tools

▶ Site search engine

▶ More Web gadgets

*T*here's a mighty big difference between a Web page and a *good* Web page. While multitudes of HTML editors, image-manipulation tools, and other software toys proclaim that using them can make your Web sites bigger and better, we've narrowed things down to ten items you just can't live without.

Microsoft FrontPage

FrontPage, a Web-publishing suite from Microsoft, can be a useful tool for both novices and experts. FrontPage (a Windows 95 or NT product) uses a similar interface to Microsoft Office to allow you to create Web pages from templates or from scratch. You can also use its Image Composer to design images for your site and its site management tools to update the site.

The Microsoft FrontPage site includes details about what the software can do and tips for working with FrontPage, as well as extensions and fixes and a gallery of FrontPage-created sites. Visit http://www.microsoft.com/frontpage.

BBEdit and Luckman WebEdit

These two packages, one for the Mac and one for Windows, get consistently rave reviews because of their excellent interfaces and their near-automation of the HTML writing process. Both are available in shareware and professional versions.

Got a Mac? Visit Bare Bones Software, and check out BBEdit at http://www.barebones.com. PC users should pay a visit to Luckman Interactive at http://www.luckman.com.

XTML

Creating tables can be annoying at best. If you have access to Microsoft Excel, however, you can use a nifty little extension called XTML to automatically convert an Excel spreadsheet into HTML. Just mock up your table in Excel, and use XTML to create the code. When you have your basic table created this way, you can modify the way it looks by changing the settings for alignment, cell padding, cell spacing, and so on.

XTML, developed by Ken Sayward, is free. Get it at http://members.aol.com/ksayward/XTML.

Adobe Photoshop

Photoshop is the software professional graphic designers use to create images. The latest editions of Photoshop are highly Web savvy, making it easy for you to anti-alias text (anti-aliasing removes those ugly jaggies), reduce the size of GIFs, and create tiled backgrounds.

The Adobe Photoshop home page can be found at http://www.adobe.com/prodindex/photoshop/main.html; Kai's Power Tools, also handy, at http://www.metatools.com.

Paint Shop Pro

If Photoshop is so great, why are we talking about another image program? Because Paint Shop Pro is cheaper, easier to use, and requires less RAM and disk space to run. What's more, Paint Shop Pro has a few features that can make your life easier in conjunction with Photoshop. The screen capture utility is one of the best available, and the Browse program enables you to view thumbnails of entire directories in batches on your screen; this is much easier than opening them one by one. But the most compelling reason to use Paint Shop Pro is that it's shareware: You can download the whole thing and test drive it for 30 days before you decide to keep it (that is, pay for it).

Jasc, the makers of Paint Shop Pro, maintain a helpful Web page at http://www.jasc.com.

GIF Construction Set and GIF Animator

Animated GIFs (those cute little pictures that move) are easy to make — if you have the right software. For PC users, the GIF Construction Set, from Alchemy Mindworks, is inexpensive and easy to use, and it lets you create polished results — not only animations, but transparencies and font effects as well. While Ulead's PhotoImpact GIF Animator doesn't have the animation wizard, it has a similar range of features and is simple to use, particularly with Photoshop.

Download and use the GIF Construction Set by visiting `http://www.mindworkshop.com/alchemy/gifcon.html`.

Try out Ulead's GIF Animator at `http://www.ulead.com`.

Flash Animator

Flash animations (which you may have known previously as FutureSplash) don't look much different from animated GIFs, but they have a couple of differences. First, Flash uses vector images — made up of lines rather than bitmaps — to create incredibly compressed files, rarely exceeding 20K in size. More importantly, however, FutureSplash animations are more than just moving images. You can put a certain level of interactivity into them, meaning that they can react to clicks and mouseovers in a way that normal GIFs can't do on their own. Flash has been incorporated into Macromedia's Shockwave family of products, but it's much easier to use than Director.

To make and see Flash animations, start at `http://www.macromedia.com/software/flash`.

Jamba

Aimtech's Jamba software, subtitled Java for the Rest of Us, enables the creation of simple Java applets with no prior knowledge of programming. Users instead click through a drag-and-drop interface, arranging objects and actions in order to create animations, sound effects, and clickable interfaces. Jamba is currently available only for Windows.

Read all about Jamba, and play with some demo applets, at `http://www.jamba.com`.

Excite for Web Servers

Even if your site is strictly organized from top to bottom, the bigger it gets, the harder it is to find stuff. What you may want is a search engine that allows both staff and users to search your site — not just by keyword, but by concept. Simply put, the Excite for Web Servers search engine uses a type of intelligent thesaurus to search your site. Excite for Web Servers is free, available for a number of platforms, and relatively easy to install.

Look into making your site searchable by perusing http://www.excite.com/navigate.

Miscellaneous Web Gadgets

We wrap this chapter up with a few useful sites that can do some of your work for you. Do you want a site that can give you the hex codes for whatever color you choose? Use ColorServe Pro. How about one that can lay out a table-based calendar in the month and year of your choice? Calendar Generator does that. What about a simple, free VRML site? Use Instant VRML. Our point is that there are a lot of time-saving tools online, and you can find many of them by exploring hotlinks on sites about Web design.

Color by numbers with ColorServe Pro is found at the following URL: http://www.biola.edu/cgi-bin/colorpro/colorpro.cgi?.

You can make a calendar with Calendar Generator, which is found at this URL: http://www.intellinet.com/CoolTools/CalendarMaker.

Finally, get Aereal Instant VRML Home World from the following URL: http://www.aereal.com/instant.

Chapter 18

Ten Types of Live Content You Can Use Today

Regular HTML provides a framework for presenting text and images to the world as well as links to information and downloadable files, such as software or sound files. But if you want to exploit the multimedia aspects of the Web and add interactivity, sound, and visual movement to your pages, you may need more than just an HTML editor and an image tool to play with. Some packages noted here are easier to use than others; they require varying degrees of programming knowledge ranging from none to a lot.

RealMedia

Progressive Networks' RealMedia software is the next generation of RealAudio, and it introduces video capabilities to the already-renowned RealPlayer. RealMedia delivers audio and visual content in streams. There's no wait for downloads; the software starts playing the audio or video as soon as it has enough information to do so. Not only is the new RealPlayer's sound quality high, but the video is relatively stutter free, and the *buffering* (the extra information that's downloaded and stored to prevent skips in the broadcast) works better than ever. You can convert audio or video files that you have on hand, and you can also set up live (a.k.a. real-time) delivery of concerts, interviews, or radio broadcasts. Keep in mind that you need to purchase server software to be able to send RealAudio or RealVideo files as streams.

From Progressive Networks' home at `http://www.real.com`, you can test the free RealPlayer and download a server package to test drive for 30 days. Don't miss the DevZone (`http://www.real.com/devzone/`), which is packed with tips for optimizing your streamed content and using it in innovative ways (like autoplaying content from within a Web page).

Shockwave

Macromedia's Shockwave is a browser plug-in that places CD-ROM–quality multimedia content into the browser window. Many of the most innovative Shockwave applications are in the form of games or movie-like animations, but Shockwave Audio is increasingly being used for putting audio on pages, because the sound quality is high and the download time is relatively low (because the files are compressed until played). You can convert any file created in Director, Authorware, or Flash into a Shockwave file, although you may want to break movies into smaller chunks to minimize download times.

Macromedia's home page, at `http://www.macromedia.com`, showcases Shockwave's capabilities, describes the software packages that are used to create Shockwave audio and movie files, and includes a lot of helpful pointers for adding Shockwave to your pages.

Internet Relay Chat

One of the oldest forms of live interaction on the Internet is Internet Relay Chat, or IRC. These chat sessions generally take place in a text-based chat client, and many Netizens already have chat software installed on their computers. There are two major advantages to hosting an IRC chat as part of your content: You don't have to run your own server (although it may be helpful), and the participants can use any IRC chat software package they prefer to participate. Roundtable discussions about specific, timely topics and celebrity chat interviews are both popular features.

Two easy-to-use software packages may make IRC sessions more appealing: (a) Global Chat from Quarterdeck (`http://www.globalchat.com`), which is compatible with Netscape Navigator and includes information about the GlobalStage chat server, and (b) Microsoft Chat (`http://www.microsoft.com/ie/comichat`), which offers text-only or comic-strip-character chat sessions and is compatible with Internet Explorer.

Java

Java has been the hot buzzword ever since Sun's debut of the language in 1995. A cousin to C++ and Objective C, the Java language is used to create *applets,* or small programs. A lot of the Java you see online has cute or otherwise aesthetic value (as in lit-up, scrolling marquees or animated logos), but Java can also be used to create word processing programs, HTML layout and design tools, database interfaces, and live chat environments. While Java until recently has been relegated to the land of programmers, some not-quite-WYSIWYG tools, such as Jamba (which you can check out at `http://www.jamba.com`) and Studio J++, enable nonprogrammers to structure simple Java applets. You can also find both applets and source code online that you can either purchase or download for free (on the IDG Books Web site, for example, at `http://www.idgbooks.com`). However, most people who want to use Java would benefit from contracting or hiring a programmer who can create or modify Java to their needs.

Two sites cover nearly everything you need to get started thinking about Java: Sun's JavaSoft Home Page (`http://www.javasoft.com`) and Gamelan, the Official Directory for Java (`http://www.gamelan.com`). Gamelan also offers a big collection of applets you can download and use on your site.

JavaScript

JavaScript is a scripting language that extends the capabilities of HTML. The advantage of using JavaScript rather than a separate Java applet is that the code is generally brief and is included in the body of the Web page; this means no additional download time to access the capabilities of the script. Creating fully functional programs, such as calculators or color converters, is possible with JavaScript, although most people reserve that type of application for Java, which is a more robust language. JavaScript is useful for randomization, redirecting site visitors, simple animations, and clever Web-page designs. Both Netscape Navigator and Microsoft Internet Explorer can handle JavaScript enhanced Web pages. (Microsoft calls JavaScript JScript.)

A good starting point for learning about JavaScript is the HotSyte JavaScript Connection, found at http://www.serve.com/hotsyte. Microsoft's JScript page is located at http://www.microsoft.com/jscript. Both sites include pointers to sample code you can start working with on your own site.

ActiveX

ActiveX is Microsoft's answer to the Netscape browser plug-ins. Programmers who are already familiar with Microsoft programming environments can use their know-how to create miniapplications, games, and animations for the Web as well as to extend HTML's capabilities into the NT server domain for things like database compatibility and online transactions.

For an overview and online help with ActiveX and related technologies, visit Microsoft's Active Platform page at http://www.microsoft.com/activeplatform.

CU-SeeMe

Real-time videoconferencing hasn't yet surpassed the first such package, CU-SeeMe. This software was developed at Cornell University for use in two-way conferences or one-to-many broadcasts. White Pine software has since licensed the commercial version, called Enhanced CU-SeeMe. NASA often sponsors CU-SeeMe broadcasts of shuttle launches as such, and you can use it to broadcast groundshaking events. All you need (besides the software) is a video camera and a microphone; but for large-scale broadcasts, invest in a dedicated server, because CU-SeeMe is fairly bandwidth (and CPU) intensive.

Download a trial version of CU-SeeMe, and test it for a while. You can find out all you need to know at White Pine's CU-SeeMe home page: http://www.cu-seeme.com.

Toward Push: Castanet and PointCast

PointCast, Marima's Castanet software, and a slew of other software tools are evolving the way the Web browser works. In the browsing model, the user traverses the Web, selecting sites or articles of interest. To experience content, the user must "pull" the content by using his or her browser to request that a server deliver the stuff. In the push model, the user specifies once what *type* of content is of interest (by selecting a "channel"), and then content of that type is "pushed" onto his or her screen in a model similar to broadcasting. Two award-winning leaders in this field are PointCast and Marimba; both companies offer plenty of information describing how to create custom content by yourself or as a partner.

The first to do the push thing was PointCast, (`http://www.pointcast.com`), while Marimba's Castanet products (`http://www.marimba.com`) became the leaders in 1997.

VRML

A VRML world, or a simulated 3-D environment created using the Virtual Reality Modeling Language, is not something you can cough up without programming ability. On the other hand, it is something that you can outsource, particularly if you already have video or film on hand that describes the environment you want to create. A programmer can then render an image of the world you envision into a computer-generated landscape that users can navigate from all perspectives as well as click through to gain access to links or to other VRML worlds. The rendering involved doesn't look as sophisticated as a 3-D video game at this point, but it has an ambiance all its own, and VRML certainly isn't a frivolous endeavor. The Internet Underground Music Archives (IUMA) and Intel are using VRML successfully to promote their sites — and thus, their brands.

Visit VRML.org (`http://www.vrml.org`) to find out all about VRML development. Then walk through VRML worlds at Intel (`http://www.intel.com/procs/ppro/intro`) and IUMA (`http://www.iuma.com/IUMA-2.0/vrml`) for a truly different perspective on Internet presentation of content.

Custom Programming

Using back-end programming, you can create the kind of interactivity the big sites use: cookies that know who the user is when she arrives at the site, shopping-cart programs that track purchases and preferences, randomization scripts that change the way a user navigates a site, agent software that queries the user's tastes and needs and finds information for him or her, and customizable home pages that are unique to a user. The possibilities are endless, and although many script repositories and companies have agent design or transaction packages to sell, you're better off if you have a knowledgeable programmer on your side — and on your site.

Take a look at these examples of what custom programming can do: Amazon.com's shopping cart (http://www.amazon.com), Firefly's Agents (http://www.firefly.com), MSN's custom home page (http://www.msn.com), and Pathfinder's cookies and redirects (http://pathfinder.com).

Index

• *K* •

(continued)